Modern Studies
Britain Today
Third edition

Other titles in the Modern Studies series

Consulting editor
Alasdair G Nicolson
Assistant Principal
Jordanhill College of Education
Glasgow

Wright: **The World Today, Fourth Edition**
Wright and Nicolson: **Europe Today**

Britain Today

Third edition

Alasdair G Nicolson
Assistant Principal, Jordanhill College of Education

James G Kellas
Reader in Politics, University of Glasgow

James J Tumelty
Senior Lecturer in History, University of Glasgow

McGraw-Hill Book Company (UK) Limited

London · New York · St Louis · San Francisco · Auckland · Beirut
Bogotá · Düsseldorf · Johannesburg · Lisbon · Lucerne · Madrid
Mexico · Montreal · New Delhi · Panama · Paris · San Juan · São Paulo
Singapore · Sydney · Tokyo · Toronto

Published by
McGraw-Hill Book Company (UK) Limited
MAIDENHEAD · BERKSHIRE · ENGLAND

British Library Cataloguing in Publication Data

Nicolson, Alasdair G.
 Britain today. — 3rd ed. — (Modern studies series).
 1. Great Britain — Social conditions — 1945 —
 I. Title   II. Kellas, James Grant   III. Tumelty,
 James   IV. Series
 309.1'41'0857   HN383.5   77-30213

ISBN 0-07-084224-8

Copyright © 1978 © 1970 McGraw-Hill Book Company (UK) Limited.
All rights reserved. No part of this publication may be reproduced, stored in a retrieval system, or transmitted, in any form or by any means, electronic, mechanical, photocopying, recording, or otherwise, without the prior permission of McGraw-Hill Book Company (UK) Limited.

12345 WC & S 80798

PRINTED AND BOUND IN GREAT BRITAIN

Preface

It was in 1962 that the first edition of this book was published. This, the third edition, is a radically different animal from the original one. Then, the book was aimed primarily at those taking courses in the new subject of Modern Studies—a Scottish product geared to the needs of pupils in the 14–15 age range. That earlier text described a society moving into an era of almost infinite expansion—at least in some aspects of social and economic life—a society largely unimpeded by the constraints with which we are now so familiar: price inflation, the oil and energy crises, and the wider problems of persistent unemployment; all of which now appear of such compelling significance in day-to-day policy-making.

The last decade has altered quite substantially some basic features of our contemporary society and, added to the above changes are the structural changes within the fields of both central and local government. Inevitably the issues raised by these must be reflected in a text of this kind.

Within the social subjects, too, very extensive changes have been taking place. In Scottish schools, the courses in Modern Studies are now very popular and the new Ordinary Grade examination will alter quite markedly the content of courses and the techniques used in the classroom. In the rest of the United Kingdom the structure of courses in social subjects has been changing rapidly and, in preparing this text, we have been mindful of the range of examinations in Social and Economic studies. Pupils will, we hope, use this as a background text for Higher or Advanced level work in GCE and it should prove attractive to students of social sciences at the post-school level.

We are most grateful to all those who have helped us to bring this edition to life...to Kit Hamilton for efficient editorial help and invaluable suggestions... to Peter Clark and Anne Williamson of Jordanhill College Library...to our wives whose patience has been outstanding.

We trust that we have gone some way in providing guidance to a complex and changing society. We hope you will enjoy reading this book.

ALASDAIR G. NICOLSON
JAMES G. KELLAS

Contents

Preface		v
Chapter		
1	Britain: change and challenge	1

Population 1 Standard of living 5 Specialization 10 The industrial revolution 12 The twentieth-century challenge 14 Postwar developments 14 A note on the National Income 16

2A	Major industries: old and new	19

The changing structure of British industry 19 Iron and steel 20 Engineering 27 Motor vehicles 28 Aerospace industry 29 Electrical engineering and electronics 30 Shipbuilding 31 Textiles 33 Chemicals 36 Other industries 39

2B	Energy	40

Sources of energy 41 Organization and location 44 Gas 47 Oil 49 Electricity 51 Future consumption 53

3	Industry: organization and location	54

Private enterprise 54 Public enterprise 57 The rise of the large firm 65 The location of industry 70 Government influence 73 Policies since 1972 74 Industry then and now: a summary 80

4	Scotland: study of a changing society	82

Population 82 Economy 82 Industrial decline 84 Industrial expansion 87 Iron and steel 95 Shipbuilding 96 Coal 98 Textiles 99 Smaller Scottish industries 99 New industries 100 Other developments 104 Scottish politics 106 Postscript on Northern Ireland and Wales 108

5	Agriculture and fishing	109

Government and agriculture 114 Agriculture and the European Community 116 The Community and the 'Green' pound 118 The Common Agricultural Policy 119 The pattern of British farming 120 Fishing 123

6	Commerce, transport and trade	126

Commerce defined 126 Transport by water, land, and air 127 Distributive trades 134 The retail trade 136 Consumers and traders 140 Advertising 141 Origins of banking 142 Advantages of banks 143 The money market 144 Bank organization 145 The Bank of England 145 Overseas trade 146 Commercial policy 154 Balance of Trade 156 The Balance of Payments 157

7 Economic problems and policies　161

The main problems 161　The Balance of Payments problem 162　Possible solutions 163　Economic growth: efficiency and productivity 165　Investment 167　Government finance and the Budget 170　The Budget 177　The National Debt 178　Government influence on economic growth 180　The need to restrain inflation 182　Increasing prosperity 187

8 Social welfare and the citizen　189

The Welfare State 189　Attack on poverty 189　National Insurance 190　Child benefits, family income supplement, and supplementary benefits 191　National Health Service 193　The NHS: finance and organization 193　Unemployment and its causes 197　Creating full employment 199　The meaning of poverty today 201　Housing 201　Town and country planning 202　Education 205　Social welfare today 208

9 Industrial relations　210

Then and now 210　Human relations in industry 211　The rise of the trade unions 212　Unions: types and organization 213　The Trades Union Congress 215　Trade unions and politics 216　Collective bargaining 218　The Government and industrial relations 220

10 Government and politics　224

The Constitution 224　Development of the Constitution 226　Election procedure 227　Electing MPs and choosing a Government 227　The party struggle 228　Party system in Parliament 231　Party ideologies compared 232　Supporters and 'floaters' 235　Party organization 235　The Liberal Party, the Nationalists, and the Ulster Unionists 236　Some objections to the party system 237　Pressure groups 237　Consumer protection and citizen action groups 239　The press and broadcasting 239　Effects of public opinion on Government 240

11 Parliament　242

House of Lords 242　House of Commons 244　Making of laws 245　Control and criticism of the Government 249　Control of the raising and spending of money 252　Twentieth-century decline? 254

12 Ministers and civil servants　256

The Crown and Monarch 256　Government and Parliament 256　Prime Minister and Cabinet: development 257　The Prime Minister 258　The Cabinet 261　Government departments 262　Ministerial responsibility 263　The Civil Service 264

13 Local government　266

Scotland 266　England and Wales 267　Local government services 268　Elections 269　The committee system 270　Permanent officials 270　Where the money comes from 271　Where the money goes 272　Relationship of local authorities to the central government 274　Changes in the future 275

14 Maintenance of law and order　277

Criminal Law and Civil Law 277　Scottish Law and English Law 278　The police 278　The courts and the judges 279　Criminal procedure 282　Jury system 283　Civil procedure 284　The Rule of Law 284　Why it is important 285　Some complaints 286

Questions to consider　288
Bibliography　291
Index　294

1. Britain: change and challenge

In area the United Kingdom, i.e., Great Britain (England, Wales, and Scotland) and Northern Ireland, does not rank high among the countries of the world. Her 94 000 square miles (244 000 sq. km) would put her in seventy-fifth place in a league table based on size. But if we compiled a table based on population, then the United Kingdom with about 56 million people would be placed tenth. If, finally, we ranked the world's countries by density of population, i.e., by the number of people per square mile (or square kilometre) of land, Britain would come in fourth place with a density of 596 per square mile (229 per sq. km). Only Japan, West Germany, Belgium, and the Netherlands are more densely populated. Britain, then, is a very small country and a very crowded one.

Population

The overcrowding is more intensive than the general density figure suggests, since the population is not distributed evenly throughout the island. There are various ways of analysing the distribution. In terms of countries, England is more thickly populated with over 900 people per square mile than Wales with 340 or Scotland with 170. Perhaps a more useful classification is in terms of the Economic Planning Regions (see Table 1.1). These regions are used for a number of statistical purposes; and their relation to economic planning makes their population figures very meaningful.

What stands out here is, of course, the heavy clustering of population in the South East, which has over one-third of the people in about one sixth of the area; whereas the South West, for instance, although almost as large in area, has only about one-thirteenth of the population.

This classification does not convey the full picture. It does not reveal the most interesting aspect of the population distribution: the over-whelming extent to which it is urbanized. Eighty per cent of the British people live in urban districts. Moreover, many of the remaining 20 per cent, while living in what are classed for administrative purposes as rural districts, go to work or school in urban areas.

Table 1.1 Populations of new standard regions: United Kingdom. (Source: *Social Trends*, No. 7, HMSO, 1976)

	Mid-year estimates (millions)							Projections (1974-based)			
	1961	1971	1972	1973	1974	1975	1976	1981	1986	1991
Wales	2·6	2·7	2·7	2·7	2·8	2·8	2·8	2·8	2·9	2·9
England and Wales	46·2	48·9	49·0	49·2	49·2	49·2	49·3	49·4	50·1	50·9
Scotland	5·2	5·2	5·2	5·2	5·2	5·2	5·3	5·3	5·5	5·6
Great Britain	51·4	54·1	54·2	54·4	54·4	54·4	54·5	54·7	55·5	56·6
Northern Ireland	1·4	1·5	1·5	1·5	1·5	1·5	1·5	1·6	1·6	1·6
United Kingdom	52·8	55·6	55·8	55·9	56·0	56·0	56·1	56·3	57·1	58·2
North	3·1	3·1	3·1	3·1	3·1	3·1	3·1	3·1	3·1	3·1
Yorkshire and Humberside	4·7	4·9	4·9	4·9	4·9	4·9	4·9	4·8	4·9	4·9
East Midlands	3·3	3·6	3·7	3·7	3·7	3·7	3·8	3·9	4·0	4·1
East Anglia	1·5	1·7	1·7	1·7	1·8	1·8	1·8	1·9	2·1	2·2
South East	16·1	17·0	17·0	17·0	17·0	16·9	16·9	16·8	17·0	17·1
Greater London Council	*8·0*	*7·4*	*7·3*	*7·3*	*7·2*	*7·1*	*7·0*	*6·5*	*6·1*	*5·7*
Outer South East	*3·7*	*4·4*	*4·4*	*4·5*	*4·5*	*4·5*	*4·6*	*4·9*	*5·1*	*5·4*
Outer Metropolitan Area	*4·4*	*5·2*	*5·2*	*5·3*	*5·3*	*5·3*	*5·3*	*5·5*	*5·7*	*6·0*
South West	3·7	4·1	4·1	4·2	4·2	4·2	4·2	4·4	4·5	4·7
West Midlands	4·8	5·1	5·2	5·2	5·2	5·2	5·2	5·2	5·3	5·3
North West	6·4	6·6	6·6	6·6	6·6	6·6	6·6	6·4	6·4	6·5

During the nineteenth century this urbanization reached its most characteristic form in the great cities. These still have heavy concentrations of people; but, as Table 1.2 shows, most reached their peak numbers in the 1950s or earlier. The development of public transport, the spread of car ownership, and overspill policies—rehousing dwellers from old parts of the city further out or

Table 1.2. Population of conurbations and cities and towns with over 200 000 persons at mid-1971: United Kingdom. (Source: *Facts in Focus*, 3rd edn, Penguin, 1975)

	Mid-year estimates (thousands)			Density at 1971 Census (persons per sq. km)
	1951	1961	1971	
Cities and towns				
Birmingham	1112	1105	1013	4860
Glasgow	1093	1056	894	5580
Liverpool	789	741	605	5420
Manchester	700	657	546	4930
Sheffield	540	537	517	2840
Leeds	504	508	501	3020
Edinburgh	475	474	453	3210
Bristol	444	437	426	3900
Teeside	334	374	395	2230
Belfast	444	416	360	5560
Coventry	266	316	334	4120
Nottingham	308	311	297	4050
Bradford	290	295	294	2850
Kingston-upon-Hull	299	302	284	4030
Leicester	285	286	282	3870
Cardiff	263	284	276	3020
Wolverhampton	243	261	269	3910
Stoke-on-Trent	278	276	264	2860
Plymouth	237	240	245	3020
Newcastle-upon-Tyne	291	268	220	4950
Derby	196	212	219	2810
Sunderland	206	218	215	4190
Southampton	190	205	213	4400
Portsmouth	216	225	205	5280
Conurbations				
Greater London	8206	7977	7441	4720
West Midlands	2257	2370	2371	3500
South East Lancashire	2411	2419	2399	2430
Central Clydeside	1760	1804	1723	2220
West Yorkshire	1693	1699	1736	1370
Merseyside	1382	1380	1263	3250
Tyneside	835	853	803	3440

in new towns— all helped to check the continued concentration inside the city boundaries.

In many ways a more realistic unit than the city is the conurbation: a densely populated urban region consisting of built-up areas clustering around a great city. There are seven conurbations and $17\frac{3}{4}$ million people—one out of every three of the population— live in them. The conurbations are around London, Manchester, Birmingham, Leeds, Liverpool, Newcastle, and Glasgow. With the greater mobility conferred on people by the car, the conurbations, too, are becoming a little less densely packed or, at least, have slowed their rate of growth.

Again, this reflects overspill policies and the individual's ability through improved public and private transport to live farther away from his work, plus his readiness to do so in return for fresher air and quieter surroundings at home. But the characteristic native of these islands is still an urban or suburban animal. One Englishman in five is a Londoner; one Scotsman in five is a Glaswegian.

The overcrowding is likely to continue. The 1961 population represented an increase of $2\frac{1}{2}$ millions on the 1951 census; and the census in 1971 revealed that there had been a further increase of 3 million. This was not the pattern expected as recently as the 1940s. Throughout most of the last century the birth rate remained high—around 35 per 1000—while the death rate fell to around 20 per 1000: the rate of natural increase was high (see Fig. 1.1). During the present century, while the death rate came down to 12 per 1000, the birth rate fell to about 15 per 1000 by the 1930s. The decline reflected the drop in the size of families from the mid-nineteenth-century average of six children to the twentieth-century average of about two children. Had this continued, the population would have begun to decline from the 1970s. After the Second World War, however, the birth rate rose again, especially in the immediate postwar years—'the bulge'. A bigger proportion of the population is getting married than in the 1930s; and a far higher proportion of women are marrying and starting families in their early twenties. At the same time, the factors working to keep the death rate down—higher living standards, better nutrition, improved hygiene, advances in medicine, the greater availability of medical services, and so on—are continuing, so that people are living longer. Calculations now suggest—though they could be falsified by events, as those of the 1949 Commission on Population were—that the population of the United Kingdom should reach around 58 million by 1991.

For the most part the people of the United Kingdom are closely unified. They are a mixture of peoples, but most of the mixing took place centuries ago; and later, smaller additions have been assimilated. English, Scots, Welsh, and Irish still feel conscious—and proud—of their separate identities, but people from all parts mingle without feeling that they are among foreigners. In modern times there has always been a steady influx of people from Southern Ireland (which was for a time part of the United Kingdom).

During the last 20 years, particularly since the 1950s, growing immigration from Commonwealth countries, especially from the West Indies and Pakistan, has caused some concern and stirred up some feelings of colour prejudice. Numerically this influx has been small; there are about 1.8 million 'coloured' people in Britain today. Because the immigrants are concentrated in a few areas of London and some Midland cities, a false impression of their total numbers is easily formed. There have been demonstrations against these immigrants by people who feel that they are complicating the problems of the social services, above all housing. Restrictions on immigration are embodied in the Immigration Act 1971. To try and check the growth of discrimination against immigrants, a Race Relations Act was passed in 1965, which made it illegal to discriminate against anyone on grounds of his colour, race, ethnic or national origin. The Act set up a Race Relations Board whose main task is to encourage conciliation; where its conciliation committees do not succeed,

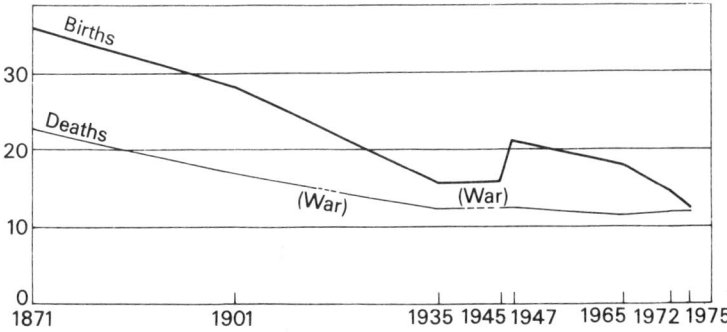

Fig. 1.1. Birth and death rates per 1000 population in the United Kingdom (note fall in birth rate)

however, the Board has powers to bring the matter to court. A 1976 amendment to the Race Relations Act (Section 70) came into effect in the Spring of 1977.

Standard of living

Despite a favourable climate, good soils, and fishing grounds in the surrounding seas, Britain cannot provide all the food that her population needs. The island can meet less than half of its requirements; the rest must be imported from abroad. Over half of the wheat, one-third of the meat, all of the tea, coffee, and cocoa, and nearly all of the sugar have to be imported. So does four-fifths of the timber needed for furniture, paper, and building. Britain cannot grow cotton, rubber, or tobacco. The home supply of wool is only one-tenth of the demand.

Nor is Britain self-sufficient in mineral resources, with the one great exception, coal. Her coal deposits are good for several centuries yet, which means she has a source of power, industrial fuel, and domestic heating. There are valuable deposits of iron ore, but they satisfy only about half of the island's needs. Apart from those two important ones, her resources are slim. We have no supplies of key minerals such as aluminium, asbestos, nickel, copper, tungsten, tin. But recently large discoveries of oil and gas in the North Sea have altered this picture. Indeed, by 1980 Britain should become a net exporter of oil and should be able to increase her production and sales for at least thirty years ahead.

Notwithstanding the limitation of natural resources and inadequate food production, Britain is a prosperous country and her people enjoy a high standard of living. We cannot calculate this as accurately as we can the population of a town, but there are number of pointers we can use. The most

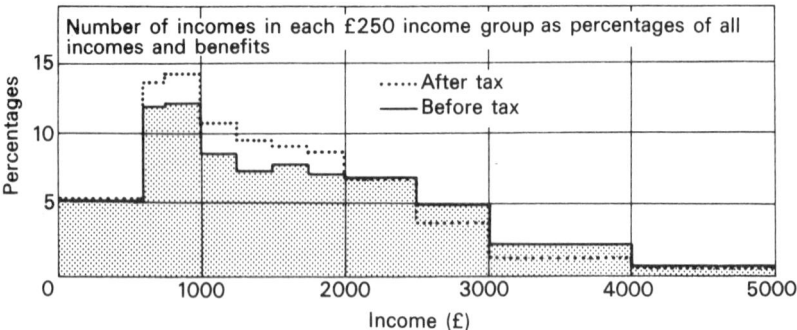

Fig. 1.2. Distribution of personal incomes before and after tax, 1973/74 (Source: *Social Trends*, No. 7, HMSO, 1976)

significant of these is the National Income. This is a measure of the total goods and services—the real wealth of the nation—produced in the course of a year. All this production involves the exchange of money: it is for our part in producing these goods and services that we all receive our incomes. Thus the total of the incomes of all engaged in production gives a guide to the value of the real wealth which has been produced.

This concept is so important—we need it to represent a country's wealth, to find out how its economy is growing from one year to another, and so on—that it demands treatment in its own right: this involves some lengthy explanations, which are given at the end of this chapter. For our immediate purposes it may be sufficient to say that the National Income of Britain in 1974 was £64 363 million.

A National Income of over £64 000 million means, by simple division, a *per capita* income of about £1140, which puts Britain among the top ten of the world's richest countries. In practice, of course, the National Income is by no means distributed equally. Nor does everyone receive an income. We can get a more realistic idea of the distribution of personal incomes from Fig. 1.2. Figure 1.3 shows distribution of household income, not only the broad spread of incomes from under £20 a week to over £150 a week, but also the way they are distributed within active and non-active groups. Thus some retired persons enjoy the highest levels but the great bulk of this group has an income of less than £20 a week.

There is, however, some redistribution of income. This comes partly through the system of direct taxation, which is graduated so that the rate of tax rises with the amount of income. The higher incomes, therefore, bear a correspondingly heavier burden of direct tax. Much of the tax revenue is used by the State to subsidize a variety of services so that they are made available free or at

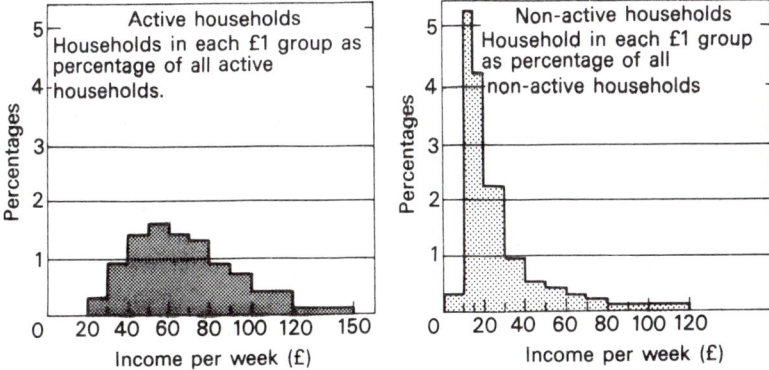

Fig. 1.3. Distribution of household incomes: active and non-active households, 1974. (Here, active households are where the head is in full-time employment; non-active households are where the head is over the national insurance age, is retired, and unoccupied. The households with incomes over £150 per week are not shown.) (Source: Social Trends, No. 7, HMSO, 1976)

least much more cheaply than they would otherwise be, e.g., education, housing, food. Moreover, a large part of the social security system is paid for out of general taxation. Hence, some income is being taken from those in the higher income groups and redistributed to those in the lower income groups.

Although we need to be cautious in working with averages, they do give a general guide. The average manual worker earns around £65 a week. The average white collar worker earns around £80 a week. However, many household incomes are increased because the wife works as well: one married woman in three goes to work in Britain today, a much higher proportion than in pre-war years. This might suggest that their husband's earnings are insufficient to make ends meet, but recent enquiries do not support this. Some women (about one-third) gave this as their reason, but more explained it was for the pleasure of mixing with people, or to earn money for luxuries or special additions to the home. Despite moves towards equal pay, culminating in the

Sex Discrimination Act 1975, women working full time earn on average £46 a week. For those doing manual work, this is reduced to under £40—some £26 a week less than their male counterparts. This could be misleading, however, as the male figure includes bonus, shift, and commission payments of various kinds. It is reasonable to say that for most people incomes are higher in real terms, i.e., despite rising prices, than at previous periods or by contrast with many other countries in the world..

Another indication of living standards is the level of nutrition. This for most people is high and still rising. An enquiry into the average diets of households showed that people were getting much more than the level required to sustain them in their activities. The average individual drinks 5 pints of milk a week, and eats $2\frac{1}{2}$ pounds of meat, $1\frac{1}{2}$ pounds of sugar, 7 pounds of fruit and vegetables, about 3 pounds of bread, and $\frac{1}{2}$ pound of butter. Recently the steady rise in levels of consumption has evened out.

The most striking sign that the British not only eat well, but enjoy generally good living conditions, medical services, and so on, is the expectation of life at birth. For men, this is now about 70 years; for women, about 75. A child born in Britain today has more chance of reaching the age of 60 than one born at the opening of the century had of reaching the age of 5. Moreover, he has a far better chance than children in poorer countries where the expectation of life is much lower: in India, for instance, it is about 40 years.

Today's child also has a better chance of improving his conditions during his life through the greater availability of educational opportunities. Again, these are far from equal: children from wealthier, middleclass homes start with advantages which weight things relatively in their favour at every stage of the educational process. Still, by contrast with the past, the opportunities for all are greater. Of those aged over 65 today, only 10 per cent were educated beyond the age of 15; of those aged between 20 and 30, over 30 per cent were at school beyond 15.

Along with improved incomes has gone an increase in leisure time and opportunities. The average working week is forty-two hours, though this is even more deceptive than most averages, since it excludes overtime working. The five-day week is now common in industry and most workers get at least two weeks holiday with pay a year.

The combination of more money and more leisure has brought changes in living patterns, inside and outside the home. Much of the increase in spending power goes on household furnishings and equipment, notably on items which were once confined to the homes of the wealthy. Table 1.3 shows how recent and how rapid the spread of these goods has been.

The most marked and significant increase has been in the number of homes with television sets. By 1976 the number of viewing licences issued was 17·7 million, over half of which were for colour sets. All agree that television is of great social importance, though there is much uncertainty as to television's precise effects. It has been praised and blamed for most things which people like or dislike in modern society: from strengthening the family and spreading knowledge, to increasing the crime rate, promoting indecency, and undermining respect for authority. Television is no doubt partly responsible for the decline in the popularity of the main entertainments of the 1930s and 1940s: the shift away from sound radio, the fall in cinema attendance (down from 1430 million in 1949 to 395 million in 1962 to 142 million in 1975), and the fall in football 'gates' (down from $41\frac{1}{2}$ million in 1949 to 28 million in 1975. Television has been accused of encouraging passiveness, but there is no sign that the national taste for hobbies and active pastimes has diminished. Britain is still full of private enthusiasts, e.g., pigeon-fanciers, dog lovers, gardeners, coin collectors.

Table 1.3. Percentage of adults in homes with certain consumer goods, 1952-75

Year	Cars	Refrigerators	Television sets	Washing machines	Vacuum cleaners
1952	—	6	11	10	40
1963	—	37	85	52	80
1975	57	85	95	72	90

Television has played a part in the spread of more cultural activities. The printed word has certainly not declined. There were over 35 600 books published in 1975 as against 26 000 in 1966. Here the major development has been the paperback explosion, providing an enormous range of cheap reprints, both fiction and non-fiction. Nor has music suffered. Gramophone records, which had their own 'revolution' with the advent of the long-playing record in 1951, now sell at about 140 million a year. The attendances at live concerts are higher than ever, and more people are making their own music of all kinds.

More money and leisure is also reflected in the growth of new enthusiasms: gliding, snow-skiing and water-skiing, skin-diving and indoor bowling, camping and caravaning. There is far more dining-out than there used to be, and a greater readiness to try other than familiar national dishes: Chinese, Indian, and Italian restaurants are now found in most large towns. Whether more money has transformed workingclass attitudes into middleclass ones is debatable and doubtful; but in some areas of life it has made the former differences less marked. This is especially so in dress, where the emergence of stylish clothes at reasonable prices has made this particular distinction between classes harder to detect. This is above all true among the younger generation. Whatever the family background, where fashion and taste are concerned, the gap is between young and old rather than between social classes.

One great British pastime has survived and thrived on more money: gambling. The traditional forms of gambling—on horses, dogs, and football—have been reinforced by the growth in popularity of bingo, and the spread of betting shops and gaming clubs. The turnover in horse and greyhound betting alone is estimated at about £1800 million per year.

With more money has come more—and more adventurous—holiday-making. About 40 million people now take an annual holiday; 5 million of them take a second break. Whereas in 1951 only 1½ million of them ventured abroad, in 1976 almost 7 million did so.

But the greatest instrument of social change in postwar Britain has been the car. In 1952 there were 2½ million private cars on the road, by 1975 there were over 18 million. Around 57 per cent of households now have a car compared with 47 per cent in 1967. The car has increased enormously people's mobility and freedom to travel when and where they choose. It has given a special stimulus to the growth of greater enterprise in holiday-making. Over 60 per cent of all holiday-makers now go by car, and many take their holiday in a car, on tour, or with a caravan. Activities previously limited by the vagaries of public transport have been opened up, whether Sunday excursions in the country or late nights-out in town. The car's effects go beyond this widening of leisure-time opportunities and horizons. By enabling people to live farther from their work in towns and cities, the car helped to change the distribution of population and patterns of housing. It has changed the face of Britain by the massive developments it entailed in road systems and motorways, parking-spaces, service stations, and the virtual reconstruction of urban centres. Nor are the car's effects always a blessing. The transformation it demands of road and traffic systems is very costly. It can lessen the pleasures of life with fumes, noise, and the confusion and frustration of traffic jams. It can help to disfigure the very countryside it enables people to visit. In 1975, an average year, it killed 6400 people and seriously injured 77 000. Controlling the car's less pleasant effects is made more difficult by its continual expansion: in 1975 there were about 18½ million cars on the roads, by the end of the century this figure will have risen to about 30 million.

Specialization

How did Britain, overcrowded and with small resources, manage to achieve this high standard of living? The answer is by specializing in manufacture and trade, i.e., by making and selling articles that other countries wanted but could not make for themselves so cheaply or so well. By selling these goods, Britain earned the money with which to buy from abroad the food and raw materials that she needed but could not produce from her own land and also those manufactured goods of which other countries were the specialist producers.

Table 1.4 illustrates this specialization. it shows that about 7½ million of Britain's workers are engaged in manufacture, whereas only about ½ million are engaged in agriculture. No other country has so few of its population engaged in farming. A further sign of the advanced state of the economy is the high proportion of workers who are not engaged either in the primary, extractive industries or the secondary, manufacturing ones, but in the tertiary industries which provide services. In less developed economies the great concentration is in the extractive industries, especially agriculture: very few hands can be spared from growing food to provide the apparently non-productive services. Indeed, in Britain today this trend is now being blamed for some of the economic ills. In 1961, 3·02 million people (around 16 per cent of the total labour employed in the market sector) were employed in services. By 1974 the figure was 4·37 million (24 per cent). By mid-1976 the figure had risen again, to almost 4·75 million—over 27 per cent were thus employed in non-productive services.

Table 1.4. Employees by industry group: United Kingdom. (Source: *Facts in Focus*, 3rd edn, Penguin, 1975)

	Thousands 1971 Census
Total employees in employment	22 121
Agriculture, forestry, fishing	432
Catering, hotels, etc.	691
Construction	1 262
Distributive trades	2 610
Gas, electricity and water	377
Insurance, banking, finance and business services	976
Local government service	914
Manufacturing	8 058
Mining and quarrying	396
Miscellaneous services (excluding catering, hotels, etc.)	1 255
National government service	596
Professional and scientific services	2 989
Transport and communication	1 568

As for trade, Britain is still one of the greatest trading countries in the world. About one-third of the goods Britain produces are sold abroad. The island is the world's biggest importer of wheat, meat, butter, tea, tobacco, and wool. Her ability to import so much, whether food or raw materials for her manufacturing industries, depends on her ability to keep selling her manufactures abroad, i.e., her standard of living depends on her efficiency in manufacture and trade.

These characteristics of Britain today have developed fairly recently. Two hundred years ago the population of Britain was only about seven million, and increasing slowly as the high birth rate was largely offset by a high death rate.

Then for various reasons, such as improvements in agriculture, greater prosperity as manufactures developed, advances in medical services, the death rate was reduced. More and more people survived to an age where they could marry and have children, who in their turn had a better chance of staying alive till they could marry and have children.

Moreover, of those seven million people in eighteenth-century Britain, most lived in the country, not in towns, and most of them worked on farms, not in factories or offices. The great change from this rural agricultural way of life to the present urban, industrial one, is the result of the Industrial Revolution.

The industrial revolution

The discovery of coke as a smelter of iron, the invention of textile machinery, and the invention of the steam engine—all contributed to the successful exploitation of natural resources. The new supplies of basic materials, the new machinery, the new power to drive it, and new techniques of production: together these made up the revolution which made Britain the leading industrial nation in the world.

Not only were the discoveries made in Britain but, in addition, she was in a position to make the most of them. Coal was the great foundation of the new techniques, and coal was Britain's most abundant mineral. This was the source of the new power to drive machinery and transport. From iron, her second mineral, the machinery was made, e.g., steam-engines themselves. From the steamdriven machinery in growing volume poured the goods, especially textiles, the articles for which the new methods were used first and most fully. Countries that wanted cotton or woollen goods, hardware, machinery, steam-engines, railway engines, naturally turned to Britain. So Britain became the workshop of the world, earning a living by making goods and selling them abroad. She was banking on doing this so well that she would earn more than enough to buy from abroad the food and raw materials without which her people would go hungry and her factories slow down.

With industrialization came urbanization and that concentration of people in certain regions that marks modern Britain (see Fig. 1.4). The iron industry moved to the source of its new fuel, the coalfields; manufacturers in general moved there to be close to the source of the new power. As the new industrial establishments sprang up on the coalfields, the people working in them were housed nearby. The many needs of these growing manufacturing populations attracted still more people to cater for them: shopkeepers and publicans, builders and plumbers, transport workers and entertainers. So the new industrial towns began to cluster on the coalfields of central Scotland and Tyneside, Lancashire and the West Riding of Yorkshire, the Midlands and South Wales.

For many years the great industrial lead Britain had built up enabled her to

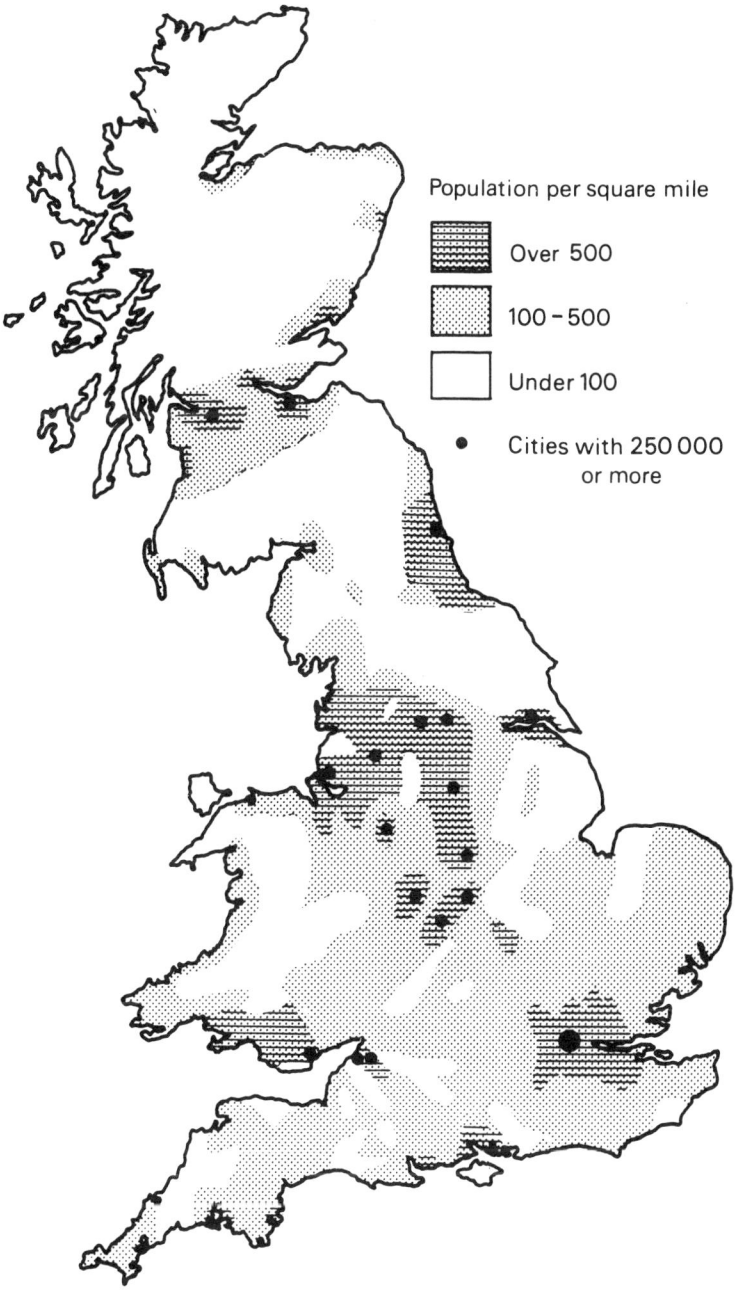

Fig. 1.4. Great Britain: population spread

achieve comfortable success in the role of factory and shopkeeper to the world at large. In the twentieth century, however, the task became harder, and new rivals came to challenge her position.

The twentieth-century challenge

By the early 1900s Britain's great asset, coal, had been undermined by the competition of other coal-producing countries and by the emergence of new alternative sources of power—electricity and oil. From 1914 the amount of coal produced in, and exported from, Britain began to decline. Iron and steel suffered from American and German competition and the growing use of new alternative metals and alloys. The textile industry, the third great base of Britain's earlier prosperity, was the most badly damaged of all. India and Japan developed their own textile industries and captured important markets in Asia from British cotton. The results were seen in the steep fall in the value of Britain's cotton exports. At the same time, an overvalued pound meant that British export prices were very high. In addition, the depression in world trade generally in the 1930s came as an especially serious blow to a country so dependent on trade.

In fact, the money Britain was earning from the sale of her manufactures abroad was no longer enough to meet the bill for the food and raw materials she was importing. There were, however, certain other assets which eased the position. During her great days of prosperity in the nineteenth century, Britain had invested vast sums of money abroad. These earned a large annual income in the shape of interest payments by the foreign borrowers. When these payments were added to Britain's normal export earnings, there was more than enough to meet the cost of imports, so Britain was still paying her way, though not simply on what she could make and sell abroad.

Postwar developments

The Second World War (1939–45) weakened Britain still more. To pay the huge bills for urgent war supplies, she had to sell most of her overseas investments. That extra source of annual income which had enabled Britain to keep meeting the cost of her imports was therefore lost. And while what other countries owed her had dwindled, what she owed foreign countries had swollen enormously: big new debts had been incurred in wartime. The conversion of her industry to wartime production naturally meant that normal exports had declined; by 1945 Britain was exporting less than half the amount of 1938. Many markets had been lost because other countries had stepped in while Britain was making munitions instead of consumer goods for those markets. A great part of the merchant fleet that carried Britain's exports abroad had been destroyed by enemy action. The factories that made the goods, the railways that carried them to the docks, and the docks themselves had likewise been damaged by war.

Consequently, although Britain had won the war she was struggling in the economic field in 1945. The basic problem of selling enough abroad to pay for imports was not new: that was always present from the time that Britain had decided to specialize in manufacture and trade. But it was far more difficult to tackle than it had ever been before. Britain would have to export a good deal more than in 1938 in order to import the same amount as in that year. She would have to export still more to pay the interest on those debts she had incurred since 1938.

Worse still, the prices of the foodstuffs and raw materials which Britain bought were higher after the war than the prices of the manufactured goods she sold. She had to sell 130 tons of exports in order to buy the imports that 100 tons would have bought in 1938. Moreover, for several years after the war, many of her pre-war sources of supply were unable to provide all the materials Britain wanted. Britain had to turn to the American continent for many of them. But the Americans wanted payment in dollars, and the kind of goods Britain had to sell to earn these dollars were often goods the Americans were making for themselves. Sales to the 'dollar countries' were especially necessary yet especially difficult.

Thus even to get back to the 1938 position was a big task. But the British people wanted to do more than this. Houses and towns needed rebuilding; people had gone short of many consumer goods they were anxious to acquire. They wanted better social services, and large sums also had to be found to keep up the nation's defences. If the goods and the money for all these purposes had to be forthcoming as well, then production would have to be increased even more. The steel that went into a car for the home market could not also go into a car for the export market, yet both were needed. Britain would simply have to produce more steel. Yet the big export industries, like coal and textiles, had been lagging even in 1938; and other basic ones, like steel, were in no position to produce quickly the increased amounts required to expand the export trade.

The British people responded well to the postwar challenge, though they needed, and got, assistance from the United States. The results of this drive were impressive. In 1958 the Gross National Product (GNP) had increased by over 30 per cent since 1936; by 1966 it had doubled. The restrictions, controls, and rationing of the immediate postwar years were steadily removed during the 1950s. The number of people engaged in production also increased during these years. We would, therefore, expect them to produce a greater total. But the growth in output exceeded the growth in the number of workers, i.e., the amount that each worker produced had also increased. Production methods had become more efficient. Moreover, much of this production went as exports to foreign markets. As early as 1948 exports had climbed back to their pre-war volume. In 1948 they earned about £2000 million; in 1960 they doubled this amount; by 1966 they were earning over £5000 million a year.

Yet this impressive achievement was not enough. On the contrary, Britain's difficulties are not over. The amount of money we spend on imports has also risen enormously so that the task of increasing exports remains a big one. In the course of the 1960s Britain found that year after year her export earnings were insufficient to pay for her imports. Moreover, rival trading countries began to make greater headway than Britain, often in the same products. Although the National Income grew year by year, the rate of growth was not impressive, whether measured against the performance of other countries or against what Britain herself was capable of achieving. During this period, the benefits which accrued from the increases in output were reduced by the more rapid increase in prices.

Unemployment and inflation, export and import levels: these are the problems which face Britain in her attempts to keep improving the living standards of the people. There are many tasks to be done in making Britain a better and more civilized country—not just a more wealthy one. But most of them require wealth if they are to be done. The basis of that wealth lies in Britain's ability to increase her production and sell enough of it abroad. Unless she can do so, then the standard of living must fall and many admirable plans for improving our society founder for lack of resources.

A note on the National Income

The National Income is a measure of the total goods and services produced in the nation in the course of a year. It is measurable in money terms since the economic activities of producing goods and providing services involve exchanges of money. Since we receive our incomes—whether in the form of wages, salaries, profits, or rents—in return for the goods and services we provide, the sum of all the incomes provides a guide to the value of what has been produced.

It is not a precise measure nor is it a simple one to make. There are services provided which are unpaid—cooking by a housewife, for instance—and these do not enter into the account: whereas if the meal were prepared by a cook who was paid a salary, then that service would be countable. Again, only incomes which are received for economic activities are counted. Old age pensions, for instance, are not given in return for some goods produced by the pensioner; so they have to be excluded from the calculations.

The National Income may be approached from a second angle—expenditure. We can add up the amounts paid out by people in purchasing goods and services throughout the year. As one person's expenditure is someones else's income, then this total ought to come to the same as the first; but as it is calculated from different sources, the two act as a check on each other. Imports need to be deducted, however, because they represent production in another country while exports have to be added.

A third calculation can be made through production. We could add up the value of the output of goods and services of each industry in the country, though here there is a need to avoid the error of double counting, i.e., items

Table 1.5. Gross National Product: United Kingdom. (Source: *Facts in Focus*, 3rd edn, Penguin, 1975)

	£ million 1974		£ million 1974
Expenditure		**Factor incomes**	
Consumers expenditure	51 282	Income from employment	51 360
Public authorities current expenditure on goods and services	16 440	Income from self employment	7 651
Gross domestic fixed capital formation	16 280	Gross trading profits of companies	9 865
Value of physical increase in stocks and work in progress	781	Gross trading surplus of public corporations	2 384
		Gross trading surplus of other public enterprises	138
		Rent	5 433
Total domestic expenditure at market prices	84 783	Total domestic income	76 831
Exports and property income from abroad	28 993	*less* Stock appreciation	−5 812
less Imports and property income paid abroad	−32 405	Residual error	687
less Taxes on expenditure	−11 339	Gross domestic product at factor cost	71 706
Subsidies	2 921	Net property income from abroad	1 247
Gross national product at factor cost	72 953	**Gross national product at factor cost**	72 953
		less Capital consumption	−8 590
		National income	64 363

produced by one industry for processing by another must not be counted for both. In any of these ways—by adding up incomes, expenditure, or output—we could arrive at a total figure expressing the value of all goods and services provided in the country during the year—the National Income.

The figure finally arrived at can be 'processed' a little further and presented in one of three ways:

(a) Gross Domestic Product (GDP). This is the total value of goods produced within the country.

(b) Gross National Product (GNP). A certain amount of income accrues to Britain during the year as earnings for services provided in the form of investments overseas. When this is added to the GDP the final figure is the GNP.

(c) Net National Income. Neither GDP nor GNP allows for the fact that some of the nation's output each year needs to be subtracted to allow for making good the wear and tear to equipment. This has to be deducted from GNP to obtain the Net National Income. In practice, this figure of 'capital consumption' is just an estimate; and we are normally content to work with the gross figure, whether GDP or GNP.

The figures are usually cited as at 'Factor Cost'. The point here is that the prices we pay for goods often include an indirect tax. This means that the price is higher than the cost of the factors of production which went into making the article available—wages, profits, rent, interest. When we deduct the amount of tax on the article, we have its value at factor cost. In some cases the market price may be lower than the factor cost: there may be a subsidy which allows it to be sold more cheaply. Such subsidies would therefore have to be added to the market price to obtain the factor cost.

Comparisons of GNP or GDP over a number of years are likely to be more meaningful if we can eliminate the effect of price changes during the period. It is therefore customary to take prices prevailing in one year—1958 is the one used—as a base, and revalue the figures for other years in terms of these prices. On this basis of constant prices we can see how far the National Income of the country has grown or diminished over the years.

Table 1.5 illustrates how the National Income was arrived at from incomes in 1974.

2A. Major industries: old and new

The changing structure of British industry

The role of industry in general is clearly of crucial importance to Britain's economy. The manufacturing industry accounts for over one-third of the GNP. It is responsible for over 80 per cent of Britain's exports. It gives employment to more than 34 per cent of the working population. Some branches of industry are of especial importance and interest, and merit closer consideration: coal, iron and steel, engineering, textiles, and chemicals. All these are major groups; some old, some relative newcomers, some in difficulties, some thriving. Their different fortunes represent the changing structure of British industry which characterizes the middle decades of the twentieth century. Before looking at these activities individually, it is convenient to bring together some basic information about them in a form which allows this process of change to be seen quickly and easily. Figure 2.1 shows the relative decline (since 1961) of the numbers engaged in mining and textiles and the rise of those in engineering (with vehicles singled out as of particular importance), chemicals, and iron and steel.

Falling numbers need not mean falling production: technological improvements may enable an industry to turn out more goods while using fewer men. Table 2.1, covering the same groups for broadly the same period, however, confirms the picture suggested by Fig. 2.1. While the output of industry as a whole increased twofold over the period, mining output positively declined, and although textile production increased, it did so far more slightly than industry in general whereas chemicals increased output sevenfold, engineering fourfold, and iron and steel production trebled.

Table 2.2 shows recent variations in output per head for production and manufacturing industries. In mining, both employment and output are falling; in textiles, the decline in employment is still more marked, but production has increased, although at a rate unimpressive by comparison with others; in metals, both employment and output are growing; while chemicals and engineering are also growing but more impressively, at a rate higher than that of the manufacturing industries as a whole.

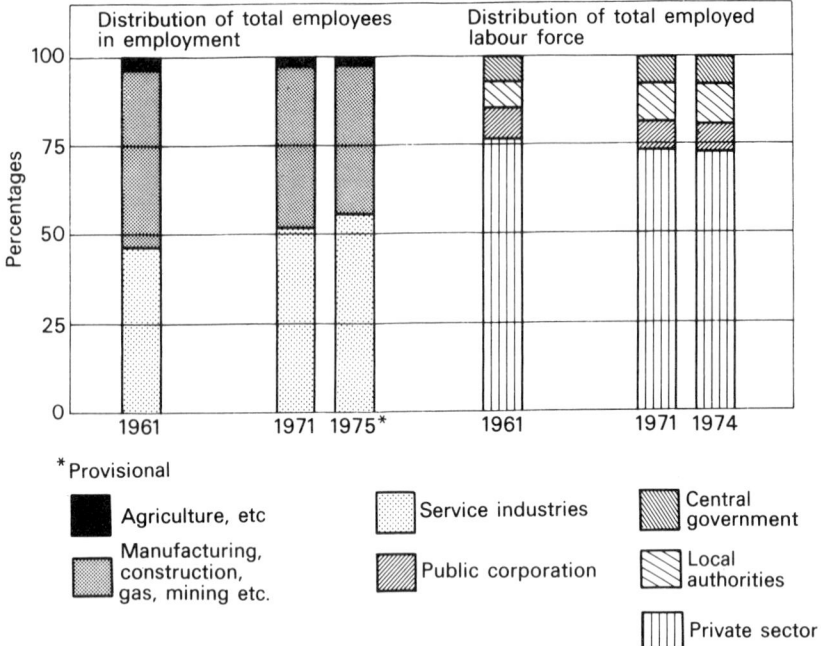

Fig. 2.1. Distribution of people at work: United Kingdom. (Source: *Social Trends*, No. 7, HMSO, 1976)

Iron and steel

The iron and steel industry employs about 365 000 people—fewer than in coalmining—but it produces the essential material for the making of hundreds of articles, from railway engines to razor blades. In manufactures generally, in transport, in farming, in the building industry, steel is a basic material so it is of great importance to the whole economy. Because it is used in so many fields, the figures for steel production are often used as a quick guide to a country's industrial strength.

At one time Britain was self-sufficient in the main materials of the industry—coal and iron ore. Nowadays, however, she has to import about half of the ore from Sweden, North Africa, Canada, and Newfoundland.

Like coal, the iron and steel industry has had its difficult times in the present century. Britain's old lead in iron was maintained for a while in steel once new discoveries in the 1850s and 1860s made steel the more important branch of the industry. But by 1914 both America and Germany had far outstripped Britain in steel production, and were strong rivals in selling to foreign customers. They had the advantage of bigger and better supplies of iron ore, but they also made use of more modern equipment and methods of production.

The depression in 1929 added to the steel industry's troubles. It was those industries that had always been the biggest users of steel which were most depressed—shipbuilding above all—and so the demand for steel fell steeply.

Table 2.1. Index of industrial production, 1948–75 (1970 = 100). (Source: Britain 1977: An Official Handbook, HMSO, 1977)

Industry group	1948	1968	1970	1973	1974	1975	1948–75 Percentage change
All industries	50.5	97.2		110.2	106.3	101.0	100
Mining/quarrying	129.1	111.4		92.6	79.1	86.3	–33
Total manufacturing	47.8	95.8		110.8	108.1	101.4	112
Food/drink/tobacco	58.4	96.5		109.3	109.9	108.5	85
Coal/petroleum products	21.4	84.0		110.0	106.0	92.0	330
Chemical/allied industries	25.5	89.8		121.2	127.7	115.8	353
Metal manufacture	61.8	97.5		100.0	91.7	78.6	27
Engineering industries	34.7	91.1		111.3	109.8	106.1	206
Shipbuilding	110.3	95.1		95.1	99.4	103.4	–6
Vehicles (inc. aircraft)	39.0	101.1		105.1	101.3	94.7	143
Other metal goods	64.1	98.3		103.1	103.5	94.5	45
Textiles/clothing	73.4	98.9		110.1	103.0	99.1	35
Bricks, pottery, etc.	54.4	102.1		127.1	116.6	107.9	100
Timber, furniture, etc.	45.4	106.5		132.6	112.5	110.2	144
Paper/printing/publishing	42.7	96.2		112.1	108.8	95.6	127
Other manufacturing	30.5	95.7		116.5	114.2	103.1	241
Construction	56.3	103.5		107.3	98.3	93.3	65
Gas/electricity/water	31.4	91.6		118.1	118.6	120.4	280

Table 2.2. Output per head (1970 = 100). (Source: *Britain: An Official Handbook*, HMSO, 1977)

	All production industries			Manufacturing industries			
	Output	Employment	Output per head	Output	Employment	Output per head	Employed labour force
1966	90·6	105·6	85·6	89·2	102·6	86·9	102·6
1967	91·7	102·8	89·2	89·8	99·8	90·0	100·9
1968	97·2	101·4	95·9	96·0	99·0	97·0	100·5
1969	99·8	101·5	98·3	99·6	100·3	99·3	100·4
1970	100·0	100·0	100·0	100·0	100·0	100·0	100·0
1971	100·4	96·9	103·6	99·6	96·8	102·9	98·2
1972	102·7	94·6	108·6	102·4	93·7	109·3	98·9
1973	110·2	95·8	115·0	110·8	94·2	117·6	101·0
1974	106·3	95·5	111·3	108·1	94·5	114·4	101·3
1975	101·0	92·3	109·4	101·4	90·8	111·7	100·4

The steel firms used the breathing space to reorganize. Many firms amalgamated, pooling their resources and working together instead of against one another. They closed down old works and opened new ones using modern plant and processes, e.g., the huge works at Corby in Northamptonshire.

The Second World War and its aftermath brought prosperity to the steel industry. The spread of mechanization into all fields of industry, the erection of massive oil, chemical, and electrical plant, of power stations and a hundred other installations, the expansion of car and aircraft production: all this has meant, up till recently, a constant demand for steel. As well as feeding the huge engineering industry, steel is one of the six leading export industries. Steel output has trebled since 1935, doubled since 1945. It boasts the best labour relations of all British industries, and steelworkers are among the highest paid of all British workers.

The iron and steel industry faced many problems in adapting itself to the quite new demands of industrial and contruction firms. Highly susceptible to fluctuations in demand, it was necessary that such an important industry should be developed in a way better suited to the needs in a highly competitive European market where other nations were already well organized. As early as 1952, the Dutch, Belgians, French, and Germans had been working together in a coal and steel community in which there was such planning of productive facilities and marketing.

Thus, despite her earlier leadership as a steel-producing nation, Britain had by the late 1960s fallen to eighth place in the world league table of steel producers. The appearance of prosperity in the industry since 1945 belied the fact that often the steelworks operated at under 100 per cent capacity. In view

Table 2.3. Coal production at National Coal Board Mines: Great Britain. (Source: *Facts in Focus*, 3rd edn, Penguin, 1975)

	1969/70		1974/75	
	Output	Output per manshift	Output	Output per manshift
	(million tons)	(cwt)	(million tons)	(cwt)
All NCB mines	140·0	43·4	115·0	45·0
Barnsley	8·1	42·0	7·6	46·1
Doncaster	8·5	47·9	8·3	50·7
East Wales	7·7	27·2	8·7	—
Kent	1·1	26·6	0·8	24·5
Northumberland	6·9	42·4	14·6	37·4
North Derbyshire	10·6	56·0	7·7	58·1
North Durham	5·4	33·4	14·6	37·4
North Nottingham	11·8	58·7	10·8	58·7
North Western	7·0	36·0	12·6	46·3
North Yorkshire	9·2	49·4	8·3	52·0
Scottish North	5·0	38·5	10·0	39·5
Scottish South	6·4	35·6	10·0	39·5
South Durham	8·3	36·3	14·6	37·4
South Midlands	9·3	59·7	7·8	58·6
South Nottingham	11·2	58·6	9·7	57·7
South Yorkshire	10·1	46·2	8·1	44·7
Staffordshire[1]	8·6	50·5	—	—
West Wales	5·1	29·7	8·7	26·5

1. Included with North Western in 1974/75.

of the colossal capital costs of building new steel plants, and the kinds of risks involved in marketing the products, the Government decided to take the industry under public control. This was done by the Iron and Steel Act of 1967, which brought thirteen major steel companies into public ownership and set up the British Steel Corporation (BSC). In it were firms producing about 90 per cent of all steel products and around 70 per cent of the total manpower employed in the industry.

The steel industry has been particularly successful in the last decade in adopting its productive techniques to meet new needs. The BSC has devoted its resources to improving efficiency by concentrating on basic oxygen steel-making (BOS) and the electric arc furnace processes (replacing the older open hearth furnaces). The effects of such changes are not only rises in production per manshift, but a more effective use of the raw materials used in the plants.

Five years after its establishment the BSC adopted a ten-year development programme (1972–82) to improve still further facilities at Ravenscraig

(Scotland), Scunthorpe and Teesside (in England) and at Llanwern (in Wales). By 1976 a large-scale basic oxygen steelmaking plant had been completed at Port Talbot (along with deep water harbour and ore terminal) and a major steelmaking complex at Scunthorpe. Only through constant developments of these kinds can British Steel maintain its export record—worth over £550

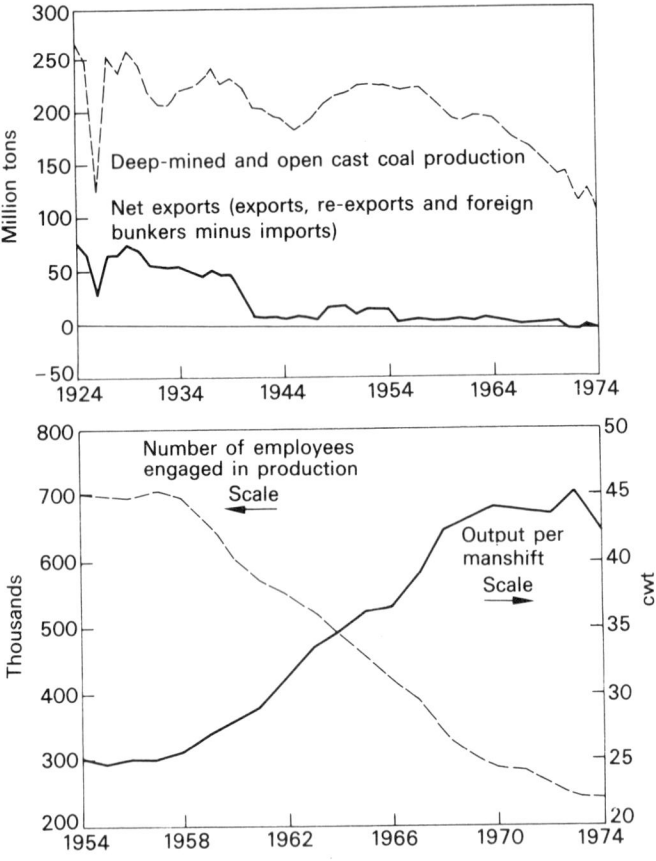

Fig. 2.2. Coal production and exports: Great Britain. Source: *Facts in Focus*, 3rd edn, Penguin, 1975)

million in 1975. Already as an industry it is highly mechanized. It is one of the foremost industries in its use of computers and automatic controls—around £15 000 of equipment is provided for each worker. Massive investment on a regular basis seems the only way to keep ahead of competitors. Public control of the industry appears an essential element in assuring financial support on such a scale.

The main centres of iron and steel production are South Wales, the North East, the Sheffield region, and Scotland.

South Wales: The presence of iron ore deposits and forests in the north-east of this region encouraged the early growth of iron working. When coal became the main fuel, local supplies enabled the industry to expand without any shifting of site. Merthyr, Aberdare, Ebbw Vale, and the rest of the 'iron' towns

Table 2.4. Iron and steel. United Kingdom. (Source: *Facts in Focus*, 3rd edn, Penguin, 1975)

	1964	1969	1974
Steel			
Number of steel furnaces in existence at end of period	756	657	535
Total supply of steel (thousand tonnes ingot equivalent)	28 750	30 010	28 620
Home sources;			
Total	26 740	27 200	23 420
Crude steel production	26 650	26 840	22 430
Reusable material	250	230	100
Deliveries to (−) or from (+) stocks	−160	+130	+890
Imported	2 010	2 810	5 200
Distribution of supply (thousand tonnes ingot equivalent)			
Exports	4 700	5 010	4 240
Supply for home use	24 050	25 000	24 380
Net deliveries—actual tonnage (thousand tonnes)			
Exports	3 283	3 461	2 676
For home use	17 063	18 556	18 812
Iron			
Number of blast furnaces in existence at end of period	94	71	58
Iron ore production (thousand tonnes)	16 588	12 298	3 602
Pig iron production (thousand tonnes)	17 551	16 653	13 903

were not only on the coalfield but in a part where the lie of the land simplified the extraction of coal.

By the early twentieth century, however, the sites of the industry were shifting. The exhaustion of the north-east ores, and the need for special foreign ores as steel replaced iron, proved a great disadvantage. The coast was only twenty miles away, but the imported ore had to be hauled at heavy cost up from the steep sided valleys. It was more economical to set up the steelworks on the coast. So, one by one, the great works of the north-east closed down. This migration of metal making to the coast coincided with the decline in coal's fortunes, so that the north-east found both its main props removed from under it at the same time.

To ease the distress, one firm, which was proposing to leave Wales for Scunthorpe, was persuaded to set up a new, modern steelworks at Ebbw Vale, despite its inconvenient position. Apart from this, the present centres of steel are on the coast at Port Talbot, Swansea, Llanelly, and Cardiff.

There was a further reason for this shift. The great local consumer of steel was the very active tinplate industry, and the kind of steel best suited for tinplate needs foreign ore. So the steelworks were accommodating their best customer when they moved to the coast. The steel industry is still closely tied to tinplating: most Welsh steel is in the shape tinplating requires—strips and sheets. Wales now produces 30 per cent of the total crude steel output of the United Kingdom.

The North East: With the discovery, about one hundred years ago, of iron ore in the Cleveland hills, Middlesbrough became the centre of the region's iron and steel industry. Within a few miles lay the ore, Durham coking coal—the finest for smelting—and limestone from the Pennines. Its location on the Tees estuary was an advantage in the export of the massive products of the industry; it is still more so now that most of the ore has to be imported from Spain, Algeria, and Sweden. The iron and steel plants are sited right on the river banks, so that the raw material is unloaded direct at the blast furnaces; for imports and exports this situation cuts out rail transport cost. This is the leading iron district in Britain and its steel output (29 per cent of UK total) is second to that of South Wales. About one-quarter of the North East's iron is exported; the rest, and nearly all its steel output, goes to feed its own engineering and shipbuilding industries.

The Sheffield Region: The metal industries of the Don valley were carried on long before the industrial revolution. Local iron ore was worked, and the surrounding forests provided abundant wood when charcoal was the smelting fuel. When coal replaced charcoal, the district was still favoured by the existence of the great Yorkshire coalfield. What was true of fuel was equally true of power supply: the falling streams for water power, the coals for steam power later. The millstone grit of the Pennines was a good grinding stone that helped the growth of cutlery manufacture.

The natural advantages are gone or matter little today, except the coal. The ore is exhausted and Sheffield has the drawback of an inland situation, so that imported material is expensive; much comes up from Corby, but again transport costs are heavy. Nevertheless, it is the third greatest steel-producing centre in Britain. The reason is that it has acquired advantages that hold the industry there. Four centuries of metal making and production have built up the area's reputation and tradition; there is a huge experienced labour force, including highly specialized craftsmen; and all the aids and services that grew up with the industry and the population. These could not be created overnight in another region, whatever its natural advantages.

Sheffield has reduced the disadvantage of its situation by concentrating on certain types of product: small steel articles, like cutlery and tools, which use little metal and much skill; and special quality alloy steels whose value again is far higher than the simple amount of metal in them. Sheffield firms were the pioneers in alloy steels: Hadfield's produced the first of them, manganese steel, following it with silicon steel. Firth's developed stainless steel. In effect, wherever a special quality steel is needed, Sheffield can supply it: armour-plating, guns, shells, highspeed tools, engine parts. Because these products are much more valuable than the bulk of raw material in them, they can command a high price that more than repays the cost of transporting them—and the necessary raw materials—overland for long distances.

Scotland: This is covered in Chapter 4 (see page 95).

Engineering

For the real giant of British manufacturing industries today, we must turn to the engineering industry. This is really a collection of industries all engaged in making some kind of machinery out of iron and steel. Mechanical engineering, electrical engineering, vehicles (cars and aircraft), and shipbuilding are the main branches. Nearly half of all the people employed in manufactures are in engineering. It has been the most flourishing of Britain's industries since the war. It accounts for about one-third of the output of all manufactures, and it provides more than half of Britain's exports.

Mechanical engineering itself employs about one million people. It covers many things: textile machinery, agricultural and office machinery, stationary engines, machine tools, cranes, boilers, heavy industrial plant and equipment. This is the biggest branch of the engineering industry. It is Britain's leading export industry.

This great expansion since the war is a result of the growing mechanization of British industry. For instance, in 1938 farming used 150 combine-harvesters; now it uses over 60 000. The coal industry, as we saw, makes far more use of machinery than it did. Forty firms are kept busy producing machinery solely for the steel industry. Over 200 concentrate on making the complicated equipment for the growing chemicals industry. When even unlikely places like offices and farmyards are clamouring for machines, mechanical engineering cannot help but grow quickly.

The engineering industry satisfied another modern want by developing a range of labour-saving devices that gave the British housewife more time to herself: vacuum cleaners, irons, washing machines, spindriers. From being the luxury articles for a few, they became part of the normal equipment most women expect to have in their homes.

Motor vehicles

The vehicle industry is mainly concerned with cars and commercial vehicles. This part of the industry is dominated by four car giants—British Leyland (under public control), Ford, Chrysler UK, and Vauxhall (General Motors). These together account for over 95 per cent of cars and commercial vehicles. In addition, buses, coaches, sports cars, and specialist vehicles are produced by some smaller firms. The industry now has manufacturing and assembly plants in Wales, Merseyside, and Scotland as well as in the original strongholds of London and the Midlands. This is a twentieth-century industry. The key invention that made it possible, the internal combustion engine, using petrol as the fuel, was developed in Germany in the 1880s. However, it was ten years before the first car firm appeared in Coventry, and another thirty before the first popularly priced car, the Austin Seven, appeared on the British scene. In 1938 the industry was producing about half a million cars a year; now it turns out over three times as many, and keeps nearly 500 000 men busy making them. By 1974 almost 600 000 cars were exported, with a total value of over £425 million.

Cars now play a bigger part in Britain's export trade than any other single engineering activity. Better jobs and higher wages in Britain and many foreign countries since the war have brought the car within the reach of millions who could never have dreamt of buying one in the 1930s. The industry has been quick to satisfy these wants. No other industry uses so many automatic processes. In the British Leyland's glass-walled, push-button factory in Birmingham six men can produce what, fifty years ago, required over 100 men. Along the conveyor chains—sixteen miles of them in this factory—move the engines, chassis, bodies, axles, in a steady stream; each component arrives at the right moment in the right place to be joined by another swinging out from its own stream; a ghostly procession of car parts putting themselves together with few human beings handling them.

It is not an industry in which fortunes are to be made easily. The international competition is severe, especially from the Japanese, who passed Britain as the world's leading exporter during the late 1960s. At home, the car industry is among the most sensitive to government tax policies: changes in hire-purchase terms can easily upset the industry's calculations and its programmes. Its nature as a component industry, dependent on the inflow of thousands of parts from hundreds of places, makes it peculiarly vulnerable to costly strikes, for a stoppage of work at the firm making batteries or brakes can halt the whole assembly line. Assembly line working breeds its own tensions in the workmen, tensions made no easier to handle by a multiplicity of unions. In addition, changes in production are costly, since new models mean expensive modifications in equipment; and risky in that fashions change and the bright new model can be a total flop. Gradually these tough conditions have led to mergers to form companies big enough to compete efficiently. Thus in 1951 Austin and Morris merged to form the British Motor Corporation. In 1966 they acquired Jaguar, which itself had taken over Daimler in 1960, and became British Motor Holdings. In 1968 the Leyland-dominated group, Standard Triumph International, merged with BMH into one company. In 1975 this in turn became British Leyland. This controls nearly half of all Britain's vehicle industry.

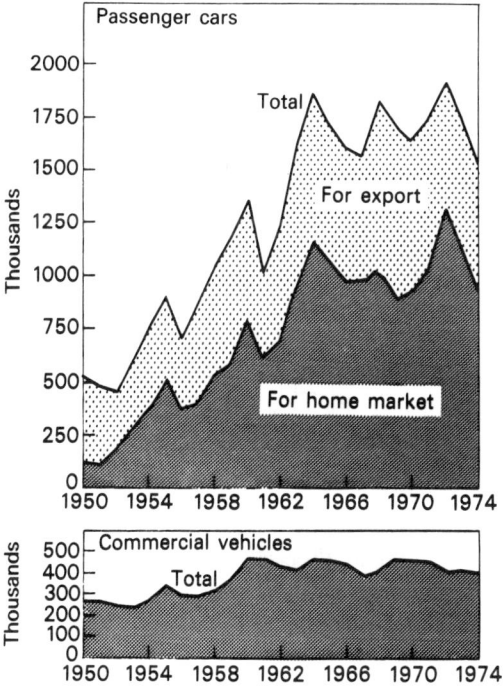

Fig. 2.3. Motor vehicle production: United Kingdom. (Source: *Facts in Focus*, 3rd edn., Penguin, 1975.

Aerospace industry

Known until recently as the aircraft industry, this important sector of Britain's industry covers a wide range of products, including civil and military aircraft, and also helicopters, guided weapons, hovercraft, and space vehicles.

The industry got a tremendous boost from the developments and inventions of the war period 1939–45. Indeed, within six years a wide range of developments took place, not only in engine development but in the structure and design of aircraft. The invention of the gas turbine engine was only the most spectacular of dozens of such improvements. After the war, the peacetime industry benefited greatly—in the case of the gas turbine it led to the jet-engined aircraft which pushed the industry to the fore on the world map up till the early 1960s. Unfortunately, international competition in this field is intense and already the USA has overtaken Britain in some of these developments.

Despite this, Britain's aerospace industry is one of the most advanced and most comprehensive in the world. Current production includes civil planes like the Hawker Siddeley HS 748, Trident, and 115 Executive jet, the BAC One-eleven, the Shorts Skyvan, and the Islander/Trislander light transport aircraft produced by Britten Norman. Concorde, which was the result of a joint Anglo-French project to develop a supersonic airliner for international travel, is operating on several routes, with the earliest British leg of the service being between London and Bahrain on the Persian Gulf—a flight that takes just over four hours for the distance of 3515 miles.

On the military side, developments such as the Hawker Siddeley Harrier, which can rise either vertically or with a short take-off (and land in the same way) has pushed Britain to the fore in sales of such planes abroad. The Puma, Gazelle, and Lynx helicopters, which were developed jointly by Britain and France, led to further joint efforts in the field of guided missiles. Altogether it is an industry geared to the twenty-first century, with extensive (and expensive) research into space systems and 'satellite' communications.

Not only is Britain the leading producer of hovercraft which are already widely used for cross-Channel passenger and car ferries, but many of these speedy vehicles are sold abroad. They contributed to the massive £631 million earned by export sales of the industry in 1974. The total value of the output was then around £1234 million, and around a quarter of a million people were employed in the industry.

The aerospace industry was dominated by two large airframe manufacturers—The British Aircraft Corporation and Hawker Siddeley Aviation. In 1977 the Government took both of these companies—along with Hawker Siddeley Dynamics and Scottish Aviation—under public control. The new concern is known as British Aerospace. The object of this public takeover is to provide coordinated financial support for an industry involving massive research and developmental work.

Electrical engineering and electronics

With around 840 000 employed in the manufacture and installation of a wide range of electrical and electronic equipment, this is a huge industry in money terms. In 1974 the total value of all production reached almost £5000 million. Exports of machinery and appliances reached £1131 million, and the range of products sold covered all types of generating, transmission, and electronic equipment, electric motors, television and radio receivers, computers, domestic electric appliances (kettles, irons, toasters, etc.), and specialized electronic equipment.

Apart from this, there are around 700 firms in Britain manufacturing and supplying electrical machinery like generators, switchgear and control gear, transformers, convertors, etc. In this section of electrical machinery manufacture nine major firms are responsible for over one-third of the total output, although the total workforce employed is around 140 000.

Electronics An important and clearly separate sector within the electrical industry in general is the field of electronics. Production of electronic equipment employs over 400 000 people, and the range of work includes telecommunications, components, computers, and capital equipment. Britain is a major exporter of telecommunication equipment, and British scientists have made important contributions to the developments in the industry. While the consumer side includes manufacture of high fidelity audio equipment, tape recorders, televisions, etc., the computer sector of this industry provides the whole range of control processes, from large-scale data processing to mini computers for use in automated communications systems.

The whole engineering industry is in fact led forward by the electronics branch. New telecommunication systems, railway modernization, computers, advances in navigation instrument, modern weapons, remote control missiles—all these make electronics among the most exciting as well as most rapidly expanding of all industries. However, in respect of electronic microcurrents (i.e., silicone 'chips') Britain has not only failed to match her American and Japanese competitors. She has so far been forced to import almost all of these essential components for electronic calculators. The electronics industry has the further advantage that its discoveries can transform the techniques and output of a host of other industries. Steel, oil, chemicals, cars, as well as banks and offices, make use of the automatic aids devised by the electronics industry. It is an important exporter, especially of navigational devices for ships and aircraft.

The electronics industry is not tied to the places favoured by the basic industries. It does not depend on the systems of mineral reserves such as coal. For these reasons, it can be a boon to any area with employment problems. To establish a plant or factory requires basically a supply of electricity (to be 'on the grid') and a supply of labour (most of it unskilled). With competent technical leadership and the capital required for initial establishment firms could be set up where required in terms of government regional or local policies. It is a 'new' industry. And it is fairly easy to arrange new locations for plants or factories to suit local employment needs.

Shipbuilding

An older branch of engineering—shipbuilding—has had a more chequered postwar career and faces more difficulties than the others. In the years straight after the war there was a big demand in the world for new merchant ships: many had been lost in wartime, many had got into a bad state of disrepair and needed replacement; and the revival of world trade with the return of peace meant that more ships were wanted. Shipyards in all countries found their order books full.

By now, however, the urgent needs have been met, and there are simply more shipyards in the world than the demand for new ships warrants. As a result, competition for orders is severe, Continental and Japanese yards being particularly powerful rivals of British yards.

The fact that Britain's shipbuilding is an old industry means it has a bigger job to modernize its equipment and methods. The full order books after the war may have bred an optimism which made changes seem unnecessary. At all events, British yards were slower than their rivals, the Swedes, Germans, and Japanese, to introduce more modern techniques. The British Government gave less encouragement in the form of subsidies which most foreign Governments gave their shipbuilders in one form or another. Relations between management and men in British yards were far from good. This was not unexpected in an industry where demand can fluctuate widely, so that workers never feel secure in their jobs. The frequent disputes and stoppages of work often led to late deliveries and setbacks to Britain's reputation as a shipbuilder. An enquiry in 1966 (the Geddes Report) concluded that there were too many shipyards in the country and that they were too small. It recommended large-scale reorganization, with the more efficient yards in a region joining together to act as a group. Fewer, bigger units comprising the best of the existing yards would stand a better chance of competing in the world's markets.

Despite the long tradition of successful shipbuilding British yards have been forced to embark on extensive programmes of modernization. Reorganization of the yards through several mergers of old-established firms had led to a lower and a hopefully more competitive structure.

In Chapter 4 there is a case study of what happened to shipbuilding on Clydeside. There the industry is now concentrated in two huge groups—Upper Clyde Shipbuilders and Scott Lithgow—and in north-east England there are now three major groups. A further group controls shipbuilding in east Scotland, while activities in the south of England are dominated by one large corporation. If we add to these the Merseyside and the Belfast group (Cammell Laird) they account for nine-tenths of the total tonnage built in Britain.

Substantial progress has been made in improving industrial relations and raising productivity, and one of the most significant steps has been the completion of covered production bays which enable craftsmen to continue full-scale work on new ships both summer and winter—and, if required, night and day. Only when such facilities became commonplace in the shipyards can Britain hope to compete successfully with the high speed, high production yards of Japan and South Korea. In the first mentioned, unskilled labour has been trained within a few weeks to produce large bulk carriers to designs produced in Scotland for the original use of Scottish shipyards.

Clearly, then, international competition is very keen, and the new trends in world shipping, favouring the much bigger bulk carriers and oil tankers, present a real challenge to British firms. Already some of these firms are diversifying their work—some yards carry out repair work, maintenance, conversion, and refitting as well as building. Success in this work is already in sight. By 1974 over £250 million was earned in this way.

Shipbuilding, as a capital industry which provides the basic facility to transport world trade, is very susceptible to any swings in such trade. The world trade recession which began in 1973 affected orders for new vessels, and this in turn affected the future employment of many thousands of craftsmen, who were faced with empty order books for the future. This was the situation in the 1930s: shipbuilding was one of the first industries to suffer from the economic recession in world trade then, and history would appear to be repeating itself now.

In view of the importance of the industry to the community, the Government passed a Bill in 1977 to take shipbuilding under public control, and set up a new public corporation—British Shipbuilders. With the financial backing this gives to the industry, combined with the large-scale reorganization already under way throughout the industry, the future prospects seem more promising.

Table 2.5. Merchant shipbuilding: United Kingdom (vessels of 100 gross tons and over). (Source: *Facts in Focus*, 3rd edn, Penguin, 1975)

		1964	1974
Orders on hand			
Value (£ million):	Total	316	1538
	For export	48	474
Number of vessels			
under construction:	Total	188	171
	For export	32	38
not yet laid down:	Total	118	210
	For export	28	72
Net new orders			
Value (£ million):	Total	141	364
	For export	16	285
Number of vessels:	Total	207	140
	For export	32	52
Completions			
Value (£ million):	Total	103	228
	For export	15	62
Number of vessels:	Total	193	134
	For export	39	31

Textiles

Textiles as a whole employ over half a million people—half of whom are women. Britain has since medieval times been important as a producer of wool and worsted products. By 1976 over £800 million worth of such goods were produced. Nowadays, however, the textile industry overall is not a major growth industry—certain sections of it are in decline, for instance, cotton.

During the nineteenth century cotton was the king of British industries, far and away the biggest item of Britain's exports. But changing world conditions in the twentieth century undermined cotton's position.

Countries that used to be valuable customers of Lancashire's cotton firms—USA, South America and, above all, India—built up their own cotton industries and made their own cotton goods. In America, heavy import duties were imposed on British cottons so that they could not compete with the growing home industries. In India, dislike of British rule led many Indians to refuse to buy British goods.

Moreover, in many markets, especially in the huge Asian one, fierce competition from rival cotton-producing countries proved too much for Britain. The Japanese were the main rivals and in most respects they had advantages over Lancashire. Their workers were paid much less and they worked more shifts. Japan was nearer to sources of raw cotton and to the Asian markets, so transport costs were less. Like all the newer cotton-producing countries, Japan had much better equipment—even in 1946 only 1 in 20 of Lancashire's looms was automatic.

With Government help the industry is being streamlined, old factories closed down, the remaining ones equipped with new machinery. As a smaller industry, making quality goods, there may be a future for British cotton, but the days when it commanded a massive world market seem to have gone for good. At present it employs only half the people it did in 1938, produces only about a quarter what it did then, and as an export industry it has been surpassed by others such as hosiery and knitwear, which sold abroad over £80 million in 1974 against the £22 million sold by cotton firms in the industry.

The great centre of the cotton industry is still Lancashire. The region had good supplies of soft water for washing processes, and the same fast-flowing streams from the Pennines were a valuable asset when the first water-driven machinery was invented. The change to steam power did not bring the industry, here, it was already established; but Lancashire's coalfield meant the new power was at hand too, so that the industry could stay and expand instead of migrating. The mills, which had been strung out along the banks of the Pennine streams in water power days, simply moved down on to flatter land and clustered together in evergrowing numbers. The damp climate was an advantage to spinning, as cotton fibres snap easily in a dry atmosphere. The local soft water and the convenient saltfields of Cheshire were ideal for bleaching, and in Liverpool the region had a fine port with established connections with America, the major source of raw cotton in the nineteenth century.

By the mid-1950s, however, change was necessary throughout the industry. The days when the world was clothed in the products of a few grimy Lancashire towns are gone for good, for reasons we have already seen. Lancashire appreciated the changed position, and under the Cotton Industry

Act (1959) the industry began to adapt accordingly. Half of its capacity was scrapped, the machinery broken up, the mills closed, and the sites cleared for new activity. Burnley, which had 300 mills, has under 25. In the smaller, more compact industry, up-to-date equipment improved efficiency; and it is geared to the manufacture of high quality yarn and cloth, abandoning the cheap lines to its Far Eastern competitors who have squeezed Lancashire out of the world market for these.

Table 2.6. Textiles: United Kingdom. (Source: *Facts in Focus*, 3rd edn, Penguin, 1975)

	Unit	1964	1974
Wool			
Virgin wool (clean weight):			
Imports	Million kg	179	88
Home production	Million kg	38	33
Production of tops:			
Wool and hair	Million kg	120	44
Man-made fibre	Million kg	26	55
Deliveries of worsted yarn[1]	Million kg	106	77
Production of woollen yarn[1]	Million kg	148	123
Deliveries of woven fabrics (woollen and worsted excluding blankets)[1]	Million sq. m	272	175
Deliveries of blankets	Million sq. m	28	28
Cotton and man-made fibres			
Imports of raw cotton	Th. tonnes	334	152
Production of cotton yarn (including waste yarn)	Million kg	230	101
Production of cotton cloth	Million lin. m	946	409
Production of man-made fibres	Th. tonnes	374	628
Production of spun man-made fibre and mixture yarn (incl. waste yarn)	Million kg	66	88
Production of man-made fibre and mixture cloth	Million lin. m	558	505

1. Includes man-made fibres and mixtures.

Wool has declined also, though less than cotton (see Table 2.6). It was never so tied to foreign markets as cotton. It never enjoyed so huge a sale. Its losses began earlier and were more gradual. British woollens always had a name for quality, which put them in a stronger position in the more limited markets they served. Finally, wool is less hit by competition from the new artificial fibres than cotton. In recent years blends of wool and man-made fibres have proved very successful. So, although the woollen industry has suffered, it is more fortunate than cotton. It is now a much more valuable export item than cotton—a striking reversal of the nineteenth-century position.

There are other textiles apart from the big two, and if we take these into account, e.g., rayon, nylon, jute, hosiery, carpets, then the industry still employs over 800 000 people. And it is still a useful exporter as well as supplying our own clothing demands.

Yorkshire is still the heart of Britain's woollen and worsted manufacture. Unlike cotton, which was a newcomer in the eighteenth century, wool had been established for centuries, the most important of Britain's manufactures and carried on widely throughout the country. But supremacy did not just fall into Yorkshire's lap. For technical reasons steam-driven machinery came later to wool than to cotton, and Yorkshire had taken the lead before the new machinery was widely used; coal confirmed its lead. And even while many processes were still being done by hand, Yorkshire had begun to forge ahead of its rivals. Yorkshire organized its manufacturing processes more efficiently, its business men showed acute sense in their judgment of the types of cloth to make and the time to switch to other lines. In addition, there was more urgency: East Anglia and the West Country were better farming land and so had alternatives open to them; the bleak moors and poor soils of the West Riding offered a dismal prospect if wool failed. Finally, the success of its neighbour and rival, Lancashire, introduced a sense of rivalry that adds an extra edge to business as much as to sport.

Yorkshire enterprise, together with natural assets, made the West Riding supreme in the industry. At present over 90 per cent of Britain's worsteds and over 80 per cent of woollens are produced here. Local wool has long been of little importance; about 90 per cent of the raw wool has to be imported from Australia, New Zealand, South Africa, and India. For reasons we have seen, wool has not suffered so severely as cotton in the twentieth century, and still holds its own more steadily than cotton.

Within the region there is much specialization, as with cotton, but the differences are not between the *processes* of spinning and weaving but between the *products*. In general, the north-western towns like Huddersfield, Halifax, and Bradford go in more for worsteds, the others for woollens. Rather different fibres and methods are needed for each, so concentration on one or the other was natural. Bradford is the main worsted town; Huddersfield has a special reputation for fine serge; Halifax is famed for its carpets. Dewsbury, the 'Rag Capital of the World', takes old clothes, sorts them, tears them up, and remakes cloth. Leeds specializes in the textile-using trades, notably the clothing industry.

Chemicals

The chemicals industry is another that is growing rapidly. With a labour force of over 400 000 its range of manufactures includes toilet preparations, paint, soap and detergents, synthetic resins, plastics and synthetic rubber, dyestuffs and pigments, fertilizers, and general chemicals. By 1976 the value of exports of this industry was well over £2000 million, and about £1 out every £7 earned in exports came from chemicals. It is important to note that petroleum-based chemicals, or petrochemicals, accounting as they do for four-fifths of all the organic chemicals produced, are the main source of many of the plastic materials and man-made fibres in everyday use. The effects of North Sea oil on this part of the industry, until recently dependent on costly imported petroleum, will prove most beneficial to British industry.

The industry takes a few natural substances and transforms them into dozens of different materials, which in turn can be put to hundreds of uses. Britain is rich in three of the most important substances—limestone, salt, and coal. In a fourth—petroleum—she was not, until the advent of North Sea gas and oil, and her exports have been so extensive that the British petrochemicals industry is the second biggest in the world.

By breaking down these substances, the industry produces innumerable byproducts, e.g., acids, alkalis, explosives and fertilizers, dyes, drugs and detergents, plastics, rubber, paint, insecticides, glass, soap, bleach, and artificial fibres like nylon and Terylene. Some of these products (e.g., plastics) have given rise to whole industries; and most of them are valuable to a host of different industries. Alkalis, for instance, are essential for the making of paper, glass, soap, artificial silk, and high-grade steel.

The growth of the chemicals industry in this century has been encouraged by government measures. The First World War made Britain aware of the importance of the chemicals industry and from 1921 high tariffs were introduced to protect it from outside competition. With this assurance, firms were encouraged to develop. Advance has been speeded up enormously by research which has found more and more new materials. In plastics there was bakelite in 1907, perspex in 1933, polythene in 1937. In fibres, rayon was made in the early years of the century, cellulose acetate in the 1920s. Nylon was not discovered until the 1930s, and not till later still did Imperial Chemical Industries set up Britain's first nylon factory. Terylene was invented by two British chemists in 1941, though the first factory—ICI's at Wilton—only went up in 1955. Inside five years it had to treble the size of its plant to cope with the demand. In 1957 production began of still more recently discovered fibres, Orlon and Acrilan. These man-made fibres have now pushed the natural ones, cotton and wool, into second place. They are as attractive and they are cheaper. From a national point of view, they have the extra attraction in that they have a lower import content and so help to keep down import costs.

Another branch of the chemicals industry which demonstrates the role of scientific research in fostering advance is that of pharmaceuticals and drugs. It has been claimed that as many as three out of every four medicines and drugs available today were unknown before 1945.

The whole petrochemical branch of the industry is barely thirty years old in Britain. The first plant was set up in 1942 by Shell and Courtaulds. There are a dozen now, the main ones being Shell's at Stanlow, the Esso refinery at Fawley,

ICI's at Wilton, and BP's at Grangemouth. We should not imagine these great installations are just to produce petrol. Petrol is distilled from the crude oil, so are paraffin, fuel oils, and lubricating oils. But other products remain after distilling. These go through the 'cracking' plant, which breaks down their molecules and regroups them so that they emerge as different substances that are then used to make detergents, rubber, paint, and other things. The growth of this industry is easily understandable. Its products are of use to dozens of other industries. They produce materials which have promoted the expansion of certain industries, providing ideal substitutes for materials that have become very dear or scarce. For instance, the radio and electrical industries could not have grown so quickly without bakelite. The new fibres have enabled textile firms to develop drip-dry and crease-resisting fabrics. Perspex is a useful substitute for glass. Nylon has over a hundred industrial uses. The car industry values the synthetic rubber products. Again the nation benefits, for this is one of the import substitutes produced by this industry which helps keep down the bill for imports.

Along with constant attention to research and technological advance, the chemicals industry is marked by the massive amounts of capital it applies—and requires—to improve production. This in turn has fostered the amalgamation of firms into units big enough to command the financial resources needed to undertake such great investment programmes. No small firm could stand the pace, when plant is so expensive and technological and scientific progress so rapid that frequent, costly replacements are essential if a firm is not to fall behind its rivals.

Production in the chemicals industry more than doubled between 1938 and 1958; since then it has doubled again. The plastics branch alone now turns out twenty times as much as it did thirty years ago. The whole industry gives work to about half a million people. Although it cannot rival engineering as an export industry, it accounts for about 10 per cent of Britain's exports, and its earnings are now more than those of cottons and woollens put together.

The main centres of the chemicals industry are in the North East, Merseyside, and Grangemouth on the Firth of Forth.

The North East: In this area local raw materials—salt deposits, limestone, and coal—encouraged the establishment of chemical manufactures at Billingham, near Stockton. Nearness to the coast and a site on the River Tees were further assets. But it was the First World War that established the industry. German naval activity blocked the import from Chile of sodium nitrate, essential for explosives. To make good the shortage from Britain's own resources, a big drive was begun and the Billingham works extended. This development enabled Billingham to take advantage of the great advances made in industrial chemistry thereafter. The huge ICI plant there spreads over a thousand acres; and the new one at Wilton, across the river, is bigger still. Together they constitute the biggest chemical plant in Europe.

Merseyside: On Merseyside the chemical industry developed because of the chemical needs of textiles and the presence in Cheshire of the largest salt deposits in Britain. From salt was produced chloride for bleaching textiles, and hydrochloric acid for the metal-using industries. Combined with local limestone, salt was the basis for alkali manufacture. Its soda ash, used with a type of sand and limestone found near St Helens, produced glass. With sulphur from Sicily or Texas it made sulphuric acid, with vegetable oil from West Africa, it made soap; and Merseyside was a natural receiving centre for these raw materials from abroad.

So there grew up a large chemical industry centred on Widnes and Runcorn, with glass at St Helens and soap at Port Sunlight—first home of the firm that was to become Unilever. The newer branches of the chemical industry have followed—the big oil-refining and petrochemicals plant at Stanlow; an important dye industry at Manchester, based on local coal tar.

Local raw material and access to ports for essential imports explain the original locations of these chemical industries. But it so happened that coastal sites were a vital element in locating the oil refineries which were established after 1945. By settling in areas where chemicals were already established, close links between oil and chemicals could be forged. It is these links which mark the newest, most rapidly expanding side of the industry, petrochemicals.

Grangemouth: see Chapter 4 (page 101).

Other industries

It should be stressed that the industries we have discussed are just the main mining and manufacturing industries in Britain. There are other important industries such as the food, drink, and tobacco group which imports most of its raw materials but employs 760 000 people to turn these raw materials into bread, biscuits, chocolates, sweets, beer, and cigarettes. Another 678 000 people are busy in agriculture, growing crops and raising cattle. Over another $1\frac{1}{2}$ million are employed in building and construction.

Moreover, over half of Britain's workers are outside the factories, mines, and farms altogether. About 12 million people work in the service industries, not producing goods but performing necessary work. About 3 million people are kept busy seeing that the products reach the people who want them. They are engaged in the distributive trades, with shop assistants forming the biggest section. About 5 million people provide special professional services: doctors, dentists, teachers, lawyers, accountants, and so on. Some $1\frac{1}{2}$ million people are engaged in the transport and communications industry—of these nearly $\frac{1}{2}$ million are in the postal and telecommunication sector. Over 700 000 people work in government offices. Without producing material articles, all these workers nevertheless make a contribution to the well-being of the community.

We can see from this survey that the pattern of British industry has changed greatly during the twentieth century. The Britain of coal and iron, cotton, and ships, is still there, but is being overshadowed by a Britain of oil, electricity and steel, cars and aircraft, electronics and chemicals.

2B. Energy

Every factory, every bus, every household in Britain depends on the production of some form of energy. The energy to produce power for machines can be electrical, or steam or internal combustion. The bus or car depends almost completely on provision of petroleum or diesel fuel oil. Houses are heated by oil, coal, gas, or electricity. All of us in our daily lives are dependent on some form of energy—and energy fuels are expensive.

The total UK energy bill came to the huge sum of £11 500 million in 1975: this was for industry alone—it did not include private consumption at home or in transport. But our resources were until recently very limited. The total value of all minerals produced in the United Kingdom in 1974 came to £1719 million. Each year our energy consumption increases by 1·5 per cent. By the end of the century we will require to increase our energy supplies by 50 per cent. Such an increase requires a massive boost in our production of home-produced fuels and minerals. If we do not produce enough our choice will be a

Table 2.7 Trends in energy consumption

	Unit	Amount 1960	1975	Dist. % 1960	1975
Primary sources					
Coal	Million tons	196	180–200	74	48
Oil	Million tons	39	95–105	25	42
Hydro-	Th. million kW	2·5	5–6	1	1
Nuclear power	Th. million kW	2·1	55–65	1	7
Natural gas	Th. million therms	—	1–0	—	2
Final conversion					
Coal	Million tons	91	40–50	35	10
Coke	Million tons	30	25–26	12	6
Oil	Million tons	32	75–85	21	31
Electricity	Th. million kW	105	300–360	24	46
Gas	Th. million therms	2·6	4·5–5·00	7	7

difficult one—whether to cut (drastically) our production of goods and services, with all this would mean to our standard of living, or pay very high prices for buying fuels and then find that all the goods in our shops are all the more expensive. Indeed, the primary cause of our recent inflationary spiral was the sharp rise in prices of imported oil in 1973.

With a fourfold increase in the price charged by Middle East oil-exporting countries there was a sharp rise in the prices of all products, and exacerbated by the demands of working people for compensatory rises in money wages to match those rising prices, the inflationary spiral which developed took prices up 30 per cent in a year (that was the annual rate—with 1 January 1974 price level as 100, the level soared to 155·6 in June 1976).

Clearly then, energy and the fuels behind its production are vital aspects of the highly industrialized British economy. What are these fuels and how do we plan out our use of energy?

Sources of energy

The main primary sources of energy used in Britain are petroleum, coal, natural gas, and nuclear power—together with some water power. From these come secondary sources such as electricity, town gas, and coke. In Britain about half of our energy requirement is supplied from domestic fuel

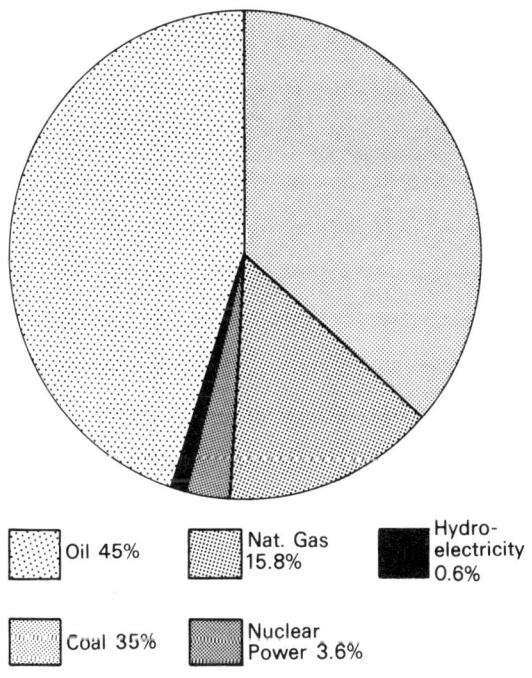

Fig. 2.4. Primary sources of energy

minerals—petroleum, coal, and natural gas. Of all the energy consumed, coal comprises just over one-third, a dramatic fall from its dominant position in the 1950s—a point underlined even more when we find that in industry today coal's share has fallen to 21 per cent (around one-eighth). It can be seen from Fig. 2.4 which fuels are the real providers of today's industrial energy. And industry uses only 4 out of each 10 units of energy produced, as Fig. 2.5 illustrates. Even more is consumed by the other users: houses use over one-quarter; the public authorities use 7 per cent; transport alone takes one-fifth of all the energy; and other users account for the final 7 per cent.

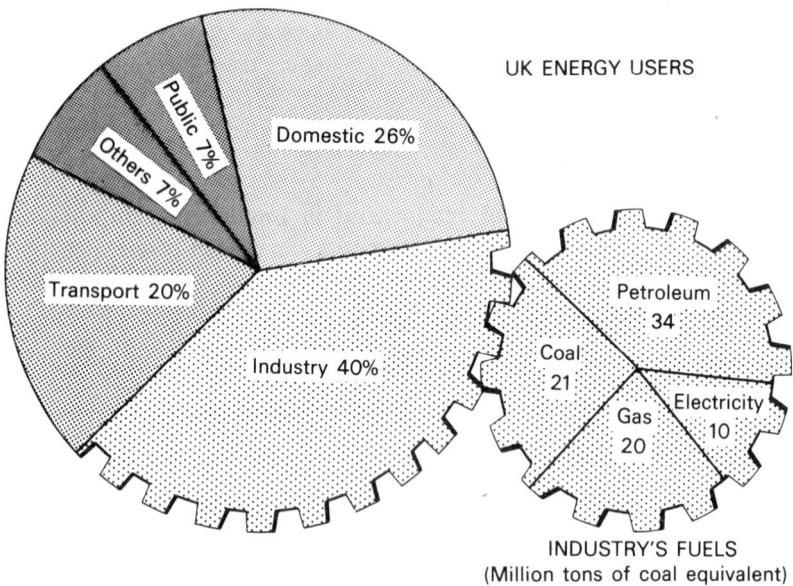

Fig. 2.5. UK energy users. Industry's fuels are also shown. (Source: *Employment News*, No. 32, HMSO for Dept. of Employment, May 1976)

These users have made a choice about the kind of energy they use. One point seems clear, they are moving towards greater use of sources other than coal.

Coal Despite its relative fall in importance compared to last century, coal production in the United Kingdom is still high. In 1974 109 million tons were produced. Although this was a dramatic fall of 80 million tons per year compared to nine years before, it is possible that coal will now tend to stabilize in its annual production. There are 255 National Coal Board collieries, and with a colliery workforce of 240 000 the industry is urgently considering ways of marketing coal to industry and to domestic consumers.

Coal appears to have many assets in its favour in such efforts. It has been worked in Britain for perhaps 1200 years. For the last 300 there has been an organized coal mining industry—200 years longer than any other country. Some 60 to 70 per cent of Britain's electricity is produced by coal-fired stations (though it is true that oil and a little natural gas and water power are used). British coal exports dominated the world market until around 1910. In 1913—the peak production year—the industry produced 287 million tons, sold 94 million tons abroad and employed a million workers. These were the heydays of the coal industry. By 1965 exports were down to 4 million tons, the workforce to under 300 000.

Fig. 2.6. Decline of coal in the twentieth century

Why the decline? The reasons are:
1. Other countries, like Holland and Spain, which had previously relied on Britain for their coal, now began to develop their own resources. They also began to export to what had been British markets.
2. After 1920 industry was suffering from economic recession, demand for coal fell off, and some industries began to seek out ways of getting cheaper sources of energy.
3. Allied to this was the history of bad relations between management and workers—culminating in the 1921 coal miners strike, which became one of the causes of the General Strike of 1926. Mine owners were loath to spend money to modernize production and mechanize the mines; they were content to cut wages and hope that the industry would ultimately return to a healthy state. The workers naturally refused to cooperate in a low wage policy, and the scene was set in 1921 for almost thirty years of bitter industrial strife and ill-feelings.
4. The main reason has, however, been the switch in industry and household to the use of cleaner and more controllable heating—oil and gas, about which we will hear later. Suffice it to note that the picture is not all dismal.

Table 2.8. Coal: example of decline. (Source: NIESR)

	Million tons			
	1955	1960	1975 (proj.)	
Total consumption				
Total	213·5	195·5	180·200	
Domestic	38·1	34·1	18–24	
Iron and steel	6·1	2·6	1–2	
Gas	27·9	22·1	10–12	
Gross National Product	1960		1975	
(at market prices + GDP factor)	23 931	22 248	40 000	36 850

In spite of all the disadvantages and the subsequent fall in production and sales, it would appear that by 1976 at least some progress has been made in stabilizing the industry. Between 1974 and 1975 coal production started to increase—from the 109 million tons noted above to 127·2 million tons—an increase of 4·7 per cent. This increase has been achieved through greater productivity—this means that each miner is producing more coal during each shift in the pit. Indeed, during the 1950s and 1960s, when demand for coal was falling off rapidly, such 'productivity per manshift' increased steadily. Indeed, it has more than doubled in the last twenty years and in 1975 the figure was 7·8 tons per manshift. It has made possible a rundown of the workforce from 700 000 in 1947 to 248 800 in 1975.

Overall production is now concentrating on the more productive coal mines, and there is a deliberate and advanced mechanization programme which has not only speeded up production but has put effective powered energy in the hands of the individual faceworker, and has revolutionized the transportation and handling of coal from the coalface to the consumer.

Organization and location

In Chapter 3 we shall see how industry has developed round the sources of energy like coal. Because of the bulky nature of the product and the difficulties of transportation, the heavy users of coal clustered around the mining areas. Even the switch to alternative fuels has not altered radically this association. From Fig. 2.7 we can see where our main coalfields are situated.

Yorks–Derby–Nottinghamshire: This is easily the biggest and most efficient coalfield in Britain. It accounts for about half of total production. It extends 60 miles from Leeds to Nottingham, and it is 20 miles wide in places. Nowadays it has modern collieries, and great reserves of coal still lie below the ground. So far this field has suffered little from the falls in export sales of coal—it never depended on such sales. As it is a profitable field, it is being further developed by the Coal Board. The main mining towns are Barnsley and Doncaster (where the newest and most efficient mines are to be found).

Fig. 2.7. The main coal-bearing areas in Britain. (Source: *Britain 1977: An Official Handbook*, HMSO, 1977)

Northumberland and Durham: This field was active long before the industrial revolution, when coal was used simply as a domestic fuel. This was because the field is coastal, and the Tyne and Wear, near which the early shafts were sunk, are navigable rivers. Consequently, sea transport, the only way there was of moving coal over distances in the days when land communications were very poor, was available. While Britain's inland coalfields were little worked, their markets being confined to their own immediate neighbourhood, the North East was producing vigorously for distant markets like London and the coastal regions of the Continent.

With the discovery of coal's value as a power source, the industry loomed bigger than ever; it aided local industrial development and, unlike, say, Lancashire coal, shot ahead as the main industry and biggest export of the district. This very dependence on selling to foreign markets meant it was badly hit as these declined after 1914. Though it is a big supplier of southern England and exports a little abroad, output is far below its 1913 peak. The reserves in the western field are running low and are awkward to work, so activity is concentrated on the eastern coastal strip, especially around Blyth. But it is still the second largest coalfield in the country and the National Coal Board is still the biggest single employer of labour in the region.

South Wales: This coalfield came into its own with the industrial revolution, when it developed rapidly, serving local industry and exporting coal throughout the world. It was the variety and quality of Welsh coal that explain this widespread demand. The eastern part of the field was rich in a type with fine coking qualities, particularly suitable for iron and steel manufacture. In the western part were large deposits of anthracite, producing great heat without much smoke or ash—very useful to the baking and malting industries. From the centre, along the Taff and Rhonda valleys, came a type of coal especially good for raising steam. The development of the steamship sent the demand for Welsh steam coal rocketing upwards.

The nearness of the coalfield to the sea enabled the region to respond fully to the world's demands. Canals and railways ran down the short river valleys, linking the mines of Pontypool and Merthyr, Pontypridd and Rhondda, with the ports of Cardiff, Newport, and Swansea. Cardiff, as the main exporting centre, grew from a small town of 2000 in 1800 to its present size of 250 000.

The decline in the world's demand for coal between the wars hit South Wales hard, since so much of its production had been for the world market. Unemployment rose steeply, men left the dismally depressed mining towns for the Midlands and London. Output now is less than half of its 1913 peak, exports only one-eighth of what they were then.

But the industry is healthier than it was in the 1930s. Many pits where reserves were low, working difficult and equipment old, have been closed. But on the more profitable parts of the field—the western and the southern edge—mines have been mechanized and modernized.

The coal industry, as we saw, was in a state of uncertainty between 1910 and 1945. Loss of exports, competing fuels, bad industrial relations, and lack of capital to promote adequate re-equipment of obsolete mines—all these factors led to a complete reorganization of the industry in 1947. The Coal Industry Nationalization Act 1946 brought the industry under the authority of a National Coal Board. The Board's first chairman was Alfred Robens (later Lord Robens), an active and enthusiastic organizer and spokesman for the industry. Many of the outdated mines were closed, and a radical streamlining of the whole industry was set in motion.

The NCB raises its working capital by borrowing from the Secretary of State for Energy or from abroad. An industry which has undergone such massive reorganization requires heavy capital investment. Indeed, by 1973 the Board had accumulated a massive deficit (or debt) of some £450 million. Under the Coal Industry Act of 1973 not only was this debt written off, allowing the industry to be free to develop new policies, but different grants and loans were arranged to aid the NCB in completing its plans for redeployment and redundancy of staff. As a result of this reorganization, the Board was able, for the year ending March 1975, to announce an operating profit of some £34 million.

The future looks good—or better than the past. The plan for coal accepted by the NCB, the trade unions, and the Government as a blueprint for the ten years to 1985 is a bold one. There will be new capital investment of some £600 million; an estimated 100 000 million tons of coal deposits are known—and, of this, 4000 million are felt to be worth extracting. A new mine is planned at Selby with its 1000 million tons of known reserves. And major schemes have been set in motion to expand pits in Durham and at Betwys (Dyfed), as well as the massive undersea mining complex project at Ellington in Northumbria.

Gas

Public supplies of gas date back to 1807, when London streets (Pall Mall was first) were lit by gas. Up till the early twentieth century town gas was used to light streets in many towns—in some cities, including Glasgow, there are still a few lamp lighters employed to light gas lamps in some tenement areas. In the main, however, gas is now used just for cooking and heating, supplying some $13\frac{1}{2}$ million customers throughout Britain. Around one-fifth of the total energy used in industry comes from gas, and the proportion rises each year with the vast discoveries of natural gas in the North Sea.

The main single source of gas is now natural gas. Some 90 per cent of the total comes from this source. The whole gas industry came under public control in 1949, and there are now around 100 000 people employed in it. There were, however, major changes required in the late 1960s to meet the new flow of natural gas supplies. In 1973 the British Gas Corporation replaced the old Gas Council, and it set about its many tasks of developing and maintaining an efficient coordinated and economical system of gas supply. Its powers include the right to search for new sources; and when we consider that in five years alone (1969–74) the quantity available increased by over 140 per cent, we can appreciate the massive growth in supplies.

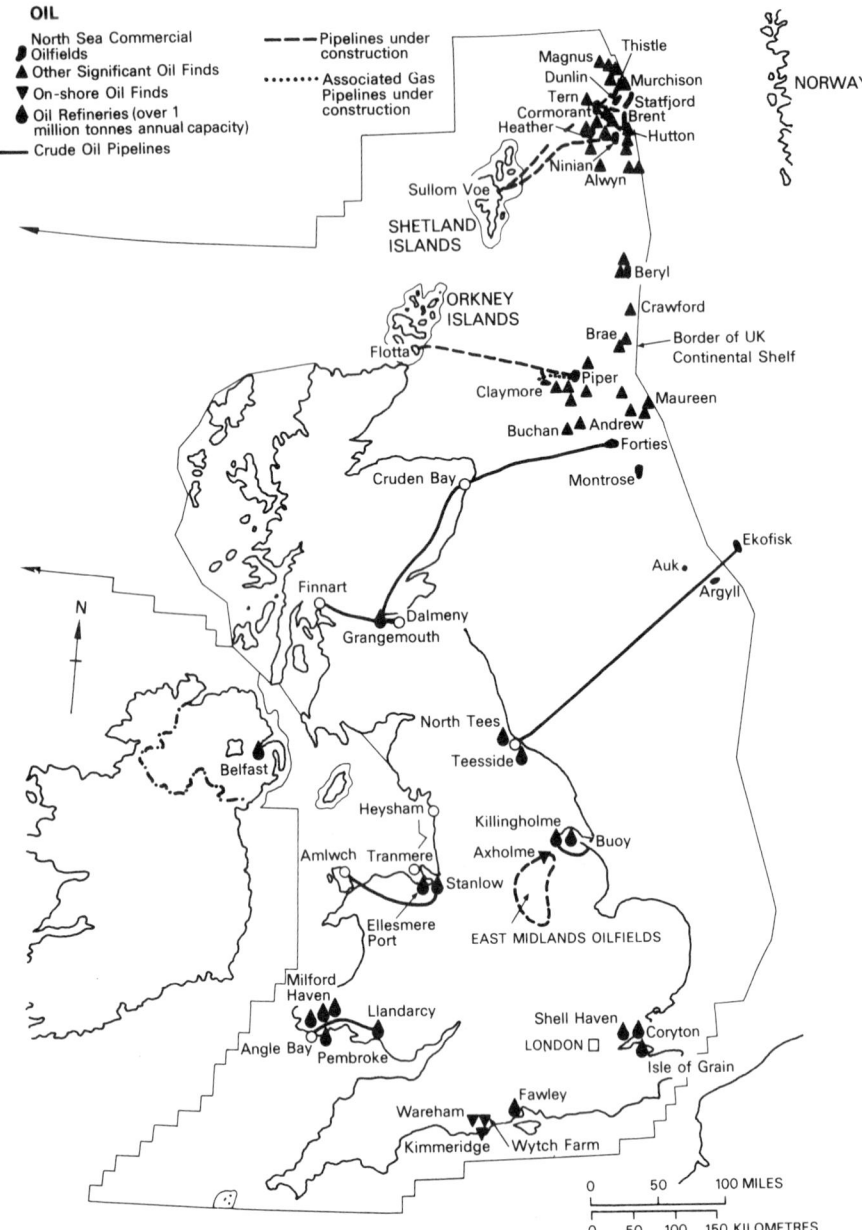

Fig. 2.8. Britain's Oil reserves. (Source: *Britain 1977: An Official Handbook*, HMSO, 1977)

The first discoveries of natural gas in the British sector of the North Sea are only some eleven years old. By 1974 five major gasfields were already in production (see Fig. 2.8)—Lemon Bank, West Sole, Hewett, Indefatigable, and

Viking—and by 1977 two others, Rough and Frigg, were in full production too. The amounts found have changed the whole pattern of local supply. By 1975, only ten years after these first developments, the number of local gas works had fallen from 246 to 50, and of those left some are already being adapted to produce substitute natural gas (SNG).

The costs of this series of developments, including the conversion of over nine out of ten of all consumers to natural gas by early 1975, have been very steep. With an investment of £28 million in 1967, the industry has now passed the peak and is hoping, through the steep rise in consumption, to pay for the capital developments carried out. With sales of gas continuing to increase steadily, the future of the industry seems secure.

Oil

Of all the sources of energy oil has become the one which has dominated the economy (and in Scotland the politics too), and the others have found it difficult to impede the rapid rise in its share of the total energy picture. Over one-third of industry now uses oil—compared with around 10 per cent some twenty years ago. As we saw, the effects of the Arab oil boycott and subsequent price increases in late 1973 were catastrophic to the whole British economy. By 1975 our 'oil deficit'—that is, the gap between the imports (which we have to pay for) and exports of crude oil (from which we could receive some payments)—was the equivalent of £63 for every man, woman and child in the United Kingdom. In this situation, any developments of new sources of oil in our own waters were very welcome indeed.

The first important UK oil find was by BP in the Forties field in 1970. Figure 2.8 shows that this field is far out to sea. It has taken the construction of a 105-mile-long undersea pipeline to bring oil ashore from what is believed to be one of the largest oilfields in the world. By mid-1976 some dozen more commercial fields had been identified, and as early as June 1975 tankers were bringing oil ashore from the Argyll field; in 1976 the Beryl and Auk fields started production. Fuller details of the effects of such discoveries can be found in Chapter 4 (Scotland), as it is in Scotland that most of the earlier effects are being found. In our companion volume, THE WORLD TODAY, the international implications of oil for Britain are treated in a fairly detailed way. Here we look only at the British scene.

Nevertheless, it is useful to remember that oil refineries (like that on Teesside) handle vast amounts of imported foreign oils and re-export abroad as well as operating for North Sea oil refining. Indeed, Teesside in one year can handle and refine oil equivalent to one-fifth of the total UK consumption. By 1980 we should produce enough to meet our own annual needs. Reserves of oil seem to be enough to last us for twenty-five to thirty years. Then perhaps we shall face another energy problem.

This takes us back to our energy prospect graph—see Fig. 2.10 at the end of this chapter.

The Government has already considered some of the problems arising from the recent discoveries of North Sea oil and the implications for the industry and for Britain in the next twenty years: a British National Oil Corporation has been established with its headquarters in Glasgow. BNOC exists to maintain government control over licenses to produce oil and it already has North Sea oil interests in the Thistle and Hutton fields. It can extend its interests to the refining and distribution of oil, and the public should ultimately benefit from

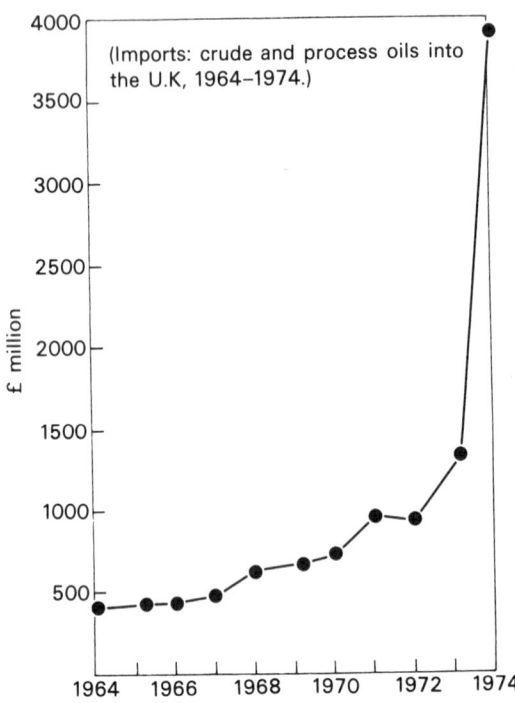

Fig. 2.9. Oil deficit: the cost. (Source: *Employment News*, HMSO for Dept. of Employment, April 1975)

the petroleum revenue tax, the corporation tax, and royalties on the exploitation of oil—all of which will increase as the oil flow increases.

Elsewhere we note the effects of the discoveries on the shore-based industries and trade, and here even prior to the North Sea developments British oil firms had already anticipated a steep rise in oil consumption and had set in motion vast capital plans for new oil refineries. By 1975 twenty-two refineries were already in operation, and these alone give Britain a refining capacity of 150 million tons a year (more than 130 million tons of oil are anticipated from North Sea in 1980) and some of these refineries, like Fawley near Southampton (18·5 million tons a year) and Stanlow in Cheshire (18 million tons a year), could each have handled all our requirements in oil of some twenty years ago. Indeed, these two plus the massive three refinery complexes at Milford Haven could alone have coped with our total refining demands as recently as 1968!

Thus the whole picture of oil is one of massive expenditure by the main oil firms—all multi-national giants which make arrangements to merge, combine, and split as they feel necessary, in the frantic search for 'black gold'. The rewards are worth while. So long as the British North Sea oil maintains its price relative to Middle Eastern oil, the successful oil explorers in the North Sea should in each field be able to recoup all their developmental costs in some four years of operation. Despite all the taxation and controls, this is a fair return on the capital invested. The future as seen by Shell, Esso, BP, etc. is bright indeed.

For the community the need is to maintain a steady control over operations so that safety levels, scenic beauty, and local industry are safeguarded in a consistent and responsible way. As yet, we do not know how successful we have been.

Electricity

As a form of energy supplied to the public, electricity can trace its origins to 1881 when it was first available in Godalming, Surrey. The industry from as early as 1919 was subject to public supervision through the Electricity Commissioners, who were responsible for the reorganization of the industry. Later, a Central Electricity Board was set up. And in 1943 the North of Scotland Hydro-Electric Board was established to develop, on a large scale, the vast water power of the Scottish Highlands. By 1948, all the municipal and private electricity producers were brought under public control. Nowadays, with a workforce of 195 000, the industry is organized into fourteen regional boards. Of the total public supply produced in 1974 (around 250 500 gigawatt hours; N.B. 1 gigawatt hour = 1 million kilowatt hours = 1000 megawatt hours) conventional steam-power stations provided 86 per cent, nuclear stations provided 12 per cent, and hydroelectric stations 2 per cent.

Despite the rapid rise in the use of energy by industry and consumers as a whole over the last decade, it would now appear that since 1974 the level of output has stabilized—indeed, the amount of electricity generated in 1974 was 3 per cent less than in 1973.

Electricity production in the United Kingdom accounts for over half the British consumption of coal and around one-fifth of our consumption of oil.

In terms of the conventionally powered generating stations there has been considerable competition between coal and oil to get access to what is a most profitable outlet for their product. As a result of such competition, we occasionally find attempts to meet the views of both pressure groups involved. For example, a dual-fired station to burn either coal or oil has been opened at

Kingsnorth, Kent, and two other stations have been converted to use either natural gas or coal. At Peterhead in Scotland a new station opening in 1978 will burn natural gas (from North Sea) as well as oil.

Nuclear power in Britain has been seen most clearly as a source of energy in the production of electricity. As we saw, about one-eighth of the total public supply comes from nuclear stations—with Britain producing almost one-fifth of the world nuclear energy. Britain had the first commercially viable nuclear power stations at Calder Hall in Cumbria and at Chapelcross near Dumfries.

Most of Britain's nuclear generated electricity comes from stations owned by the electricity authorities. By 1972 there were nine of these in operation, but already there are plans to use a system known as the fast breeder reactor and to boost 'nuclear' electricity output from the late 1970s. The fast breeder reactor (already a proven success at Dounreay, Scotland) can release up to one hundred times as much energy as the present nuclear power stations. It is of vital importance in the future search for energy resources.

Finally, in terms of energy for electricity comes hydroelectric power. This type of electricity generator uses water supplied from high level reservoirs—to be found almost exclusively in Scotland and Wales. By March 1975 there were fifty-six hydroelectric conventional stations in the North of Scotland, including the massive Loch Sloy station. Even larger, however, is the potential of the Loch Awe scheme: here electricity generated in offpeak periods is used to pump water up to much higher levels from which it can descend at the required peak periods and operate the generators to produce electricity. Already other such stations are planned, including one at Dinorwie, Gwynedd (Wales).

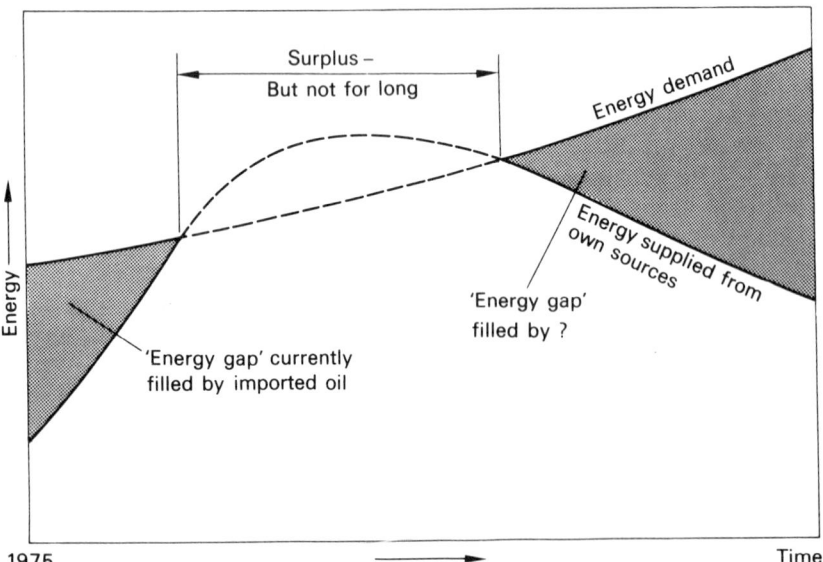

Fig. 2.10. Projected UK energy demand and supply. (Source: *Employment News*, No. 32, May 1976, HMSO for Dept. of Energy)

Future consumption

Having assessed the potential of our energy producers, let us turn to the pattern of future consumption. In Fig. 2.10 we can see that, despite the North Sea oil bonus and irrespective of our nuclear developments, a serious gap will be with us again by the end of the century or earlier. Any steps we can take to postpone such a crisis are to be welcomed.

In 1974 the Government estimated that voluntary conservation measures could have saved up to 2 per cent of the total supplies used. In industry every effort to save energy is now being encouraged. Government loans are given to help in this, and publicity is also being given to better insulation of homes, shops, and factories to save fuel. In addition, any subsidies which still mask the real costs of lighting and fuel are being removed—VAT on petrol has been increased to 25 per cent to discourage its use; speed limits on roads have been reduced; advertising and display lighting in shops are actively discouraged; and government publications like *Employment News* devote great space to encouraging an all out campaign in industry to reduce inefficient use of energy.

3. Industry: organization and location

Industrial activity does not occur by chance. It has to be organized, decisions must be taken about what to produce, and in what quantity, and where to set up the factories. Money to pay for equipment, materials, and workers has to be forthcoming. The basic unit which sees to this organizing is the firm. We can talk of men working in an industry, but in practice they work for some firm which is engaged in that industry. Firms vary enormously, not only in the products they make but also in size and in the ways they are owned or controlled.

Private enterprise

Most British firms are privately owned. Private individuals put up the money to start the firm, and pay the costs of production. They take all the decisions that have to be taken on their own responsibility. They do this because they believe people will be willing to buy their product, in amounts and at a price which will more than cover what it cost to make. In other words, private enterprise is inspired by the *profit motive*.

But even within this field or private enterprise, there are different kinds of firm. There is the one-man firm in which a single individual owns and runs the business. This need not be small: the man may own several factories. He provides the money for premises, equipment, wages; he decides what to make; whatever profits the firm earns are his and his alone; so are any losses it suffers if he has misjudged what the public are ready to buy, or the goods cost more to produce than is earned from selling them. In manufacturing industry the one-man firm is not of much importance now, though in the retail trade it is still very common (the small shopkeeper).

The partnership firm is more common, though it, too, is not of much importance in industry today. In this type two or more persons are joint owners of the firm. Each partner contributes to the firm's capital, and profits are shared out among them. Partnerships have the advantage over one-man firms in that they can command more capital, since they can draw on the pockets of several owners instead of just one man. They can use the special talents of each partner in running the business; one to look after the buying of materials, another after the actual production side, a third giving all his time to advertising the product, another to the sales side, and so on. The disadvantages are that agreements made by one partner are binding on them all, and that each partner can be held liable for the total debts of the firm even if these were the result of activities by other partners. The risk involved in partnerships is therefore very great, and many a man has been ruined because an unscrupulous partner has plunged a firm into debt and then fled, leaving his unfortunate partners to settle the accounts.

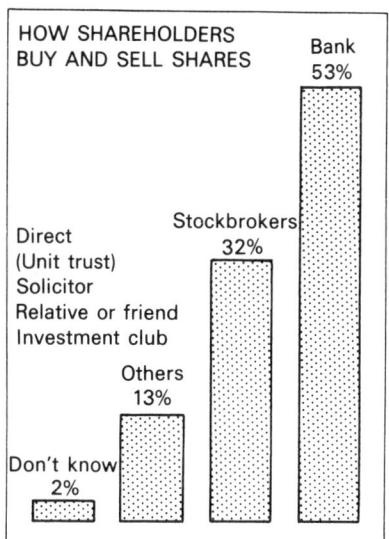 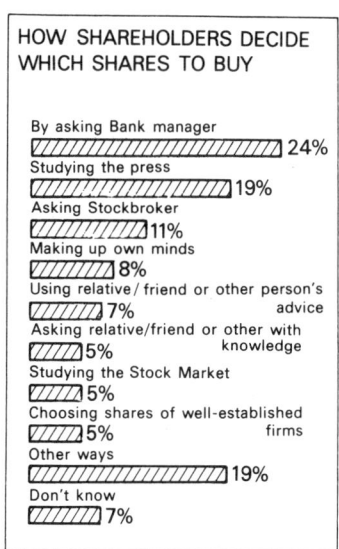

Fig. 3.1. How shareholders decide what to buy and sell. (Source: J. Nobbs, *Social Economics*, McGraw-Hill, 1975)

By far the most common type of firm in British industry today is the joint-stock company. There are about 250 000 of these. They get their capital not from one man or a few partners but from hundreds, perhaps thousands, of people. Each person contributes a certain amount—it may be quite small—and in return receives shares in the company to that amount. These shareholders who have supplied the capital are the owners of the firm. Of course, thousands of owners, widely scattered, cannot run a business in the sense that a single owner or a few partners can. They elect a board of directors to see to this, and these directors make the decisions, appoint a salaried manager to carry out the policies in the factories and workshops, and so on. The board has to answer to the shareholders, the real owners of the firm (even if they have never been inside any of its factories or offices), for the success or otherwise of the company.

Any profits the joint-stock company makes are distributed as dividends among the shareholders according to the amount and type of the shares they hold. The main types are, first, *preference* shares. As the name suggests, holders of these have first claim on a share in the profits, but, as against this, the percentage dividend they receive is fixed and limited (about 5 per cent). Even in a year of enormous profits, the preference shareholders still get no more than this fixed rate of dividend. Second, there are *ordinary* shares, the holder of which has less priority. He must wait till the preference shareholders

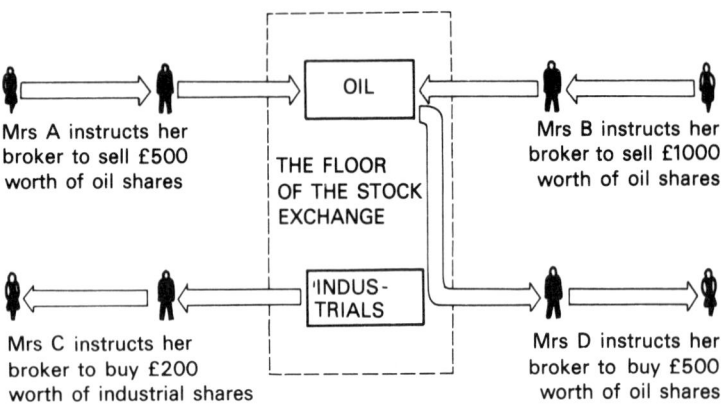

Fig. 3.2. The working of the Stock Exchange. (Source: W. Outhwaite, *Commerce for Schools*, 2nd edn, McGraw-Hill, 1977)

have had their dividends paid in full, so that in a poor year he may get no dividend. On the other hand, there is no ceiling fixed for him, and in a very good year he may get a very high rate of dividend. A third type, the *debenture*, is not strictly a share in the company at all. The debenture holder has made a loan to, not an investment in, the firm; and he is guaranteed an annual rate of interest which the firm must pay, even if it has made no profit at all in the year.

The joint-stock company is the most widespread type of private firm because it has distinct advantages over the other types. First, it enjoys the great boon of limited liability, hence the word 'Limited' which must always appear in its title. This means that no shareholder is liable beyond the amount he has actually invested in shares. The risk of investment is reduced because the individual investor knows the maximum he can possibly lose should the company fail. Moreover, a shareholder can get his money back quickly, if he wants it, by selling his shares to someone else. The Stock Exchange is the special market where the buying and selling of company shares take place. Because a man can invest a quite small sum, risking no loss beyond that amount, and considering the relative ease with which his money can be recovered should he so wish, thousands of people unable or unwilling to sink money in a one-man firm or partnership are quite ready to invest in joint-stock companies. So the savings—often the small savings—of the community at large are attracted to finance industrial undertakings.

From the angle of the firm as well as the individual investor, the joint-stock company has advantages. For various reasons that we shall see later, production in modern times has tended to concentrate in bigger units. Production is often more efficient and cheaper if done on a large scale. While there is often more money to be made from operating on a large scale, it takes more money to set up on this scale. This is where the joint-stock company comes in. The one-man firm or the partnership is rarely in a position to command the huge amounts of capital that large-scale production demands. The joint-stock company can tap the savings of the whole community, and by raising moderate sums from hundreds of thousands of investors can acquire vast amounts of capital more easily.

There are two kinds of joint-stock company, the private and the public. The private company cannot have more than fifty shareholders and cannot offer its shares to the general public. On the other hand, it does not have to make public so much information about its activities. The public company is permitted to offer its shares to anyone and is not restricted in the number of shareholders it may have. But, for these reasons, people need to have assurances about it. It has therefore to make public many more details about its finances and its business activities.

The private companies are more numerous; over 95 per cent of all joint-stock companies are of this type. But the public companies are much bigger organizations. There is far more money invested in these than in all the private companies put together.

Public onterprise

Britain is a mixed economy. This means that certain industries in Britain are not owned by private enterprise in any form. They are publicly owned. The most important of these are coal, electricity, gas, steel, railways, airports and air transport, commercial road transport, and postal services. At one time most were in the hands of private firms, but in recent years the State has taken them over, compensating the previous owners on quite generous terms. Indeed, around 8 per cent of all workers are employed in public corporations and around a quarter in the public sector.

By any standards, the nationalized industries occupy a central role in the economy. Together they account for more than one-tenth of the national product and nearly one-fifth of total fixed investment. (The four largest employers in the country—after central government—are nationalized industries.) They occupy a dominant position in energy, steel, and transport. They account for about one-third of all the plant and equipment bought by British industry, and for several sectors they are the sole domestic customer.

The reasons for this 'nationalization' of some industries were many and varied. There was a general feeling that private firms running them with the aim of making profits might not pay much attention to the interests of the community. What was good for some firm's business might not be good for the nation. So, in the case of important industries, it seemed better that the State should own them and run them with an eye to the community's interests.

Certain industries, e.g., coal, are of key importance because so many others depend on them. Poor production or high prices in these can hold up advances in other industries, check the nation's prosperity, and so damage the interests of millions of people. Such industries should be run with this in mind, not the profits of a few private persons. Even if firms were running these industries efficiently, many people still felt it was unsatisfactory for a few people to control firms in such a powerful position in the nation's economy.

Some of the firms, however, were not being well run. Both the mines and the railways needed overhauling to bring them up to date; the private owners were unable or unwilling to spend money on this. Yet the country could not afford to let such vital concerns as power and transport stagnate.

Then there were essential services like electricity and gas where it was wasteful to have several private firms competing. If these firms were not privately owned but constituted a public concern, the people would get not only the benefits of large-scale production but a safeguard against the danger of being exploited: a private firm might be tempted to cash in on its control of this essential service. For such reasons as these, certain industries have been nationalized and the nationalization of others, including shipbuilding and aircraft production, are at present under consideration.

Not everyone, of course, is convinced by this kind of argument. Some maintain that nationalization is a recipe for inefficiency. They argue that the playing down of the profit motive removes the main criterion of commercial success. Whereas the private businessman stands to lose his own money unless he makes a go of his business, the public corporation has no such personal stake. Again, the private firm has to raise its finances in the capital market, and will only succeed if it can show evidence of good performance and promise. Up till recently, the nationalized industries could have loans arranged for them by the Government and, if need be, could get subsidies from public funds at the expense of the taxpayer: in this way, the incentive for efficiency in management may be blunted.

This lack of incentive may also result from the diminishing of competition.

Private companies competing for customers endeavour to keep prices down and services up: one great state monopoly dominating the field lacks this stimulus, and can become slack and complacent. Even if not run directly by the Government, many believed that the nationalized industries would succumb to the fate which, in the popular mind, is reserved for government enterprises—suffocation by forms and strangulation with red tape. This seemed all the more likely as the vast scale of these organizations makes them very cumbersome and difficult to run.

After 1945 the Labour Government went ahead and nationalized some major industries.

The nationalized industries are not run directly by a government department. The Minister most concerned with the particular industry, e.g., the Minister of Energy in the case of coal, appoints a board to run the industry, rather in the way that a board of directors looks after the running of a private joint-stock company. The public corporations, as these boards are called, are not composed of civil servants, but of men from other walks of life, picked for their experience and ability. Lord Robens, first chairman of the National Coal Board, was formerly a Labour politician; British Rail chairman (until 1976) Richard Marsh was previously an MP and Cabinet Minister. To reorganize the railways in 1961 Dr Beeching was brought in from the board of directors of ICI; Sir Ronald Edwards of the Electricity Council used to be a professor of economics. The corporations see to the day-to-day running and the commercial management of their particulur industry. They have, however, to keep the Minister fully informed.

The Minister, apart from appointing (and dismissing) board members, including the chairman, can issue general instructions on the broad policy of a nationalized industry, though in practice these big policy decisions are made in consultation with the Board. The Minister is answerable for the industry and submits its annual reports and accounts to Parliament. In 1957 a special committee of the House of Commons was set up to examine these and provide Parliament with its own reports on them. This was to enable Parliament to obtain better information on the nationalized industries, to hold more effective debates on them, and to question the Minister more thoroughly. The Minister is also expected to see that the interests of the industry's customers are protected. Consumers' councils have been set up to consider complaints and suggestions from customers, and to advise the Minister and the Board on the changes they think necessary.

The main nationalized industries are:

Coal: The coal industry was taken over by the State from private owners under an Act of 1946. It is run by the National Coal Board, consisting of a chairman and about a dozen members appointed by the Minister for Energy. The Board has exclusive rights to mine for coal, though the distribution side is still left largely in private hands. The Board conducts its operations through twelve area boards, each responsible for a group of collieries in its region.

Electricity: This industry was nationalized under the Electricity Act of 1947. The main authority is the Electricity Council with a chairman and a dozen members, again appointed by the Minister for Energy. The Council, working through the Central Electricity Generating Board, controls power stations (outside Scotland) and the National Grid transmission system. It supplies electricity to twelve area boards which are responsible for distribution.

Gas: The Gas Act of 1948 took the industry from the hands of nearly a thousand separate gas undertakings. There are, as in electricity, twelve area boards each of which sees to the manufacture and distribution of gas in its region. The central body is the Gas Board, with a chairman and about a dozen members which coordinates the activities of the area boards.

Transport: This industry has had a more chequered career than coal, electricity, or gas. The 1947 Transport Act took over railways, docks, canals, road transport, and London passenger transport. All were placed under the control of the British Transport Commission. In 1953 the Conservative Government denationalized road transport. In 1963 it was decided that a single body, the BTC, was not adequate to run operations covering so wide and varied a field. Accordingly, an Act dissolved the BTC and replaced it by four boards, one each for British Railways, London Transport, British Transport Docks, British Waterways. Each board is responsible to the Minister of Transport, who appoints the members. British Railways, the best-known board, operates through six regional boards.

Civil aviation was nationalized under an Act of 1946. The running of the industry was placed under two corporations, British European Airways (BEA) for the United Kingdom and the Continent, and British Overseas Airways Corporation, (BOAC) for the longer flights beyond Europe. In 1960 the corporations lost their monopoly, as freedom was given to independent operators to develop services. In 1971, under the Civil Aviation Act, the Civil Aviation Authority was established to control many aspects of air transport, and a new board—British Airways—was set up to merge BEA and BOAC. There are now about thirty independent operators, but the bulk of air transport still falls to British Airways, which has a chairman and a board of a dozen members under the general eye of the Department of Trade.

Iron and steel: This is another industry with a chequered history of nationalization. In 1951 the Labour Government took it over from the private owners, but the Conservatives, in 1953, denationalized it, returning the companies to the private owners in the course of the next few years. In 1967 the Labour Government nationalized it once more, putting it under the control of the British Steel Corporation. The thirteen steel companies are divided into four groups on a geographical basis. But people are conscious that the industry has not benefited from the uncertainty and the shifting back and forth since 1951. The Corporation has so far been content to keep the existing company names and allow the company boards to remain.

Shipbuilding and Aerospace: Both these industries were brought under

Fig. 3.3. Electricity generating stations: United Kingdom. (*Britain 1977: An Official Handbook*, HMSO, 1977)

public control in 1977 as 'British Shipbuilders' and 'British Aerospace'. The nationalized industries have certainly encountered difficulties. Not all made losses, but during the 1950s BOAC, coal, and railways showed mounting deficits. Their performance was compared to, to their disadvantage, with that of the big private enterprise firms. The comparison was not altogether fair. It was true that they could obtain their investment needs more easily than private industry through the Treasury, but any new capital has now to be financed by interest-bearing bonds—quite a costly way to raise money. Railways and coal had been in poor shape when they were taken over, with heavy liabilities and out-of-date plant and equipment. They were restricted in their control of their price policies. They had to try and cover annually not only their operating costs but also heavy interest charges as part of the compensation due to the former private owners. Above all, there was great ambiguity in the 'founding' statutes as to their obligations. If not expected to make massive profits, the nationalized industries were not to ignore commercial principles. They were expected to break even, taking the good years with the bad. But they were also expected to operate with a special regard for public service, not just profit. They were to be 'the high custodians of the public interest'. What this meant in practice was that the railways kept running services that were financially a dead loss; that electricity supplies had to be laid on at great expense for isolated rural communities; that BOAC expected to favour the products of the British aircraft industry even when some foreign aircraft was superior and better suited to its needs. Nor were these public corporations free from competition. Oil emerged as a powerful challenger to coal, road services competed with the railways.

As the losses grew, the Government became alarmed, and issued a new set of guidelines for the industries in a White Paper in 1961. This stressed that the nationalized industries 'are not and ought not to be regarded as social services absolved from economic and commercial considerations'. They were now to operate on a five-year accounting period, for which financial targets of profit—or at least 'break even'—were set. New investment programmes would not be sanctioned unless they held out promise of a certain rate or return. The industries were given greater freedom to adjust the prices they charged. Since then new chairmen have aimed at overhauling the industries in the interests of efficiency and profitability.

The best known instance is British Rail. It was losing money every year. By 1961 the accumulated deficit was over £700 million; in 1961 alone it was over £130 million. In that year a new Chairman of the Board, Dr Beeching, began an enquiry, *The Reshaping of British Railways*, which was published in 1963. This showed that only a few sectors of rail traffic were paying their way: the transport of some heavy freights, especially coal, mail services, and some of the faster passenger services. All the other services were costing the railways more to provide than they were bringing in. One-third of Britain's railway track carried only 1 per cent of all passenger traffic. Most suburban and slower passenger services were not covering their costs. Such services should be abolished or reduced, little used lines abandoned, thousands of small stations closed down. The railways should concentrate on improving those services where they already had an advantage: more speed and comfort on fast intercity passenger trains, special freightliner trains, more electrification and diesels. A policy of streamlining and modernizing the railways, coupled with freedom to charge more realistic prices would produce in time an efficient and profitable system.

Yet the 1961 White Paper still left the obligations of the nationalized industries ambiguous. Governments have not in fact carried out all the Beeching recommendations. It must be remembered that all government policy towards nationalized industries is subject to the approval of Parliament. In the House of Commons, the Select Committee on Nationalized Industries (which investigates other public corporations too, including the Independent Broadcasting Authority, Cable and Wireless Limited, and even certain activities of the publicly owned Bank of England) did in fact discuss these recommendations and there was considerable opposition expressed to them by the MPs.

Also, Governments since 1961 have been impressed by the powerful, but non-commercial objections that were made against the recommendations. If, it was asked, the reduction of rail services meant forcing more traffic on to the already overcrowded roads, would not the national transport system as a whole become worse? Again, the closing of a branch line might save the railways money but might mean economic decay for some small community dependent upon it; or grave social hardship for the people, few though they might be, who found their usual, perhaps their only, form of transport removed. Values and costs were not always a matter of mere commercial accounting. These were valid reasons for not carrying out all Beeching's proposed cuts and closures; but they meant that the railways were still being run on something other than a simple commercial basis.

This difficulty still remains for the nationalized industries. All are much more competitive than in the 1950s: all, for instance, go in for vigorous advertising campaigns; the Gas Board with its 'High speed gas, heat that obeys you', is perhaps the most enterprising of all. But the railways are still struggling to get out of deficit, and coal finds it hard-going against its rivals. And the nationalized industries are still supposed to consider the public interest as well as profit. This is commendable but whether the cost of carrying socially valuable but commercially unprofitable services should be included in the industry's accounts is questionable. Whenever Government decides that such a service should be continued—and this is a decision for politicians not businessmen—should not the cost be borne out of taxation and removed from the profit and loss accounts of the industry? This was done in the case of the railways under the Transport Act of 1968. Now, under the Railways Act 1974, the Board receives direct compensation from the Government for operating a railway passenger network, which is providing a social service unlikely to exist in a purely 'profit motive' industry. In the subsequent inflationary period it has been difficult to assess as yet the effects of this method on the efficiency of the railway system.

Nationalization is less prominent as a subject of dispute than in the years just after the Second World War. Then it was novel, the great socialist principle from which its advocates expected marvels, its opponents feared disaster. Now these industries are a familiar part of the daily scene. They have not fulfilled the highest hopes of their friends nor the worst fears of their critics. Workers in them are not inspired by some special zeal lacking in those employed by private, profit-hunting enterprises. As railwaymen and airline pilots have shown, they are still ready to strike for remedy of grievances. Change of ownership is not apparently reflected in any increase in efficiency or production, the issues which loom so large today. To many workers in these vast organizations, the change of ownership may mean no more than new faces in the boss's office. Some would argue that had the change been accompanied by more worker participation and control, then it might have had a marked effect on performance. On the other side, it would be hard to maintain that men like Lord Robens are any less thrusting or concerned about efficiency than the managers of private industry. Of course, when any new nationalization proposals come up, the dispute flares up again. The Post Office has now come under a public corporation instead of being a department of state under a Minister, but this is not the takeover of a private firm.

More recently, Government has adopted different ways of acquiring a stake in industry. It does not take over industries entirely but takes a certain share in them. In some companies, e.g., Cunard, it has acquired a financial stake. Again, in 1966 it established the Industrial Reorganization Corporation. This body, composes entirely of businessmen, tried to encourage private firms to merge and rationalize their structure in the interests of efficiency; or at the Government's request, assisted particular firms to develop. It did so by making loans, buying shares, providing machinery—by any means, in fact, which seemed suitable. In the 1960s it put up £25 million to aid the merger of BMH and Leyland, £15 million to help English Electric and Elliott Automation merge, a modest loan to enable Nuclear Enterprises, a small but impressive Scottish firm, to extend its operations. The IRC was abolished in 1970.

In the 1970s the pace of such activity and involvement has quickened. Massive loans to Chrysler UK in late 1975 were essential to keep this car firm operating in the United Kingdom with all this means in employment and social terms. In 1975, too, only an injection of £100 million into British Leyland Motor Corporation and its subsequent transfer to public control as British Leyland kept this huge car firm going. (Even then, the Government had to commit itself to total investment in the firm of up to £2800 million by 1982 before its future could be assured.) Many people now accept that the scale of industrial operations and the vast risks involved call for instant 'lifesaving' by the only body with cash on the scale required—the Government. Such loans, grants, etc., have to be linked with some say in the use to which the cash is put. The logic of this argument led in 1975 to the setting up of the National Enterprise Board, under Lord Ryder, himself a topline industrialist.

One function of the new Board is to coordinate all of the policies so far pursued with regard to state shareholdings in private firms. Another is to participate in the activities of any company which seeks government support. Thus by the late 1970s we have a real mixed economy—with public corporations, public/private firms, public firms (the Government having the majority of shares), and private firms—all coexisting under the 'benevolent', or watchful, eye of Government, which is now acutely aware of the need to maintain healthy industrial enterprises and all this means in terms of capital replacement and modernization. Thus, for the future, the share of Government in industry may well continue to grow. Critics often referred to this trend as 'creeping socialism' or 'nationalization through the back door'.

Most people, however, now expect the State to maintain high rates of employment—even when this means intervention in the affairs of privately controlled firms or industry. They expect the Government to encourage the growth of the economy and boost exports—things which might not strike any private firm as being its concern. And in doing these things, the State has to keep interfering with private firms in a multitude of ways. As we shall see, it can persuade industries to set up in particular districts and prevent them from setting up in others. It encourages some industries by grants or easy loans. Its use of devices like the regional employment premiums, and special investment allowances can affect the fortunes of particular private firms.

The rise of the large firm

Size is not necessarily another word for efficiency, but in many cases it does offer advantages not otherwise obtainable. Indeed, in some industries it is very difficult for small firms to operate with much chance of success. In the motor industry, or chemicals, or oil, the cost of plant, the need for constant research, the likelihood of frequent expensive scrapping and replacement as innovations undermine existing methods—all these demand the kind of huge financial resources which only big firms can command. Certainly, some industries in the past—coal for instance—suffered from too many small companies, none big enough to contemplate the huge investment required to bring about the thorough modernization which the industry needed.

There are industries where the big firms seek to cooperate internationally to find a basis large enough to support the great costs required if they are to keep on improving their position. The development of the Concorde aircraft needed the cooperation of French and British firms, backed by both Governments.

British firms come in all sizes, from the small company with one factory to the giants like ICI with over 100 000 employees on its books, or Unilever controlling over 400 firms. There are far more of the smaller type, but in many fields the few big firms are responsible for more of the total production than all the pygmies that swarm around them. Table 3.1 gives some indication of this.

Over the last fifty years the rise of the big firm has been a feature of British industry. Single firms have grown bigger, and these bigger firms have merged together into still larger concerns. Nearly every major industry today—cars, oil, chemicals, tobacco, and electricals—is dominated by a handful of giant companies. In Britain the largest 100 firms account for over half of all profits and employ around a third of the total industrial and commercial workforce.

Table 3.1. The major trading groups and Europe's largest firm in each group

Group	Company
Food, drink and tobacco	Unilever NV/Ltd (GB/NL)
Chemicals and plastics	Royal Dutch Shell (GB/NL)
Engineering, electrical and transport equipment	Philips' Gloeilampen NV (NL)
Ferrous and non-ferrous metals	ICI Limited (GB)
Textiles, clothing and footwear	Farbwerke Hoechst AG (W. Germany)
Paper, printing and publishing	British-American Tobacco Co. Ltd (GB)
Construction	Mannesmann AG (W. Germany)

This process of industrial concentration into fewer and fewer very large firms is speeding up. In the 1960s the spending on takeovers (where one firm buys up the assets of the other and takes control of it) was in the region of ten times that of the 1950s. Indeed, from a total value of £550 million in 1966 it rose in two years to some £1600 million and then by 1972 to a peak of over £2500 million. Another feature of this is the scale of the operation: most of the mergers and takeovers are between already massive enterprises—Thorn–Radio Rentals; BMC–Leyland; Unilever–Allied Breweries; Boots–Timothy Whites; AEI–GEC; Imperial Tobacco–Courage. One estimate of the effects of this whole movement is that about one-fifth of the total assets of manufacturing industry was transferred to new owners during the 1960s.

It is useful to note also that these mergers sometimes took place between non-competing firms, e.g., Unilever, with its soap detergent image, linking up with Allied Breweries. There are two main reasons for this growth and concentration among industrial firms.

The first is that producing goods on a large scale is often more efficient and lowers the cost of making each article. The big firm can make use of machines that it would not pay a small one to use: tractors are fine if you have a big farm, but a waste of money if you have an allotment. Big firms can afford to have their own research staff seeking ways to improve the product, so that the small firm's articles can become outdated. Because they buy in such huge quantities, big firms get their materials at cheaper prices. All this is an advantage to the big firm, to the industry which is kept up to date, and to the customer who buys a better and probably cheaper article. This, of course, only holds good if the market is a large one. In many things there is such a large market: people's wants have increased, so have their earnings; transport and communications have advanced, bringing distant places closer together. Thus large-scale production can be profitable. For example, the cost of £12·10 per ton to build a plant to produce 100 000 tons of iron a year would be slashed to £5·60 a ton for a 1 million ton plant. Again, doubling of car production in a motor plant from 50 000 to 100 000 can lower costs per car by 15 per cent. These are known as technical economies of scale.

The second main reason for the merging of firms is one that appeals more to the firm than to the customer; it enables competition to be reduced. When a number of quite independent firms are competing for custom, each tries to make an article that is better or cheaper than a rival's product. The customers benefit from this. But firms may decide that it would be better for all of them to stop trying to undercut each other's prices, and combine or work more closely together instead. If between them they produce the great bulk of the article in which they deal, they will, as a result of merging, be able to command the market for it without fear of competition from any possible rival. So they are in a position to hold the customer to ransom. They may fix the price of a product at a level that suits them, and anyone wanting it will have to pay that price, however steep, or go without. So all the firms can benefit from merger or association, and all this without the constant strain of having to keep production costs low and profits slim as they had to do when competing with one another.

This does not mean that every merger or agreement between firms is a plot to defraud the public, to stop squeezing each other and combine to squeeze the customer. But this is the danger that goes along with the benefits that large firms can provide. On the one hand, they can be more efficient, make articles better and more cheaply, and so bring advantages to the public. On the other hand, they may abuse their dominating position to exploit the public. How to keep the advantages of large-scale organization while getting rid of its dangers is a tricky problem.

In Britain there are laws forbidding firms to adopt unfair practices such as fixing prices by agreement, though the practices are not always easy to prove. Since 1956 the laws have been made stricter, and a special court has been set up to deal with cases of business associations who make restrictive agreements. There is a Monopolies Commission empowered to investigate cases where a firm controls more than a certain proportion of an industry's output. Under an Act of 1965, the Government can hold up any proposed merger until the Commission has carried out its enquiries.

Despite such controls, however, the trend towards bigger and bigger industrial firms goes on. In steel, oil, cars, chemicals, and heavy engineering a small number of giant firms are responsible for most of the production in their respective fields. The firms are household names.

In the car industry: (1) British Leyland (resulting from a series of mergers the last of which linked Leyland to the British Motor Corporation); (2) Chrysler (UK) Limited, which was the result of the merger with Rootes which had itself been the result of earlier mergers of Hillman, Sunbeam, and Commer.

In the oil industry takeovers usually result in the dominant partners holding the name and the smaller groups disappearing: the main firms here are Shell,

Fig. 3.4. ICI in Europe. (Source: *Sunday Times*, 1 June 1975)

British Petroleum (51 per cent British Government controlled until some shares were sold off to private buyers), Esso.

In chemicals there is ICI (Imperial Chemical Industries) employing about one-third of all chemical workers. Since Britain joined the EEC the position of ICI as an example of the new multi-national giants has become clearer. If we look at Fig. 3.4 we can see the scale of the operation. Ranging from pharmaceuticals in Italy to paints in Hamburg, from Terylene in Oestringen to nylon in Kerkrade, the business is continental in scope. In the last fifteen years ICI Europa has been the fastest growing sector of Britain's biggest company. The sales records are impressive—between 1973 and 1975 ICI's sales to Europe leapt up from £235 million to £565 million, and despite our inflationary trends in that period the volume of real goods being sold has probably increased by at least half as much again in that time. ICI Europa, which is only one section of the massive company, earned £100 million profit in 1974–75. A look at Table 3.2 will show how this enterprising group pushed up sales to Europe. Thus, with a workforce of over 100 000 in the United Kindgom alone, this firm's importance to the British standard of living can be appreciated as can the need to ensure its efficient operation.

Distillers Company Limited own nearly all the best-known names in Scotch whisky (as well as Gordons gin).

Table 3.2. ICI sales to Europe. (Source: Sunday Times, 1 June 1975)

	Exports from Britain to the Continent (£m)	Total sales on the Continent (£m)
1960	33	33
1961	35	35
1962	38	40
1963	43	66
1964	56	76
1965	59	84
1966	57	95
1967	60	129
1968	90	155
1969	109	192
1970	116	207
1971	120	218
1972	131	235
1973	201	364
1974	314	565

In electrical engineering there is GEC/AEI. In manmade fibres there are two famous names, ICI and Courtaulds (a proposed merger between these broke down in 1966).

Nowadays the tentacles of these giants stretch out into many fields. General Electric will make anything from a nuclear power station to an electric light bulb. Unilever, which began as a grocer's shop in Bolton, is now responsible for over 1000 products, many of them household words: Persil, Domestos, Vim, Omo, Squezy; Wall's sausages and ice cream; Stork, Summer County, and Blue Band margarines; Birds Eye frozen foods; MacFisheries products; Gibbs, Signal, and Pepsodent toothpastes; Lux, Lifebuoy, Knight's Castile soaps. ICI, as we saw, produces paints, plastics, explosives, nylon, Terylene, and drugs. Vickers began in steel but now makes ships, aircraft, plastics, and rubber.

Even in the early 1960s chemicals had brought the big oil and chemical firms closer together. The Steel Company of Wales and Monsanto Chemicals combined in the production of nylon.

The location of industry

Although we can find industry being carried on in most parts of Britain, it is not evenly distributed throughout the country. It is much more heavily concentrated in some regions than in others. Moreover, not all these industrial regions are engaged in the same industries: some specialize in certain lines, others in different ones. Why should this be the case, instead of industry being more evenly spread over the country?

The short answer is that a firm interested in a certain branch of manufacture decided that one region offered more advantages to it than another. It afforded easy access to one or more of the things that the firm would need if it were to carry on its business successfully.

In the first place, the region may contain abundant supplies of the power a manufacturer needs to drive his machines. When the early cotton machines, driven by water power, came into use, factories had to be near fast-flowing streams; and that meant in the hilly northern and western parts of Britain. When steam power was discovered, coal became the major source of power. But coal was very bulky and costly to transport, so it paid firms to establish their factories on the coalfields to keep down their transport costs.

Nearness to the source of the raw material used by an industry is another important consideration, especially if it is used in large quantities. A firm would save in this case by building its works in the district where the raw material is found. If this happens to be a long way from the source of power required, then firms must choose between rival localities.

The iron and steel industry has been faced with this choice and has moved about as the circumstances have changed. At first, it used rich ores from a little of which a good deal of metal could be made, whereas great amounts of coal were needed as fuel and power. So it paid to set up furnaces on the coalfields and bring the less bulky ore supplies to them. But as the industry exhausted the rich ores and turned to using poorer quality ore the position was changed. So much of this poor ore was needed to produce a small amount of metal that it was cheaper to set up the furnaces on the ore fields and have the coal transported to them. Finally, the industry found it had to import its iron ore from abroad: it then paid to have the furnaces on the coast near a port to save the extra costs of carrying the iron ore overland into the interior of Britain. Thus the iron and steel industry has moved its location from coalfields to ore fields and then to the coast.

Marketing is the third consideration: an industry is attracted by nearness to a large market where it hopes to sell its product, as this again saves the cost of transporting the finished articles over long distances. Makers of heavy mechanical gear for foreign markets, for instance, prefer to be near a good port. The cost of moving massive equipment any distance overland is very high. Makers of household goods, like vacuum cleaners, are keen to set up near huge centres of population where their customers are on the doorstep of their factory. They are quite prepared to transport the power supplies they need (usually electricity) and their raw materials (seldom very bulky) to a site that is close to their markets.

Once an industry has begun to set up in a region, this gives the place a greater attraction as time goes on. The local people acquire the special skills of the industry. Workers come to know the business—cotton or steel or shipbuilding—inside out. Related industries, when developed, cooperate with the main ones. For instance, where shipbuilding was established, we found industries making marine engines, boilers, steering gear, navigation equipment, cabin furniture.

Other valuable services are built up to cater for manufacturing industries: banking and insurance firms, warehouses and docks, roads and railways, often specially adapted to suit the needs of these industries. Different firms or different towns start specializing in one part of the industry, and great improvements result in each through this concentration of effort. As a result, the place gets a reputation for this product. Other firms wanting to go in for this line will be tempted to come to this same region where so many of the things they will need are already available.

In time these 'acquired' advantages can keep attracting or holding an industry in places when the natural advantages of power sources, materials, and markets no longer exist or matter. We saw a typical example of this when we looked at the cutlery industry in Sheffield (see page 27).

The reasons for the location of many industries, then, often lie in the past. They would not, perhaps, operate in the same way today if an industry were being established from scratch. Thus a hundred years ago the pull of the coalfields on industry was enormous. Here lay the most effective source of power, and transport was so costly that it was advisable to set up the factories on the coalfields. As iron and steel moved there for power and fuel, the metal-using industries were also attracted, because iron castings and steel plates were their 'raw' material. With the concentration came those additional advantages: the masses of available workmen, the special engineering skills and crafts, the road and rail services—all the things calculated to attract still more industrialists to the region.

As you can see in Fig. 3.5 this pattern of concentration on the coalfields is still a feature. But it is no longer so true as it was sixty years ago. The pull of the coalfields has slackened greatly, mainly owing to the development of alternative sources of power to steam. Electricity is easily carried through the grid system over long distances, so industrialists pay more attention to things other than power when picking their sites.

This explains the drift of industries southwards during the last few decades.

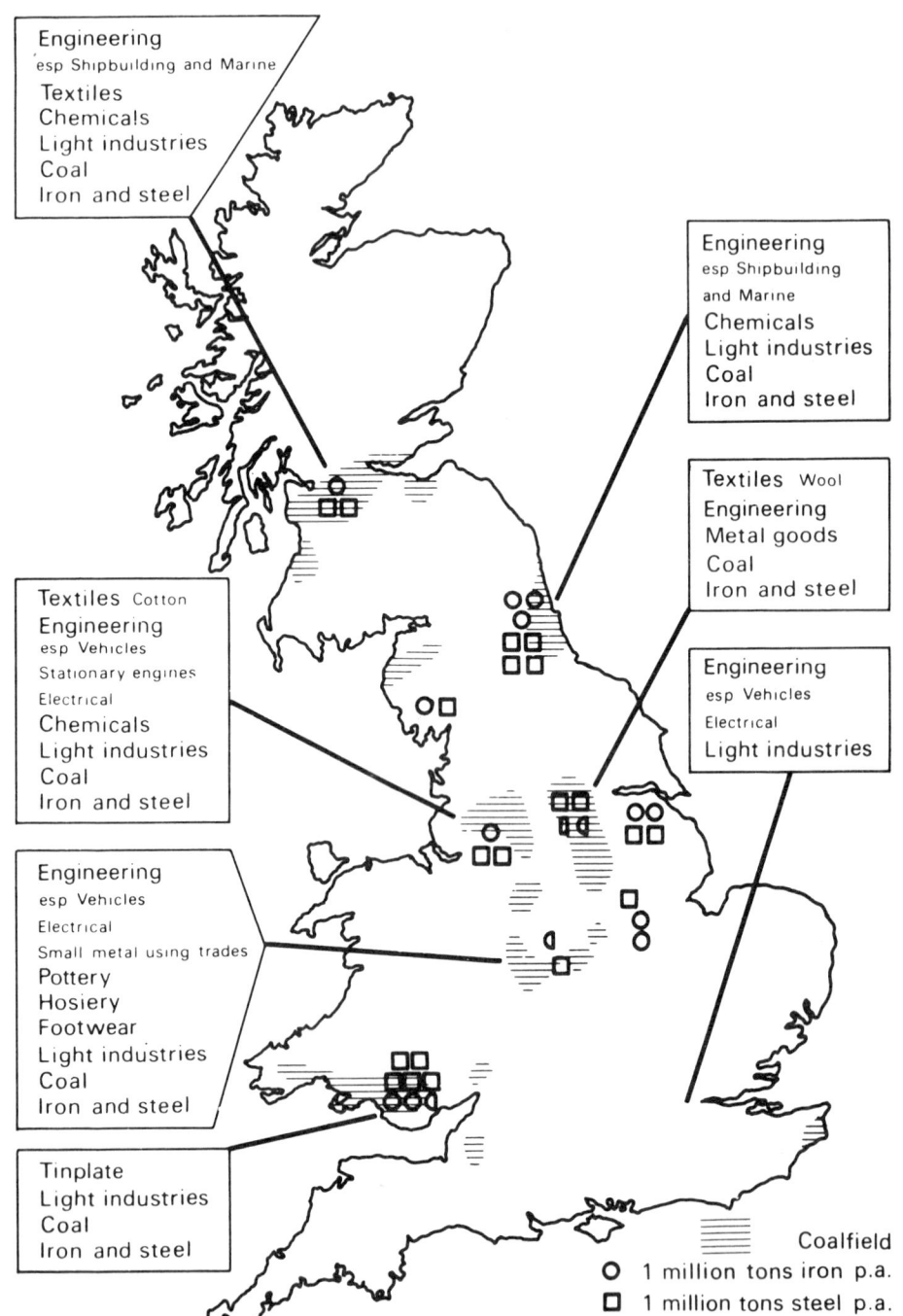

Fig. 3.5. Great Britain: main manufacturing and mining

The light industries, i.e., those making the articles for ordinary, everyday use as distinct from ships, machinery, cranes, girders, and so on, were pulled towards the great markets of the South and the Midlands. London's eight million people offered a huge market, accessible with hardly any transport cost if factories were established nearby. They also offered a large supply of labour, which is another valuable asset, for men are reluctant to move away from home to work. As most of these industries are assembly industries, which simply put together parts made elsewhere, there was no need for special craftsmanship. What was needed was a good system of communications so that the flow of parts into the assembly region was assured: and here, too, London, the centre of the nation's road and rail services, filled the bill.

Until the 1939–45 war businessmen starting up in manufacture decided the site by weighing up such advantages as power, materials, markets, labour, communications, transport. In addition, of course, personal preferences mattered; e.g., the existence of good leisure facilities, of access to pleasant countryside, etc.

Government influence

After 1945 a new and important element emerged—regional planning. As a result of the experience gained by government departments in moving and developing industries during the war, and also because of the need to develop economic policies which would benefit people throughout Britain, there was ready recognition by Government of the need to avoid wide disparities of standards of living as between different regions of the country. Not only so, but evidence existed of widespread differentials in income, employment levels, and general living conditions as between the parts of South-east England, with the highest standard of living, and Scotland, Wales, and Northern Ireland where all three of these were different to the London area.

Often this imbalance has been gradually developing for reasons we noted earlier—drift of light industries to the South East, and the decline going on steadily in the areas of the older basic industries like coal, shipbuilding, and cotton, which were less able to sell their products in foreign markets. As orders shrank, mines, mills, and shipyards began closing down and millions of men were put out of work. Areas specializing in these industries—Clydeside, Tyneside, Lancashire, South Wales—became 'depressed areas'. Related industries, whose success was bound up with the main ones, likewise declined. Once the industries that had provided so many of the pay packets of the local people ceased to do so, there was less money to spend. The result was that many shopkeepers also were unable to earn a living and had to put up their shutters. Hence those dismal streets with rows of empty shops that made parts of the depressed areas seem like ghost towns.

Nor have the effects of this contraction of some major industries ceased to make themselves felt. In some parts of the country such industries, e.g., coalmining and shipbuilding, are still important but still shrinking. Table 3.3 shows how in three such areas this process has meant a substantial rise in unemployment over the past decade. Some of these workers found jobs in other occupations, some left the region to find work elsewhere. Nevertheless, unemployment figures in such areas, termed Development Areas, remain above the national average. Successive Governments tried to promote alternative sources of employment in these regions by encouraging new industries to move in.

Since the Second World War, the measures became much more extensive. Unemployment and poor amenities, derelict buildings, and migration from the areas were all features of such regions as Scotland, Northern Ireland and Wales, and also places like Merseyside and the North East of England. Successive Governments made the elimination of this regional imbalance a basic feature of their planning policies. Financial and other aid was given on an ever-increasing scale. The sequence of legislative steps is shown in Table 3.4. It is useful to

Table 3.3. Rates of unemployment show up three depressed areas: Northern Region, Wales and Scotland. (Sources: *CSO Annual Abstract of Statistics*, HMSO, 1976)

	Percentage annual average		
	1965	1970	1975
Northern Region	2·5	4·7	5·9
Wales	2·5	3·9	5·6
Scotland	2·9	4·2	5·2
England	1·1	2·3	3·9
Great Britain	1·4	2·5	4·1

remember that even after a quarter of a century of such aid the average annual income in the South East of England (including the London area) was 10 per cent higher than in the rest of the country. Also, even today, while parts of the South East suffer from serious noise and congestion problems which reduce the value of their living standard differential, there are still real pollution hazards in some of the disadvantaged areas to add to their other problems of income and employment.

Policies since 1972

While there have been many detailed changes in the machinery used by Governments to effect improvement in regions, the most recent steps have been based on the Industry Act of 1972. As we see from Fig. 3.6, areas are now graded according to the assessment made of their needs. Three categories

Table 3.4. Government policy on regions

Regional development grants
Available on investment in buildings, plant, machinery, e.g., *development areas*—20 per cent; *special development areas*—22 per cent; *intermediate areas*—20 per cent (buildings only)

Regional employment premium (phased out in 1977)
At £2 per employee, encouraged labour-intensive industry to move to development areas

Industrial development certificates (IDC)
For over 5000 square feet building outside development areas. Area limits now raised and effects weakened

Selective financial assistance
Assistance under Section 7 of 1972 Industry Act, i.e., for maintenance and safeguarding of employment in assisted areas. Used in a discretionary way—often relief grants only

(Scotland) Scottish Development Agency
SDA from 1975 and Highlands and Islands Development Board (HIDB) from 1965. Large-scale financial support to locally based industry

---

appear—*special development areas* where the economic situation and continuing high rates of unemployment provide the case for urgent assistance; *development areas* with less severe problems; and the distinctly less disadvantaged areas, the *intermediate areas*.

The Act provided for regional development grants to meet costs of buildings to be used mainly for manufacturing, construction, or mining—and in the first two categories give help towards actual plant and machinery as well. If profits are likely to maintain or safeguard employment, then loans or low interest grants are made to the firms concerned in bringing or maintaining business in the area. The opposite course was pursued for the wealthier regions—industrial development certificates are not granted and planning permission is difficult to obtain to set up a new factory. Together with other measures introduced before 1972 (such as the regional employment premium, which was an additional payment to firms for each male employee but was scrapped in 1977), it is hoped that these regional selective assistance measures alone will lead to an increase of 58 000 new jobs by 1980. As we saw earlier, it will require more than this to compensate for the 300 000 jobs already lost in the basic industries in the last twenty years.

Nonetheless, these steps have been, and are, important. For example, when firms move into development areas they are welcomed. Industrial development certificates are granted readily. Special grants for training workers are made available; purpose built factories may be available, and tax and credit favours are granted for the first few years. And, as important, the variation in government policies often caused by balance of payment problems do not

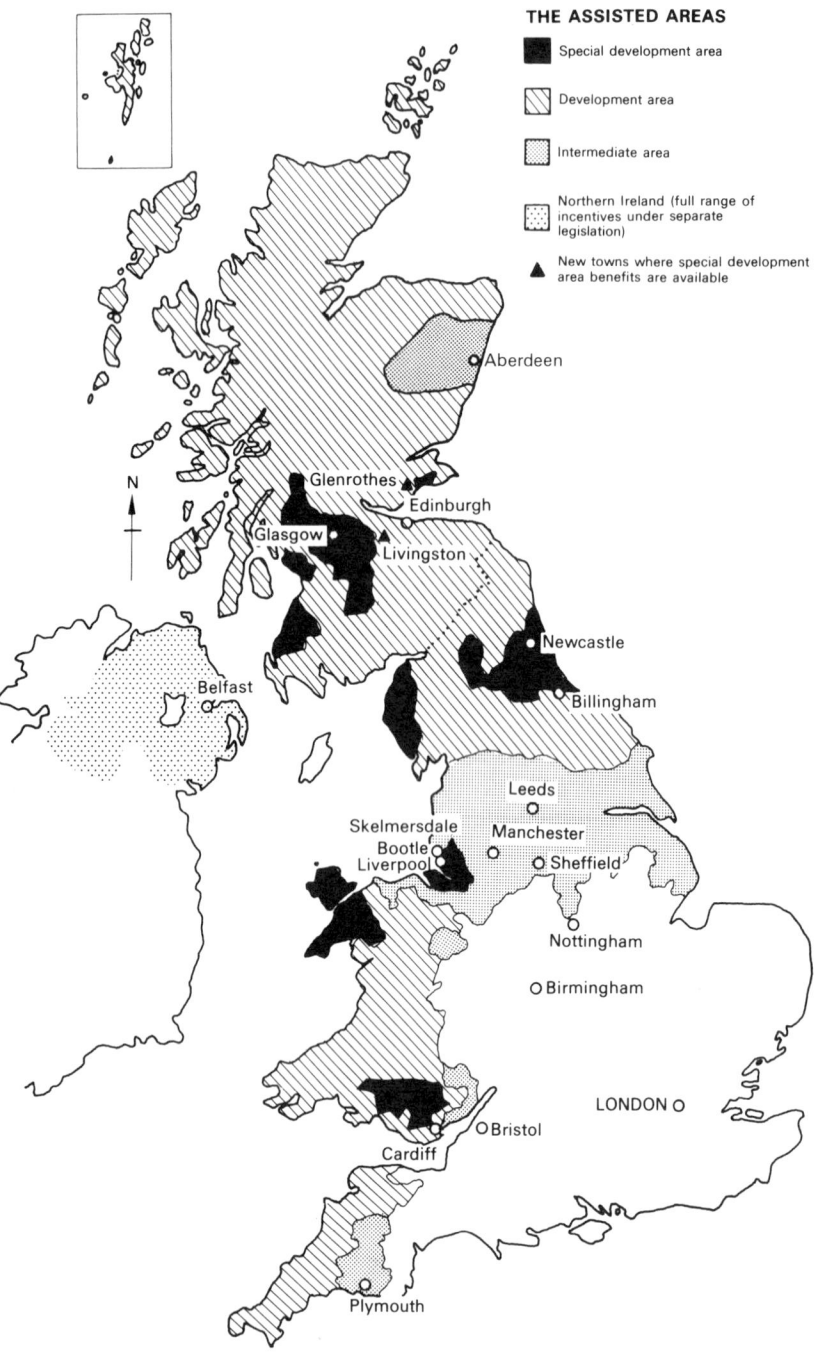

affect these policies—most of the government cuts and credit squeezes are modified in respect of these areas.

The scale of these activities is impressive. For 1974–75 some £213 million was paid in regional development grants. During the 1950s expenditure on them was about £10 million a year, in the 1960s it had risen through £100 million a year and in 1967 was over £200 million. Under the Local Employment Acts in the 1960s about 5000 projects received assistance, providing 370 000 jobs. Over fifty industrial estates are in existence, all crowded with factories; and there are 250 factories built on individual sites with assistance under the development area schemes. There are now about 250 000 people employed in these factories.

Under these incentives a host of new industries have moved into the development areas. On Merseyside, a new and different Liverpool is emerging: it has been described as 'a Liverpool of penicillin, chocolate biscuits, and the Treble Chance'. Fords were encouraged to expand at Halewood. On the industrial estates at Aintree, Kirkby, and Speke dozens of new manufactures are carried on: aircraft engines, telephone equipment, household electrical goods, rubber, chocolate, jam. Many workers have left the docks for these new industries, and the city's prosperity is less completely tied to the ups and downs of world trade.

On Tyneside, thirty industrial estates and two new towns have created thousands of new jobs to replace those lost as the traditional local occupations in coalmining and shipbuilding declined with the contraction of these industries. Light engineering, clothing, plastics, radio sets, electric lights, biscuits, and a hundred other manufactures have been persuaded to move in.

Forty years ago no region had fewer basic industries than South Wales. Today the scene is very different. On over twenty industrial estates a wide range of light industries has been established: electrical equipment and appliances, clothing, foodstuffs of all kinds, cars, nylon. The impact on Scotland has probably been most impressive of all (see Chapter 4) although oil has contributed much to new prosperity there.

The attempt to improve employment and prosperity in the development areas remains a major part of Government's concern with the regional economies. But during the 1960s that concern began to go further than these rescue operations in selected places. It became apparent that even prosperous regions had their problems. They did not suffer from unemployment but they experienced labour shortages, traffic congestion, overcrowding in housing and schools. If, as calculations suggested, Britain's growing population continued to crowd into the already congested South East, these problems could become

---

Fig. 3.6. The parts of the country where assistance is offered by the Government to encourage industrial development and service employment. (Source: *Britain 1977: An Official Handbook*, HMSO, 1977)

intolerable. Moreover, regions not so prosperous as the South East nor so depressed as Scotland, e.g., Yorkshire and Humberside, were worried about their relatively slow growth; and feared that the steering of industry and investment to the Development Areas might result in their own economies falling further behind.

In the poorer regions there were clearly resources, especially of manpower, which were underused. In the wealthier regions the pressure on many

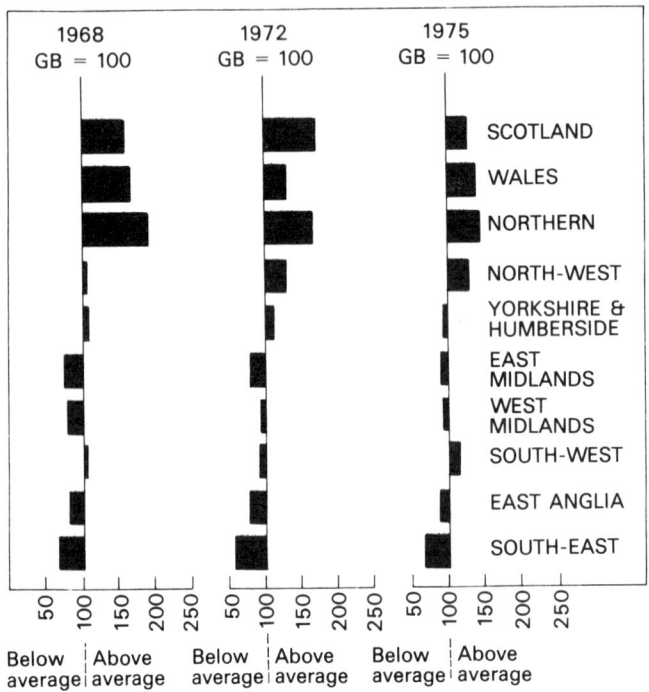

Fig. 3.7. Change in relative unemployment by region. (Source: *Economic Progress Report*, COI, August 1976)

resources—housing, schools, transport—was extremely severe. Left unattended, the latter would grow as natural increase and immigration swelled the population.

These regional difficulties clearly affect the national economy. In the interests of this, as well as of the region itself, the problems of the imbalance between regions and the conditions within each must be tackled.

The operation of the whole regional planning system is under the Department of Industry. In Scotland and Wales, however, Development Agencies have been established in 1975 to organize aspects of regional policies relevant to these countries, and since July 1975 the control of selected financial aid, which is under the Department of Industry in England, is in Scotland under the Secretary of State and in Wales under the Welsh Office.

The Department of Industry operates outside Scotland and Wales through the regional industrial development boards. There are eight economic planning regions—five of these have boards. These boards (North, North West, Yorkshire, Humberside, and South West) advise the Department on regional

Fig. 3.8. Economic planning regions

industrial opportunities, and make suggestions and recommendations for the redevelopment of their own regions. The position in Northern Ireland is different where the problems of industrial development are very difficult indeed. Grants are available at 30 per cent of cost for new buildings, machinery, and equipment for any of the manufacturing, construction, or mining industries. Rent free or rent reduced factories (government built) are available along with grants towards operating costs for any new firms setting up in business.

Industry then and now: a summary

Britain's industry in the last quarter of the twentieth century has changed strikingly from what it was only sixty years ago. The preceding pages have illustrated this, but it may be useful to sum up at this stage.

First, industry has expanded enormously in volume. Britain is more industrialized than ever.

Second, many new industries, based on technological advances have appeared on the scene, and are growing in importance. New sources of power and fuel, such as oil, electricity, and nuclear energy; key inventions like the internal combustion engine and the radio valve; new materials like plastics and artificial fibres—these have enabled a host of new products to be made, and created the foundation of a whole range of new industries. Thousands of people are earning their living in jobs that did not exist in their grandparents' day—the inventions, the fuels, the materials these jobs depend upon had not emerged. About one-quarter of the things we handle today were completely or almost unknown a few decades ago.

Third, the older industries have been greatly changed, too, by these advances. They may still make the same goods, but their materials have often altered, their equipment been transformed, their production methods revised.

Fourth, the relative importance of individual industries has changed. Some of the old giants have shrunk, others are being outstripped. New industries, infants sixty years ago, if they were even born, are looming larger every year.

Fifth, along with the rise of new industries has come some shifting in the location of industry. The old pattern of concentration on the coalfields is still apparent, but the last forty years has witnessed the beginning of a wider dispersion of industry and some moving of industry from north to south; the first reversal of the tide that set in 200 years ago. The great concentration of people, wealth, and activity is now spanning the Midlands down to London. It is variously described as an ellipse, a semicircle within a fifty-mile radius of London, or a 'coffin-shaped wedge'.

Sixthly comes the influence of the very large firms—operating as we saw earlier across national boundaries—what we called the *multi-nationals*. Each year they increase their control not only over one product but over wide ranges of products. With the great corporations there has come a structure of industry as complicated as the machines they use; their interests are spread in space across the globe, their activity is felt throughout a hundred fields. Many people are now becoming seriously worried lest the influence of these firms, often foreign owned, should dominate the British industrial scene—taking decisions and changing industrial location to suit their own interests, not always beneficial to the local employees and with no firm commitment to support British social or economic policies. (You can read more about multi-nationals, and their influence internationally, in THE WORLD TODAY, fourth edition.)

Among the most impressive changes is the much closer link between science and industry. Most of the innovations described in earlier pages are the fruit of this collaboration. They demand special scientific knowledge for their discovery in a way that earlier ones did not. A workman operating a simple machine for years might think of a way to improve it; but he could dig coal for a lifetime and never dream it could produce nylon stockings. In all the big industrial concerns teams of trained scientists are employed on fulltime research to find new products and materials, and improved versions of the existing ones. Even lower down the line, in the workshop itself, scientific training is needed to perform many of the operations in manufacture.

Just as noticeable, and just as important, has been the change in the part played by the State in industry. About one-fifth of industry is under direct government control—the nationalized industries. In still others it has a share or an interest. Yet more, though in private hands, have been helped by government subsidies. Hardly less directly, Government has affected the fortunes and the location of industries through its policies for the regions, for development areas, and for the distribution of industry. Less directly but still powerfully, there is the fact that Government now is expected to assume a general responsibility for the economy, and in particular for the handling of big issues like exports and the Balance of Payments, securing full employment, tackling inflation, seeing that investment and savings are encouraged. Its measures to deal with any of these can have important consequences for industry. Government fiscal or financial policies have long affected the fortunes of industry; but even in this more traditional field, the huge scale of government taxation and expenditure today gives this an increased importance in industry's development. In all this we can see evidence of the evergrowing role of Government in industry and in the economy as the twentieth century progresses.

4. Scotland: study of a changing society
with a Postscript on Northern Ireland and Wales

Population

Scotland, a separate country and Economic Planning Region, is less densely populated than England or Wales. In area—nearly 30 000 square miles—she accounts for about one-third of Britain; her population of about 5 206 000 forms only about one-tenth of the British total. Perhaps this fact, along with familiar travel posters, suggests a country of crofts and farms, with people scattered evenly and thinly throughout the wide open countryside. The distribution is, in fact, far from even; and any picture of Scotland as a peasant country is quite wide of the mark.

Great stretches of the North, the Highlands and Islands, are very mountainous; much of the southern belt is rugged hilly country. These regions are thinly populated—about twenty people to each square mile in the Highlands. There are a few towns and manufacturing industries, some of them flourishing, e.g., tweed, knitwear, whisky distilling, but in general these regions are more rural in their character and more agricultural in their economy than Britain as a whole.

But the vast majority of the Scottish people are not found in these regions. Four Scotsmen out of every five live in the narrow belt, the Central Lowlands, where the population density is nearly 1000 per square mile. Half of them, in fact, are crammed into a strip twenty miles long and five miles wide, stretching from Clydebank and Paisley through Glasgow to Airdrie and Motherwell.

Economy

In many respects Scotland is as highly urbanized and industrialized as England. Agriculture, which less than ten years ago, accounted for about 5 per cent of the total labour force, now has less than 3 per cent (a fall from 78 000 to 49 000 in seven years, 1968–75). Nowadays around 20 per cent are engaged in manufacturing industries and well over half of all Scottish workers are engaged in non-productive service industries. Such a pattern of industry is one common to highly advanced economies (like Sweden or West Germany). Unfortunately Scotland's manufacturing industry, which provides the production base for all the other wealth is not as yet in a sound enough state.

During the period 1962–71 about two-thirds of all the new manufacturing plants set up in central Clydeside came from firms which were controlled from outside Scotland. (Compare this with the English west Midlands where during the same period almost two-fifths of the new jobs came from firms established in, and belonging to, the local area.) Thus there is a real lack of Scottish enterprise in the manufacturing areas. The situation by 1973 had improved very little—indeed, despite the fact that for Scotland as a whole some 72 per cent of

Table 4.1. Production comparison: Scotland/GB, 1961–71

	Index of production (1961 = 100)	
	Scot.	GB
1961	100·0	100·0
1962	100·0	100·9
1963	102·7	103·9
1964	110·7	112·8
1965	115·2	116·2
1966	117·0	118·1
1967	115·2	119·6
1968	118·8	126·7
1969	121·4	130·3
1970	121·4	130·4
1971	120·5	131·0
1972	n.a.	132.7

the manufacturing plants were owned and controlled by Scottish-based firms the remainder (some 28 per cent), which included English and US-owned firms, accounted for over half the workforce employed.

Furthermore, the rate of production increases needed from this fairly small manufacturing sector (compared with the non-productive service sector) have not been forthcoming. Although Scotland has shown itself able to produce as efficiently as UK industry in general, the overall rate of improvement in productivity (production per manshift per week) has not kept pace with what is required if the economy is to prosper. Investment by Scots in Scottish industry is too low. Movement away from productive industry needs to be checked, and reorganization of some of the basic industries is an urgent priority.

What used to be a source of concern was the high rate of emigration—the net loss or outflow of potential producers from Scotland to other countries

(England or abroad). Table 4.2 shows how this outflow has tended to fluctuate in recent years and the latest figures indicate a marked reduction in this loss to the Scottish economy.

Table 4.2. Estimated net migration from Scotland (Source: Scottish Abstract of Statistics, 1975)

Year	To overseas	To rest of UK	Total
1955/56	−13 200	−14 000	−27 200
1960/61	− 8 700	−25 900	−34 600
1965/66	−21 500	−21 700	−43 200
1970/71	−10 500	−11 200	−21 700
1971/72	−12 800	−14 800	−27 600
1972/73	− 6 700	− 4 000	−10 700
1975/76	4 400	− 400	− 4 800

Industrial decline

At the root of problems like unemployment and population drift lie the changing fortunes and structure of Scottish industry. During the last century Scotland was well placed for developing the industries which underpinned the great prosperity of Victorian Britain. She possessed important local deposits of coal and iron. Within a small area she had a source of steam power, the raw materials for an iron and steel industry, and, in these metal supplies, the basis of engineering activities. Together with navigable waterways, they fostered the growth of a great shipbuilding industry, once metal had replaced timber as the building material and steam replaced sail as the driving power. Moreover, Scotland still possessed, in some areas, thriving textile industries, the basis of much of her wealth before the rise of heavy industry. With these assets she enjoyed good, convenient ports as departure points for the markets of a world waiting for her products. Coal, iron and steel, textiles, shipbuilding: these became the main pillars of Scotland's prosperity and the providers of jobs and incomes for her people.

Her high degree of concentration of these activities made Scotland, like the north of England, especially vulnerable when they began to run into difficulties during the twentieth century. As we saw, the rise of native industries in countries previously supplied from Britain, the emergence of strong rival industrial and trading nations offering similar products, the discovery of alternative products often more efficient and more attractive to the world markets, these together with the high price of Britain's exports and the slump in world trade dealt crippling blows to regions specializing heavily in these industries and in export activity. Scotland was among the hardest hit.

There was some easing in the immediate postwar years. Shipbuilding picked up with so much of the world's stock of merchant shipping in need of repair and replacement. The clamour for coal from industry and the domestic consumer was more than the pits could satisfy. Iron and steel were in demand for the massive reconstruction required in many fields. But in the 1950s the difficulties re-emerged. The world demand for new shipping was largely satisfied: a share of the much diminished market had to be fought for in the face of fierce competition from other shipbuilding countries. The metals industry felt the pinch as big consumers like shipbuilding and allied industries declined. The demand for coal began to go down as oil became more common. New kinds of product were in demand.

This shift, an experience familiar to British industry, generally, has been felt more acutely in Scotland because her economy is so closely geared to the industries most severely affected. In general, manufacturing industry accounts for about the same proportion of Scotland's economy as it does for Britain as a whole; but its makeup is still significantly different.

Scotland has a bigger proportion of her workers in industries which are contracting or growing very slowly—shipbuilding, textiles, metals—and a smaller proportion in those which are expanding most rapidly, e.g., chemicals and vehicles. In addition, Scotland has a rather bigger proportion in agriculture, another industry where improved methods and machinery are thinning out the numbers of men needed. In coal, another contracting source of employment, the same percentage of workers are involved. Again, even Scotland's similar proportion in the expanding 'engineering and electrical' is a little optimistic: this includes some activities which are on the decline, e.g., vehicles includes railway rolling stock, an industry which is contracting as the programme for modernizing the railways proceeds. Moreover, Scotland, with its great tracts of thinly populated land, had more than its share of half-empty trains trundling along miles of track through little-used stations. It is, accordingly, feeling the effects of the cuts and closures carried out by British Railways. As the traditional industries declined with the diminishing demand for their products, so did their need for, and their ability to employ, the great number of workers required in their more prosperous past. Even when they fought back against their difficulties, this was still likely to result in a reduction of jobs: the battle for efficiency involved more machines and the more economical use of labour, rather than an expansion of the workforce. So Scotland's big share of such industries has meant problems of unemployment. It has been calculated that the rundown in these shrinking industries meant the loss of 190 000 jobs between 1960 and 1970; and this is without considering the losses in related industries; or that the population—and hence the number requiring jobs—has been increasing.

Parts of England, notably the North, had experiences similar to those of Scotland. But in Britain as a whole, as we saw, new industries were developing in the years between the wars. These have now gone far, whether as sources of prosperity or employment, to recover the ground lost by the contraction of the staple industries of the nineteenth-century economy. Unfortunately for Scotland, the centres in which the new industries arose were the English

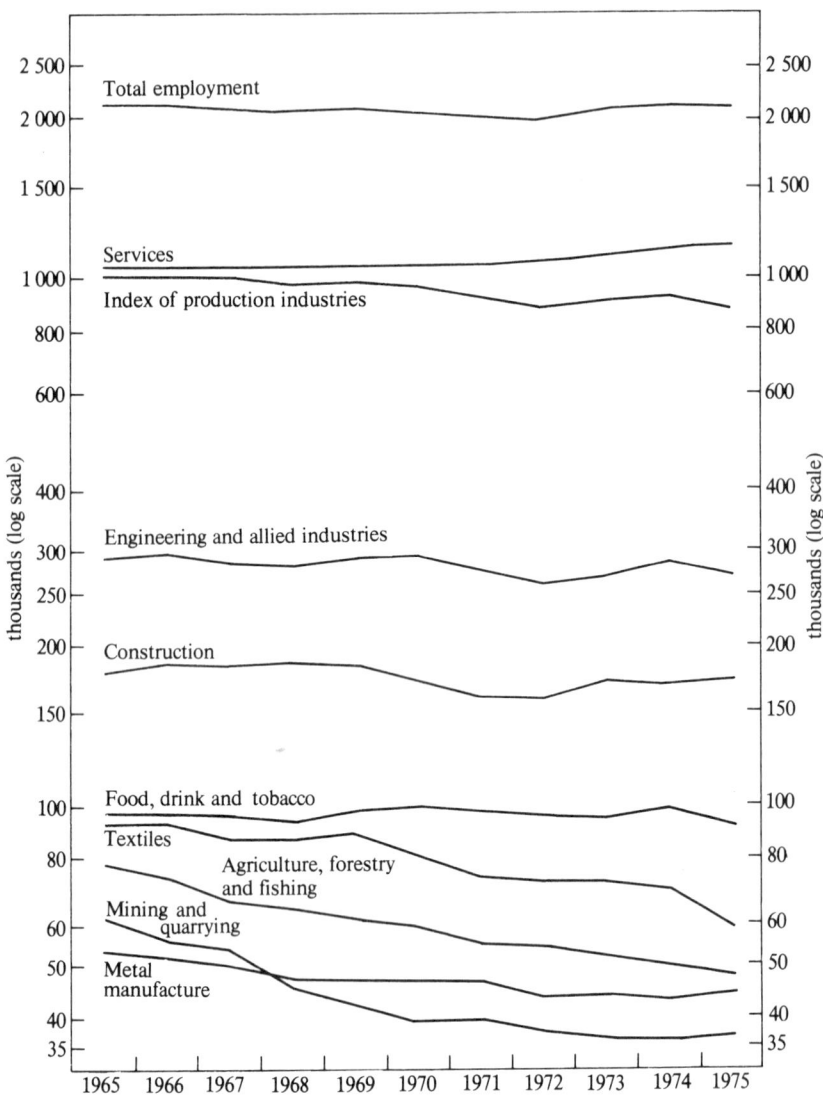

Fig. 4.1. Employees in employment: Scotland (Source: *Scottish Economic Bulletin*, no. 12, 1977)

Midlands and South East. Scottish industry did not find it easy to adapt to the new products, even when they were in the engineering field where the Scots possessed expertise. Scotland's engineering was geared to the production of heavy, specialized articles in relatively small quantities, like ships or locomotives. The new industries were geared to the production of smaller articles in mass quantities for huge markets, whether individual consumers or other industries needing them as components: transistors and electric light bulbs, radios and cars, television sets and typewriters. These demanded a quite different approach to production and marketing from that needed to build and sell an ocean liner.

Moreover, the newer industries were especially interested in having access to a mass domestic consumer market. From this angle, the attractions of southern England were irresistible, above all the vast potential market in and around London. As the new industries became established, the South East gained those advantages which made it still more likely that businessmen, embarking on these industries, would select this region as the most attractive location for their firms.

Conversely, those parts of Scotland where the contracting industries had been thickly located became less attractive. Unemployment and falling prosperity cast an air of gloom. 'Where there's muck there's money' had been a favourite saying of industrialized Britain in earlier decades: now the money was going but the muck remained. Housing, roads, public amenities—all tended to share in the decline, so that physical decay, squalor, and dirt, if they did not actually increase, at least became more noticeable and less tolerable.

In short, Scotland's difficulties were that she was losing on the roundabouts without gaining enough on the swings. She had been too dependent for prosperity and jobs on the traditional industries which were contracting, and hence less well able to provide either. Even when an industry prospered it was usually as a result of better capital equipment or technological improvements reducing the need for manpower so that unemployment was not eased. The newer industries which might replace the old as a source of wealth and employment have been slow to take root. So the unemployment figures remain high. This has a bearing on the other disturbing figure, emigration; one reason why the Scots keep leaving their country is the lack of prospects there and the greater promise held out south of the border or across the seas.

Industrial expansion

The situation has not been accepted passively; a great deal has been and is being done to try and remedy it. But for this, the unemployment and emigration figures would have been far more depressing.

Whatever its difficulties of late, Scotland does possess advantages that are ready to be developed and exploited. The community is highly industrialized with a long tradition and wide variety of skills. It is well supplied with sources of fuel and power, particularly hydroelectric power. The main area, the Central Lowlands, is compact; distances here are short and communication systems readily developed. It is served by good, convenient ports. And if some towns are unattractive, few places in Britain can offer such outdoor attractions within such easy reach of the crowded towns: Loch Lomond is only twenty miles from the centre of Glasgow. The advantages have not been ignored. Some foreign firms in particular were attracted by the surplus of skilled labour capable of retraining for new skills, and by the scope for expansion as their enterprises developed. They moved here rather than to the already congested Midlands or south of England, where labour was in short supply and space for future expansion limited. At the same time, leading figures in Scottish public life—businessmen, trade unionists, MPs, councillors—have been actively trying to promote Scotland's interests. They stressed how great the country's potential was, how readily it could be built up, how urgently it needed developing. A landmark here was the Report on the Scottish Economy produced in 1961 by a committee of enquiry under Sir John Toothill, chairman of Ferranti's. The Scottish Council (Development and Industry) a non-profit-making body, worked to promote industry and commerce through publicity and research. Native enterprise was not lacking. Oil and chemicals at Grangemouth were 'old' industries in the sense that they were already growing before the Second World War. Whisky was as flourishing a concern as anything in Britain. Steel, jute, publishing—in all these fields Scottish businessmen showed that they were not waiting on outside help.

While the role of the Scots themselves is crucial, government policies towards the regions have provided the most striking instrument for tackling the country's problems. Scotland figured prominently in all those schemes which we have already seen in considering the effect of regional policy on industry generally. Under the Special Areas Acts of the 1930s, the industrial belt was classed as a special area. It was under these Acts that Scotland's first industrial estate, Hillington, near Glasgow, was established. Under the next main Act, the Distribution of Industry Act in 1945, the central Lowlands and some regions farther north, became development areas. As such, they enjoyed all the inducements which, as we have seen, were used to encourage firms to move into these areas. Under the Local Employment Act of 1960 when any district with over $4\frac{1}{2}$ per cent unemployment became eligible for special treatment, Scotland was peppered with them but, as a 1963 Report pointed out, this Act was too restricting: it often made better sense to introduce development schemes not in the particular town suffering unemployment, but in some nearby area where there was a better chance of progress. A number of such growth areas were designated in Scotland and given special attention. They included the new towns, East Kilbride, Cumbernauld, Livingston, Glenrothes, and Irvine; the Grangemouth–Falkirk district, and areas in Lanarkshire, Fife, and Dunbartonshire. Then under the Industry Act of 1966 the whole of Scotland, except for Edinburgh and its neighbourhood, was scheduled as a development area. A firm coming into Scotland could pick a suitable location almost anywhere in the country and still be entitled to all the favourable treatment once limited to firms going to special local 'black spots'.

The whole battery of measures already outlined on page 75 were brought to bear. The measures were applied through a variety of agencies. At the head stands the Secretary of State for Scotland working through the departments known as the Scottish Office. These include some with a direct bearing on the economy, e.g., town and country planning, roads, electricity supply. In addition, the Scottish Secretary carries responsibility for economic development planning. For this he works through the new regional bodies, the Scottish Economic Council and the Scottish Economic Planning Board, introduced under the 1965 Act.

In the meantime Scotland's economy also had a boost in the establishment in 1965 of the Highlands and Islands Development Board, which is now under the chairmanship of Professor Kenneth Alexander. It is an ambitious attempt to tackle the problems of the Highland Region. It is able to give direct financial aid to anyone 'carrying on any industrial, commercial, or other activity which in the opinion of the Board will contribute to the economic or social development of the Highlands and Islands'. Grants in aid to the value of £790 000 were received by the Board in its first year, and by 1974–75 these grants exceeded £5·7 million. The visible results of its work over a dozen years are to be seen throughout the area. From promotion of a vast aluminium smelter complex at Invergordon in 1971, through electronics works at Tobermory in Mull, thermostatic components assembly in Barra, to venetian blinds assembly in Fort William. The Board has provided low rental advance factories, has made grants and loans available for hotel extensions, and has had hotels built at Craignure, Mull and in Barra to help the tourists trade. Not only so, but with extensive surveys being undertaken into mineral resources, the Board hopes to expand its work into exploration, development and mining of a wide range of minerals—from non-ferrous metals to potash, uranium and silica, copper and chromite. The plans are numerous and ambitious—they need to be. Figure 4.2 indicates the vastness of the land area involved and the great problems of an extensive shoreline.

Thus since 1966 a whole battery of measures has been brought to bear on Scotland's problems. The scale of success in new jobs can be gauged from Tables 4.3 and 4.4. Each year the number of firms coming in has kept growing. Some were small firms and did not grow rapidly in size; others like Honeywell Controls began with sixty employees in 1948 and had 2500 by 1966. Also, the older industries' loss of jobs slowed up, and the rundown of these industries seemed to be over. Even in 1968 such policies were expensive and Scotland received then over £100 million.

Since 1972 there has been a marked change in the system of industrial and regional incentives, and the whole of Scotland has become eligible for 100 per cent first-year allowances on plant and machinery. Added to the special

regional development grants and the grants (of up to 20 per cent) paid in development areas on plant machinery and buildings came the advice on selective assistance to industry from a new Industrial Development Advisory Board, with powers also to provide additional employment or to safeguard existing employment. Manufacturing, mining, and even some service industries gained from this help.

Table 4.3. Total assistance offered and estimated associated employment—Section 7, Industry Act. (*Scottish Economic Bulletin*, No. 9, 1976)

Period of Act August 1972–March 1975 offers made

	Number	Value £000	Estimated associated employment
Scotland			
Loans	100	25 033	10 807
Removal grants	35	643	626
Interest relief grants	251	13 264	24 064
Totals	386	38 940	35 497

Assistance was further stepped up in 1974 with the inclusion of Edinburgh as a development area eligible for full assistance, and with the doubling of the Regional Employment Premium (REP) (scrapped since 1977) to allow for the loss of value through inflation. In 1975 (July) the Secretary of State for Scotland took over full power for selective regional assistance, and December 1975 saw the establishment of the Scottish Development Agency (SDA) under Sir William Gray.

Incorporating the Scottish Industrial Estates Corporation and the old Small Industries Council for Rural Areas of Scotland, the SDA was given a budget over five years of up to £200 million (plus an additional £100 million if Parliament approved).

The Agency took over the Derelict Land Clearance, environmental improvement schemes, and, for the first time in Scotland, was authorized as a body to participate directly in industry—being able to pump cash into existing industrial firms to promote development and employment. This is already a potentially vital instrument in the field of Scottish economic planning. A measure of this importance is the Government's intention to place the SDA under the control of the Scottish Assembly, which will appoint half of the members of its board.

Fig. 4.2. The Highlands and Islands: general location map. (Source: D. Turnock *Scotland's Highlands and Islands*, OUP, 1974)

Table 4.4. Identifiable public expenditure on assistance to industry in Scotland: current and capital. (Source: *Scottish Economic Bulletin*, No. 9, 1976)

Years	1960/61	1966/67	1967/68	1968/69	1969/70	1970/71	1971/72	1972/73	1973/74	1974/75
			£ million							
1. Local employment acts	3·4	18·7	12·7	9·9	6·7	12·1	3·7	14·2	9·1	−2·9
2. Investment grants	—	—	43·2	57·0	69·4	68·0	54·2	34·6	19·8	5·6
3. Regional Development grants	—	—	—	—	—	—	—	3·0	32·0	61·6
4. Regional employment premium	—	—	13·1	38·3	42·0	40·8	39·2	37·1	38·4	57·2
5. Selective employment premium	—	3·4	10·6	9·6	11·0	2·8	—	0·1	0·1	—
6. Regional support and regeneration—other								8·0	9·4	10·5
7. Industrial innovation								26·6	32·4	36·2
8. General support to industry—other	n.a.	11·5	18·9	23·8	33·1	25·2	42·8	27·6	29·3	44·2
9. Support for nationalized industries—other								0·1	0·1	1·7

Another source of aid is Europe. With over £10 million of grants from the Regional Fund—leading to £1 million boost to a Shetland airport—and loans of almost £17 million from the European Investment Bank for the Sullom Voe tanker harbour, European commitment to Scotland's future seems assured.

To limit our survey to jobs is to underrate the extent of the changes. In terms of productivity, the advance has been marked. Recent estimates indicate that the Scottish rate of improvement here has been higher than the British average. Male manual workers' earnings have climbed to the national average: in 1960 they were 90 per cent, in 1968 they were 96 per cent; in 1975 and 1976 they were over 100 per cent (of the UK average).

In terms of the make-up of Scotland's economy the changes have been significant. They are bringing about a readjustment of the country's industrial base. For the new jobs are not a collection of minor activities, turning out biscuits or bottletops. They include important modern industries, notably cars, chemicals, and electronics. Each year the share of these new activities in the composition of Scotland's national product is growing, while that of the older, declining ones is diminishing. This is important. It means that, increasingly, Scottish industry—and Scottish workers—will be linked with the high wage, high productivity industries, and less with the low wage, low productivity ones. It means that there is far greater diversification in Scottish industry than before. This provides more security against depression. Even if the older industries continue to decline, their reduced importance as sources of jobs and wealth means that the effects of this will be less disastrous than in the past.

In addition, many of the newcomers offer prospects for expansion. This is not merely to say that they are expansion minded, confident, and expect to get bigger. It is that they are more science based, and more actively concerned with technological advance. This is most obviously true of petrochemicals, electrical engineering, and electronics. Conscious of the great benefits—the 'spin-off'—derived by California and Boston from the presence of so many high-powered technologists and scientists, Scotland hopes for similar results. An institution like the National Engineering Laboratory (NEL) at East Kilbride is not meant just to provide jobs for the men actually working in it. It is hoped that it will turn out ideas and improvements which will enable other industries to expand and new ones to spring up. So, too, with the growing links between the universities and industry. Strathclyde University, already working closely with NEL, has set up a Centre for Industrial Innovation: any firm with a problem or an idea can call on the aid of this collection of hundreds of scientists and technologists—a pool of scientific brainpower which firms could not hope to assemble for themselves. A new body, the Scottish Industry–Scottish University Committee in Engineering has also been established.

The readjustment of Scottish industry is apparent not only in its occupational spread, but also to some extent in its geographical distribution. The predominance of the Glasgow conurbation remains, but there are signs of a wider spread. Glasgow's own share of manufacturing has fallen. New areas have assumed importance and are likely to enhance their position with time. Grangemouth, with its oil and petrochemicals, stimulates the whole area around it. Each of the new towns and overspill areas has attracted new industries and the scatter of industrial estates also provides more small centres of activity. The vehicle industry is centred in Renfrewshire and West Lothian.

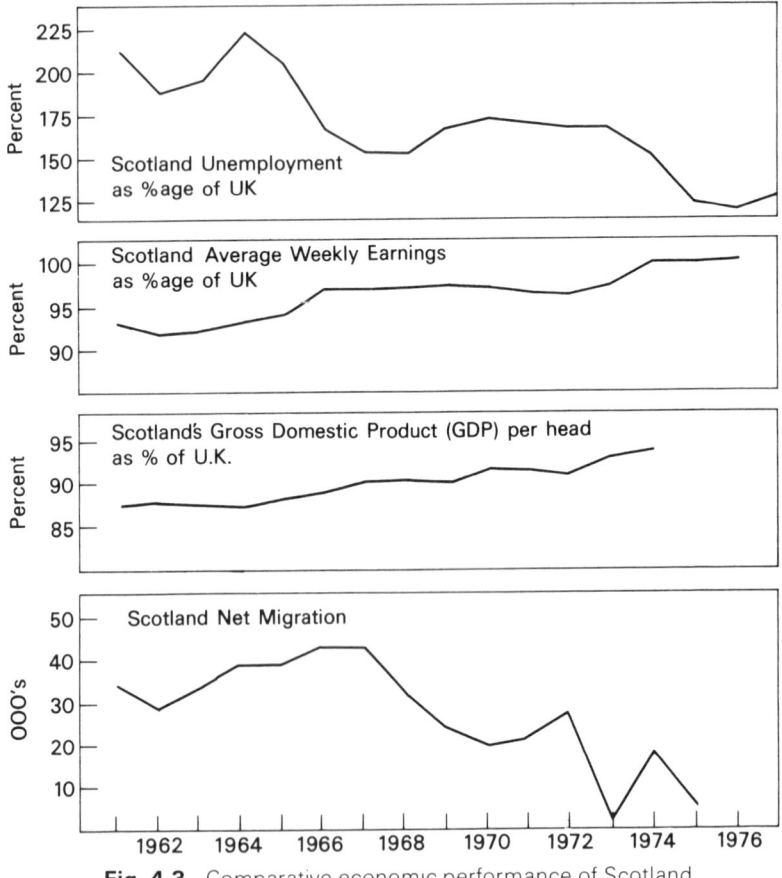

Fig. 4.3. Comparative economic performance of Scotland

The Edinburgh region has attracted much new industry, as has the Falkirk–Stirling area. There are concentrations in central Fife and around Dundee.

Not all Scots regard these developments with unmixed approval. Some feel that there has been too much concern with the short-term aim of providing jobs for the unemployed and not enough with the longer term one of encouraging economic growth—which requires industries with good prospects of playing a permanent and expanding role in Scotland's economy, not just any firm to fill a hole quickly. Most of the new firms are branches of English or foreign, especially American concerns. This has raised the fear that should the parent firm run into difficulties, these outlying branches in Scotland will be regarded as expendable and hence be the first to be closed down. The continuing trend in business towards the amalgamation of firms and the centralization of decisions may tell badly on Scotland. First, because the decisions about so much of her industry will be made increasingly outside the country. Secondly, because any Scots wanting to reach the top in these firms will have to move out of Scotland: there will be a drain of the very people most required to ensure that Scotland's industry remains dynamic. These may well be dangers. Even without them a great deal more time and effort is required before the position in respect of employment, security, and prosperity is restored. But then the task is nothing less than the transformation of the structure of the Scottish economy: it is not one to be accomplished in a year or two, without some setbacks and disappointments. The Scots can well insist that Scotland is not a country in decline; like Britain as a whole, it is a country in process of change, as a closer look at some of the major industries will confirm.

Iron and steel

Central Scotland was not an ancient centre of iron working. It was the child of the eighteenth-century technical advances in iron production. The discovery that iron ore could be smelted with coke instead of charcoal was the origin. In 1759, using local coal and iron deposits near Falkirk, John Roebuck opened at Carron the first great ironworks in Britain using coal as the fuel.

Local enterprise improved on Nature's gifts to the region. The work of David Mushet and James Neilson in the early nineteenth century enabled the huge deposits of blackband iron ore around Airdrie to be smelted more easily. Thereafter, though Falkirk remained, as it still does, an iron centre the blast furnaces crowded into the triangle formed by Airdrie, Motherwell, and Glasgow. Once steel began taking over—from the 1870s, when Colvilles opened their plant at Motherwell—this, too, concentrated in the same triangle.

Local ore is now exhausted and has to be imported from Sweden, North Africa, and Newfoundland. So, too—from Durham—must come some of the high quality coking coal that steelmaking requires, for Scotland's coalfields are running short of this. Despite the loss of these original advantages, the industry, especially on the steel side, continues to flourish.

The losses were partly countered by other advantages. Both the Falkirk and Clydeside areas have the next best thing to a local ore deposit: the great Firth estuaries and the ports of Glasgow and Grangemouth present easy means of importing supplies of the bulky raw material.

Clydeside had further assets. In steelmaking, scrap metal can be used as raw material, and the local shipbreaking yards provide quantities of this. And the equally close shipbuilding yards and engineering works are the markets where the finished steel can be sold. Thus transport costs are kept low, an important item when the materials and products of an industry are massive and expensive to move far overland. About 80 per cent of steel output is for local use.

Although a century-old industry, steel is more than holding its own in the changing Scottish economy. There has been some reduction in the labour force: the figure of 44 000 in 1975 is 13 000 fewer than in 1959. But production in 1976 of $2\frac{1}{2}$ million tons of crude and 2 million tons of finished steel represents an increase on that year, so that the productivity of the industry has increased. (Reports for 1977 indicate that output of all kinds reached record heights.)

There have been major developments, notably the building of a new £60 million continuous strip mill at Ravenscraig, near Motherwell. Despite recent cuts in investment and employment the prospects are good, especially as the British steel industry is increasingly using foreign, cheaper, ores. This gives an advantage to steel plants sited near deep water, where the giant ore carriers can berth. Earlier plans for a new terminal at Hunterston, able to accept 8 million tons of ore a year (as against the 2 million tons which is the limit of the present Glasgow Terminus Quay), have been revised to double the ore imported there. The limited capacity of this quay in the past set limits to Scottish steel production.

There have also been cuts in steel production plants to prepare for such future developments and to meet the needs of a modernized steel industry. In July 1973 BSC announced the closure of the old Tollcross foundry and the future closure of Clyde Bridge 'open hearth' steelworks. In August 1974, to meet the need for specialized steel plate in the North Sea developments, they announced a facelift for the Clyde Bridge and Dalzell works (costing £4·3 million).

In August 1975 a boost was given to the industry in Scotland by proposals from the Secretary of State for Industry. These followed Lord Beswick's review of the industry and confirmed some earlier proposals for modernization:
1. To increase the ironmaking facilities planned for Hunterston on the Clyde.
2. To develop and expand Craigneuk steel foundry,
3. To expand capacity for threaded pipes for oil/gas well casing.
4. To build electric arc plants at Hunterston and Ravenscraig and to increase capacity at Hillside (in Lanarkshire).

With new facilities for access to its raw material and new customers as the vehicle industry expands in Central Scotland, the steel industry could play an important part in the prosperity and employment of a changing Scotland.

Shipbuilding

Ample, convenient supplies of metal, coal for power, and the navigable waterway of the Clyde for launching: these fostered the growth of a great ship-building industry, once iron and steel became the building material and steam the driving power. But the river needed deep dredging to take large ships, and special launching arrangements had to be worked out in narrower parts.

From the 1860s the industry grew until Clydeside became the biggest shipbuilding centre in the country. Up till the 1960s around one-third of the tonnage launched in Britain each year was built there. Along the twenty miles from Glasgow to Greenock stretched over twenty shipyards with world famous names.

The prosperity of the region depended heavily on the fortunes of this industry. In the years just after the Second World War these shipyards flourished through the worldwide demand for new shipping. From the late 1950s, however, demand dropped while foreign competition grew. As we saw, this development spelt trouble for British shipbuilding in general. The situation in the Scottish industry reflected this. The number of men employed fell from over 70 000 in 1959 to 48 000 in 1967, a reduction of over 30 per cent: only the coal industry has experienced a more drastic decline in employment. By contrast with the better years of the mid-1950s, production fell by about the same amount.

The industry fought back. Part of the reduction in manpower represents the drive for greater efficiency of production through amalgamating shipyards. On the lower reaches of the river, Scott's and Lithgow's merged. On the higher reaches, John Brown's, Fairfield's, Connell's, and Alexander Stephens came together to form Upper Clyde Shipbuilders. All embarked on schemes of modernization. Lithgow's had long been among the most active of British yards in introducing new techniques and equipment. Unions bargained away their restrictive practices in productivity agreements. In Fairfield's, the unions agreed to put some capital into the firm, along with the Government and private business. UCS launched the biggest container ship yet built in Britain. Scott Lithgow studied the feasibility of building ships of one million tons. They felt no doubts about their ability to capture orders once they had the working capital required.

Thus the industry attempted to respond to the changing conditions—but not quickly enough. By the early 1970s the problems had multiplied. British shipbuilders were accused of three main faults: failure to deliver on time; non-competitive prices; and shoddy workmanship. Whether such accusations were fully justified or not, the effects were grave. Other nations took Britain's place as shipbuilders to the world's merchant fleet.

Despite all the efforts made by Scottish yards to modernize, others, abroad, were going one step ahead. In 1975 Spain had launched more ships than Britain. By 1976 (following almost two years of world depression of trade), with glowing prospects envisaged by most merchant shipping companies, the outlook for Scottish shipyards was bleak. With around 40 million tons of ships laid up through lack of trade, competition for new orders was keen. Scottish yards on the Clyde were by late 1976 facing the possibility of closure: Govan Shipbuilders, which had been based on UCS with a workforce of 5300, had no orders beyond 1976; Scott Lithgow had orders only up to late 1977; and a similar story was true of shipyards elsewhere. The irony was that Govan

Shipbuilders, which had been based on the 1966 Fairfield experiment (worker participation, long-term planning; job security; work study; modernization), now offered little job security at all. The effects on the local area were serious—around 60 000 people in Govan depend on the prosperity of the yards for livelihood. The Government having announced the plans for taking over the shipbuilding industry throughout the United Kingdom defined the immediate needs—modernization (including undercover production bays); flexibility to meet changing needs of buyers; speedier production schedules; greater quality control; effective price pruning.

Already some British yards have led the way in some of these matters. In Sunderland, Austen Pickersgill, making a regular profit, has been producing ships (and selling them) at the rate of one every 120 days. Indeed, each ship takes only eleven weeks to build and a further six to fit out. Foreign yards, however, are very difficult to match in competitive terms, and it will require great Scottish initiative and skill to meet the Japanese and South Korean challenge to our long-established shipbuilding tradition.

Coal

Coal, one of Scotland's oldest industries, is, as we have seen, in considerable difficulties. Year by year the decline continues. The years between the wars were not the industry's greatest by any means, but in 1938 it produced 31 million tons of coal and employed a workforce of 90 000 men. In 1956 the output was down to 21 million tons, the workforce to 84 000. By 1975 production had fallen to 10 million tons, the workforce to 36 000. From supplying just over 60 per cent of the country's needs of fuel in 1965 coal has slumped so much compared with natural gas and oil that by 1980 it will contribute less than a quarter of Scotland's total energy needs.

As in so many cases, this in fact represents a great increase in productivity, in that in 1956 output per manshift was 21 hundredweights, in 1975 it was almost 40 hundredweights, the result of the introduction on a large scale of sophisticated mechanical equipment. But just as with the coal industry in Britain as a whole, this is not enough to turn the tide in favour of coal. Though still in demand in Scotland, where most of its output is consumed by industrial and domestic users, coal is losing ground to its rivals. The Electricity Board is an important customer, but its most recent plans for the future envisage a massive new nuclear generating station at Hunterston and an oil-fired plant at Inverkip, neither of which development will help the coal industry's sales. The use of natural gas has expanded rapidly in Scotland during the 1970s. The oil industry, already strongly based at Grangemouth, is expanding also on Clydeside. At Hunterston, Chevron, the giant oil company, is seeking to establish a large oil refinery and related terminal.

In these circumstances even coalfields which are running profitably at present find the going hard. The Scottish division of the Coal Board shows a deficit every year. This reflects to some extent the difficulties of working the fields. Much of the older, more accessible fields in Lanarkshire and Ayrshire have been worked exhaustively. The Fife fields are less worked and more promising, but even here there are difficulties and extracting the coal is expensive. Mining machinery is very costly. Hence even the most attractive of Scotland's coalfields often prove uneconomic and pits have had to be closed down. Given the even fiercer competition which coal seems likely to meet in Britain generally, and the lower production targets set for it in the 1970s, the Coal Board may well look even more critically at those divisions which produce with difficulty and at a loss. Some further thinning out of this Scottish industry seems likely during the late 1970s.

Textiles

The textile industry is a traditional one. It used to dominate the region; but from the mid-nineteenth century Clydeside turned to metals, engineering, and shipbuilding, and the textile industry went into decline.

It remained of importance in some localities. There was still some cotton industry in the central belt, jute concentrated around Dundee, wool in the Border country. But in the years between the wars, Scottish textiles had the same hard times as their English counterparts. Cotton, apart from thread at Paisley and carpets in Ayrshire, practically vanished.

The history of difficulty and decline has continued, for the textile industry no longer provides the jobs it did. Jute has encountered postwar problems in the form of native jute industries in East Pakistan (now Bangladesh); and, though still a big employer of local labour, has recently lost its title of the biggest employer to the engineering industries which have established themselves around Dundee. In the Borders, wool, hosiery, and knitwear remain the major sources of employment. Here the trouble is the shortage of trained workers. In 1951 textiles as a whole employed 125 000 workers, in 1975 it employed only 59 000. Its output, however, remains about the same, so that, in a more modest way than earlier in the century, it continues to play a part in Scotland's economy.

Smaller Scottish industries

There have been other industries in Scotland which have been important to the very existence of remote areas and have indeed prospered despite the smaller numbers employed: the whisky distilling industry, Scottish fishing are two of these—both are well known at home and abroad as representing differing aspects of the Scottish personality.

Whisky, in terms of export sales, has for many years been one of the most important of Scotland's assets. Despite very heavy taxation on home consumption the production and sales of whisky have continued to rise rapidly in the last ten years or so. For example, in 1963 total production of grain and malt whisky stood at 88·3 million gallons. By 1973 this had increased to 104·8 million gallons—an average *annual* increase of around 8 per cent. Even here, however, with an annual demand growing at around 9 per cent, there is still a huge supply of bonded whisky—indeed between 1963 and 1973 the stocks almost trebled—posing problems of overproduction even for this otherwise prosperous industry.

The Scottish fishing industry reflects the diversity of the Scottish seaboard—from the fairly urban fishing ports of Aberdeen and Peterhead on the eastern coast, to the more remote hamlets like Kinlochbervie and Carradale on the west coast of Scotland. For many hamlets, fishing is the mainstay of the economy. There are still some 10 000 fishermen with another 20 000 jobs available on shore, and in terms of value Scotland has recently increased her share of the UK landings of fish, e.g., in 1969 it was 27·6 per cent of the UK total, in 1972 it was almost 37 per cent—and during the same period fishermen's earnings doubled. For the future, much depends on the EEC's new fisheries policy. One basic principle of this 'Common Fisheries Policy' is equality of access to and rights to fish within EEC members' territorial waters—allowing French, Belgian ships to fish in British waters with exactly the same rights as Scotsmen. The operation of this principle was postponed until 1982, and it was agreed that in most waters where dangers of over-fishing became evident UK vessels would have the sole rights of fishing up to twelve miles out from shore. (This was particularly helpful to areas solely dependent on fishing.) Thus the Shetlands, Orkneys, and the north and Cape Wrath to Berwick on the east coast became protected areas.

On the rather gloomier side, the possibilities of a severe cutback in the fishing fleets operating in the Faroes and off Iceland will result from the recent agreements with Iceland (see WORLD TODAY, fourth edition, and Chapter 1 earlier). Indeed, cuts of up to 50 per cent in the fishing fleet are expected, with very serious effects on the trawler bases at Aberdeen and Granton.

At the moment some 100 trawlers operate from Aberdeen and twenty from Granton. And as each trawler costs in the region of £500 000 any plans for future building or replacement of these ships depends very much on the profits expected; even in this industry the prospects are rather cloudy.

New industries

The older industries are not necessarily down and out, though they are coming to occupy a smaller share of Scotland's industrial base than in the past. But it is the wide variety of newer industries which is the most distinctive development since 1945: these embrace a host of light engineering activities and other manufactures, from pressure cookers to jet engines and machine tools. All are contributing to the broadening of the industrial base, but some are of outstanding importance: oil and chemicals, vehicles, and electronics.

The oil and chemicals industries are newcomers in the sense that the great expansion, a consequence of the link-up between the two, is essentially a post-1945 development. But the original oil refinery at Grangemouth was established as part of the much older business of processing shale oil from West Lothian; and the existence of this refining plant made Grangemouth an obvious choice for the much more elaborate refining and chemicals industry that came later. This is a long step from early moves to refine a local mineral.

The whole picture of the oil industry in Scotland has now altered completely in the last few years. In this respect Scotland has pulled far ahead of the rest of the United Kingdom—at least so far as exploitation of the new-found reserves in the North Sea are concerned (see Chapter 2B for discussion of North Sea oil and its effects on Britain as a whole). Indeed, it is difficult to treat North Sea oil as only of benefit to the Scottish economy. The dimensions of the developments are international in scope and the range of effects in Scotland itself very diverse.

It is only since 1964 that Scotland has come into the oil picture in a big way. Only in 1964–65 were the first discoveries made of what later proved to be massive deposits of oil and natural gas deep down in the treacherous waters of the North Sea. Without here reciting the dangers and technical problems of locating and checking on such deposits during persistently choppy weather, it is important to remember that human life was constantly subjected to very high rates of risk throughout all the stages of the oil and gas exploration.

Apart from dangers and lack of previous technical experience of developments on this scale there was always the possibility that the money required to promote these developments would not be forthcoming. However, international oil consortia were formed to advance these earlier discoveries, and by 1970 thirty-one wells had been drilled in the North Sea—giving new exciting names to an area hitherto remote and notorious for its treacherous seas, names like the Montrose field (1969), the Forties field (October 1970), the Piper field (1974), and many others. Indeed, by 1975 some eighty-one wells were being drilled—nearly all of them to the east of Scotland and many off east Shetlands (see Fig. 2.8).

The Shetlands was one area immediately affected by such developments. Before 1966 it had been one of the areas normally associated with the prevailing Scottish problems we saw earlier—an ageing population, high emigration, a low percentage of new service-based industries, and low level of investment in local industry. Over the last ten years all that has changed, due to the impressive energy of an enterprising Islands Council. Faced with the urgent need for shore-based installations and storage facilities, agreements were made with the large oil companies which conceded excellent terms for the Shetlands in not only undertaking to conserve the quality of the area, but giving a substantial share in the profits made from the North Sea exploitations. The economy of the Shetlands has now altered from its previous moribund state to one of great prosperity, burgeoning industries, thriving shops, and a well-paid and well-organized workforce—no longer losing its vital young people to jobs outside the islands. There is now a net migration into the Shetlands, and the future, including the development of the largest oil base in the United Kingdom (at Sullom Voe), appears safeguarded for the population.

In fact, the two main effects of oil exploration on Scotland have come from, first, the vast expenditure by the oil companies in seeking supplies for their offshore developments and, secondly, the overall employment boost given by these developments to the whole Scottish economy.

At one stage the scale of the exploration expenditure was truly vast: in the late 1960s the cost of a drilling rig leased to an oil company for checking and exploiting the initial exploration was in the region of $50 000 per day! With such substantial profits available to oil-rig firms there was a rush to build and supply such rigs, with their inevitable increase bringing the rates down to below $20 000 per day by 1974.

Nevertheless, Scotland gained from the needs of these new offshore wells. There emerged the 'onshore' oil industry—helicopter transport at Dyce airport, sea freight transport to and from rigs, fuel supplies, food supplying (and catering), and above all storage facilities. Cost in providing these services for the oil industry are high—one estimate is that a large well could cost £10 million per year, about half of which will be 'onshore' costs of this type. And it is not only money. For every Scottish rig which provides a total of 260 jobs, between 90 and 120 people will be offshore (at sea) and 140 to 170 may be on land-based work. By 1976 around fifty such rigs were still working in Scottish waters. This does not take into account the many semisubmersibles and their structures which are now stationed in the sea as visitors exploiting the underwater minerals on a long-term basis.

The peak year for developments was 1976. By the end of the year eight new production platforms were installed. And with around 100 000 people involved in the varied range of jobs created in the last twelve years it is now (in 1977) estimated that the Scottish oil industry has passed its peak so far as new jobs are concerned. Already it is clear that about 70 per cent of the new jobs have been created in the North East and in the Highlands and Islands—with very few, so far, actually created in the Strathclyde and Central regions where the needs for new jobs are much greater. Hopes have grown recently, through the BP announcement (January 1977) of a vast £1000 million investment in North Sea oil including vast orders for a range of related manufactures.

The projected developments at Inverkip and Hunterston are vital to those regions, along with the earlier Finnart (Loch Long)—Grangemouth (BP refinery) oil pipeline which was a farsighted effort to bring imported oil supplies to the very heart of industrial Scotland. Its story goes back to 1947, when the petrochemical industry was introduced to Scotland. Its history is one of rapid growth, though it is an industry which depends more on elaborate plant than on a large labour force. Grangemouth itself is the biggest producer of ethylene outside the United States. The oil refinery now processes 7 million tons of crude fuel a year. Soon there could be a wider distribution and expansion of these industries. American oil companies have already shown an interest in the Firth of Clyde.

The rise of the vehicle industry represents one of the most dramatic and promising developments in Scotland's recent economic history. It is almost entirely the result of government policy. In the 1950s the vehicle industry did not loom large on the Scottish industrial scene. Then, under government persuasion, BMC came to Bathgate in 1962 and Rootes moved into Linwood in 1963. Now (1977) there are 40 000 Scottish workers employed in vehicle production—more than in mining and about the same as in shipbuilding.

Bathgate had problems. With no tradition of vehicle production in the area, the rate of production in the new industry was low compared to the Midlands. There were problems of training and quality control, but even during the period of depression in late 1976 British Leyland confidently announced plans to invest approximately £10 million in its two Scottish truck factories at Bathgate and at Scotstoun, Glasgow, where Albion Motors (a Leyland subsidiary based on an established Scottish firm) produces heavy vehicles. Indeed, even now, these two factories together account for one-third of all British Leyland's commercial vehicle output.

The modern production plant at Linwood had been expected to change the ailing fortunes of the large Chrysler Corporation's British investments. However, failure in export sales over several years, coupled with a series of misunderstandings within the plant led to a grave crisis in 1975. For a time the whole Linwood project hung in the balance; then the Government pumped in a massive loan aimed at boosting the modernization of the plant to take the new Sunbeam model. By late 1976 not only were the fortunes changing, but with the orders growing both at home and abroad Chrysler appears able to weather the variations in its Scottish fortunes.

It was hoped that the introduction of this industry would in turn stimulate the development in Scotland of allied components industries. This has happened in one instance, tyres: Uniroyal make them at Edinburgh and Newhouse; Dunlop (India) at Inchinnan; Goodyear at Abbotsinch. But apart from these exceptions, the growth of a Scottish components industry has yet to be seen.

Electronics is another industry helping to change the pattern of the Scottish economy. It is virtually a creation of the last thirty years: hardly anyone was employed in this occupation in 1940. In 1943 Ferranti Limited, the first of the electronic firms to appear, came to Edinburgh. Others followed, until by now there are over forty companies including most of the leading names in the business: Honeywell, Burroughs, IBM, NCR, Elliott Automation. They are widely dispersed throughout the central belt—from Glasgow, Airdrie, and East Kilbride to Edinburgh, Fife, and Dundee. The industry employs 30 000 people. Its production is valued at more than £30 million a year, and much of it goes for export.

The electronics industry has an additional advantage in that its products can promote, in dramatic fashion, the output of other industries—steel and ships, cars and chemicals, building and banking. Its basis in advanced science could foster the growth of science graduates in the country, ensuring continuing progress in this field, the crucial one for the industrial revolution of our day. From the buildup of this industry, the Scottish Council hopes also to promote the benefits of 'spin-off' so that the effects are cumulative.

This has yet to happen. Most Scottish electronics firms still make equipment designed elsewhere. Only one, Ferranti, has established research centres so that products can be invented and designed as well as produced inside Scotland. But in employment, production, and potential electronics is one of the outstanding newcomers to the Scottish scene.

Other developments

It was appreciated that if new industries were to be attracted, and if, having come they were to expand, they needed the assurance of basic supporting services such as power supplies and good communications systems. As to power, Scotland has long been well endowed. Apart from coal, her facilities for hydroelectric power were far better than most parts of the island. Electricity, from a variety of sources, has advanced with great strides in recent years. The amount used has doubled since 1958. The growing demands of industry were foreseen. In 1968 a big new generator was opened at Cockenzie, near Edinburgh. At Longannet in Fife the biggest engineering project ever undertaken in Scotland is complete: a massive station whose four generators have a capacity of 2400 megawatts. Together with gas and natural gas, whose consumption has also risen markedly, industry seems hardly likely to go short of energy.

Developments in road communications have been less impressive, but 300 miles of new motorway have been completed and there have been substantial improvements on the A74 linking Scotland and England and on the A9 and M9 linking Inverness with the South and Edinburgh. In terms of new bridges Scotland has done well. To the earlier new Forth Road Bridge (1964) and Tay Bridge (1966) have been added the Erskine Bridge over the lower Clyde, the Kingston high-level bridge over the Clyde within the city of Glasgow, and the Ballachulish Bridge opened in 1975 linking the South with the West Highlands. When Prestwick became a civil airport in 1946 it handled 80 000 passengers; in 1968 it dealt with 500 000 and handled about 10 per cent of Scotland's exports. A new domestic airport at Abbotsinch was opened in 1966; within two years Glasgow Airport was used by over one million passengers.

At the same time, social development has accompanied this economic change. Incoming industries were more likely to prefer clean, pleasant areas; and the changing geographical distribution of industry has meant social change too. People were moving to new places and requiring houses, school, shops, transport, as well as jobs. Again, the desire of cities like Glasgow to thin out their dense population by moving people out to some thirty-six overspill areas or new towns had similar wide implications. Glasgow in less than ten years lost over 100 000 people and its numbers are still falling.

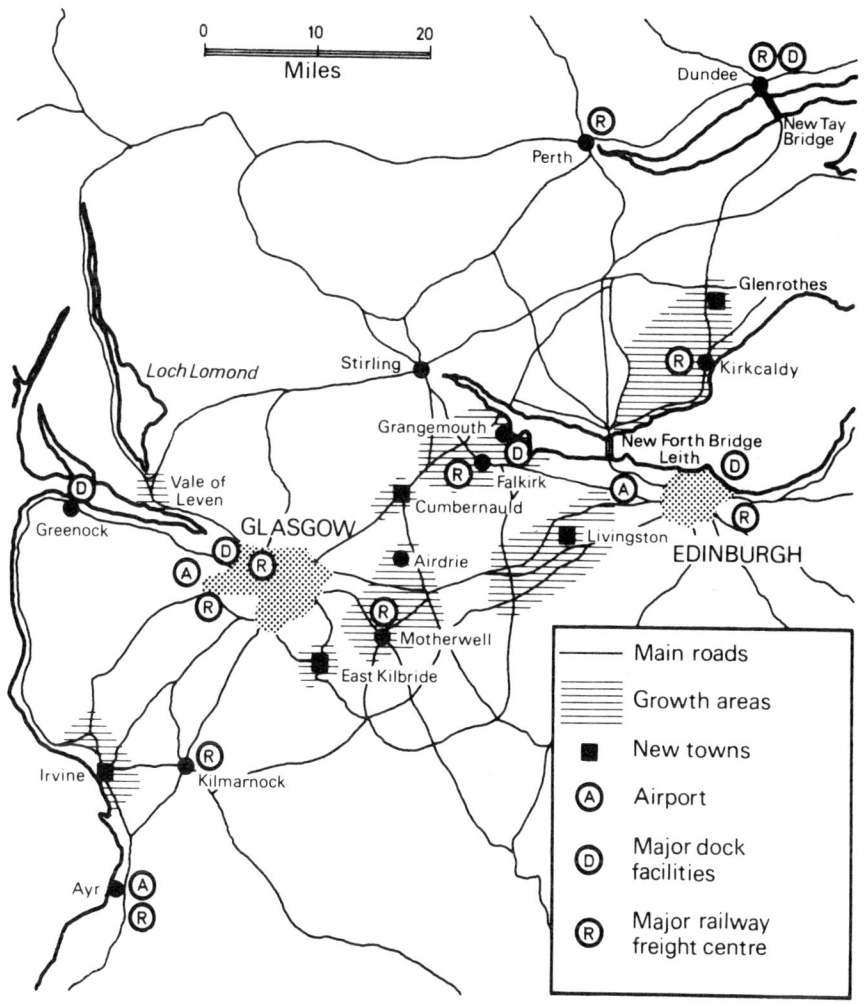

Fig. 4.4. Central Scotland

The new town of East Kilbride, for instance, had 2400 people in 1947; in 1975 it had 57 000. Here, then, was a new community. It proved attractive to industry, so the job needs of the people were met. As for the host of other needs, the opportunity was taken to experiment with new concepts for residential areas, shopping centres, traffic systems. Scotland has five new towns: East Kilbride, Cumbernauld, Glenrothes, Livingston, and Irvine. Cumbernauld has already won international awards for its architecture.

Not everyone can live in new towns or overspill areas. But even the older towns, made more conscious of their stretches of decaying and derelict property by the new developments taking place around them, have been undergoing facelifts. In Glasgow, new housing projects have got rid of some of the old eyesores. The imaginative redevelopment of the Anderston area, for instance, coupled with the massive demolition involved in building the Inner Ring road, have between them transformed the appearance of a great stretch of the city. High-rise flats, new commercial development, and the clusters of new university buildings have already altered the city's skyline out of recognition in the last few years. In 1976 the SDA announced a grand plan, Glasgow Eastern Area Renewal (GEAR), costing £120 million to improve this vast urban area. Thus a changing physical and social, as well as industrial, scene marks the development of Scotland.

Much remains to be done: Scotland still has more employed in the shrinking industries, fewer in the growing ones, than Britain as a whole. She still has a high rate of unemployment. The drift of people away from the country has not been halted; and among those leaving are many of her younger folk and many of her highly trained graduates—two elements on which any country depends heavily for its future prosperity. If Scotland's economy has improved of late, it needs, because of her problems, to do better. She possesses in the Highlands and Islands, and to a lesser extent the Borders, her own problem regions which require treatment. She still has, despite all the urban renewal, some of the worst housing in Europe.

Scottish politics

The political life of Scotland is in many ways different from that in the rest of Britain. There are special political institutions for Scotland alone, and the proposed introduction of devolution means that Scotland could have its own Government and Parliament (or Assembly) for the first time since 1707. At the moment, however, most of the administration of Scotland is in the hands of the Secretary of State for Scotland.

Secretary of State for Scotland In the late nineteenth century it was felt that Scottish affairs needed more specialized attention than they could get from Ministries that had to look after the rest of the United Kingdom as well. In 1885, therefore, a special department was set up to deal with Scottish affairs. It was in the charge of a Scottish Secretary, who was promoted to full ministerial rank in 1926 as Secretary of State for Scotland. He now has two Ministers of State and three Parliamentary Under-Secretaries to assist him.

The Secretary of State for Scotland carries out his duties through five departments centred in Edinburgh: the Scottish Education Department, the Scottish

Home and Health Department, the Department of Agriculture and Fisheries for Scotland, the Scottish Development Department and the Scottish Economic Planning Department. Together these are known as the Scottish Office, which also has an office in London at Dover House, Whitehall. The Scottish Secretary is responsible for administering in Scotland affairs that in England are divided among several Ministers.

Prisons and police, road safety, the laws affecting shops and cinemas are his concern. He supervises the National Health Service in Scotland and the setting up of new towns. He administers the Education (Scotland) Acts, and is responsible for the training of teachers. He puts into effect government schemes for encouraging farming in Scotland.

Questions in Parliament about the M1 motorway are dealt with by the Minister of Transport, about teachers' discontent in Birmingham by the Minister of Education, about cattle disease in Norfolk by the Minister of Agriculture, about policemen's pay by the Home Secretary. But questions about the M8, about Glasgow teachers, Aberdeen cattle, or the conduct of a policeman in Edinburgh are all fired at the one man—the Scottish Secretary.

Devolution Devolution to Scotland means an elected Scottish Assembly to pass laws for Scotland, and a Scottish Executive to form the Scottish Government. The powers to be given to the Scottish Assembly are similar to those exercised by the Secretary of State for Scotland, and they include education, local government, health and economic development. But the office of Secretary of State for Scotland will remain, as part of the British Government, and it will continue to exercise functions which demand more uniformity with those in the rest of Britain. Such functions include agricultural subsidies, industrial incentives, and law and order.

The Westminster Parliament remains 'sovereign' over all parts of the United Kingdom, and the Acts of the Scottish Assembly are subject to the veto of the UK Parliament. It is expected, however, that by convention such a veto will not be often used, and where powers are 'transferred' to the Edinburgh legislature, Westminster will not seek to make laws for Scotland. This leaves the UK Parliament with considerable powers, over the principal social and economic policies, as well as foreign policy. The Scottish Assembly is to receive finance from London in the form of a block grant, which is negotiated between the United Kingdom and Scottish Governments. Once the total amount has been decided, the Scottish Government may spend it according to its own priorities.

Scottish parties and pressure groups The proposal to introduce devolution owes much to the way Scots have voted in elections during the 1970s. The Scottish National Party (SNP) rose to 30 per cent of the vote in the General Election of October 1974. Ten years previously the SNP had only $2\frac{1}{2}$ per cent of the vote. While the SNP wants to see Scotland an independent state, many of its supporters at the polls do not wish to go further than a system of devolution, and with this in mind the major parties (Labour and Conservative) adopted a devolution policy.

All the political parties have Scottish organizations and conferences, and there is a separate Scottish Labour Party. Many pressure groups and organizations are Scottish rather than British—for example, the teachers' unions, the Scottish Football Association, and the local government association, the Convention of Scottish Local Authorities. These bodies press their wishes on the Government and they keep Scottish politics in some ways separate from politics in other parts of Britain. The big question mark over Scotland in the late 1970s is whether these differences will lead on to total independence, or whether Scotland will continue to be an integral part of the United Kingdom.

Postscript on Northern Ireland and Wales

Northern Ireland and Wales, like Scotland, are distinctive regions within the United Kingdom. Northern Ireland had a system of devolution from 1921 to 1972, and again from January to May 1974. Since that date, there has been no Government or Parliament in Northern Ireland, and the system of central administration there now resembles that in Scotland and Wales. There is a Northern Ireland Office, with a Secretary of State for Northern Ireland in the Cabinet.

The political situation in Northern Ireland is very different from that in the rest of the United Kingdom, with civil unrest and violence between two communities, Catholic and Protestant. Many Catholics wish to unite Northern Ireland with the Republic of Ireland, while the Protestant 'Unionist' majority proclaims its loyalty to the United Kingdom. This division has led to continual conflict, especially since 1968, and the British Army has been concerned with peace-keeping in the Province since 1969.

Wales has never had devolution but since 1964 there has been a Secretary of State for Wales, as head of the Welsh Office, in the Cabinet. There is a strong movement to promote the use of the Welsh language in Wales, and in the 1970s many place-names reverted from English to Welsh. Welsh is also used in official documents in post offices, etc., alongside English, and is widely taught in Welsh schools. Wales is less politically nationalist than Scotland. The Plaid Cymru (Welsh Nationalist Party) won 11% of the Welsh vote and elected three MPs in the general election of October 1974. A form of 'executive' (non-legislative) devolution has been proposed for Wales.

5. Agriculture and fishing

Of these two, agriculture is the more important. Indeed, of every 100 workers in civil employment in the United Kingdom around three are engaged in agriculture. Some 678 000 people work in the industry, and in 1974–75 they produced about £4921 million worth of food. In doing so, they used up around 80 per cent of total land available (i.e., 47 million out of 60 million acres). The effective use of this land is the key to effective and profitable farming.

Land used for farming is divided up into land under cultivation (for crops or grass) and land for rough grazing. In Britain around half of all land is under crops or grass. When all other uses of land (for rough grazing, woodland, and so on) are added together, we can understand how it is that four-fifths of all land is used by the agricultural industry. What is left is either mountain or forest, or is used for urban developments—housing, factories, and towns.

Despite this, Britain cannot really be called an agricultural country. Her economy is not dependent on agriculture—the annual output is in value only around one-twenty-fifth of the value of the nation's total production. She is very far from being selfsufficient in food. Not for the last 150 years has Britain been able to feed her citizens from her own resources. During the Second World War serious efforts were made by the Government to encourage increased production by farmers. At the time the survival of the nation was at stake, and home-produced food played a vital role in freeing shipping for other vital war supplies. Great campaigns were launched to increase the home production of food, and generous grants and subsidies were given to farmers to help them improve their farms, extend or intensify their cultivation, and so step up their output.

After the war, the steady expansion of the industry in terms of yield per acre continued. Livestock in the form of cattle and calves now totals over 15 million (1974) as compared with $8\frac{1}{2}$ million in 1938 (see Table 5.1). In the last ten years the number of pigs has increased by a quarter, and egg supplies have increased by one-tenth. Each day, 3 million dozen eggs, 6000 tons of meat, over 8 million gallons of milk, 18 000 tons of potatoes are produced by British farms.

Table 5.1. Manpower, land use, produce and livestock. (Source: *Britain 1977: An Official Handbook*, HMSO, 1977)

Item and unit	Averages 1936–38	1964–66	1974	1975	1975 imperial unit equivalents
Manpower in agriculture ('000)	¹	¹	678	657	
Land use ('000 hectares)					
Total crops and fallow	3 605	4 809	4 838	4 819	11 907³
Temporary grass	1 692	2 663	2 316	2 138	5 284³
Permanent grass	7 588	4 943	4 920	5 074	12 538³
Rough grazings	6 668	7 214	6 564	6 555	16 198³
Woodland on agricultural holdings	²	²	212	225	556³
Other land on agricultural holdings	²	²	161	171	423³
Total	19 552	19 628	19 010	18 984	46 911³
Main crops					
Cereals: area ('000 hectares)	2 145	3 623	3 747	3 654	9 029³
harvest ('000 tonnes)	4 513	13 307	16 382	13 823⁴	13 605⁹
of which—					
Wheat: Area ('000 hectares)	751	941	1 233	1 035	2 557³
harvest ('000 tonnes)	1 677	3 813	6 130	4 438⁴	4 368⁹
yield (*tonnes per hectare*)	*2.23*	*4.05*	*4.97*	*4.29*⁴	*1.71*⁵
Barley: area ('000 hectares)	376	2 234	2 214	2 345	5 794³
harvest ('000 tonnes)	777	8 146	9 133	8 433⁴	8 309⁹
yield (*tonnes per hectare*)	*2.08*	*3.65*	*4.12*	*3.60*⁴	*1.43*⁵
Oats: area ('000 hectares)	972	411	253	233	574³
harvest ('000 tonnes)	1 971	1 232	955	802⁴	798⁹
yield (*tonnes per hectare*)	*2.03*	*3.00*	*3.77*	*3.44*⁴	*1.37*⁵

Potatoes: area ('000 hectares)	293	295	214	204	504[3]
harvest ('000 tonnes)	4 951	7 074	6 791	4 516[4]	4 449[9]
yield (tonnes per hectare)	16·82	24·00	31·60	22·14[4]	8·82[5]
Sugar beet: area ('000 hectares)	136	181	195	193	488[3]
harvest[6] ('000 tonnes)	422	888	568	635	625[9]
yield (tonnes per hectare)[7]	3·11	5·9	3·6	4·3	1·7[5]
Livestock ('000 head)					
Cattle and calves	8 675	11 425	15 203	14 717	
Sheep and lambs	25 786	29 842	28 498	28 270	
Pigs	4 466	7 564	8 544	7 532	
Poultry	76 236	118 486	139 672	136 572	
Livestock products					
Milk (million litres)	7 069	11 307	13 280	12 999	2 859[8]
Eggs (million dozen)	558	1 088	1 081	1 093	
Beef and veal ('000 tonnes)	587	892	1 194	1 155	1 137[9]
Mutton and lamb ('000 tonnes)	198	164	260	257	253[9]
Pigmeat ('000 tonnes)	442	875	928	811	788[9]
Poultry meat ('000 tonnes)	90	412	646	657	647[9]

1. Complete figures were first available in 1971 when the number was 716 000.
2. Figures not collected before 1972.
3. Provisional.
4. Tons per acre.
5. Sugar production 1936–38: raw equivalent basis; 1964–75: refined basis.
6. Sugar-in-beet per crop hectare.
7. Thousand acres.
8. Million gallons.
9. Thousand tons.

Discrepancies between totals and their constituent parts are due to rounding.

Table 5.2. Economics of farming: United Kingdom. (Source: *Facts in Focus*, 3rd edn, Penguin, 1975)

	£ million	
	1969/70	*1974/75*[1]
Output		
Livestock and livestock products	1473	2815
Horticulture	268	512
Farm crops[2]	434	987
Sundry outputs	12	32
Sundry receipts[3]	31	32
Production grants	100	157
Total receipts	2318	4533
Work in progress	+82	+388
Gross output	2400	4921
Input		
Feedingstuffs	545	1234
Machinery	162	326
Seeds	51	106
Livestock	71	107
Fertilizers and lime (before subsidy)	140	305
Farm maintenance	94	152
Miscellaneous expenditure[4]	161	336
Total expenditure	1223	2566
Gross input (total expenditure *less* change in stocks)	1225	2578
Gross product (gross output − gross input)	1175	2343
less Depreciation	178	405
Net product	997	1938
less Labour, net rent and interest[5]	438	806
Farming net income	557	1133

1. Forecast in December 1974.
2. Includes receipts from crops sold off farms, and subsequently bought back, cereal and potato seed, but excludes deficiency payments on retained cereals.
3. Deficiency payments on animal disease compensation, cereals retained, etc.
4. Electricity, rates, veterinary expenses, pesticides, etc.
5. Net rent = gross rent *less* landlord share of maintenance and depreciation. Interest on commercial debt for current farming purposes.

It is clear that agriculture is a main plank in our economic policy. The more food we grow ourselves the less money will we need to spend on buying food from abroad, and this saving will ease our Balance of Payments problem. Britain now produces over half of its total food requirement. This itself is no

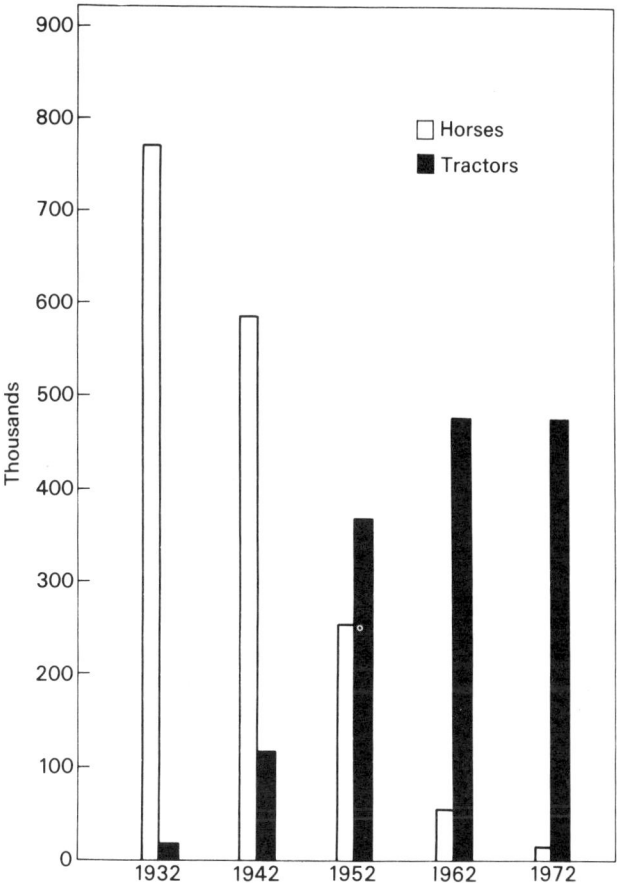

Fig. 5.1. Progress in mechanization of farms. (Source: *Facts in Focus*, 3rd edn, Penguin, 1975)

mean feat. Rising living standards lead to increasing consumption of foods. Despite this, in the last twenty years we have been able to improve our provision of home supplies of many food products in daily demand, e.g., milk supplies are totally home produced; so is more than two-thirds of our wheat (under one-fifth twenty years ago); over three-quarters of our meat (less than two-thirds in 1956)

Figures in Table 5.1 compare production in the mid-1960s with that in the late 1930s. Lately the pattern of food consumption has tended to settle down, and this is reflected in less radical changes in the composition of our farming supplies (see Table 5.2).

A significant feature is the fact that British farming is based largely on livestock. Indeed, 70 per cent of total farm output is in the form of livestock or livestock products. This is reflected in the expenses incurred by farmers. Around 40 per cent of all spending is on foodstuffs. In Fig. 5.1 we see the changing pattern of energy/power in farming. Tractors and machines have replaced horses, and they now account for one-fifth of all farm expenses. Now with one tractor to every 34 acres of land, Britain's farms are among the most mechanized in the world. With the use of over 60 000 combine harvesters and a wide range of harvesting and milking machines many farmers find that a useful way of sharing equipment without the outlay involved in purchase is through membership of a machinery syndicate, whereby, for a fee, they have access to mechanization whenever they really need it. This saves the individual farmer from spending vast sums on the purchase and upkeep of such machines.

Farmers are dependent on a regular income for the planning of future crops, and, despite the overall development and progress of the industry, little would be possible without guidance and help from the Government—at several levels.

Government and agriculture

Government encouragement to agriculture takes various forms. Up till 1973 the main form (which had been laid down in the Agriculture Act of 1947) was a guaranteed price to farmers for most items of agricultural produce, and it worked in the following way.

Every year in February representatives of the Government and the farmers met to weigh up the prospects for agriculture in the coming year. As a result of their survey and discussions, the Government then guaranteed farmers a certain price for each of their main products. The price varied from one commodity to another. The farmer then grew his produce and sold it in the ordinary market—to wholesale dealers, shopkeepers, or consumers—at whatever price he could get. But if that price was less than the one guaranteed at the 'February Review', then the Government made up the difference to the farmer. This was called the 'deficiency payments' system. This system is now undergoing a complete change (see p. 116).

In some items, e.g., milk, the farmers found it more convenient to set up marketing boards (whose members are mainly elected by the farmers themselves) to look after the selling side of the business. The farmer simply sold all his milk direct to the Milk Marketing Board. By avoiding the need to find individual customers, argue about prices, arrange deliveries, and so on, he was able to give all his time to the job of producing. The appropriate board saw to the selling of the produce in the ordinary market. The difference between the price it received and the guaranteed price was made up by the Government.

For some produce, notably vegetables and fruit, there was no price guarantee. These were protected by tariffs and quotas imposed on rival foreign produce that might otherwise have undercut the home product in the British market and so forced the farmers to reduce their prices—perhaps to a level where it would not have been worth while for British farmers to carry on growing them.

Table 5.3. Estimates of the proportion of UK food requirements derived from home agriculture and fisheries. (Source: *Facts in Focus*, 3rd edn, Penguin, 1975)

	Percentage			
	All food products		Indigenous food products only	
Years	Home output	Imports	Home output	Imports
1968/69	51·5	48·5	64·0	36·0
1969/70	52·4	47·6	64·7	35·3
1970/71	53·5	46·5	66·0	34·0
1971/72	53·9	46·1	67·0	33·0
1972/73	54·0	46·0	66·9	33·1
1973/74	56·0	44·0	69·8	30·2

Agriculture was further helped by a wide range of financial grants and subsidies available to farmers who wanted to make their farms more efficient, e.g., by improving the drainage system of their land. For other schemes, now covered by grants, the farmer could often get a loan on easy terms.

There are numerous institutions whose services are available to farmers. There are agricultural committees, with representatives of the Government and farmers, operating in each county. They give advice and assistance to the local farmer on his problems. There is an advisory service, with branches in every district, where expert help on all kinds of problems—farm machinery, animal feeding, soil chemistry, plant diseases—may be obtained. There are about fifty agricultural research stations. Apart from universities and agricultural colleges, there are many courses in agriculture run by local education authorities.

The deficiency payments scheme described above had the advantage that it guaranteed prices for the farmer and so assured Britain of a high domestic production of food. It enabled us to buy home-grown food more cheaply than we could if the farmer lost his deficiency payments and had therefore to demand a higher price from the consumer. Nevertheless, not everyone agreed that this was the best way to help the industry. Some people felt that the cost was too high. They saw the deficiency system as encouraging the inefficient farmers, and they felt that there should be concentration on production from the most efficient farms—even if this meant that there was less farming; poorer farms should go; extravagant crops should go. Any loss in production would be made up by the savings in subsidies. Such savings might then be used, in part, to purchase abroad any of the hitherto home-grown crops from those inefficient farms.

Others felt that the price to pay for maintaining British agriculture was a small one. Fears of world overpopulation, and all that this would mean in terms of food shortages, convinced many that Britain must keep up domestic food production. The fear of another era of food shortages due to war or worldwide famine has, up till now, led governments to pursue a course of generous help for agriculture.

Agriculture and the European Community

Since February 1973, however, Britain has no longer had a final say in such policies. Under the 'Common Agricultural Policy' (CAP) adopted by the European Community a system quite different to the previous deficiency payments system has been in force, and with Britain joining the EEC we have had to set about adapting ourselves to the new system. The EEC has an Intervention Board for Agricultural Produce which administers the CAP. The agricultural Ministries, however, remain reponsible for the overall policies, and through their Annual Review they build up an overall picture of the production trends, market requirements, and consequent subsidy costs for the ensuing years throughout the Community. In Britain the total cost of subsidizing agriculture in 1974–75 was £296 million—under the CAP arrangements £193 million was paid by Britain. Of this, however, £147 million was reimbursed from the European Agricultural Guidance and Guarantee Fund (i.e., FEOGA).

Concern for Britain's agriculture was one reason why some people disliked our decision to join the Common Market. Each of the 'Six' protected its farmers by tariff walls against foreign produce. They hoped for a gradual lowering of these barriers between themselves until the whole region could become one large market open equally to the farmers of all member countries. There is a tariff barrier around the boundary of the region to protect agriculture inside the Common Market from the competition of non-member countries. The Dutch farmer finds no trade barriers to hinder him selling his produce in Paris, or Rome, or Bonn; French, German, and Italian foodstuffs will find no trade barriers thwarting their sale in Rotterdam.

Until 1973 Britain did not rely much on tariffs to protect her farmers. She used subsidies. It was not difficult for foreign produce to enter Britain, but the

British farmer, through the deficiency payments, was assisted to ensure that he would 'hold his own ground' against it. He was able to keep his prices down, knowing that he would not lose—the Government would make good to him the difference between his selling price and the one he was guaranteed at the Annual Review. As a member of the Common Market, Britain could hardly expect to continue this system, for its effect would be to deny other members access to the British market on open and equal terms. Britain would then be retaining special advantages for her farmers and evading her obligations to her partners.

The effect of the change in this system will not be fully felt until the end of this decade. For most commodities, Britain has agreed to adopt the Community support level system over a five-year transitional period. Thus during the next few years there will be free trade between Britain and other EEC members so far as the main agricultural products are concerned—subject to special arrangements being made for the differences in price levels and currency values (see below—'Green' pound). There is also a market intervention scheme to be used when items of particular importance to certain member countries are dealt with. In such cases, the Community authorities will support the prices by bulk purchasing so that such items are not sold at a loss to producers. At the same time, there are minimum prices for imports from abroad which might otherwise cause undercutting in prices of marketable commodities.

There were many arguments put forward before 1972 about the adverse effects of the new EEC system on British agriculture. These were:
1. That the abandonment of the subsidy system would lead to the decline of British farming. European produce would flood into the country and domestic food production would slump in face of this intense competition.
2. The prices of food in Britain were lower than they might have been, because the farmer could afford to sell cheaply—even at a loss—to the consumer, knowing that the Government would make it up to him through the deficiency payments system, but once the subsidies were scrapped the whole burden of paying for food would have to be borne by the consumer. Food prices would rise. The poor, who pay little in taxes towards the subsidies, would feel this burden the most.

The effects of EEC membership have been difficult to assess. Prices of food products have risen steeply (e.g., since 1973 butter prices are up by about 50 per cent). However, these rises have been due not only to the EEC system but also to the pressures of inflation itself. We do now pay more for food as consumers, but perhaps this may be countered in future by a reduction in our payments as taxpayers. The Government has attempted, through strict vetting of price rises, to alleviate the worst aspects of the situation.

As to the ruin of British agriculture, so far this has not happened. Some branches have met difficulties: horticulture, for instance, faces powerful competition from Dutch growers. Inefficient and wasteful farming also suffers, but to protect this was never the aim of the subsidies. Many British farmers are as efficient as any in the world and can stand up to foreign competition in the British market.

The EEC system has caused some complications for Britain's Balance of Payments (see Chapter 7). All EEC members contribute to a special agricultural fund. The contributions are based on food imports, and Britain, as a big importer, pays large sums to the fund. The annual loss to her Balance of Payments is over £200 million. We could, on the other hand, gain (as has happened through EEC support for the 'green' pound).

The Community and the 'Green' pound

Since Britain confirmed her membership of the EEC there has been considerable discussion about ways of aligning British policies to those of the other members of the Community. To the British consumer it has appeared unfair that the move from our deficiency payments system should be towards a system based on higher food prices. To the European countries it appears unfair that Britain should be allowed to subsidize the 'real' cost of food and permit consumers to receive food more cheaply than citizens in fellow member countries.

The argument has also focused on two aspects of the CAP—the support being given to Britain from the Agricultural Fund and the 'green' pound.

The EEC agreed to support British transition to the higher prices of the Common Market by a subsidy of around £1 million a day. This is a heavy burden for European taxpayers and many want to see it ended.

The 'green' pound is the currency used by Britain when operating Common Market farm policies. 'Green' currencies (pounds, francs, marks, etc.) are really the rates at which the members exchange currencies for farm products. As a rate of exchange it was fixed some time before the British pound (£) began its rapid fall in value in the financial centres of the world. Thus the 'green' pound gives the £ a rate of exchange much higher in terms of farm prices than in the industrial or commercial field. Britain, having a greatly overvalued 'green' pound, can buy European farm products much more cheaply than would be possible if the £ were given the same exchange value for farm prices as it has for other industrial trading goods. In effect, the European members are subsidizing British consumers who are paying less than their continental neighbours for EEC farm products. Indeed, President Giscard d'Estaing of France has already declared that the current allocation of 25 per cent of the Community's expenditure to maintain this 'unrealistic exchange rate' is quite unacceptable.

The effect of any devaluation of the 'green' pound for the British consumer would be an immediate and fairly steep rise in farm products—a rise that, allied to the inflationary trends, would be bad news for the British housewife but good news for British farmers, who would receive more cash for their produce.

In 1976, several attempts to alter the 'green' currencies and the British exchange rate within the system were stalled by prompt British opposition. Nevertheless, as the British £ continued its downward trend in the normal international money Exchanges pressure built up in the EEC to change the system. Our fears of steep price rises are real ones and our statesmen in Brussels have fought strongly to maintain the present position as long as possible. This controversy marks another stage in the movement towards European integration—with all the problems which arise for those involved. Britain and Europe have many such problems to solve before the Agricultural Community becomes a meaningful term.

The Common Agricultural Policy

Overall the aims of the EEC with regard to agriculture are embodied within the scheme known as the Common Agricultural Policy (CAP). The main aims are to stabilize markets and to provide adequate supplies at reasonable prices (to the consumers). As described above, there is generally free trade on commodities within the Community with a common system of levies (often varied) on imports from third countries. Also, there is a system of common support prices within the Community designed to give producers a fair return from sales. If a glut develops in a particular commodity (e.g., the butter mountains which were publicized in 1975 and in 1977) then the Community could authorize support buying to clear the surplus products from the Market.

In general, the former system of the Annual Review is still in operation in Britain. It is used by the agricultural Ministers to determine the guaranteed price level for the next year for cereals, potatoes, fat sheep, milk, and wool. But this system will change. At the end of 1977 the guarantees for all commodities for which the Community has a common market organization ceased. Even now, there is no such organization for sheep, wool, or potatoes. For fat cattle, such guarantees ended as early as March 1973, for eggs in March 1974, and for sugar beet in June 1974. After 31 July 1975 there was no guarantee for fat pigs. While the interim scheme operates, there are still deficiency payments designed to close the gap between the price obtained for the commodity on the open market and the price guaranteed by the Government. Such guaranteed prices are themselves subject to the rules of the Treaty of Accession.

So far as Marketing Boards within the United Kingdom are concerned, the system works as follows: in the case of milk there are five Boards. The Government pays to the Boards a guaranteed price on a 'standard quantity' which they assess as being roughly equal to anticipated total production for the year (say, 1975–76). Any milk produced in excess of this would be sold for manufacturing, and the Boards, after estimating the returns from this source and from government grants, decides on the 'pool price' to be paid to milk producers. If, as was the case in 1975, the Government decided to subsidize the retail prices, then there would be a deficit for the Boards which would require to be compensated direct from the Exchequer.

In terms of potatoes, the situation is different. The appropriate EEC Ministers fix, annually, a target acreage which they estimate should achieve selfsufficiency. In Great Britain the Potato Marketing Board tries to ensure that this target is achieved, and if there is any surplus of potatoes it can, with government support, buy up and resell such stocks for animal feeding. In Northern Ireland the Department of Agriculture would undertake this operation and the Government would pay for it.

One of the major problems of the EEC in terms of British relationships with the Commonwealth centred round the sugar trade. Up till the end of 1974 we were committed, under the Commonwealth Sugar Agreement, to take certain quantities of sugar annually from Commonwealth exporters. The ending of the Agreement, it was feared, would destroy the main source of revenue for Commonwealth countries—particularly in the West Indies—who depended on sugar exporting for survival. However, after much hard bargaining within the EEC, where some continental interests tried hard to exclude such sugar imports, it was agreed (Convention of Lomé, February 1975) that the EEC be committed to accept certain quantities of sugar annually from developing sugar exporting countries at a price which would be similar to that obtaining within the Community. Thus one thorny problem appeared to have been solved—and it was believed that (in any event) most of such sugar would still come to the United Kingdom for refining.

From this review of the EEC system, it is clear that overall the importance of price guarantees has already declined and will continue to do so. The basic aim of EEC philosophy is free and healthy competition, and the main help which farmers can expect now is through inducements to increase productivity. This, although direct government aid fell from £290 million to £230 million between 1974 and 1976, substantial grants are still given to maintain breeding herds of cattle and sheep, to encourage suitable meat production, and to help towards the cost of certain capital expenditure, and for effecting farm amalgamations and farm structural improvements.

The pattern of British farming

Farming depends more than other industries on natural elements like climate, land relief, and soil. Britain, generally, has a temperate climate with mild winters and moderately warm summers, the seasonal difference in temperatures being modified by the surrounding sea. Rain, as the guidebooks say, 'is fairly well distributed throughout the months of the year'. There is no wet season, just wet weather.

But there are variations, the most important being in rainfall. The eastern side of the country, with less than 30 inches a year, is much drier than the west, with 40 to 60 inches. In temperature—less ranging and less important—we may distinguish in winter between the west and east, the former being milder; in summer, though, the dividing line is between north and south, the latter having the warmer weather. In hours of sunshine, too, the region south of a line from the Wash to the Severn scores higher than the northern parts.

In relief there are many gradations, from the mountains of Scotland and Wales in the north and west to the plains of Midland England and the still lower lying Fenlands reclaimed from the sea. Soils, depending largely on rock formations, of which Britain has many, vary in quality and kind: sands, clays, limestone, chalk.

We can see these factors at work in a general way in the pattern of British farming. On the more mountainous part of the country, where height, the thin rocky soil, and the lie of the land set limits to what can be done, only rough grazing is carried on. Again, of the two main types of farming, arable (the growing of cereals or crops) and pastoral (the raising of livestock, whether for beef or dairy purposes), the former is more likely to occur in the eastern parts of Britain, the latter in the western. Cereals and crops are grown more easily in a drier, sunnier climate, in lower altitudes where temperatures are warmer, in deeper soils and on more level ground that lends itself to ploughing. Such conditions in general are more typical of the eastern side of the country, whereas the mild climate and heavier rainfall of the west make for excellent pasture grass—the main necessity in livestock farming.

On a closer look, however, the pattern breaks up. We find many cattle being raised on farms in Northumbria, and arable farming carried on along the Lancashire coast. Moreover, the most common type of farming in Britain is 'mixed'—a combination of both. The arable farmer nearly always has some cattle as well as crops, the livestock farmer often cultivates crops on some part of his land. Again, some of the land that now mainly supports dairy farming—pastoral—was at one time used mainly for arable purposes.

The explanation lies chiefly in two things. First, farming is a business, and so it is affected by economic considerations as well as geographical ones. Second, it is enterprising and scientific. Therefore, if a certain type of farming promises to pay a farmer well, he may go in for it although his land might not by nature be as well adapted to it as land elsewhere in the country. Initiative and science can both be applied to help overcome some of the natural drawbacks.

The usual motive for such effort is the prospect of a good market. This is why dairy farming became so widespread in twentieth-century Britain. Dairy products, especially milk, were not threatened by foreign competition in the way that wheat was. Being perishable, they could not be transported over such long distances. The growth of great towns and the better wages earned by the inhabitants created a growing demand for dairy produce. So dairy farming that was within easy reach of the urban centres expanded, based on grass in the better pastoral regions of the west, on fodder crops in the eastern arable districts.

Again, market gardening of vegetables and fruit needs rich soil and special climatic conditions; but chemicals, fertilizers, electric heating, glasshouses and frames enable the conditions to be created artificially. This technology is expensive, but given a large market for vegetables nearby, so that sales are certain and transport costs low, then it is worth the expense.

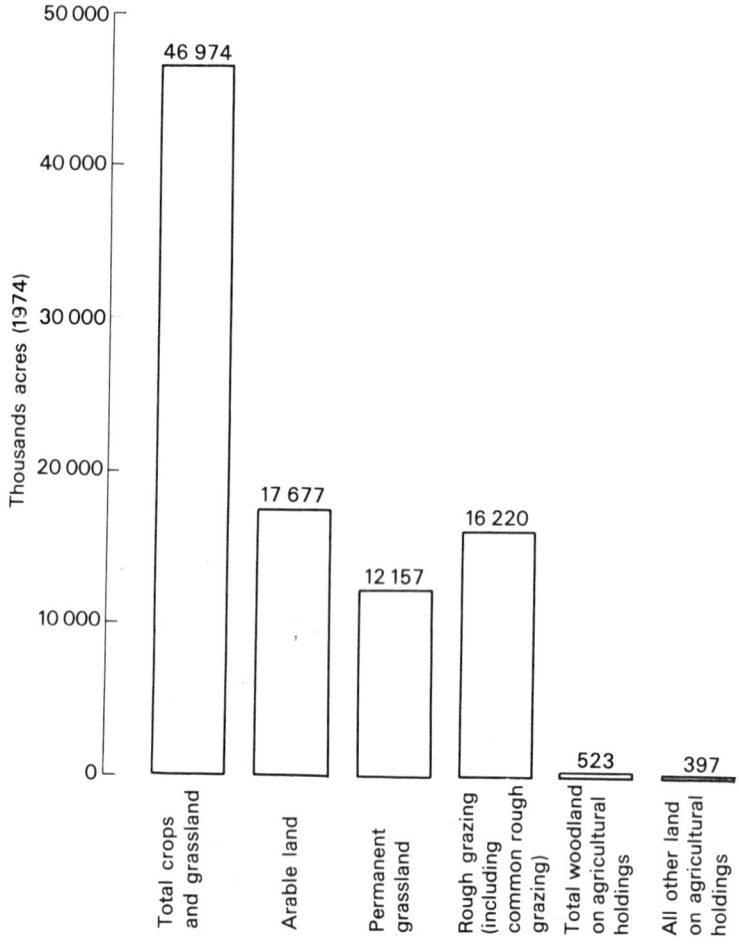

Fig. 5.2. Distribution of agricultural land: United Kingdom

Pig and poultry farming, other profitable lines, are not much affected by soils or climate, and can be carried on in most places so long as there is a market for the produce.

Thus the distribution of much farming follows a pattern that depends on markets, i.e., economic circumstances, as well as on climatic and soil conditions. The most popular of all types of farming in Britain, the mixture of arable and livestock, is so favoured because it lets the farmer make the most use of his land in turn, to prevent it becoming worn out. If he plants it with fodder crop for cattle instead of leaving it quite idle, he gains greatly. The soil is not only rested from wheat, it is enriched for the next planting, since the cattle manure fertilizes it. Moreover, having some cattle he can use for milk or beef gives him an extra safeguard if his main line—wheat or barley or oats—does badly. The farmer who is mainly concerned with cattle finds it pays him to raise fodder crops in some fields instead of leaving them all to grass, as the fodder provides food for his cattle during the winter.

The crop rotation system is an outstanding example of the way in which enterprise can improve the soil, making it far more productive than its natural state would suggest. It was the discovery of this system by Norfolk farmers, not the natural bounty of the local soil, that enabled that county to become the showplace of English farming in the eighteenth century.

Many kinds of rotation systems are now used. In East Anglia itself a six-year cycle is more common than the famous old four-year one. Six-year rotations are favoured in the Lothians, too. The crops rotated within a system also vary. A farmer may rotate his corn with turnips as fodder or with potatoes as a cash crop. His choice depends on his main lines, his soils, and his markets. But all systems have the attraction of making the farmer's land more productive for his main crop while providing him with a second source of income. Even while it is resting, the land is still working.

Another sign of the commercial and scientific element in farming is the growing importance of the larger unit. Most of Britain's 220 000 farms are small: the average size is about 140 acres. But about half of all agricultural production comes from some 40 000 large farms which are classified as 'commercial businesses'. In this way agriculture is more like industry than we sometimes think. In each case it is an advantage to have natural local resources, whether fertile soil or a convenient port. But the people of the region can do much to make the most of these and overcome natural disadvantages by skill and enterprise, whether they are industrialists or farmers.

Fishing

Fishing in Britain today is big business. In 1974 470 000 tons of fish valued at £88 million were landed. Of this, cod accounted for 43 per cent of the total value, and haddock and plaice around 25 per cent. Despite this, £58 million of fish were imported. While the negotiations on the EEC continued. Britain's fishermen pressed for adequate fishing rights for the United Kingdom in order to preserve our fishing areas and to exclude 'unwelcome' continental fishing fleets from these areas. Already in 1964 our exclusive fishing limits had been extended to 12 miles, and yet by the Treaty of Accession (EEC) any vessels registered in member states may also fish in British waters (but not less than 6 miles out and in some areas they are even excluded from the 6–12 mile limits.

Table 5.4. Fisheries: Great Britain. (Source: *Facts in Focus*, 3rd edn, Penguin, 1975)

Fishing fleet

	1964	1969	1974
Total vessels	7810	6063	6626
England and Wales	4863	3383	3872
Scotland	2947	2680	2754

Landing of fish of British taking

	1964	1969	1974
Total value (£ thousand)	56 932	65 408	151 917
Cod	23 063	27 766	61 640
Haddock	10 218	11 405	27 217
Herring	2692	3262	12 751
Plaice	5378	5429	8602
Saithe	1430	1518	5573
Shell fish	2809	5664	10 881
Other	11 342	10 364	25 253
Total landed weight (thousand tonnes)	849·5	945·1	939·4
Cod	299·2	379·0	262·5
Haddock	150·1	142·8	124·2
Herring	98·2	122·9	138·3
Staithe (coalfish)	41·9	46·9	43·3
Plaice	41·7	41·4	28·5
Shell fish	26·9	47·6	59·9
Other	191·6	164·5	282·7

British fishermen feel strongly they must retain the wide area for their own exploitation. The supplies of fish are, they say, limited, and it is essential for the preservation of the industry that preference and even exclusive rights be accorded to British ships.

Nevertheless, this argument does not apply to all British fishing. We have been seeking greater rights of fishing for our deep-sea trawlers, and here the problem has been that we do tend to infringe the rights of fishing of others—also dependent on fishing. Over the last decade or so Britain has been involved in disputes with Iceland, who claimed an extension of exclusive rights round her own coastline. Indeed, dependent on fishing for 100 per cent of her trade, Iceland took the dispute to international arbitration. Such was the heat of this dispute, involving as it did cutting of trawler nets and interference with each other's ships, that the whole question became an acute embarrassment for Western diplomacy (see WORLD TODAY, fourth edition, page 23). An agreement on fishing limits and an overall agreement on large-scale fishing was urgently required. Since January 1977 the new 200-mile limit claimed by Britain highlights the need for an international settlement of this problem. The immediate effects of any agreement would appear to mean a substantial cutting of our trawler fleet and, inevitably, a fairly steep rise in prices in the shops.

The principal fishing ports are Hull, Grimsby and Fleetwood in England, and Aberdeen, Peterhead, Fraserburgh in Scotland. These are already being affected by changes in the industry—while in 1974 there were 18 000 fishermen regularly employed, by 1978 there could be fewer than 12 000. When one considers that around 60 per cent of these men are employed in Scottish ports (where employment is threatened by the completion of on-shore oil developments) the prospects are rather bleak.

The cost of building and servicing large modern fishing trawlers (160 of them are 42·5 metres in length) is such that prospects of profits must be good. These vessels are fully equipped to deal with all weathers, and one can appreciate the need for an effective marketing and distribution system which matches such large-scale operations. Methods of processing and packaging of fish are regularly being developed and researched. With over a quarter of all catches being quick-frozen, there are new export outlets for fish—new underexploited species of fish are being examined with a view to future developments, and already fishmeal production (from white fish and herring) accounts for around 68 000 tons a year.

The prospects for the future seem dependent on agreements with our maritime neighbours and particularly within the EEC (see WORLD TODAY, fourth edition, Chapter 1). There is a Common Fisheries Policy and the common organization of the Market has applied to Britain since February 1973. There are producer organizations in the industry who are responsible for the marketing. The main aim is to assist in balancing supplies and demands of the Market. There are plans to harmonize and develop resources of each country to lead to a more rational exploitation of the seas. This covers access to waters, conservation of coastal waters, and joint measures for paying for structural improvement of the industry.

It seems clear that the EEC alone cannot solve this international dispute about fishing rights. Only a full awareness of the effects of large-scale 'overfishing' can set the scene for future agreement. At this time, agreement seems distant and prospects are cloudy.

6. Commerce, transport and trade

Commerce defined

Most of what we have been considering so far has to do with the actual production of goods in factories, workshops, or farmyards. This, though of vital importance, is only one stage in the much longer and wider process called commerce. Before a Birmingham factory can produce bars of chocolate there has to be a great deal of movement of materials. Cocoa from West Africa, sugar from the West Indies, raisins from Southern Europe all have to be moved from their place of origin to convenient ports—Lagos, Kingston, Valencia—and shipped thence to convenient British ports such as Liverpool. From there they have to be taken by train or lorry to the factory, with intervening spells in warehouses if the factory is not yet ready to receive them. Meanwhile milk has to be conveyed from Britain's dairy farms. Until there has been all this movement of materials from far and near, the skilled workmen or the elaborate machines in the factory cannot begin to make bars of chocolate.

Clearly the process is not completed even when the chocolate is produced. It has to be made available to the consumers, who cannot take a train to Birmingham every time they want a bar of chocolate. The goods have to be transported from the factory to wholesale dealers throughout the country and distributed by them to the thousands of local shopkeepers who sell them to the consumers. All this shifting around of materials and goods is the process of commerce.

Commerce involves more than might be apparent from these remarks. *Transport* is obviously an important commercial activity, so is *distribution* through wholesalers and retailers. But manufacturers want people to know that their product exists and the distributors want them to know that they have it in stock, so they *advertise* in the press and on commercial television and employ commercial travellers to persuade shopkeepers to stock the article. Again, these movements of goods require large amounts of money, so another aspect of commerce is *finance*—the raising of money for these expensive transactions and the financial organizations through which this can be done.

Transport by water, land, and air

The importance of transport is clear. Without the ocean-going steamship it would be difficult to move goods around the world in great quantities, at high speed and reasonable cost. Without good road and rail systems factories could not depend on getting their materials from the arrival ports, nor could distribution be carried out efficiently and cheaply. The great developments of the nineteenth and twentieth centuries in mechanical transport were essential to the growth of commerce. Without these developments industries were limited to local materials and confined to local markets. Unless there was a port nearby it was often too costly to bring materials from, or send goods to, the other end of Britain. The transport revolution freed industry from these limitations, and expanded the potential market from the local region to the whole world.

One indication of transport's importance is the fact that nearly $1\frac{1}{2}$ million people are employed in it, and the services they provide are vital to the process of commerce and to the country's prosperity. We are soon reminded of them when, for some reason, part of the transport system comes to a halt.

Sea transport Britain's merchant fleet used to be the main carrier of goods for the world. Nowadays some 90 000 persons are employed in operating around 10 per cent of the world's traffic. With over 31 million tons our merchant fleet is still the third in rank after Liberia and Japan. Recently there has been a quite positive effort to restore our former strength, and even since 1969 our merchant fleet has increased by 32 per cent—much of this in purpose-built container, tanker, and bulk carrier vessels. Ships themselves are becoming bigger: in the early 1950s an average oil tanker would have been around 20 000 tons, now a large one could be around 500 000 tons. Today's large container ships of around 60 000 tons can carry up to 2800 containers. This switch to containers is safe, clean, and enables rapid movement of a wide range of goods.

In the field of oceanic passenger transport Britain has fared badly. Our share of such traffic has fallen by three-quarters since the 1960s. Despite this, however, we do have a thriving trade with Europe, where holiday traffic has doubled since the early 1960s.

Canals Within Britain there are also waterways—canals. Although they were the first big advance in transport in the eighteenth century canals are now playing a minor part in transporting goods. There are still about 2500 miles (some 4023 kilometres) of navigable inland waterways, and of these some 2000 miles (3219 km) belong to the British Waterways Board, the rest are privately owned. In 1974 around 3·9 million tons of goods were carried and of that over one-third was coal and about one-third liquids in bulk, while the remainder was general cargo. Almost all this traffic was on the main commercial waterways—most of it centering on Yorkshire–Humberside, Trent and Gloucester areas. The Board is now concentrating on developing cruising on waterways for recreation, and many disused canals are being restored by enthusiasts. Although freight-carrying potential seems limited for the future, it does look as if canals will be part of the transport scene for many years to come.

Slow and awkward, canals were soon driven out of business by the railways, the real revolutionary development in transport of the mid-nineteenth century.

Railways Britain's railways network grew from 1000 miles in 1840 to over 20 000 miles. Roads, whose importance was also eclipsed by railways development, are playing a leading part again since the invention of the internal combustion engine and coming of road vehicles. The railways experienced their own problems as the twentieth century progressed. The amalgamation of the one hundred or so railway companies into the 'Big Four' of 1921 was a recognition of the need for a more rationalized structure. But funds and income remained low. Normal running costs were high, pricing policies were restricted and competition from the developing road system was keen. There was never enough money available for the companies to embark on the kind of massive investment programmes required by large-scale modernization. The deterioration of railway stock under the impact of the Second World War, the heavy extra obligations, both financial and social, placed on railways after nationalization, made their situation more difficult than ever.

The Beeching Plan, 1963 As losses mounted, a drastic review of the whole system was called for. In his plan for reshaping the railways the views of the investigator, Dr Beeching, were indeed strong. The railways had to be made to pay, and the recommendations of his Report were drastic.

Over 2300 (out of 4300) stations were to be closed down; passenger services were to cease entirely on 5000 miles of track; 500 freight depots were to be cut to 100; 375 000 wagons were to be scrapped; 70 000 railways jobs were to disappear inside three years. Along with this rigorous slimming diet, the railways were to concentrate their efforts on those few sectors where they were doing reasonably well, in order to improve their competitiveness in these, e.g., heavy freight and long-distance passenger services. Investment would go into making these better: special freightliner trains, more speed and comfort on passenger services between cities, electrification, and diesels. Socially, as we saw, there was a price for this which made Governments hold back from carrying it through in its entirety. There was also the wider economic consideration. If the traffic which the railways proposed to abandon as unprofitable were driven on to the roads, would the nation's economy be any better off? The roads were already too congested.

The Transport Act of 1968 aimed at greater integration of the public transport system. The railways were promised finance for worthwhile investment, and unprofitable services were to have their cost assessed and covered by special government subsidies. As for the roads, the Act introduced a new licensing system. All lorries over a certain weight were subjected to

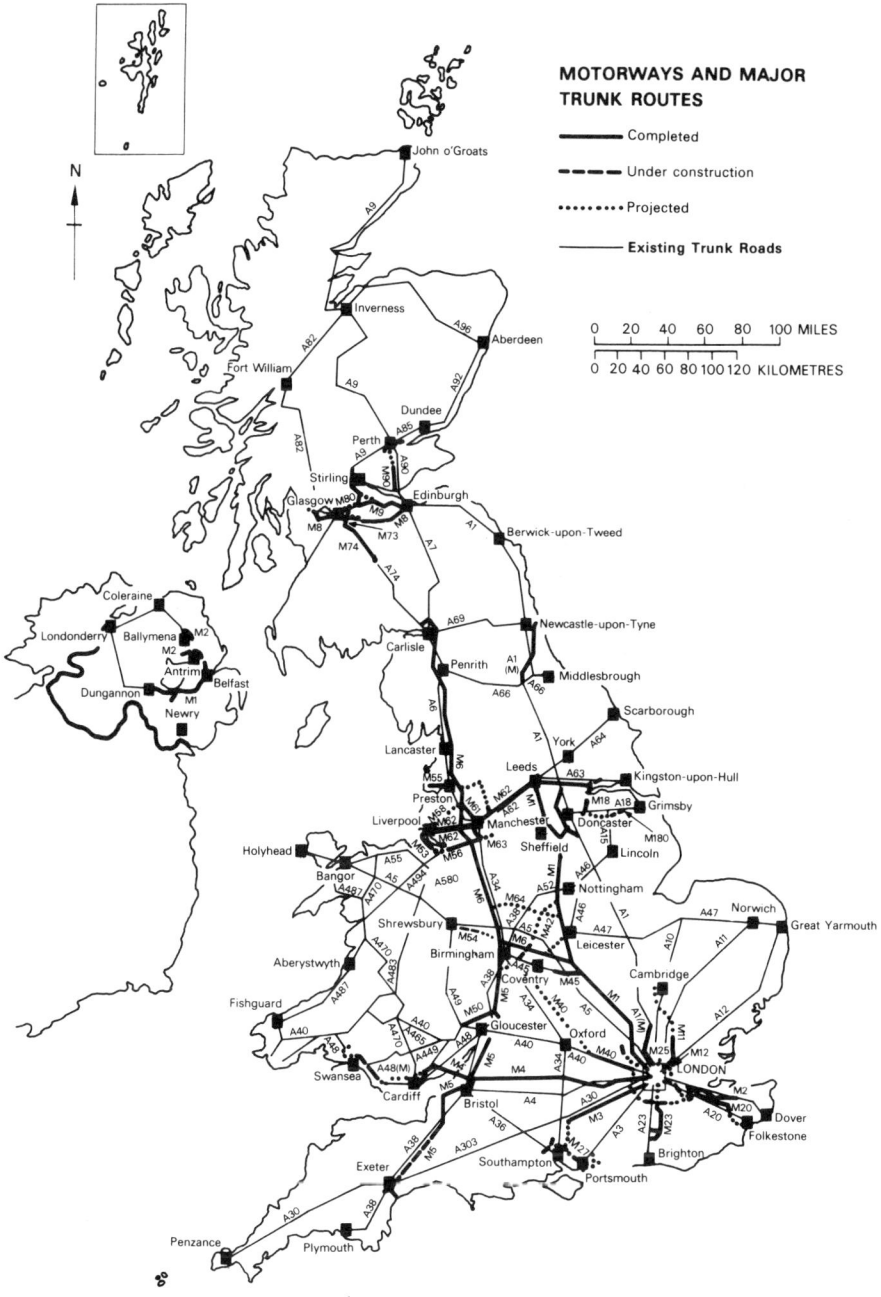

Fig. 6.1. Major roads. United Kingdom. (Source: *Britain 1977: An Official Handbook*, HMSO, 1977)

special controls before licences were granted. Taxation was increased, especially on the heavier lorries. It was an attempt to drive some of the bulkier freight at present on the roads back on to the railways.

The Transport Act established a new body, the National Freight Corporation, which spanned both rail and road. All publicly owned freight transport institutions came under the NFC, which now had greater operating power, e.g., freight carried by the NFC went by road or rail according to the NFC's decision, not the customer's: thus affording an opportunity to adjust the distribution of some freight transport between road and rail as circumstances varied. The cost of all this was heavy. Capital expenditure on the railways was about £100 million a year.

However, even this help was not sufficient to put the railways on an economic track.

Nevertheless the Railway Board had by 1974 made significant progress in reshaping its activities. In ten years the number of employees had almost halved—from 500 000 to 255 000; in five years the electric vehicles had increased from around 500 to 7156, and the switch from diesel engines had accelerated with 5000 in 1970 down to 3619 in 1974. The Board had initiated considerable improvements in comfort and safety throughout the system. Its new high-speed train was brought into service late in 1976. It now operates a fleet of vessels providing freight and passenger services, British Rail Hovercraft (with several important cross-Channel services); there is British Rail Engineering (with some fourteen workshops and 33 700 employees), and the Railway Technical Centre at Derby—all evidence of a willingness to coordinate and develop an effective railway network to meet the challenge of twentieth-century needs.

Road transport Britain has now over 1200 miles of motorway, 9600 miles of trunk roads, 20 500 miles of principal roads, and 184 000 miles of lesser roads. Despite all these imposing statistics, the transport system today still needs improving. The price is being paid for insufficient development in earlier decades. During the twentieth century road and rail operators have been keen competitors for transport traffic, and as early as 1909, when the Road Fund was instituted, it was realized that public funds were required for the regular maintenance and extension of the national road system. These funds were to come from road users themselves. This was the origin of the present car road licence fee which all car owners are now required to pay to use the public highways. In fact the Road Fund, planned as a guaranteed source of revenue for road development, has often been diverted into general government revenue. Undoubtedly road transport had several advantages over the railways. Lorries were more convenient than trains in many respects. They enjoyed more freedom of movement. They could collect and deliver on the doorstep of factories, warehouses, and shops, thus saving time and money. Roads offered advantages in price since so much of the money spent building and maintaining them came out of public funds. Britain's railways had been expensive to build and railway companies faced a constant outlay on tracks, tunnels, stations, signalling equipment, and so on; and this made them expensive to use. Roads, built with public money, presented road haulage firms with their 'track' ready made. Traffic control systems, road signs, maintenance, and improvements—all these came from sources other than the funds of the firms who were using them. Hence road haulage was in a strong position to compete with the railways.

Since 1945 the situation has changed even more, to the advantage of road transport. People were able to purchase private cars and they became used to the convenience of door-to-door travel—a facility not available from the railways. The implications were far reaching—fewer passengers on the railways, lower passenger receipts, therefore greater operating losses, higher fares, fewer passengers, and so on—a vicious circle of decline for the railways. And this decline affected the public bus companies too.

The other side of the picture is that the roads have become increasingly congested; traffic accidents, delays, and atmospheric pollution have become regular features of urban life, and the road system has been unable to cope with this massive influx of traffic users. Completely new roads and motorways had to be planned, constructed and paid for. The motor car is now the most popular form of transport. There are, however, other vehicles. By mid-1975 there were over 18 million vehicles on British roads, and of his around one million were motor cycles, mopeds, and scooters. Another vast number were goods vehicles—in late 1974 these accounted for 1·8 million of the total.

The new road pattern planned to meet this increasing challenge has meant massive road construction over quite varied terrains—with many problems of both a technical and legal nature. New land had to be acquired and adequate compensation paid. The land itself was often a problem; with wet winters and uncertain summers the task of the road builders was very difficult.

Despite these problems a new pattern is now emerging. Along with this construction went attempts to remedy shortcomings on existing stretches: more dual cariageways, clearing of the most congested urban systems, bypass roads, ring roads, new bridges (like those across the Forth, the Severn, and the Medway, all opened in the 1960s), new tunnels (like the Tyne tunnel and the Blackwall Tunnel under the Thames, both opened in 1967) (see Fig. 6.1). By mid-1976 over 1200 miles of motorway had been completed (starting from a mere 500 miles or so in 1970).

The road problem is, however, not just a technical one. Within urban areas it involves the whole quality of living. As early as 1963 the Buchanan Report spoke of a 'war between the car and the city' and of the need not just for better roads and traffic systems, or for more restrictions on the use of private cars in cities, but also 'to replace, reshape, and rebuild' cities to meet the gigantic challenge as the 18 million vehicles on the roads at present swell to 27 million in 1980 and 40 million at the end of the century. Many local authorities are making moves to discourage cars from using the city centres, or at least from abusing them, e.g., by stricter and more expensive parking systems. Ring roads are being built to take the traffic flow around the towns. In some cities and new towns cars are banned from shopping precincts: at Cumbernauld a system of different road levels was designed to keep pedestrians and vehicles apart. So far such schemes seem to have been fairly successful. For the whole country, however, the picture is not so bright.

In the last few years the figures for road deaths from traffic accidents have been around 7000 per year. In 1974 one-third of a million people were injured. This is a most glaring indictment of all road users—drivers and pedestrians alike. Hopefully we are learning. In the last three years there has been a slight decline in fatal accidents and a fairly marked drop in numbers injured.

Air transport—civil aviation Air transport in Britian is barely fifty years old. Despite this, developments have been very rapid.

Before 1939 few people could afford to travel by air. It was really the Civil Aviation Act of 1946 which set the scene for rapid development of internal services through the establishment of British European Airways, and for overseas travel through the establishment of the British Overseas Airways Corporation. These two public corporations operated separately until late 1971, when the new Civil Aviation Authority linked them into one system now known as British Airways.

The CAA is an independent statutory body, and its powers are very wide indeed. It is really responsible for the whole civil aviation industry in economic, technical, and operational terms. It overviews the air navigation services and the organization of such services at some airports. (It actually runs eight airfields in Scotland.) It is responsible for the issue of licences and certificates not only to airlines, aircraft, airports, but also to personnel at all levels—to pilots, air traffic controllers, and even maintenance engineers. CAA's main objective is to run at a profit all the services provided.

Clearly the CAA is quite different from either the Railways Board or from any organization responsible for the road transport industry. It has to work with not only the state-owned British Airways, but with a variety of private airline operators.

The pattern of services within the United Kingdom is thus determined by the effects of decisions taken at different levels with the Civil Aviation Authority. Over the years that responsibility has grown very rapidly indeed. The number of passengers carried by air services of all types has almost trebled in the last ten years (much of this being summer and winter special charter flights). Perhaps the levelling out of traffic in 1976 indicated that growth is no longer inevitable.

Civil aviation in traffic density terms is a growth industry. By 1962 more passengers were travelling to and from Britain by air than were travelling by sea. By 1975 over 31 million passengers travelled by air as against 13·8 million by sea.

As with road developments, civil aviation's progress has brought problems. First are the technical changes in the industry. Widebodied aircraft, such as 'Jumbo' jets (Boeing 747), can carry over 450 passengers on each trip, compared with the old Vanguard's 100 passengers: the problems of handling and processing such numbers have escalated sharply in the last few years. The Concorde supersonic development, the Anglo-French cooperative project which has made day-return trips to the United States a practicable proposition, poses further problems—of noise, pollution, and again airport traffic handling. These technical changes alone create new challenges for airports in strengthening, lengthening, and redeveloping runways.

The implications of these changes really constitute the second main problem. The busiest centre of international travel in the world is Heathrow Airport (London). Already underway is an £8 million programme for the modernization and extension of terminal facilities to handle the increased passenger flow anticipated in the late 1970s. A new (Heathrow to London) Underground was opened in December 1977. In 1958 London's second airport, Gatwick, was opened: now some 20 years later a complete redevelopment scheme costing £65 million or more is in progress. Similar expensive schemes are going on in Manchester, Edinburgh, Glasgow. In Aberdeen the situation is complicated further by the oil development in the North Sea. With such changes come transport and pollution problems; the emphasis since the 1960s on environmental protection made people living near airports less willing to accept a lower quality of their life—even where such trade could improve national prosperity. Nowadays each airport extension must pass very thorough and complicated sifting procedures. Planning authorities at local and national levels have to pay heed to citizens' views as well as those of the airline operators.

The third set of problems for the industry really come from international competition. While British people may be travelling abroad more often and while our airlines may be carrying more, there are many airline operators who are running at a loss. Even giants like PAN AM (Pan American) complain of falling revenues. In the last few years the pruning and merging of competing airlines has been a significant feature of the American scene. For most of the flights made there are more empty seats than passengers. Competition to cut passenger fares and fill these empty seats would, in normal circumstances, be a healthy thing, leading to the elimination of the inefficient and ensuring lower fares to the general public. (This was Freddy Laker's case, for his Sky Train, a much publicized cut-price service still in its early stages.) However, there are international agreements (International Air Transport Authority, IATA) which determine minimum fares and control any such competition. Safety at all times also precludes any drastic pruning of safety precautions or any undermanning in either maintenance or flying crews. Certain minimum standards must be maintained.

Many smaller operators really thrive only through the vast holiday charter traffic from the United Kingdom to Spain and Majorca. In winter months they have great difficulty in filling seats.

The future of those British operators will depend very much not only on the pattern of overseas holiday charter flights being extended, but on their ability to compete adequately with their British competitors and the evergrowing international competitors. Clearly the picture here is rather uncertain. On its outcome depend the jobs of many people in the British aircraft industry as well as the operators and their agents.

Within Britain the operators are divided into the private, independent airlines and the state airline—British Airways.

British Airways is itself a massive concern with a turnover of £748 million in 1974–75, of which over half was earned overseas. Alone it carried some 13 million passengers in 1974, and in 1975 it employed some 59 000 staff; had assets of £408 million in terms of aircraft and spares, and £89 million worth of land and buildings. It has the largest route network of any world airline, and it covers around 200 destinations and visits eighty-eight countries. Indeed it is the world's largest passenger fleet which operates international services, and in 1975 it had some 196 aircraft, including fifteen Super VC 10s. Already five Concordes have been ordered by British Airways and by 1976 direct services using Concorde aircraft had begun to Bahrain, on the Persian Gulf, Washington, D.C., and more recently to New York.

The massive size of British Airways could not be equalled by independent operators. Nevertheless, collectively the private operators carried around 6 million passengers in 1973 on scheduled services (just under half the BA figures). The largest of these is British Caledonian Airways, which with some thirty-one aircraft and carrying well over one million passengers on scheduled flights, offers BA quite firm competition on some internal routes.

As a component of the transport industry civil aviation is vital. Many islands and remote areas are dependent on the services provided and even, in the case of illness, are dependent on the air ambulance facilities for urgent and speedy hospitalization of patients.

Distributive trades

Transport is vital, but we need establishments in our own neighbourhood which are easily reached and where we can be sure of getting the article we want. These are provided by the distributive traders, the most important being the wholesale traders and the retail traders or shopkeepers.

In these trades nearly three million people are engaged, i.e., six times as many people are busy preparing and passing goods over the counter as are out growing food.

Most people can see that the retail shopkeeper is indispensable, but many doubt the usefulness of the wholesale dealer. Nevertheless, it is simpler for the retailer and the manufacturer if there is a middleman who carries large supplies of the various brands. Then the shopkeeper need contact only one local

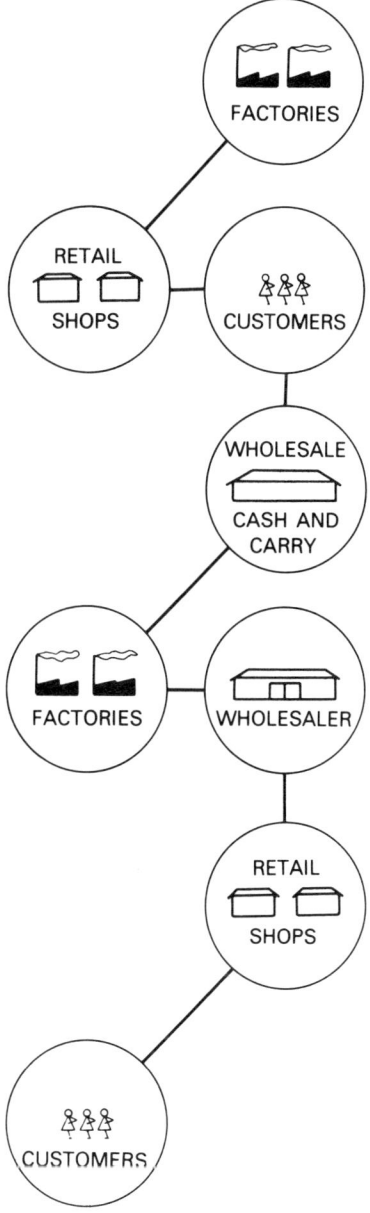

Fig. 6.2. The function of the wholesaler. (Source: *Britain 1977: An Official Handbook*, HMSO, 1977)

wholesaler listing all his wants. The wholesaler, collecting many small orders from local retailers, can order in large quantities from the makers, which is handier for them.

Even here there have been two big changes in the last ten years. First, many factories are indeed cutting corners by selling direct to the public and omitting the wholesaler—this practice is becoming quite common in woollens and furniture where the factory producer can make substantial savings both for himself and price cuts for the consumer.

Secondly, within the wholesale trade has risen the cash-and-carry warehouses. By bulk purchasing and by cutting expenditure on premises, on credit, and on delivery facilities wholesalers are able to offer fairly large discounts to their customers who are mainly small retail traders unable to compete with the larger grocery chains or multiple stores. In fact over half the warehousing for the grocery trades is now handled by such cash-and-carry firms, and there are around 600 such stores handling over £1000 million a year in trade.

The retail trade

The retail trade is the stage of the commercial process with which we are most familiar. It is from the retail shops that all the vast variety of produce from farms and factories (at home and overseas) passes in the hands of the consumer. There are now around 473 000 retail shops in Britain, but the number is tending to drop each year. At the moment this represents one shop to every 94 people in the country. This is not the whole story. There are also around 30 000 other retail outlets—these include gas and electricity showrooms, mail order businesses, market stalls (at local markets—weekly or daily), and automatic vending machine operators. However, we normally think of the retail shop when we discuss the retail trade, and of these around 40 per cent are food shops (see Table 6.1). Among these, grocers and provision dealers are the most numerous. Clothing and footwear (80 000) are the next biggest group. Fed, clothed, and shod, it seems we next demand cigarettes, newspapers and sweets (52 000). About 70 000 of our shops deal in household goods—hardware, furniture, and electrical goods shops being the three most numerous types in this category. Beyond this we may deduce something about the British people today from the existence of 18 000 chemists shops and 19 000 jewellers.

In addition to shops selling goods, there are others providing services of some kind. Once again the bulk of them are concerned with food—hotels, restaurants, fish and chip shops (70 000) as well as 75 000 pubs. Next are the hairdressers (40 000), followed by garages (30 000) and shoe repairers (10 000).

Shops can also be classified, not by what they sell, but by how they are organized. There is great variety among retail firms just as among manufacturers, from the small shop taking less than £5000 a year to the giant store which might take that much in an hour. But in the retail trade the small one-man firm, the independent retailer, is far more common than in industry, although the larger enterprises are now expanding and the independents now account for less than half of Britain's shops and just over half of retail sales.

When we consider the bigger establishments we are more likely to find the limited company at work than the one-man firm or small partnership.

The departmental store is a large retail shop selling many different kinds of goods under one roof: food, clothing, furniture, cosmetics, electrical goods, toys, magazines, and so on. Departmental stores offer the convenience of letting people buy all they want inside the one building. Since these shops buy

Table 6.1. Retail trades by type of business (1971 Census). (Source: *Britain 1977: An Official Handbook*, HMSO, 1977)

Type of trade	Establishments		Turnover	
	Number 1971	Percentage change 1966–71	£ million 1971	Percentage change 1966–71
Grocers and provision dealers	105 283	−14·7	4 156	+42·9
Other food retailers	92 524	−11·3	2 615	+25·6
Clothing and footwear shops	81 279	− 2·2	2 372	+37·9
Household goods shops	70 342	+ 6·8	2 007	+55·3
Confectioners, tobacconists and newsagents	52 064	−17·8	1 306	+24·9
Other non-food retailers	66 724	+ 8·7	1 569	+53·9
General stores	4 775	+58·7	1 586	+48·8
Total	472 991	− 6·2	15 611	+40·2
Electricity and gas showrooms	2 359	−21·7	283	+52·5
Mail order businesses[1]	772	+55·9	633	+47·6
Automatic vending machine operators[1]	65	+16·0	12	+ 9·2
Market stalls and mobile shops	31 790	n.a.	147	n.a.

1. Number of organizations.

such enormous quantities from manufacturers, they get special price concessions. On the other hand, the departmental stores have great expenses to meet. To encourage people to wander through the shop, they have to give much space to passages and staircases; they need luxurious fittings and carpets; they need lifts and escalators; they have huge lighting and heating bills.

There are not many departmental stores and they are losing ground to the multiple trader or a cooperative society. These are large organizations with many individual shops throughout the country. Like the departmental store they may deal in a wide variety of goods (e.g., Woolworths, and Marks & Spencer), but since they have dozens of branches, none of these needs to be as massive or as costly as the departmental store. Most deal in a limited range of goods, though some are extending their range: their premises are usually no larger than those of neighbouring shops. Thus they dodge the very heavy expenses involved in a single huge building, but they still get the advantages of large discounts for buying in great quantities. And the geographical spread of their shops makes them less vulnerable to lean times in any particular district. The growth of multiples in recent years has been impressive. They now control 66 000 shops, and they command 39 per cent of all retail sales. Examples of these multiple stores are chemists, Boots; provision shop chains, MacFisheries or Sainsbury's; women's clothes stores, Etam's; men's clothes stores, Burton, Jackson, or Hepworth; shoes, Dolcis or Saxone.

A further type of retail trader is the cooperative. This differs from all the others in that it is not privately owned by one man or by a joint-stock company but by the members, the people who shop at the cooperative store. The members elect their own management committee which decides policy and appoints staff. Profits are shared out among members according to how much each has spent in the year, through a dividend of so many trading stamps per pound spent. Though still important, the cooperatives are losing ground to other big retain traders.

The most recent developments in retail trading have been, first, the rapid expansion of mail order business. Stores with a good national reputation advertise in the national press or through catalogues, and purchases are made by post. Moreover, mail order firms have been established which sell a wide range of products by this method. Few people in Britain live very far from a town with good shops, so there would seem to be less scope for mail order business than in countries like the USA where one may be living a very long way indeed from any large-scale shopping centre; nevertheless, this grew more quickly than any other kind of retail business in the 1960s. Second, there has been the growth of the selfservice store and the supermarket. The former almost trebled from 9500 in 1961 to 28 000 in 1971 while the latter increased sixfold over the same period. Most supermarkets are owned by multiples or cooperatives. Their advantages to the retailer are not hard to see. By dispensing with counters they can make the fullest use of floor and wall space to display goods. Attractive displays and selfservice promote 'impulse buying', with shoppers selecting goods they did not come in to buy and would never have thought of buying had the goods been tucked away out of sight under a counter. Much of the expansion in sales achieved by the multiples in recent years is attributed to the fact that they have extended selfservice operations in their establishments.

Thirdly has come the hypermarket. These are now springing up throughout Europe, and have already spread to the United Kingdom. The first hypermarket in Britain was opened in Caerphilly in 1972; now hypermarkets in Britain are fast becoming an established feature of our shopping scene. Hypermarkets are really huge supermarkets. Often having over 50 000 square feet of selling space their capacity to offer a wide range of goods under one roof, with adequate parking facilities for the family car, gives them an edge over other retail shops. They can launch massive price-cutting ventures, and with a situation often far from established shopping areas they dodge the irritations and competition of the urban shopping areas.

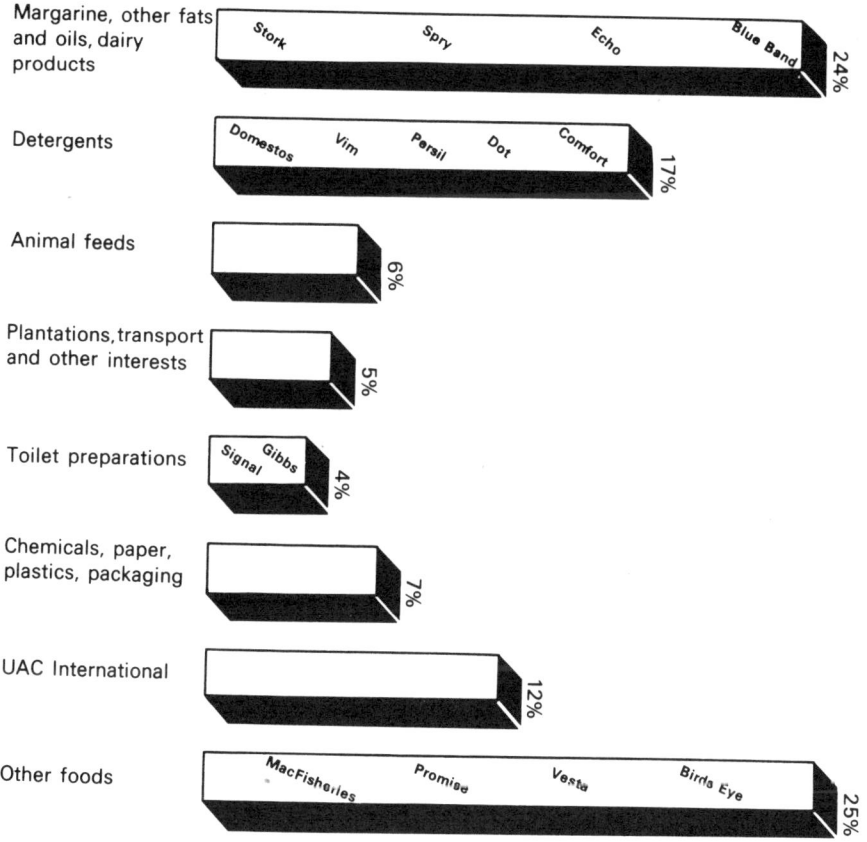

Fig. 6.3. A retail giant linked with a manufacturing giant. Unilever has 357 000 employees, and sales in markets across the world amounted to £6760 million in 1975

Much of the rapid growth in sales of household and durable consumer goods, e.g., cars, refrigerators, television sets, has been encouraged by the practice of hire purchase, buying by instalments. The terms under which this is done, e.g., the minimum deposit and the maximum time allowed for repayments, are subject to regulation by the Department of Trade. The amount of money involved in hire purchase is so large that a stiffening or a lightening of the conditions (i.e., changing the deposit requirements) affords the Government a valuable method of influencing consumer demand. In 1974 alone the new credit extended to customers was in the region of £2500 million, which means that in that one year alone, of each £20 spent £1 was a new hire purchase debt.

In distribution just as in manufacturing, this century has seen the development of giant companies, and by the same process. Retail firms in the same line of business often link up. These bigger units in turn often merge or work more closely together. Thus there comes about a huge organization like Great Universal Stores Ltd. This is the parent of a group of more than one hundred companies, some of which are themselves associations of several firms. In scope it includes stores dealing in furniture, footwear, women's wear, jewellery, musical instruments, etc. It includes several manufacturing companies—clothing, hosiery, textiles, pottery, furniture, precision engineering. It has also acquired some travel agencies.

Moreover, the big retail companies are sometimes themselves tied up with one of the great manufacturing organizations. Thus Home and Colonial Stores Ltd is a big concern, controlling over fifty food distribution companies and employing 37 000 workers in its 4000 shops and food factories. But this retail giant is itself associated with Unilever.

All this retail activity and the improvements it has brought about represent, in general, a tremendous boon to the consumer. High on the list comes the revolution in shopping which marks recent decades. Nevertheless, as the retail business grows in scale and in the sophistication of its sales techniques, there is always the danger that the consumer may be exploited unfairly. A number of safeguards to protect the consumer have been instituted. The Hire Purchase Acts of 1965 give protection to the consumer buying on the instalment system. A variety of enactments provide against faulty measure and misleading descriptions of goods and ensure standards of purity and hygiene for food. The British Standards Institution, a voluntary body, aims to set standards for a variety of consumer goods and persuade manufacturers and traders to adopt them, so that the customer knows he is buying a well-made article. The Council for Industrial Design works for improvement in the design of goods: it makes awards, so that again the customer is assured of a quality product if it has won the Council's approval.

Consumers and traders

The Government over the last few years has become increasingly involved in the process of trading, particularly in terms of protecting consumer interests. While the 'Customer is always right' was an important attitude for traders to take, it did not ensure the full protection of the consumer against shoddy goods or unfair practices with regard to the sales of goods. Linked to these problems in recent years has been the effects of inflation on the price level of consumer goods of all kinds.

In 1974 the Government set up a new department of state called the Department of Prices and Consumer Protection. The new department's first

Secretary of State was Mrs Shirley Williams, who until September 1976 (when she moved to the Department of Education and Science) had the assistance of a Minister of State and an Under-Secretary in coordinating such protection for the general consumer. Already since 1973 under the *Fair Trading Act* we have had a Director-General of Fair Trading, whose task it is to keep all consumer affairs under review. He can take action in cases of unfair trading by individuals, and encourage various trade associations to publish codes of practice. He also publishes guidance to consumers. Two of the more important bulwarks against unfair competitive selling have been the Trade Description Acts of 1968 and 1972, which make it an offence to describe goods inaccurately or to issue inaccurate statements about services being offered for sale.

For many years consumer groups throughout the country pressed the Government to give greater attention to the views of the ordinary consumer. Already several private organizations exist to do this, the largest of which is the Consumers Association. It publishes a monthly magazine, *Which?*, in which it records the results of its many tests of competing products in terms of safety, reliability, and relative value. It provides an advisory service for members, and its work is supplemented by voluntary groups like the National Federation of Consumer Groups. In 1975 the National Consumer Council was established under government auspices to ensure that the consumer's view is made known to Government and industry alike.

Advertising

There would be no point and no future in making a product for sale unless potential buyers knew of its existence and had some idea of its nature and price. To provide this information is one function of advertising. It is well catered for in Britain today. Advertising has become an industry in its own right. There are over 500 advertising agencies offering their services to promote the sales of products. The big agencies employ staffs of over 1000. Current expenditure on all forms of advertising amounts to about £1000 million a year, around $1\frac{1}{2}$ per cent of the National Income.

The main medium of this advertising is the press: national and local newspapers, magazines, and trade journals. The sum of £321 million was spent in this sector in 1974. The second main outlet is television, which accounted for about £125 million of the total. The remaining advertising expenditure—about £45 million—was through posters, films, catalogues, leaflets, window displays, and so on.

Critics of advertising practices say that some advertisements are trivial and insulting to the intelligence, and they may encourage a wrong sense of values. Specially rigged film shots or cunningly written copy blur the line between truth and falsehood. Advertisements playing up the status or prestige value of the product, or its 'indispensability', foster envy and dissatisfaction, encourage snobbery, and reinforce the notion that material possessions and outward symbols are the things that really matter in life.

The critics object to the wastefulness of advertising. One thousand millon pounds a year is a vast amount of money which adds nothing to the value of the products concerned. It would be a great gain if manufacturers saved this unnecessary expense; the money saved would enable them to lower the price of the product and this would really be a benefit.

The defenders of advertising stress that it does perform an essential and valuable service. Manufacturers turn out products in the hope of selling them. It is natural then that they want to tell the public about their product, point out its advantages and persuade people to buy it. Advertising is the means by which this is done. It has positive advantages too. It stimulates competition between firms and products, making for better quality and lower prices. New products, of high quality and reasonable price, are often only possible because of mass sales: with limited sales they would be too expensive to be worth making, or remain highly priced luxuries available only to a small minority of wealthy people. Advertising, through its market researches, can reassure a businessman, contemplating a new product, of the kind of sales he can expect; and through its selling techniques, it can help him to acquire and expand that market. The customer benefits from this. He gets access to an article which might otherwise not have appeared at all. Success enables the firm to increase and improve its output and its product—more research, more specialist staff, better equipment—and hence make the product better while keeping the price reasonable. Advertising, then, is not a wasteful, unnecessary extra. It is indispensable in a society with a high standard of living and a wide variety of goods available for consumption.

The defenders also point out that the expenditure on advertising acts to some extent as a hidden subsidy to other services which people want. Most national newspapers depend on advertisers for at least half of their revenue. Without this source of income, many papers and magazines would be unable to survive; and those that did could only do so by putting up their prices considerably. This is even more true of commercial television. It is only by their income from advertising—selling time on the air to advertisers at perhaps £10 000 a minute—that the companies meet the cost of producing their programmes.

There are limits to the power of advertising: it cannot continue to sell a product which is not basically good, reliable, and effective. Many advertisements are clever, humorous, and entertaining, giving a good deal of pleasure. As for encouraging materialism, if this is a sin it is society's not advertising's. Materialism is encouraged by the sights and sounds of everyday life, by the well-stocked windows of shops, the laden shelves of supermarkets, the increase in incomes.

Origins of banking

A highly developed system of finance is as important to commerce as good transport and distribution systems. All this movement of goods and materials requires money. Raw materials have to be paid for, as do shipping services, unloading, storage, road haulage, and railway carriage. Without the existence of money itself—a commodity which people are ready to accept in exchange for the goods, labour, or services they provide—commerce would obviously be restricted. But the mere existence of such a medium of exchange is not enough for modern commerical needs. Just as much of the usefulness of lorries would be lost without a good network of roads on which they can travel easily, so money, to be utilized fully, needs services enabling it to circulate quickly and easily.

The main institutions providing these services are the banks. Originally the banker was simply a person (usually a goldsmith) with whom people deposited money—gold, silver, coins—for safekeeping, as he had special strongrooms. The banker gave them a signed receipt for the amount they had deposited with him.

Gradually bankers became more than just guardians of money deposited with them. It became apparent that banker's receipts—notes promising to hand over the specified amount of money on presentation of the note—were just as acceptable in commerce as the money itself. Once confidence was established that the banker would indeed hand over cash on presentation of the note, then the note itself was as good as the money. It was more convenient for one merchant to transfer this slip of paper to another than to take the slip to his banker, collect a sack of coins, carry these (at risk of robbery) to the other's place of business, especially as the recipient in turn might well have to carry the money back to the same banker, hand it in for deposit, and get a slip of paper as receipt. Time, risk, and labour were all saved by the simple transfer of the slip of paper.

Then bankers found it was most unlikely that all the people who had deposited money with them would turn up at the same time and present notes for the withdrawal of all their deposits. They could therefore use much of the money entrusted to their keeping, instead of letting it lie idle in their strongrooms. They could, for instance, lend some, provided they were sure that the borrower was reliable and would repay quickly. And they could charge a small amount for this lending service. The borrower, moreover, was often content with the banker's promise that he would meet any demands up to the amount required, without insisting on having the loan in cash. The banker could make these advances with an even easier mind if he were sure depositors would not turn up unexpectedly to demand their deposits. To depositors who would promise to make no withdrawals for a definite period, the banker accordingly offered to pay a rate of interest on their deposits.

Advantages of banks

Such developments underlie the present banking system, and we can see from them some of the main purposes it serves. For the private person, as well as the commercial firm, the bank still serves as a safe-deposit. In addition to security, the banks provide convenience. The commonest instance of this is the cheque. Cheques are order forms which the bank supplies to its depositors. When a depositor wishes to pay a debt, he fills in the amount, date, and payee's name, signs the cheque, and gives it to the payee, who then sends it to his own bank. It does not matter if they deal in different banks, as all cheques go daily to a Bankers' Clearing House. Here the cheques are sorted out, and the various banks settle up among themselves. All the customer has to do is to fill in the cheque if he is the payer, or send it in to his bank if he is the payee. Thus an enormous amount of business can be done with a few strokes of the pen, without any sacks of money or bundles of banknotes being carried around, counted, checked, and so on.

Furthermore, the banks do not just hoard their deposits, they lend them out, apart from keeping a certain amount of cash in hand to meet withdrawal demands. This is an important item in commercial activity. Businessmen have money of their own, but often much of it is tied up in ways that mean it is not available quickly to meet a bill. In commerce this situation—the temporary need for a lump sum—is constantly occurring. The banks, where the savings of the community are deposited, are in a position to make these necessary advances, in return for an interest charge. They extend credit to the borrower, i.e., they agree to honour his cheques up to the amount in question, although his deposits in the bank are less than this. The banks, then, act as machinery through which credit is made available to commerce. Without this, commercial activities would be more restricted and flow less smoothly.

Banks, of course, have to be careful about the transactions for which they advance loans, since it is their customers' money they are lending out. They prefer to make loans for short periods rather than for long terms. They prefer to lend to well established concerns whose business standing is good. The *capital* for a new firm is not likely to come from a bank, because it is not certain that the concern will succeed, and, in any case, it will be unable to repay the bank for many years.

The money market

New companies, as we have seen, need to persuade the public to buy shares in them, and get the necessary capital in that way. There are other institutions that will help new companies in their attempt to raise capital, possibly by buying shares themselves, more commonly by arranging the details of the public issue of stock, contacting possible subscribers, advertising the issue, and so on. The *issuing houses*, the *merchant bankers*, and the *Stock Exchange* provide this kind of service.

All the institutions through which money can be raised, whether long-term capital advances or short-term loans, comprise the Money Market: the banks, the Stock Exchange, the issuing houses, the investment bankers, building societies, insurance companies (for these, like banks, have money deposited with them which they are prepared to lend out).

Bank organization

Banks are themselves business enterprises dealing in money instead of in goods. The shopkeeper buys goods from the wholesaler and sells them at a little more to the public, the difference being his profit. The banker borrows (buys the use of money) from some people and lends (sells the use of money) to others. By 'selling' rather more dearly than he has to 'buy' he makes his profit.

Like many business concerns, most banks are organized as limited companies on the joint-stock principle. There are six banking groups in Britain, four in England, two in Scotland. There used to be many more, hundreds of small partnership banks, but small concerns could not stand sudden heavy demands for withdrawals. Gradually the smaller banks amalgamated into the bigger ones, until the present situation of a few huge banking concerns was achieved.

It was also felt that small banks were prone to issue far more notes than their cash assets could cover, so increasing the risk of panic and crisis when more than the usual number of notes were presented for payment. Accordingly, an Act of 1844 arranged that gradually the right to issue banknotes should be vested in one bank only, the Bank of England. The Scottish banks still retain a limited right to issue their own notes.

The Bank of England

The Bank of England is a special case. From its beginning in 1694, it rapidly became the most important of the banks. A Scotsman, William Paterson, played a prominent part in its foundation. Organized on the joint-stock principle, it was the strongest bank. From the first it was the bank the Government itself looked to for loans. So, although it was an ordinary commercial bank aiming at profits for its shareholders, its size and its connection with Government gave it a special position and responsibilities. Because of this, the Bank of England was nationalized in 1946.

What are the special functions of the Bank of England? First, it is the 'bankers' bank'. All the commercial banks have large sums deposited there. They use these to settle accounts among themselves, e.g., after the daily transactions in the Clearing House.

Second, although there are still a few private customers, it is above all the Government's bank. It acts for the Government as the ordinary bank does for its customers. Government money is deposited and withdrawn from the Bank of England. It keeps the accounts of all the public departments. It keeps the nation's gold reserves and foreign currency holdings. It sees to the management of the National Debt. When the Government wants to raise a loan, it arranges it through the Bank of England.

Third, the Bank of England regulates the flow of capital into and out of the country, i.e., anyone wishing to send large sums of money to countries outside the Sterling Area must obtain its permission.

Fourth and most important, the Bank of England acts as an instrument for regulating the amount of credit available in the country. This is done by changes in the *Minimum Lending Rate* (which until 1972 was known as the Bank Rate), which is the rate of interest the Bank of England will pay depositors and demand from borrowers. All the commercial and other financial institutions, such as insurance companies, vary their own rates of interest in step with the Minimum Lending Rate. So if the Minimum Lending Rate is increased, anyone wishing for credit or for a loan from the bank will find he has to pay more interest. He will probably think twice about borrowing, and may postpone the scheme for which he wanted the loan. When the Minimum Lending Rate is reduced, money can be borrowed at cheaper rates of interest and people are encouraged to go ahead with their business projects. Since 1960 the Bank of England has enjoyed special powers to compel the commercial banks to deposit a certain percentage of their funds with it. This restricts still further the ability of the commercial banks to continue lending money at a time when this is contrary to official policy. Since so much commercial enterprise depends on the availability of credit, the Minimum Lending Rate is an important regulator of commercial activity.

Nationalization has not made much apparent change in the Bank's way of conducting its business, though the Governor and the directors are now appointed by the Government. It has strengthened the Bank's hand in persuading the commercial banks to follow its policy recommendations, for it has now great powers to intervene if they do not. The Bank comes under the Treasury. Governors of the Bank have from time to time uttered public criticisms of the Government's policy on expenditure or taxation: equally they have performed valuable and difficult services in negotiating with financial institutions abroad to arrange rescue operations whenever Britain's credit has needed strengthening as it has on several occasions during the 1970s.

Overseas trade

International trade is a natural consequence of specialization on the part of countries. Few countries are able to produce all the things they want from their own territory. In other words, they are not completely selfsupporting. Perhaps their climate makes it impossible for them to cultivate fruit or tobacco, perhaps they have no coal, or iron, or oil deposits. On the other hand, they usually have some assets in abundance, perhaps timber, so the basis for an exchange is apparent.

Even among items that it can produce, a country finds it is much better able

Table 6.2. Commodity composition of trade, 1975[1] (Source: *Britain 1977: An Official Handbook*, HMSO, 1977)

	£ million	Percent
Exports (f.o.b.)[2]		
Food, beverages and tobacco	1 428	7·2
Basic materials	561	2·8
Fuels	814	4·1
Manufactures including:	16 464	82·6
Machinery and transport equipment	*8 236*	*41·3*
Non-electric machinery	4 255	21·4
Electric machinery	1 529	7·7
Road motor vehicles	1 737	8·7
Other transport equipment	715	3·6
Chemicals	*2 179*	*10·9*
Metals and metal manufactures	*1 839*	*9·2*
Textiles	*698*	*3·5*
Other manufactures	*3 512*	*17·6*
Miscellaneous	662	3·3
Total	19,929	100·0
Imports (c.i.f.)[3]		
Food, beverages and tobacco	4 346	18·0
Fuels	4 310	17·8
Industrial materials including:	8 364	34·6
Basic materials	*2 214*	*9·2*
Chemicals	*1 409*	*5·8*
Other semi-manufactures	*4 741*	*19·6*
Finished manufactures including:	6 395	26·5
Machinery and transport equipment	*4 523*	*18·7*
Machinery	3 343	13·8
Road motor vehicles	883	3·7
Other transport equipment	297	1·2
Other manufactures	*1 872*	*7·7*
Miscellaneous	749	3·1
Total	24 163	100·0

1. On an overseas trade statistics basis.
2. Free on board, i.e. all costs accruing up to the time of placing the goods on board the exporting vessel having been paid by the seller.
3. Cost, insurance and freight, i.e., including shipping, insurance and other expenses incurred in the delivery of goods as far as their place of importation in Britain. Most of these expenses represent earnings by British firms.

to produce some than others. Rather than try, laboriously and expensively, to produce all of them, it may prefer to concentrate on those it can do well, cheaply, and easily. It can then exchange its surplus of these items with countries specializing in other commodities. These exchanges between the peoples of different countries make up international trade.

Britain is especially dependent upon trade. For some countries, the USA for instance, trade is important but not so vital, because they can, with effort, produce a great deal of what their people need from the huge, varied resources of their wide territory. Britain cannot do this, for her small land simply does not possess such resources. (We should remember that the United States, with about three times as many people as Britain, is over thirty times as big.) Britain produces only about half of the food her people eat, the rest must be imported from abroad. Even the specialized commodities she sells abroad to pay for this food—her manufactures—are themselves largely dependent on various raw materials imported from other countries. These, too, have to be paid for by

Table 6.3(a). Changing composition of Britain's imports

Commodity group	Percentage of imports		
	Late 1930s	1954	1974
Food, drink, tobacco	45	39	16
Basic materials	28	31	11
Minerals, fuels, lubricants	5	10	20
Semi manufactures	15	15	21
Manufactured goods	7	5	24

Britain's products sold abroad. For Britain, trade is not a 'fringe' activity—a matter of acquiring a few things she does not have but would rather like—it is an absolute necessity.

Despite her relatively small size and population, Britain is one of the largest trading nations in the world. Her share of international trade in manufactures, about 12 per cent, is smaller than in pre-1914 years, when it was over 30 per cent or in 1950 when it was about 21 per cent; but the total amount of world trade has grown so enormously over the period that this diminishing share represents a greatly increased amount. The value of Britain's exports in 1948, for instance, was about £1500 million, but in 1977 it is over £16 000 million; the value of imports in 1948 was about £2000 million, in 1967 it was almost £14 000 million.

Food and raw materials (including in these basic materials, fuels, and semifinished items) make up over three-quarters of Britain's imports. Among the foodstuffs the main item is meat, then fruit and vegetables, followed by cereals, tea, and sugar. Among the raw materials, petroleum is the biggest single item. It is required as fuel for industry, as a raw material in chemical manufacture, and as power for cars and lorries. Only twenty-five years ago petroleum accounted for less than 5 per cent of our imports. Its growth to about 20 per cent reflects a big change in Britain's industrial and social life in

Table 6.3(b). Changing composition of Britain's exports during the twentieth century

Year	Percentage of total exports accounted for by:					
	Non-manufactures	Chemicals	Textiles	Metals	Engineering products	Other manufactures
1919–20	17.7	4.7	42.9	11.4	6.4	16.7
1921–29	19.5	3.8	32.1	12.0	8.1	24.5
1934–33	21.6	5.9	24.8	12.7	13.6	21.3
1946–51	12.9	7.2	18.6	12.1	36.9	12.4
1952–62	14.6	8.6	9.4	13.3	42.4	11.7
1974	14.6	13.0	4.5	10.4	36.7	18.4

the intervening period (see Chapter 2B, on Energy). Iron and scrap metal for Britain's steel industry, which has long outgrown the capacity of native deposits, is the next in order of importance. Raw cotton and wood imports together remain an important item, but timber and wood pulp, considered together, far outstrip them—another commentary on the changing character of Britain's industry.

A comparison of the composition of Britain's imports over the years, reveals some interesting trends. The most noteworthy of these is, first, the diminishing proportion of foodstuffs in our imports. This partly reflects the expansion over these years of domestic agriculture. It also, however, reflects the way in which the growth of industry in general has demanded evergrowing amounts of the materials it needs. Second, within the 'materials for industry' sector, the basic raw materials have taken a diminishing share. This is partly because of the successful development of domestic substitutes and partly because an industry like cotton, which made heavy use of imported raw materials, has declined, whereas the newer industries have a relatively lower content of such raw materials. A third trend in recent years is the rapid rise in the share of our imports commanded by fully manufactured goods—from about 5 per cent in 1954 to 24 per cent in 1974. This represents a trend in world trade generally, in that the highly industrialized countries are becoming more specialized in their manufacturing industries, and trading with one another in them; by contrast with the more traditional pattern of selling manufactures to less industrialized countries in exchange for their primary products. this remarkable rise in imports of manufactures may also represent in Britain's case the more discouraging fact that, even in lines she does herself produce, foreign products are proving more attractive to the British buyer (e.g., over 50 per cent of all new cars sold in the United Kingdom in 1977 were of foreign manufacture).

The changing composition of Britain's exports over the twentieth century reveals clearly Britain's own line of specialization: over 85 per cent of all she exports consists of manufactured goods. Non-manufactured goods, i.e., foodstuffs and raw materials, have declined as a proportion of exports throughout the century. Coal is the most dramatic example of this: in 1938 it accounted for 8 per cent of Britain's exports, today it is barely 1 per cent of them. Among the manufactures there has also been a marked change in recent decades. Before 1914 textiles made up about 40 per cent of Britain's exports with cotton the most important; now they make up only about $4\frac{1}{2}$ per cent, with woollens more important than cotton. The growing giant of this century has been engineering products: machinery, electrical and non-electrical, vehicles and aircraft. These now account for nearly 37 per cent of all Britain's exports. Chemicals, dwarfed by textiles fifty years ago, have advanced steadily till they now make up about 13 per cent of all exports. Iron and steel make up about 11 per cent, a proportion which has remained fairly steady for decades.

The distribution of Britain's trade—the main areas from which she imports and to which she exports—has also been changing in recent years (see Tables

Table 6.4. Principal British markets, 1974/75. (Source: *Britain 1977: An Official Handbook*, HMSO, 1977)

Exports (f.o.b.)[1]	1974 (£ million)	1975 (£ million)	Percentage change 1974/75
United States[2]	1 777	1 789	+0·5
Federal Republic of Germany	1 026	1 304	+27
Netherlands	983	1 115	+13
France	914	1 164	+27
Belgium–Luxembourg	836	922	+10
Irish Republic	820	907	+11
Sweden	723	826	+14
Switzerland	673	805	+20
Australia	599	631	+ 5·5
South Africa	525	685	+30
Italy	510	563	+10
Canada	488	538	+10
Denmark	427	443	+ 3·5
Nigeria	222	512	+130
Iran	279	495	+77
Developed countries	12 435	14 003	+13
EEC	5 516	6 419	+16
Rest of Western Europe	2 953	3 372	+14
North America	2 267	2 332	+ 3
Other[3]	1 699	1 879	+11
Developing countries	3 591	5 202	+45
Oil-exporting countries[4]	1 210	2 278	+88
Other	2 381	2 923	+23
Centrally planned economies[5]	515	666	+29

1. On an overseas trade statistics basis.
2. Including dependencies.
3. Australia, New Zealand, South Africa, Japan.
4. Algeria, Bahrain, Brunei, Ecuador, Gabon, Indonesia, Iran, Iraq, Kuwait, Libya, Nigeria, Oman, Qatar, Saudi Arabia, Trinidad and Tobago, United Arab Emirates, Venezuela.
5. Soviet Union, Poland, German Democratic Republic, Hungary, Czechoslovakia, Albania, Bulgaria, Romania, Chinese People's Republic, North Korea, North Vietnam (Democratic Republic of Vietnam), Mongolia.

6.4 and 6.5). In terms of area, the Sterling Area—broadly but not identically the Commonwealth countries—is a major trading region, taking about 30 per cent of Britain's exports and supplying nearly as large a proportion of her imports. Today western Europe (33–40 per cent in 1974) is a bigger market for British goods than the Sterling Area; and is still bigger as a source of British imports.

The same trend is apparent in terms of countries if we compare, for instance, the shrinking role of Australia over these years with the growth as markets and suppliers of West Germany and Sweden. Growing fast as a trading partner

Table 6.5. British principal sources of supply, 1974/75. (Source: *Britain 1977: An Official Handbook*, HMSO, 1977)

Imports from (c.i.f.)[1]	1974 (£ million)	1975 (£ million)	Percentage change 1974/75
United States[2]	2 265	2 352	+ 4
Federal Republic of Germany	1 902	1 999	+ 5
Netherlands	1 637	1 873	+14
France	1 349	1 628	+21
Saudi Arabia	1 178	857	−27
Canada	984	856	−13
Sweden	929	886	− 5
Irish Republic	810	921	+14
Belgium–Luxembourg	731	952	+30
Switzerland	765	737	− 4
Italy	724	810	+12
Japan	570	672	+18
Denmark	577	622	+ 8
Iran	513	701	+37
Norway	408	593	+45
Developed Countries	16 132	17 434	+ 8
EEC	7 730	8 805	+14
Rest of Western Europe	3 469	3 566	+ 3
North America	3 249	3 208	− 1
Other[3]	1 684	1 855	+10
Developing Countries	6 376	5 940	− 7
Oil-exporting countries[4]	3 785	3 274	−14
Other	2 591	2 666	+ 3
Centrally planned economies[5]	751	753	—

1. On an overseas trade statistics basis.
2. Including dependencies.
3. Australia, New Zealand, South Africa, Japan.
4. Algeria, Bahrain, Brunei, Ecuador, Gabon, Indonesia, Iran, Iraq, Kuwait, Libya, Nigeria, Oman, Qatar, Saudi Arabia, Trinidad and Tobago, United Arab Emirates, Venezuela.
5. Soviet Union, Poland, German Democratic Republic, Hungary, Czechoslovakia, Albania, Bulgaria, Romania, Chinese People's Republic, North Korea, North Vietnam (Democratic Republic of Vietnam), Mongolia.

over the same period has been the United States, now much the biggest single-country market and source of supply for Britain. This reflects some of the developments already noted: the shift away from the older pattern of industrial countries supplying manufactures to primary producing countries in exchange for food and raw materials. The most striking trend is towards the increased trade in manufactures among the leading manufacturing countries. This represents the greater specialization inside the field of manufactures, the growth of consumer demand within these richer countries for more specialized foreign goods (for Swedish furniture, or German cars, or Italian shoes, or Japanese hi-fi equipment), the greater readiness of these countries to lower tariffs and admit more foreign competition.

Trade with the Commonwealth was predominant around 1950 for a number of reasons. First, there was still the complementary aspect of the economies of these countries and Britain: that is, many were well suited to produce the materials that Britain needed, Britain was equipped to turn out more easily the manufactures they required. Second, special agreements on Commonwealth preference encouraged this trade. Since 1932 imports from these countries had been allowed to enter Britain at a lower rate of duty than similar items imported from a non-Commonwealth country. Likewise, Britain's manufactures were allowed into Commonwealth countries at lower rates of import duty than if they had come from, say, France or Germany.

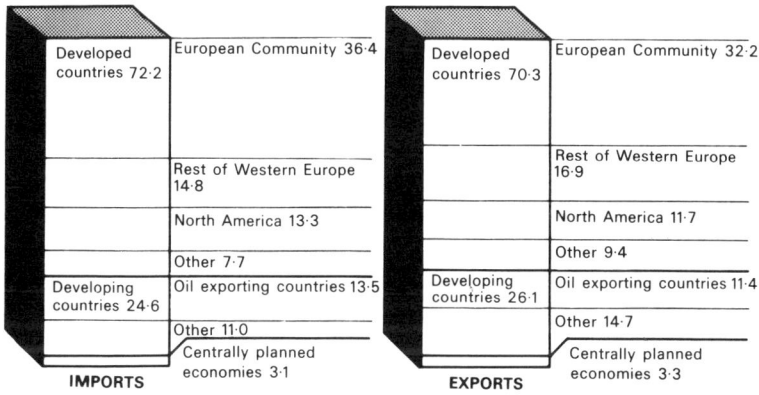

Note: Discrepancies between totals and their constituent parts are due to rounding

Fig. 6.4. Area pattern of trade 1975 (percentages of total values). (Source: *Britain 1977: An Official Handbook*, HMSO, 1977)

Third, in the postwar years Britain had a special reason for encouraging trade with the Commonwealth. It eased Britain's dollar problem. Britain had to import a great deal from the United States, which would not take payment for these goods in pounds but insisted on dollars. But it was not easy for Britain to earn dollars, as the USA, herself a highly advanced manufacturing country, was making much the same kind of things as Britain could offer.

Finally, there are long-established bonds, not only economic, between Britain and the Commonwealth. These ties of sentiment, past cooperation, language, and so on played a part. They meant that trading connections are often very old; and that even trade is not simply a matter of hard cash.

These reasons no longer hold so good as they did. Since Britain's membership of the EEC she has had to meet new conditions of trade, and

Commonwealth preferences have been ousted as preventing moves towards greater liberalization of trade. Also, many Commonwealth countries are developing their own manufacturing industries. Australia and Canada are large-scale manufacturers now, and are seeking their own world markets for their products: Australia's trade with Britain is less prominent than it used to be, but her trade with Asian countries has increased enormously.

Commercial policy

For a country so dependent on trade as Britain, commercial policy is of the greatest importance. From the mid-nineteenth century until the 1920s Britain was a free trade country. On a few items an import duty was imposed as a source of revenue for the Government, but otherwise every kind of article—food, raw material, or manufactured goods—could enter the country duty free. But in 1915 import duties were imposed on some luxury items, mainly to save shipping space for essential imports. In 1921 further duties were introduced to protect important home industries from foreign competition, e.g., precision instruments. In 1932 the tariff was greatly extended in an attempt to restrict imports and improve the balance of trade. Food and raw materials were largely untouched, but a 10 per cent duty had to be paid on every other kind of item imported into Britain.

Such protection of home industries is not now acceptable. As a member of the EEC Britain is committed to developing world trade through the reduction of tariff barriers. Even today the EEC's Common Customs Tariff (CCT), which applies to all non-members of the Community, is lower than that of several other major industrial countries. Britain is a supporter, for instance, of GATT (General Agreement on Tariffs and Trade) founded in 1948. Under this agreement about seventy countries have agreed to work towards the reduction of trade barriers, to avoid discrimination against one another in trade, to protect home industries when essential by measures more acceptable than import quotas, to give at least due warning when considering changes in their tariffs. Negotiations in 1967, the 'Kennedy Round' of talks, resulted in about fifty countries agreeing to lower tariffs on thousands of products entering their territories.

While GATT was set up as a worldwide organization, it was soon followed by more limited ones, such as the EEC and EFTA. The EEC, European Economic Community or Common Market, initially comprised six European countries (France, West Germany, Italy, Belgium, the Netherlands, and Luxembourg), who agreed in 1957 to the steady removal of all the tariff barriers between themselves, while maintaining all around the Community a common tariff (CCT) on all goods coming from countries outside. The rate at which the wealth, the production, and the trade of these countries grew was quite impressive and contrasted sharply with Britain's relatively slow rate of advance. It was the economic advantages of the EEC that were the most prominent reasons advanced by those who wanted Britain to join. Membership would open up to Britain a huge domestic market, without trade barriers, of about 300 million people. The opportunity of sales on this scale would spur industry to improve its efficiency. The partners would have equally free access to the British market, and the threat from highly efficient continental firms would make British firms sit up.

Sceptics questioned whether the economic advance which the EEC had made, were likely to be sustained. Others recognized the advantages of membership, but wondered about the price which would have to be paid. Some firms and industries did not see themselves capturing foreign markets, but saw their British market being captured from them. Some parts of Britain already felt the pinch of being remote from the thriving South East, with the centres of economic activity shifted further towards Paris or Brussels. There were doubts about the effect on agriculture, on the price of food in the shops. Commonwealth produce would no longer enter on favourable terms. For some Commonwealth countries, especially New Zealand, whose economics were geared to producing food for the British market, the effects would be harmful.

In the event, in January 1973 Britain became a member of the European Economic Community. At the same time Ireland and Denmark joined to make it a community of Nine. Although arguments still continue about the possible benefits and disadvantages of membership the majority view appears to be that the breakup of narrow nationalism, the creation of a wider trading group, the development of a new social and political community are ideals worthy of achievement—even if in the early stages there are financial losses and few real benefits for the British consumer. (Over 67 per cent of those voting in a national referendum in June 1975 favoured continued membership.)

Indeed, the entry to the Community coincided with the worst bout of inflation suffered by this country since the First World War. Thus to all the adjustments required of British industry and trade by the new Community regulations were added the additional problems of higher prices, a severe world economic recession, and a steadily falling value for the pound in relation to the other currencies of western Europe (see Chapter 7 for more details on this).

What was undoubtedly true about the membership debate was that it has shown up, even since 1973, the suspicions of each other which were a permanent feature of the pre-Community era—suspicions about social policy, industrial relations, and above all of the trade policies pursued in a highly industrialized and highly competitive segment of Western Europe. Before the third and successful bid to join Europe (made in 1970) there had already been British attempts to join in 1963 and 1967. In the earlier bids the Community members had viewed with some suspicion Britain's membership of the European Free Trade Association (EFTA) set up in 1959 as a limited attempt at reducing trade barriers. It was true that EFTA made no attempt at fixing a common external tariff (which would have kept out imports from non-members) which was a basic feature of EEC, but it did allow Britain to maintain her special relationship with Commonwealth countries and allowed her to offer special terms to Commonwealth imports to Britain—a basic cause of contention when it came to EEC/UK negotiations on possible entry.

EFTA did play a fairly important part in the pattern of British trade. Indeed, up to 1970, the EFTA group of countries (Sweden, Norway, Denmark, Austria, Switzerland, and Portugal plus Britain) increased their share of British trade—taking 15 per cent of our exports (against 20 per cent by EEC) and providing 15 per cent of our exports (against 20 per cent from EEC countries.) In each case these figures represented a doubling of the trade within a space of ten years. Also, the EFTA members were as prosperous as the EEC members in general terms. Indeed, there could have been fairly wide possibilities for the whole concept of EFTA had the whole EEC/UK relationship not redeveloped in 1970. Once Britain decided on a swift and decisive bid for EEC membership (on about any terms) the scene was set for the relative demise of EFTA as a potential competitor. With the EEC entry of Ireland and Denmark, EFTA was split and indeed so was the hitherto unified front of the three Scandinavian countries (Norway, Sweden, and Denmark). From April 1974 onwards the Nine EEC members concentrated on reaching agreement on the fairly extensive list of outstanding problems—in an atmosphere of world economic depression linked to a period of rapidly rising prices and widely fluctuating exchange rates.

The future of the Community is as yet shaky, and it will be a decade or so before adequate assessment is possible of the history of EEC or of its relationship to other world trading blocs.

Balance of Trade

All the imports and exports we have been considering are visible, physical things such as crates of fruit, bales of cotton, cars, and machinery. The difference in value between these visible imports and visible exports is called the Balance of Trade. If Britain spends less on these imports than she earns from exports, then she is said to have a 'favourable' Balance of Trade; if she spends more on visible imports than she earns from visible exports, she has an 'unfavourable' Balance of Trade.

Britain has had an unfavourable Balance of Trade for many years now. But since imports have to be paid for from export earnings, how can such a situation exist? The answer to this puzzle lies in the fact that visible exports and imports do not tell the whole story.

Trade is not confined to the exchange of physical articles. There are certain services which British firms perform for foreign firms for which the foreign firms pay, just as they would if they were receiving actual goods from Britain. For instance, British ships carry a great many cargoes for foreign firms, and thus earn money from them. Again, foreign businessmen often use the services of British banks or insurance firms, like Lloyds of London. In the past, British people may have lent money to other countries: every year the borrowers pay interest to the lenders, so that money is being earned abroad. Again, when foreign tourists spend their money in Britain, foreign money is earned just as if they had stayed at home and ordered British goods by mail and had the goods carried to them in ships as normal 'visible' exports.

The reverse, of course, also applies. When a British firm uses the services of a foreign shipping company, when British tourists travel and spend money abroad, then British money is being earned by foreign countries. These are 'invisible' imports.

To get a truer picture of whether Britain is earning enough to pay for what she buys from abroad, we have to compare the value of total exports and total imports of all kinds, visible and invisible.

The Balance of Payments

When we do compare the value of exports and imports, the difference between the two totals is called the Balance of Payments. For instance, Britain had an unfavourable Balance of Trade in each year 1964, 1969, and 1974. Her visible

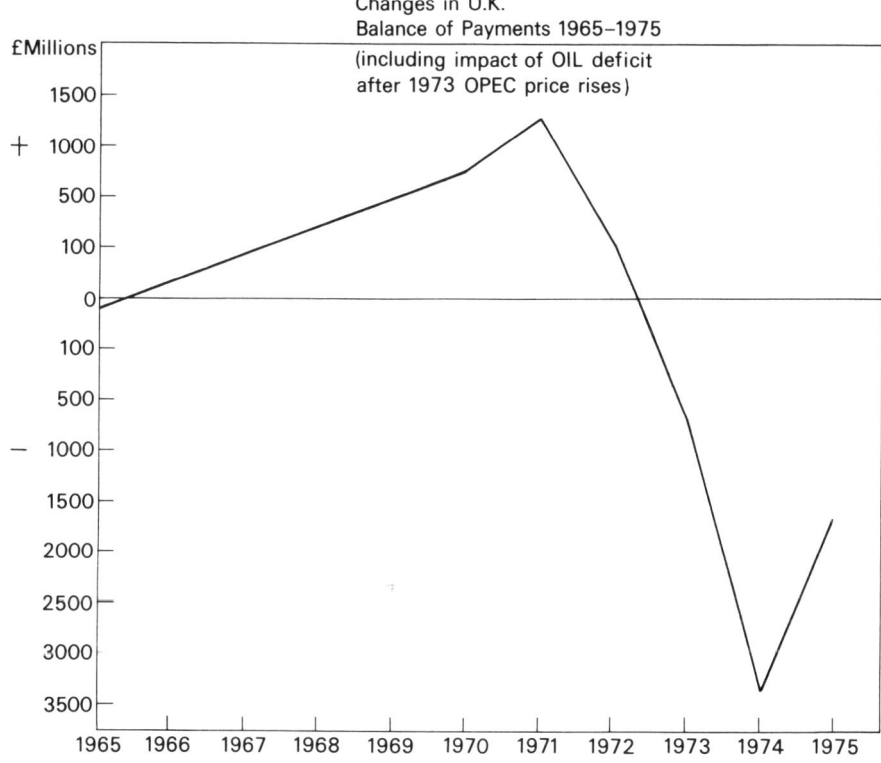

Fig. 6.5. Balance of Payments trends over a 10 year period

exports did not earn enough to pay for her visible imports. The position was redeemed by the invisible trade balance in 1969, but in the other two years the Balance of Payments remained unfavourable.

The Balance of Payments is the key figure which tells us whether or not Britain is earning enough from all the goods and services she exports to pay for all the things she imports. The immediate postwar years showed heavy unfavourable balances. This was not surprising, for reasons we have already seen: the dwindling of our invisible exports because so many of our overseas

Table 6.6. Balance of Payments on current account

Year	Imports	Exports	Visible balance	Invisible balance	Total balance of payments
1946	1 081	905	−176	−168	−344
1950	2 372	2 225	−147	+391	+244
1951	3 497	2 708	−789	+268	−521
1952	3 048	2 769	−279	−443	+164
1955	3 386	3 073	−313	+157	−156
1959	3 640	3 522	−118	+254	+136
1960	4 141	3 733	−408	+133	−275
1961	4 045	3 892	−153	+148	− 5
1962	4 098	3 994	−104	+205	+101
1963	4 370	4 278	− 83	+190	+107
1964	5 014	4 471	−543	+150	−393
1967	5 673	5 023	−650	+136	−514
1968	6 899	6 103	−796	+377	−419
1974	21 119	15 889	−5220	+1873	−3347
1975	21 972	18 768	−3204	+1531	−1673

assets had been sold off during the war; the increase in invisible imports in the form of payments on loans Britain had got from other countries in wartime; the time it took to convert industrial production from munitions back to peacetime export goods; the heavier load visible exports had to bear, because the invisibles had shrunk and import prices were rising in any case. Yet, by 1950 a favourable balance was achieved, partly through devaluation in 1949; partly as a result of a strict control of imports to keep the bill down and the encouragement of production for export as against production for domestic consumption; and partly because of large-scale aid from the United States.

During the 1960s the position worsened: 1960 and 1961 were both years of deficit, 1962 and 1963 saw a surplus restored. Since then Britain has had a regular deficit. Exports have grown but visible imports have always kept ahead of them. Moreover the invisible balance, though always favourable throughout the last twenty years, has tended to shrink in size in recent years. This was largely a reflection of the steep growth in military expenditure abroad during the 1960s: in 1950 this amounted to about £60 million, by 1968 it was over

£400 million. Both exports and imports rose after the devaluation of sterling in 1967, and within four years Britain's current account surplus shot up to a record £1048 million. Such a change of fortune, however, did not last. The rise in commodity prices (i.e., rubber, aluminium, copper, etc.) led during 1972-73 to a rapid increase in import prices—linked to a fall in value of the pound as compared with the US dollar and German mark. This resulted in a rapid rise in our visible trade deficit in 1973.

During 1973 our volume of exports improved by over 14 per cent, and but for one *major event* our trade surplus might have surpassed that of 1971. That disastrous event was the quadrupling of the price of crude oil by the Arab oil producers following the Arab/Israeli War of October 1973. Such an event could not have been anticipated, and it played havoc with the British Balance of Payments. Indeed, from 1974 one significant feature of statements about annual balances has been the insertion of a phrase 'non-oil deficit'. A move calculated to indicate the true position of our trade balances was the rise in oil import costs to be deducted. However, all the troubles for sterling did not begin with 1973. As early as 1972 the trade balance had begun to deteriorate, and despite higher exports in 1973 and 1974, the increased cost of oil imports led to a large deficit on the current account in both years.

The price rise in oil added to our problems. If this had not happened the picture would have been quite a good one. As we saw, in 1973, despite increasing competition and with the help of a massive export drive (in this case helped by the earlier depreciation of the pound which made our goods cheaper in terms of those of other competitors), the value of our exports grew by 25 per cent. This export success continued throughout 1974, and it was the massive rise in commodity prices of imports, the further fall in the value of the pound, and the fourfold oil price increase beginning in October 1973 (which became a fivefold increase in crude oil prices by the end of 1974), which really caused the disastrous drop in our overall balance in that year.

Fortunately, so far, Britain has been able to borrow from the two sources already mentioned—the International Monetary Fund (IMF) and foreign bankers. Since 1974, however, the scale of this borrowing has been a source of worry both to the Government and to foreign financiers. Every time we borrow from them or from the IMF we are rescuing the present year at the expense of greater burdens for years to come. The interest we have to pay on such loans is a heavy burden, and added to that is the fact that we must also repay the capital sums itself at some future date. Foreigners and the IMF have tired recently of having to bail Britain out of her financial difficulties. To such lenders Britain appears to be living beyond her means, and increasingly stringent conditions are applied to each new loan made. Such steps are a regular bone of contention within Britain. What the IMF and others demand is a slowdown in government spending and a balancing of our budget at home. This often requires a cutback in economic development and a restriction on wage rises and even on rises in living standards. While these policies may be aimed at achieving economic stability (see Chapter 7, page 162), the resulting tensions often lead to public complaints about the attitude of foreign bankers ('Gnomes of Zurich' is the term often used to describe Swiss financial interests). Later we shall see how the system operates.

For the immediate future Britain relies on a levelling out of the rise in commodity prices (including oil prices) to bring her payments closer to balance. Even to do this, however, she requires the help of the exporters and both sides of industry to ensure that our price level for manufactured goods is competitive enough to boost our export sales. Even given favourable conditions this itself would be difficult if the world recession in trade of 1975–76 does not begin to turn back to a period of steady expansion.

Actually the Balance of Payments did improve in 1975, and the increase in North Sea oil production should lead to fairly marked improvements in the position by 1980 (see Chapter 2B, on energy). Indeed, by October 1977 monthly trading returns indicated substantial improvements in our position, and the flow of North Sea oil combined with growing confidence in the Government's anti-inflation measures encouraged a freeing of the £/$ exchange. If the subsequent dramatic revaluation of sterling continues in 1978, Britain's poor Balance of Payments record could be reversed.

The overall picture has been gloomy until now, however. Britain has other overseas commitments not indicated in the Balance of Payments. She has, for instance, to pay out lump sums to redeem certain debts: these are *capital* payments and so do not appear, as *interest* payments do, in the current account figures. Again she makes grants of money to help the developing countries. She makes loans, especially to Commonwealth countries. These will of course earn interest and hence in the future will help increase invisible earnings, but at the moment they mean sending large capital sums abroad. Britain needs a substantial surplus if she is to cover the cost of her imports and meet these extra obligations as well: a figure frequently suggested as desirable is £1000 million surplus a year. Yet far from enjoying this she has had a deficit for six out of the last ten years.

One great help in securing immediate short-term loans has been the system of Special Drawing Rights (SDRs) initiated by the International Monetary Fund in 1970. Any IMF member may join the scheme, which works as follows. Each member who joins the scheme is allocated a share of SDRs. Any participant in the scheme accepts an obligation to provide convertible currency (when designated by the IMF to do so) to another participant who requires such currency. In return the designated participant who has given this currency will receive SDRs from the borrowing country. The lender must be willing to give up to twice the net amount of their own allocation of SDRs under the scheme. In this way Britain is able to obtain credit in times of adverse international trade balances.

7. Economic problems and policies

In late 1977 Britain had over 1½ million people unemployed. She had an inflation rate running at around 13 per cent per annum. Her Balance of Payments position was improving. Her import costs no longer regularly exceeded the value of her exports. Nevertheless, the level of her public expenditure was the subject of serious discussion both at home and abroad. When we add to this the facts of a severe world recession in trade over the last few years, and the prospect of a continuing inflation over the next few years as seen by the NIESR (National Institute of Economic and Social Research—the 'Cambridge Group'), the prospects look less grim.

Preoccupation with economic gloom should not lead us to overlook considerable developments that have been made in this field since 1945. The rapid rundown in the basic industries (see Chapter 2) and the consequent decline in demand for the manpower employed in these industries, created a considerable problem which was tackled very energetically. Britain managed in a civilized humane way to help soften the social effect of decline in her older major industries on the people and places affected. Closures and rundowns of pits, factories, and shipyards were carried out with some care and forethought for the social consequences. Generous redundancy payments were given. Attempts were made to direct alternative employment to the district. Men ready to move to other districts or jobs received assistance. Moreover, new industries were developed to replace the old, as sources of national wealth, employment, and exports: cars, engineering, electrical equipment, chemicals, consumer goods of all kinds. In many ways the task of adapting to changed circumstances was tackled with success. One proof of this success was the rise in British exports since the Second World War.

The main problems

Nevertheless, this achievement was not enough. In the last few years Britain faced four awkward economic problems. First, the need to restore a favourable Balance of Payments. Second, the need to improve efficiency and productivity in order to speed up the growth of national wealth. Third, the need to restrain inflation which can swallow up the advances made in production. Fourth, a more recent problem developed in 1974—a bout of severe unemployment (in 1977 standing around 6 per cent of all employees) which, as we saw, has destroyed the excellent record of low unemployment since 1945 when for some thirty years the average rate was as low as 1 per cent or less. This is now an immediate and continuing problem for any British Government. Any reduction in unemployment means increased production—but also increased spending power. Thus there could be a pressure on price levels leading to further inflationary price rises unless the productivity achieved by the newly employed workers more than compensated for the increase in purchasing power. So we can see that all the problems are related, though they are not the same. We might, for instance, increase the annual production of goods, but unless we manage to sell more of them abroad the increase would not in itself solve the Balance of Payments problem. None of the problems is entirely new, but there is now a general awareness that mere short-term emergency measures and general exhortations are unlikely to help. There is now much more government intervention resulting in more central planning and long-term measures.

The Balance of Payments problem

As we saw earlier, the Balance of Payments has been Britain's main economic headache of late. It is important, first, because the chronic deficit means that Britain is not paying her way; she is living beyond her means. The deficit may be feasible for a time, since she can borrow from foreign sources to tide her over. But this borrowing cannot go on indefinitely, and unless Britain can restore a favourable balance she must resign herself to a standard of living lower than that she could otherwise enjoy. The adverse balance is important in a second way, in that it has itself acted as a drag on the rate of growth of the economy. Emergency steps to reduce the deficit always include measures to restrain demand in the domestic market, partly to persuade manufacturers to put more effort into selling in foreign markets, partly to reduce imports. So the Minimum Lending Rate (i.e., the old Bank Rate) is raised, bank credit restricted, VAT and hire-purchase terms stiffened, limits put on wage rises. Domestic demand and import bills may thus be held down and the payments deficit reduced. But there is a price to be paid: business enterprises, discouraged by credit restrictions from expanding their activities, cut down their investment programmes; firms react to the reduced domestic purchasing power by cutting production and laying off workers. Often in the past, when after a while the checks were removed and expansion began again, it was found that expansion meant more imports—indispensable materials, special plant and machinery, foreign goods for British consumers with more money to spend—so that before long the Balance of Payments was upset again, the alarm grew, credit squeezes and wage restrictions were reintroduced, and the expansion of the economy was checked once more. This process became known as the 'Stop Go' policy. To achieve a favourable balance did not in itself guarantee economic growth, but without it growth was bound to be slowed down.

Moreover, the payments deficit could easily produce a further complication which made the adoption of unpleasant measures still more likely: it may contribute, as it did from 1964 to 1966, and during 1975–76, to a crisis of sterling. This comes about because holders of sterling throughout the world, nervous at a run on the pound which will cut the value of their holdings, may insist on exchanging their sterling for gold or reliable foreign currency. The reserves on which the Bank of England can draw to meet this rush of demands soon begin to drain away and only heavy assistance from foreign bankers can stop the drain, reassure sterling holders, and halt the panic. But again there is a price. Foreign bankers who help in the rescue want some reassurance that Britain will make a determined effort to set her Balance of Payments right and not come running year after year with requests for help. And the reassurance needs to be of a deflationary type—cuts in government spending and a reduction of domestic demand—which hold back economic growth. Only now there is added the rather humiliating knowledge that the British Government can be pressurized into taking such steps by outside forces.

Possible solutions

Many suggestions have been made for overcoming the Balance of Payments difficulty. Some argue that Britain could do so, not by straining to earn more through exports but simply by spending less abroad, either by cutting down on Defence (where we are committed to NATO defence) or on Foreign Aid (for which we had committed ourselves in the past to approaching 1 per cent of our National Income.) Neither of these areas could be substantially cut without effect on our allies or on the progress of the Developing World.

Again it is often pointed out that Britain might do more to reduce the amount of her imports and so keep down the bills which have to be paid from export earnings. Controls on imports are in fact used at present, for varying reasons, and not always to ease the Balance of Payments problem. Import duties are imposed on many goods entering Britain to produce revenue for the Government. There are, however, objections to the oversevere use of import restrictions. The practice runs counter to the aims of GATT and we are not free to do so *vis-à-vis* the EEC. There is the risk that countries whose products are badly hit by British restrictions might retaliate by discriminating against British goods seeking to enter their markets. Third, British industry itself is dependent on many indispensable materials obtainable only from abroad. Now we do try to develop domestic substitutes, and in terms of food, production has been stepped up from the pre-war position. We have developed substitute materials like plastics, synthetic rubber, and artificial fibres. Industry is making more economical use of imported materials. There may well be opportunities of greater savings along these lines, but they are not likely to come about overnight. The great bulk of our imports still consists of food and materials which we must have and where import restrictions, even if allowed by our EEC partners, would harm only ourselves.

More tempting is the idea of controlling the import of foreign manufactured goods, especially as the proportion of these in Britain's imports has grown rapidly—from 6 per cent in 1956 to 15 per cent in 1965, to 26·5 per cent in 1975. And for cars the situation is even worse—in November 1977 foreign cars took 46 per cent of all sales in the UK market. These goods are not essential in the way that raw materials are. Yet to restrict them means limiting the choice of the British consumer and, again, a guaranteed market at home reduces the incentive for domestic firms to find export markets. These are the main objections to a policy of controlling imports. Nevertheless, Britain may have to resort to control as a temporary measure if other policies fail. By careful selection (including taxing where required) the items required by industry could still come in; so the import bill could be lowered while industry could expand, less hampered then it is by 'unselective' measures such as credit squeezes.

Given the limits and objections to reducing the amount Britain spends abroad, the most satisfactory solution lies in increasing the amount we earn abroad by increasing exports. Attempts to do this have often taken the form of restricting domestic demand to free more goods for foreign markets, and persuade British businessmen to put more effort into the search for foreign sales. Information on foreign markets was provided and trade exhibitions abroad were arranged. Concessions were made to export firms and they are rewarded with honours for success.

Sometimes dramatic moves are necessary to close the trade gap. In 1967 Britain devalued the pound by about 14 per cent (from $2·80 to $2·40 to the £). Governments are loath to resort to measures of this kind, partly for reasons of prestige, partly because it means letting down the holders of sterling; but at the time nothing less drastic seemed appropriate to the situation, for sterling reserves were falling at a dangerous rate. Since devaluation makes the pound worth less in terms of foreign currencies, the effect is (*a*) to make our exports cheaper in foreign markets, and (*b*) to make our imports from abroad dearer. Ideally, then devaluation should make it easier to sell our goods abroad and discourage imports. In practice this is not pure gain, for there are many imports which we must have and each item costs more than before devaluation. Even so, the cheapening of British goods abroad does give a greater opportunity for increasing export sales.

To ensure that resources and efforts are directed to exports, the familiar restraints on home demands have been maintained. Rates of interest remain high (in 1976 interest rates soared—even during a depression), commercial banks go cautiously in extending credit. Devaluation, however, was never a miracle worker. It gave Britain an opportunity to improve her position. In the course of 1969 the trade figures suggested that the position was improving, the gap between import costs and export earnings was reduced. But the improvement had come more slowly and uncertainly than had been hoped when devaluation was carried through.

To keep up in the export field, however, does require more than reasonable prices, important though these are. Britain needed to be a good salesman as well as an efficient manufacturer. Firms had to keep in close touch with foreign markets to promote sales, to appreciate changes in the local tastes which may mean modifying the styling of the cars or suits or shoes that are being sent there. Britain's failings in the 'after-sales' service—dealing with complaints, replacements, and repairs—came in for much criticism. So, too, have British failures to keep delivery dates.

There may have been a time when a foreign buyer who wanted a certain article had to get it from Britain because no other country manufactured it, but that time is long past. There is nothing to compel foreigners to buy goods from Britain. Whether they buy British or not, depends largely on the efficiency of British industry and salesmanship.

Economic growth: efficiency and productivity

To increase exports may be an urgent economic objective but it is not the only one. Britain is by no means a poor country but many of the population are still far from affluent: their standards need to be raised. There are many aspects of our society which could do with improvement: more higher education, better schools, more hospitals, better social services, and so on. If we are to devote more resources to these things and, at the same time, increase the amount we export, then the total output of the economy has to be increased, i.e., the National Income must keep growing. There is no easy way to do this in a competitive world.

Increased production, however, must be accompanied by greater efficiency in production if the full benefits are to be obtained. If, for instance, 100 men in a factory produce 100 articles, and by employing another 100 men the output is raised to 150 articles, then production has gone up but the efficiency of production has declined. It has taken more effort and cost more money to produce each article in the last batch than it did in the first, i.e., unit costs of production have risen. The selling price would probably go up to cover the increased production costs and the article would be less able to compete in foreign markets and would move beyond the reach of some people at home. So with national production: it is encouraging to see it grow from year to year, but still more so if this is achieved by an increase in the amount of production per head of the working population, not by a disproportionate rise in the numbers of workers required to produce it. This efficiency of production is called productivity. It is usually measured as 'the amount of output per worker' or 'per manhour worked'.

In both these respects, total production and output per worker, Britain experienced growth in the postwar years. In the former the rate of increase was between 2 and 3 per cent a year: output in the mid-1960s was half as big again as in 1950. The population and the number of people working, it is true, both increased over the same period but not to the same degree: that is, the output per head of population or per head of the working force has also increased, though here the annual increase has been closer to 2 per cent than to 3 per cent. Both of these aspects might seem satisfactory but for the fact that in neither was Britain performing as well as other countries, nor as well as calculations suggested she could. The standard of living, therefore, was not rising as rapidly as it might. It is true that all these statistics are not absolutely precise, and that international comparisons can easily be misleading; but the general picture they present seems acceptable enough. Table 7.1 shows how Britain's total production, although it is growing again, still lags behind that achieved in other comparable countries. Productivity statistics reveal a similar position (see Fig. 7.1).

Table 7.1. Growth rates (average annual percentage increase in GNP)

Country	1973	1974	1975	1976
West Germany	+5·1	+0·5	−3·2	+5·6
Italy	+6·9	+3·9	−3·5	+5·6
Japan	+9·8	+3·1	+2·4	+6·3
France	+5·8	+3·8	−1·2	+5·5
USA	+5·5	−1·7	−1·8	+6·1
UK	+6·1	−0·1	−1·7	+1·6

Many things are involved in economic growth, whether of total production or of efficiency of production. But though often measured in terms of 'output per worker', we must not assume that growth can only be achieved by the worker sweating more over his job. A carpenter can make more articles more quickly and with less effort if, for instance, his saw, planes, and chisels are new, keen, and comfortable to use than if he has to work with blunted and worn-out tools. A good example is the housewife with a washing machine. So too, in industry, some improvement in any one of a great number of fields can increase the efficiency of production so that the workman may work shorter hours than before.

A firm might, for instance, install new plant and equipment, introduce automatic processes and computers, provide an improved version of a certain machine. By merging with other firms it might help create a more efficient unit, with better financial backing and able to afford research facilities which as a smaller unit, neither it nor any of the others could have done. Management might find a better way of transacting its business. Improved communications between management and employees could remove misunderstandings and hence the disruptions to production these cause; and better machinery for dealing with disputes when they do arise could reduce their duration and get the wheels turning again more quickly. Again a union might agree to abandon some restrictive practice (as happened recently in Govan Shipbuilders when new foreign orders were keenly sought), or manage to settle some dispute with a rival union which has been leading to stoppages of work. The Government might decide to provide better facilities for training workers, or to improve the road system. Any actions of this kind could be reflected in time in an increase in the figures for production and productivity.

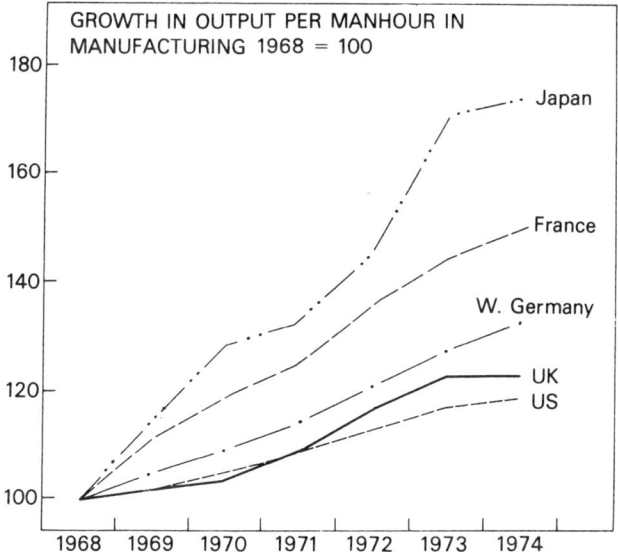

Fig. 7.1. Output (i.e., productivity). (Source: *Economic Progress Report*, COI, February 1976)

Investment

One item of great importance for economic growth is investment, i.e., the expenditure of money not on everyday needs but on buildings, plant, and machinery which have to be replaced and extended if goods are to be produced more efficiently. These things are the basic tools of industrial production. Just as it pays a workman to keep renewing his tools, so it pays Britain to keep the 'tool kit' of her industry up to the mark. As we saw earlier, one trouble with some British industries was that their equipment was allowed to get out of date—cotton, coal, railways. If the amount of investment falls too low then output and productivity cannot increase as rapidly as they otherwise could: one essential foundation for growth is not being properly laid. During the postwar years Britain's record in this respect has again been less impressive

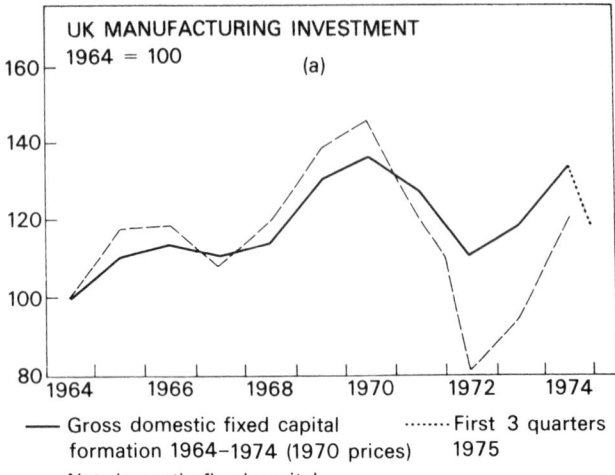

— Gross domestic fixed capital formation 1964–1974 (1970 prices)
— — Net domestic fixed capital formation (1970 prices)
······· First 3 quarters 1975

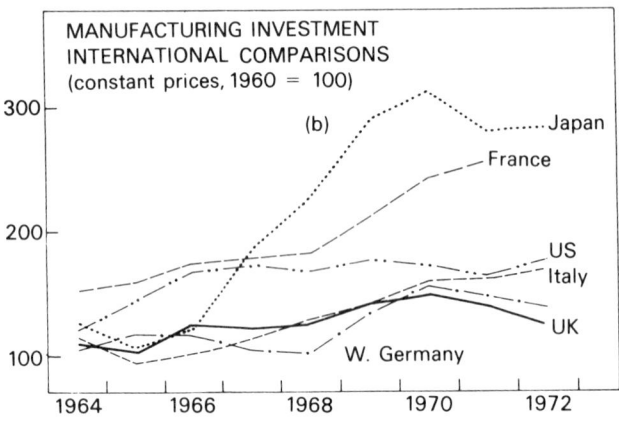

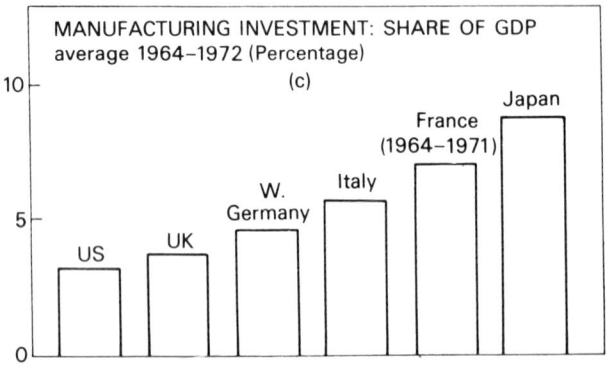

than that of rival countries. On average, throughout the 1950s, Britain invested 16 per cent of the Gross National Product each year. Germany and the Netherlands were investing about 26 per cent of theirs; France, Italy, and Belgium about 20 per cent; and the USA about 18½ per cent. Even when we limit our attention to more recent years, Britain was still investing less than others. On the other hand, the amount she invests in the vital area of 'machinery and equipment' is not so far behind most. Her investment

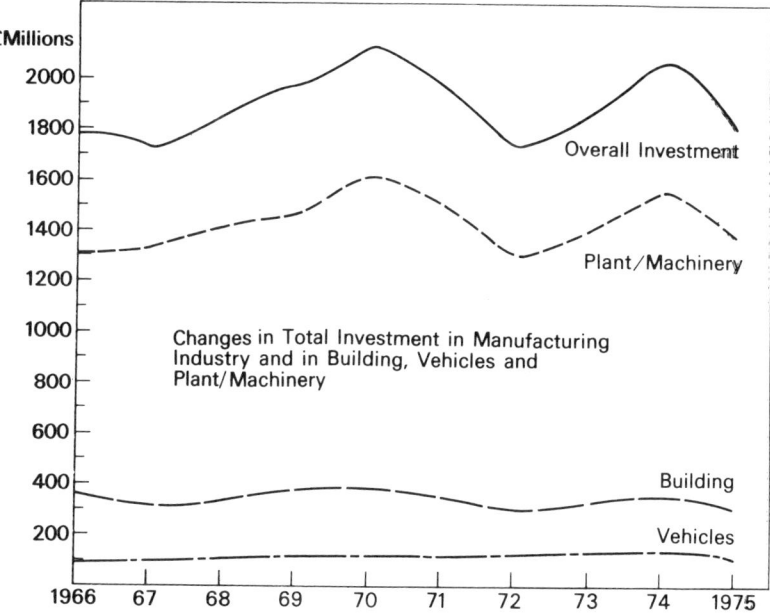

Fig. 7.3. Distribution of investment (by industry) in Britain, 1966–75

programme has been growing each year: in 1957 it was 15 per cent of the GNP, in 1967 it was 18 per cent, and in 1975 it was 22 per cent. Despite an increase of over 20 per cent between 1964 and 1974 in the annual volume of UK manufacturing investment, the actual share of the GNP devoted to manufacturing investment was lower for the United Kingdom than for any other industrialized nation (with the exception of USA).

Of course investment goes into many fields beyond manufacturing industry. Some of it is 'social' investment in new houses and schools. Some goes into transport to build new roads, electrify railway tracks, construct more diesel trains, and so on—a valuable investment, since delay through Britain's

Fig. 7.2. (a) UK manufacturing investment; (b) international comparisons; (c) Manufacturing investment: share of GDP. (Source: *Economic Progress Report*, COI, February 1976)

crowded traffic system adds to the costs of industry. Some is destined for the fuel and power industries; about one-fifth goes into the crucial manufacturing sector. It is, of course, important that the investment be placed carefully: quantity matters but so does quality. Being directed to unprofitable developments would reduce the value of the investment.

Where does this investment come from? It comes from savings. Some people or organizations in the country do not spend all the money they receive, but put some aside, making it available for capital expenditure on factory building, railway development, new power plant, and so on. In Britain today there are three main sources of savings. First, there are public authorities, the central and local governments. They save by collecting more in taxes and rates than they need to pay the everyday costs of the services they provide; the money not spent on these is available for investment. Second, there are business firms: they save by not paying out in dividends all the profit they make. They hold on to some and plough it back into their industry as reinvestment. ('Saving-up' for a few weeks in order to spend the lot on a spree is not the same, of course: such savings are not being made available for investment.) The individual can make his savings available in several ways: by taking up shares in a company himself, i.e., he lends his savings to a business firm which uses them to acquire or extend its basic equipment; or by depositing them with a bank or insurance company—institutions which in turn invest them; or perhaps by putting them into National Savings, i.e., he lends them to the Government, which uses them to advance its own investment programme—roads, hospitals, power stations, and so on. These personal savings are an important source of investment today.

Government finance and the Budget

Earlier we noted that one aspect of Britain's economic problem was the substantial expenditure by the central government which could be a contributory factor in any trend towards inflation. Governments do control the money supply and do have tax-raising powers. It is important therefore to know how the Government does raise and spend such moneys. This is a crucial aspect of economic policy.

Public expenditure has risen very steeply in money terms over the last decade or so. In 1964 total public expenditure was £12 750 million. By 1973 this had risen to almost £32 000 million—almost a threefold rise in nine years. In the next year, 1974–75, public expenditure rose by almost 40 per cent in money terms. If this were the whole story it would be frightening; fortunately, in real terms (i.e., in terms of an actual proportion of national income devoted to public expenditure in relation to all other items) the position is not quite so bad. Nevertheless, in real terms the increase between 1964 and 1974 was around 66 per cent, or a two-thirds increase. There are, however, justifiable reasons for such an increase.

What is the money being spent on and are some sectors spending more

Table 7.2. Public Expenditure, 1974/75. (Source: *Britain 1977: An Official Handbook*, HMSO, 1977)

	£ million
Defence and external relations (UK)	
Defence	4 169
Overseas services	698
Commerce and industry[1]	
Trade, industry and employment	2 626
Agriculture, fisheries and forestry	1 264
Nationalized industries[1]	
Nationalized industries' capital expenditure	2 911
Environmental services[1]	
Housing	4 059
Roads and transport	2 053
Other environmental services	2 036
Law, order and protective services	1 270
Social services[1]	
Social security	6 966
Education and libraries, science and arts	5 871
Health and personal social services	4 719
Other services[1]	
Other public services	588
Common services	547
Northern Ireland[2]	1 099
Total programmes	40 876
Debt interest	3 851
Total	44 727

1. Excluding Northern Ireland.
2. All services shown above except Defence and external relations.

proportionally to others over the years? There is a very wide range of items involved in public expenditure: within this heading comes defence; support to commerce and industry (including support for the regional employment policies we noted earlier in Chapter 4); roads, transport, housing; law and order; the nationalized industries (around 10 per cent of the total is capital expenditure in these industries), and the social services. It should be noted that the local authorities spend around one-third of the total which they receive as grants of various kinds, and the remainder is spent direct by the government agencies.

The changes in share of the total 'cake' are quite revealing. In 1960 social services took around 35 per cent of the total. By 1975 they took about 40 per cent, whereas defence found its share had dropped from 17 per cent to 9 per cent in the same period. Figure 7.4 shows the share taken by the major items of public expenditure.

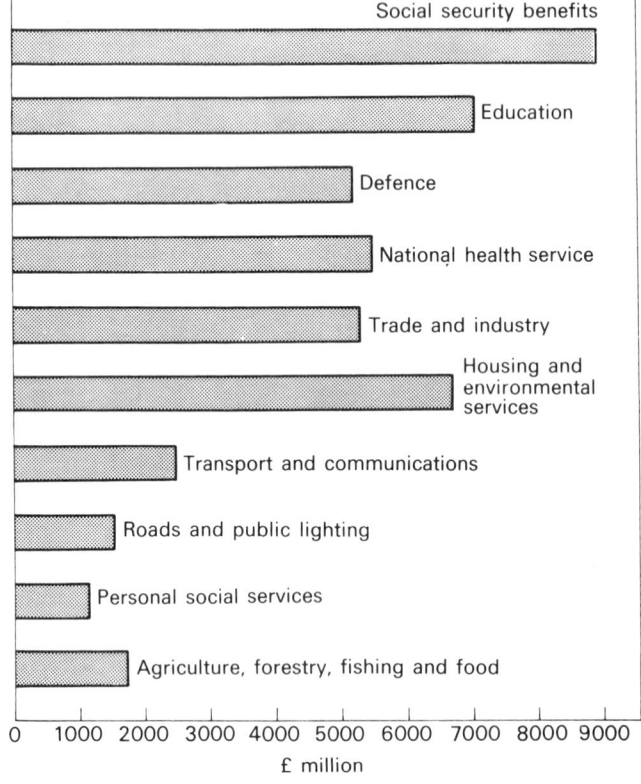

Fig. 7.4. Major items of public expenditure, 1975/76: United Kingdom. (Source: *CSO Annual Abstract of Statistics 1976*, HMSO, 1976)

Because of the variety and scale of things which the Government is expected to do, the amounts of money involved are bound to be vast. It must not be thought, however, that there is no check on such rises in expenditure nor on the actual expenditure itself. The Treasury and the House of Commons and Departments themselves are active on this, as well as the Comptroller and Auditor-General whose function this has been since 1866. Indeed all such expenditure needs to be authorized by Parliament although some, being already settled by special statute, does not come up for review each year (these include payments made direct from the Consolidated Fund, i.e., payments to the Royal Family, salaries and pensions of judges, etc.).

One check on the costs of economic policies at present under way is the annual Public Expenditure Survey, which looks at the whole field of government expenditure and covers five years ahead; thus Ministers can assess the cost of their own department's activities in relation to all other departments over the period of up to five years ahead. The overall economic outlook has to be considered, and amendments to present expenditure plans can be made accordingly.

A second check through the House of Commons Select Committee on Expenditure can lead to special reports which, if critical, can lead to full debates both on actual expenditure and also on economic policies in general.

At departmental level, estimates are prepared each autumn of the needs for the following financial year (i.e., from the next 1 April), and by December these are in the hands of the Treasury, which, if it approves of them, will submit the *Supply Estimates* to Parliament before the Budget (see below). These then form the main source of discussion and debate by the Commons over a period of twenty-nine days (called 'Supply days'), and again broad issues of economic policy can normally be discussed at this time as well as actual valuation of the projected expenditure as outlined in detail in these Estimates. Even after Parliament has approved the Estimates, there is still a fairly strict control by the Treasury over any new items of expenditure not originally authorized.

Thus there are effective instruments for checking on public expenditure which operate at different stages in the process of government finance. In addition to all of these, the House of Commons Public Accounts Committee plays an important role in exposing waste and inefficiency in departments whose submitted accounts seem to indicate a wrongful use of public money.

Nevertheless the total expenditure by government departments still seems to grow and grow in *money* terms as the central government becomes the dominating influence on all aspects of the economy: the Government is responsible for the direct or indirect employment of around half of the total workforce; its influence and power increases with every grant to, and public investment in, an ailing industry; and the growth in efficiency and operation of nationalized industries themselves (the Post Office as an independent corporation operates at a rising profit each year and British Airways is one of the most profitable airlines in the world).

In this situation we have to be concerned not only that we get value for the taxes we pay but also about the whole question of government policy with regard to the financing of its vast expenditure. Much of the expenditure referred to above is paid for by various types of taxes levied on the citizens at some stage or another in our daily lives. The Government gets income from various sources including personal income tax (see Table 7.3). In recent years income tax rates have increased steeply: one estimate in October 1976 indicated that in effect it had doubled in three years, i.e., for the person with an annual average income of £3400, and that the total effect of tax changes in the same period had depressed the standard of living more acutely than had any other factor,

Table 7.3. Taxation and miscellaneous receipts, 1975/76 and 1976/77

	1975/76		1976/77 forecasts	
Taxation	Budget forecast	Outturn	Before Budget changes	After Budget changes
Inland Revenue				
Income tax	14 008	15 068	17 977	17 045
Surtax	85	109	30	30
Corporation tax	2 125	1 987	2 694	2 650
Capital gains tax	325	386	400	400
Estate duty	165	211	70	70
Capital transfer tax	150	116	219	212
Stamp duties	220	282	300	293
Total Inland Revenue	17 078	18 159	21 690	20 700
Customs and Excise				
Value added tax	3 275	3 415	3 875	3 650
Oil	1 550	1 538	1 600	2 025
Tobacco	1 675	1 676	1 760	1 790
Spirits, beer, wine, cider and perry	1 475	1 560	1 705	1 850
Betting and gaming	275	265	295	295
Car tax	170	163	190	190
Other revenue duties	10	9	10	10
Protective duties, etc.	530	507	555	555
Agricultural levies	40	43	60	60
Total Customs and Excise	9 000	9 176	10 050	10 425
Motor vehicle duties	773	781	835	835
Total Taxation	26 851	28 116	32 575	31 960
Miscellaneous Receipts				
Broadcast receiving licences	234	230	237	237
Interest and dividends	145	152	140	140
Other	880	919	860	860
Total	28 110	29 417	33 812	32 197

including inflation. The person responsible for government policy in this is, of course, the Chancellor of the Exchequer, who not only assesses the needs of Britain in terms of overall public expenditure but has—in his Budget—to consider the whole question of how best to increase government revenue to meet the new and growing needs of our society.

Taxation is thus one of the major sources of revenue (or government income). There are three principal sources of taxation revenue: first, the taxes on income; second, taxes on capital, which include transfer tax and capital gains tax; and third, taxes on expenditure (including protective and revenue, VAT, local rates, stamp duties and licence duties (motor vehicles)).

Direct taxation Direct taxes are imposed on the income or property of individuals or companies. Such taxes have the merit of being related to a person's capacity to pay, so that the wealthy pay more, the poor less. A graduated system, whereby the greater a man's income the greater the rate of tax he pays, permits the tax burden to be still more fairly adjusted in proportion to people's capacity to bear it. And since the Government uses the revenue to pay benefits to the poorer sections of society, direct taxation acts as a means whereby some wealth can be redistributed: the rich are paying more in taxation, the poor are receiving more in benefits. The main direct tax, the biggest single source of government revenue, is Income Tax. Every man or

Table 7.4. Yield from direct taxation. (Source: *Britain 1977: An Official Handbook*, HMSO, 1977)

Tax	(£ million)		
	1956/57	1965/66	1975/76
Income tax	2 114	3 678	15 068
Surtax	158	203	109
Profits tax, etc.	200	438	398
Corporation tax	—	—	1 987
Death duties	169	293	211
Capital gains tax	—	—	386
Total	2 641	4 612	18 150

woman enjoying an income, unless it is very small indeed, is liable to pay tax on it. After deducting from a man's income a number of allowances—a personal allowance, one for his wife, children, various expenses—to which he may be entitled, the remainder is taxed at a certain rate. The number of new pence he pays on each pound of his taxable income increases as his taxable income rises. He may even reach the point where his income is so high that he has to pay higher grade tax. Surcharge for investment income, which is a further tax payable in addition to the standard rate. The precise rate of standard income tax may be altered from year to year by the Chancellor of the Exchequer in his Budget proposals.

Companies pay a Corporation Tax, a proportion of their undistributed profits. As their distributed profits are liable to income tax as well, the corporation tax has a twofold motive. It is partly to raise revenue; but it also aims at encouraging firms to distribute less of their profits in the shape of dividends to shareholders, and to put them back into their firm in order to improve its efficiency.

Capital Transfer Tax is levied on the estate or property a person leaves when he or she dies. The rate of the tax increases, just as income tax does, with the value of the estate. If it is very valuable, as much as 80 per cent of it may be taken in tax.

The Capital Gains Tax is imposed on the profits a person may make by selling property or shares whose value has increased since they were purchased. It is essentially aimed at taxing large profits from speculation: it does not apply to the individual selling his house and getting more for it than he originally paid.

Indirect taxation Indirect taxes, or taxes on expenditure, are imposed not on a man's income or wealth but on particular goods or services, e.g., petrol or beer or cigarettes. Unlike direct taxes they are regressive, that is they fall on rich and poor alike. On the other hand, such taxes can be avoided, unlike direct taxation, by not buying the goods or services. In practice this is not easy, unless one is prepared to live a very spartan life. Still, by not drinking, smoking, gambling, going to the pictures, watching television, driving a car, or keeping a dog, a man could avoid paying the taxes each of these involves. For Governments they have the attraction of being less visible and less directly felt. After initial grumbles, people get used to the increased price of petrol, if the Chancellor puts another penny on the gallon in tax. Direct taxes deducted from a man's pay, are more keenly felt and cause more discontent.

Value added tax (VAT) As a result of British membership of the EEC it was agreed that our tax system be adjusted to conform with prevailing practices on the continent in terms of indirect taxation. Thus instead of having revenue duties levied on imports and having purchase tax on internal goods it was decided to convert all into one system where taxes would be levied on the value of the product. Thus the greater the value or basic price of any goods subject to VAT, then the higher the final price. The main instrument to adjust prices is the changing of VAT rate. The Chancellor now has the power to vary rates of VAT by up to 20 per cent between Budgets, and this can be used as a 'regulator' to reflect changes in the economic policies of the Government. VAT is collected at each stage in the production and distribution process, but the final tax (with all the bits of tax incorporated) is passed to the consumer in the final price he pays for the goods or service. The trader or shopkeeper is responsible for paying the Customs and Excise the correct amount of tax for each sale. Some goods have 'zero' rating—most types of food, books and periodicals come into this category; also included in this are exports, buildings, clothing, footwear, drugs and medicines. There is a standard rate of 8 per cent for many goods but the higher rate of 25 per cent applies to television sets, hi-fis and electrical equipment, boats, aircraft, caravans, cameras, etc.—all items where there is no essential need for the product as contrasted with basics like food, and so on.

Indirect taxes, however, do require more frequent adjustment. Direct taxes, being tied to incomes, automatically produce a greater yield as incomes rise. Indirect taxes are tied to quantity not price—so much on a pint of beer. Though prices may rise for a variety of reasons, the yield from indirect taxes may soon lag behind these price rises. Unless the consumption of an item increases rapidly, the Government must put up the tax to increase the yield. Again, while direct tax falls on the whole of a person's income, expenditure taxes do not fall on the whole of his spending. Important items, notably food, are not taxed. This again helps explain why the yield of indirect taxes tends to rise more slowly than that of direct taxes and to require more frequent adjustment.

The most profitable indirect tax to the Government is that on tobacco. The tax on petrol is not far behind—is indeed ahead when other motor duties, such as the car licence, are added. The tax on alcohol in its various forms is another useful source of government income.

The Budget

The proposals for changes in taxation to produce the revenue required are presented annually to Parliament by the Chancellor of the Exchequer in the Budget. In one sense, then, the Budget is a simple financial statement: 'So much money is required, this is how we propose to raise it.' But the days when the Budget was just a statement of this kind are long past. People expect the Government to play a big part in the social and economic prosperity of the country. The Budget is one of its main instruments here: it is a social and economic statement as well as a financial one. When we ask nowadays of some tax change 'Why has the Chancellor done that?' we are rarely satisfied with the answer 'Because he wants the money': we are looking for some additional purpose behind the measure.

Thus the Budget can operate as an instrument of social policy. Income tax, as a highly progressive tax, can be utilized to redistribute income. Even indirect taxes, regressive though they are, can be shaped with an eye to their social impact. Even in a tough Budget, the Chancellor selects his tax changes so that they fall less heavily on those less able to bear the extra burdens.

The use of the Budget as a means of regulating the country's economy is a much more recent development. The mere fact that government expenditure is so large makes it one of the leading influences on the economy in general. The Chancellor has always to ask himself what effects the sums he raises and the ways in which he does so are likely to have on different parts of the economy.

The Treasury is dealing in vast amounts of money. Where the Chancellor gets them from (and how) is bound to affect economic activity. Hence he has to examine the way in which the economy is developing: what is happening to production, to exports, to imports, to the Balance of Payments, whether domestic demand is rising or falling, whether investment is lagging, whether the rate of unemployment is rising. He wants to encourage growth and so he will try to raise his revenue in such a way that it produces the desired effects on that part of the economic scene which requires attention. If, for instance, unemployment is rising he might reduce taxation so as to put more money into circulation, encourage the demand for goods, and so check the unemployment rise. If government expenditure were kept up at the same time, this would reinforce the effect. Conversely if the demand for goods is high, and prices rising rapidly, and the domestic market swallowing up too many items to the detriment of exports, then the Chancellor could raise taxes thus taking money out of circulation, and putting goods beyond the reach of individuals and so freeing more for export. If at the same time government spending is cut there would be still less money available. Whereas special rebates for articles exported could stimulate activity in this sector.

The Corporation Tax was not devised as a mere money raiser. It is intended to encourage investment by treating more favourably profits which are invested than those which are distributed.

There are many ways in which the Budget may be used as an economic instrument according to what the Government thinks are the needs of the economy.

The National Debt

The National Debt is the money Governments have borrowed in the past, especially in wartime. Its total is about equal to one year's total government expenditure, and the Government has to pay interest on this every year to those who loaned them the money, e.g., depositors in Post Office Savings Accounts, investors in British Airways stock. This interest now accounts for well over 10 per cent of government expenditure.

Despite all the checks on spending not only does expenditure rise but it is a constant subject of debate and dispute, especially as it is rising (in both money and real terms) and taxation has to rise along with it. Critics complain that Government keeps exhorting people to save, and, by increasing taxes, leaves them with less to spend; yet its own spending continues to soar. Many direct these attacks on particular items of expenditure. Some feel that defence costs could be cut even further without endangering the nation's security. Others focus attention on the social services: they claim that more selectivity in distributing benefits, more scope for private provision by those who are able to make this, would keep down taxation, and be socially desirable without lowering the quality of the social services for those who really need them. The level of taxation is a constant subject of complaint.

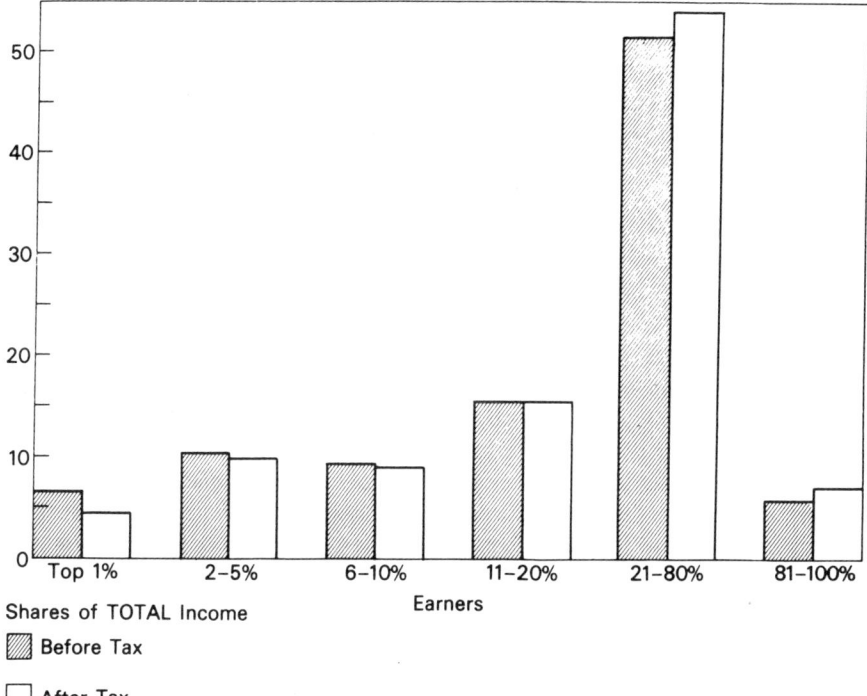

Fig. 7.5. Distribution of personal income in the UK before and after tax, 1976

Taxation is no doubt high; it may be so high for certain individuals that it reduces their incentive to work. But the popular notion that Britain is the most highly taxed country in the world is a misconception (see Table 7.5). Moreover, while government spending is rising, the increase is partly explained by rising

Table 7.5. Proportion of personal income paid in direct taxes and social security contributions: comparison of industrial nations

Country	Percentage of taxation
Sweden	34·4
West Germany	27·8
UK	21·5
Canada	20·1
France	19·8
USA	19·3
Australia	15·9
Japan	10·8[1]

[1] The figure from Japan is for 1970, the other figures are for 1974.

prices. The rise in the Estimates over recent years is less when this is allowed for.

Attempts are made to hold down the rate of increase. Since 1973 the position has worsened because of three new features of the economy. First, the quadrupling of oil prices by Arab oil producers in late 1973 affected the costs of industry and government alike, and pushed prices up for all kinds of goods and services. Secondly, the subsequent inflationary spiral which developed in 1974-75-76 (reaching a rate of inflation of 28 per cent per year in 1975) destroyed all previous bases for controlling expenditure. Thirdly, the high unemployment of 1975-76 led to a steep rise in government expenditure to support regional policies as well as injecting money into ailing industries (massive sums to British Leyland and Chrysler UK in 1975).

Everyone is now very conscious of the dangers of overspending. The Social Contract with the Stages I and II of the Government's pay policy accepted by industry and trade unions alike in two successive years (1975-77) led to a more concerted public scrutiny of all aspects of not only public expenditure but also pricing policies as applied to both the public and private sectors. People now realize the links between costs and prices, and there has been for some time a developing debate on the most effective ways (in real terms) of providing a stable or growing standard of living for as many of our citizens as possible.

The major political parties differ in their views as to how to achieve improvements in social provisions—education, medical services, hospitals, housing, roads, etc. All such items require more expenditure. The question is: Who is to pay? Inevitably the scale of capital expenditure on some items like roads, schools, and hospitals demands public provision. All agree that the needs are there and the parties also agree that some of the costs must come from the public purse. Even such limited agreement implies increased public expenditure no matter which party is in power. The level of public expenditure seems an inevitable bone of contention among political parties but also a pretty inescapable burden for the British taxpayer in the years to come. Most people want improvements in the social services. For these we, as a society, shall have to pay an increasing proportion of our resources. What we require is a regular and sustained growth in our National Income and in our stock of assets, which we usually call the National Wealth.

Government influence on economic growth

Recent years have seen the growing intervention by Government in improving the speed with which national wealth increases. Government has an interest in faster growth if only because it is expected to be concerned with so many things which themselves affect growth and are affected by it: getting the Balance of Payments rights, securing full employment, checking inflation. In the case of the first, as we have seen, the customary policies of restricting demand by monetary and fiscal measure has proved no more than temporary stopgaps; they provide no lasting solution and discourage the growth of the economy. A concentrated effort on achieving a rapid growth might work better. In any case, as we have seen, Government is now the biggest single factor in the national economy. It controls, through the nationalized industries, a huge slice of Britain's industry. Investment in these is bigger than the investment of all private industry. It is far and away the biggest spender in the country. Consequently, its decisions on investment, on expenditure, on taxation affect the plans and performance of all other parts of the economy. Government is vitally involved in economic growth. It must aim to encourage it and do what it can to promote it.

In the 1960s not everyone agreed that such involvement meant that Government should intervene still further, assuming a bigger responsibility for the economy than it already possessed. They pointed to the United States, which could outproduce almost any country in almost anything, and Japan, whose record of growth was outstanding, as countries which did not practise national planning for economic growth. Give private enterprise more encouragement and less restriction was the critics' formula for growth. Others, including the Labour Government, thought that a more deliberate effort to forecast possibilities and anticipate problems by cooperation under government sponsorship, made better sense.

Accordingly, between 1962 and 1976 Governments took a number of steps to oversee the developments in the economy. In 1962 the National Economical Development Council was set up with the proposed aim of bringing together Government, industrialists and the trade unions to discuss the most effective ways of developing government planning policies. Each industry, it was realized, had problems specific to that industry, and through the establishment of different NEDCs ('Neddies') for each major industry a clear effort was made to bring the planning of government policies down to 'shop-floor' level—identifying the problems hampering increases in production, finding ways of overcoming such problems, and persuading the people concerned to act together to solve them.

Despite the failure of a fairly ambitious National Plan in 1965 which tried to set targets for production right across the economy the basic idea of overall targets and productivity drives had even then taken root in the establishment of the Ministry of Technology, with a responsibility for encouraging innovations in industry and, through research, locating the best growth points in the field of electronics, computers, and telecommunications. Many useful inventions and developments have received its support.

To improve the potential of the individual workers effective training is essential. The Industrial Training Act of 1964 had set out to ensure better training through a system of Industrial Training Boards—one for each industry providing firms (through a levy) with incentives for better training schemes. These measures were later strengthened through injections of over £5 million between 1975 and 1977 for programmes of retraining under the Training Services Agency (TSA) to alleviate the heavy unemployment of that period.

Government also recognized that, as we have already seen, one way whereby firms could often improve their efficiency was by amalgamation in order to achieve the economies which can accompany large-scale operation. This was the object behind the introduction, in 1966, of the Industrial Reorganization Corporation. Its task was to help bring about the mergers of firms whenever this promised to lead to greater efficiency. It was empowered to advance money if need be to assist such mergers.

Planning and intervention extended to the regional as well as national level. A system of regional councils and boards was introduced in 1965 to encourage a fuller use of the resources of each region. They compiled surveys of their regional resources, drafted plans to make better use of them, and advised on how their own region fits in with national plans. They were merely advisory bodies, but their studies provided a more thorough knowledge of local resources as well as stimulating plans for improving their regions.

In addition, however, there were frequent attempts between 1974 and 1976 to offer selective assistance to industry on not just a regional level but on a selective industrial level, e.g., in July 1975 £20 million was granted for the modernization of the clothing industry, in August 1975 £25 million for ferrous foundries and £20 million for machine tools. In 1976 in a climate of heavy unemployment the National Enterprise Board (under Lord Ryder, whose task is to stimulate industry through direct involvement with government money and resources) discussed with the machine tool industry the possibility of a stockpiling policy to prepare for economic recovery—finance to be available from the Board. All of these instances reflect the growing involvement of Government in the effective running of industry.

The need to restrain inflation

One phenomenon in postwar Britain has gone far to limit these advances —inflation. This is a continuing decline in the purchasing power of money. The most obvious sign of inflation is a continuing rise in prices: the same amount of notes or coins buys fewer goods or services. Britain's experience of this process is apparent from Table 7.6. It shows the rise year by year of retail prices.

There are a number of ways in which this state of affairs can come about, but two are of particular importance. One comes from an increase in the demand for goods bigger than the output can satisfy, so that the price tends to rise as people clamour for them. This is inflation stemming from demand. The second, cost inflation, has the opposite cause. For whatever reason, the cost of producing particular goods goes up and the manufacturer, to recoup his extra costs, puts up the selling price. It may be, for instance, that the cost of some imported raw material, vital in his production, has increased: there were cases of this after the outbreak of the Korean War in 1950, and in 1956 after the Suez crisis and after the more recent oil price increases. Until that oil price rise of 1973, a more common reason for increased production costs in recent years has been increases people have achieved in their incomes without any corresponding increase in their output, so that production costs have risen and the manufacturer has had to pass this on in the shape of higher selling prices. What the Arab-influenced oil price rises did was to accentuate the trend overnight.

Table 7.6. Movement of prices in the United Kingdom, 1966 to mid-1976 (1972 = 100) (Source: *CSO Social Trends*, HMSO, 1976)

Year	Retail prices
1966	60·7
1967	73·1
1974	108·5
1975	134·8
1976	156·3

The policy of full employment since the Second World War has aided this inflationary trend. With labour in short supply, trade union bargaining power increased; they found it easier to negotiate higher rates of pay. Indeed, even the officially agreed rates were often lower than actual earnings. Agreements on the factory floor enabled workers to secure a still better deal from employers loath to face a strike or loss of labour. The increased costs of production, through higher official wage rates plus this 'wage drift', were passed on to the buying public. This in turn led to a further upward twist. The buying public, in their capacity as workers who had not had their incomes raised, pointed to the rising cost of living and claimed that their own earnings be raised to match this. Unless these income gains were accompanied by increases in output then prices continued to go up. Indeed, since there was often much more purchasing power in the community without a corresponding increase in goods and services, the increased demand for goods encouraged prices to rise.

Figure 7.6 shows how Britain's total output grew by about $2\frac{1}{2}$ per cent a year up till 1973, but over the period 1971–75 money incomes (wages, salaries, and profits) rose more steeply by about 6 per cent a year. Since 1948 productivity has grown and output still more, but the increase in wage costs was far greater than either.

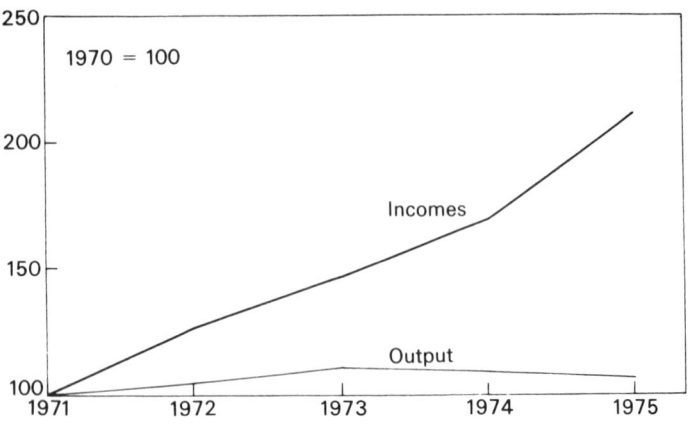

Fig. 7.6. Incomes and output in the United Kingdom, 1970–75

Inflation has serious effects. Members of strong trade unions who can insist successfully on wages increases may be all right: they can keep their incomes moving up, perhaps ahead of rising prices. Even so, the increases they gain are less valuable if higher prices gobble them up: a doubling of the money in the paypacket is no real gain if the prices of the things that the money will buy have also doubled. But many people are not in strong trade unions, and some, like old age pensioners, receive fixed incomes. These suffer great hardship from inflation: prices keep rising but their income does not go up nearly so fast. Indeed since 1972 the pace of inflation accelerated rapidly. Reasons, as we saw, were complex but the trigger was the sharp rise in oil prices in October 1973. Figure 7.7 shows how within four years the price level almost doubled; despite wage rates increasing at around an average of 30 per cent per annum 1972–75, real wages remained the same and those people on fixed incomes suffered again. By late 1977, government action through a fairly effective prices and wages policy had restrained inflation to a lower rate of 13 per cent—still two and a half times that of West Germany and twice that of the United States. The prospects of reduction of the inflation rate to below 10 per cent per year are still in doubt.

On exports the effect of inflation can be severe. If the prices of British goods rise, it is easier for foreign producers of similar articles to undersell Britain. It is true, of course, that they too feel the effects of inflation; but it is not always as marked as in Britain, so this is little consolation. Inflation then adds to the difficulty of solving the Balance of Payments problems. And should British goods price themselves out of a foreign market, this could have the further effect of shrinking the British industries producing these goods.

Inflation can also react on savings and so on the investment coming from them. The point here is that people, discouraged by the way in which the value

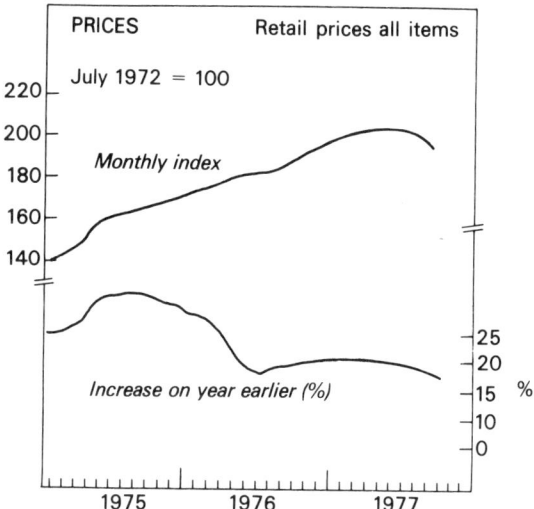

Fig. 7.7. Index of retail prices. (Source: *Economic Progress Report*, No. 83, COI, February 1977)

of money falls year by year, may decide that the sensible thing is to spend it before it depreciates further; or to invest it in items such as jewellery or pictures rather than in stocks and shares producing only a small rate of interest made smaller still by the declining value of money.

Hopefully, and assuming no further oil price 'explosion', we could avoid inflation and its consequences if we ensured that any increase in earnings is matched by an increase in productivity. This is precisely what Governments have been attempting to do. Fully aware that British prosperity depends on the prosperity of industry, particularly of manufacturing industry (giving 30 per cent of our total output and 80 per cent of our visible exports) the Government sees inflation as preventing industrial regeneration and improved exports. Inflation has to be accepted as the main enemy and destroyed—even where it might mean some restriction on ideas of free wage bargaining accepted hitherto as basic freedoms of our society. For then there would be no shortage of supply and excess of demand; the two would keep in step, and prices could remain stable. If productivity is increased, a wage increase can really mean a higher standard of living without any of those inflationary effects. More efficient production means cheaper production. The employer could therefore increase wages out of the savings this has brought, and would not have to pass the cost on to the buyers. Employees would get more money, the employer still gets his profit, the purchaser still gets the article at the previous price—perhaps at a lower price. The bigger paypacket really would buy more goods, the person on a fixed income would not be hurt, and prices abroad would remain competitive.

Government's normal way of trying to cope with inflation has been to reduce, by using monetary or fiscal measures, the purchasing power and thus lessen the pressure of demand. For instance, they have increased Minimum Lending Rate, put up VAT, budgeted for a surplus, i.e., raised more in taxes than is needed to meet expenditure, thus removing some purchasing power. As recently as 1976 tough deflationary Budgets cut Government's own spending schemes as well and held back still more money which would otherwise have gone to increase the pressure from demand. These methods were aimed at producing a quick deflation. Unfortunately, they also meant increased unemployment, though one school of thought argued that a higher normal level of unemployment was the best way to insure against continuous inflation. Not only so, such measures defeated any attempts to increase the rate of growth of national production.

In the 1960s a more direct attack on inflation was attempted through measures to restrain the growth of incomes beyond increases in output which accompanied them. The argument was that if the extra wages bill were matched by bigger output, there would be no increase in production costs and hence no need for increased prices; while the increased demand represented by higher wages would be readily accommodated since output also would have gone up. Government stressed that this was not a policy of preventing wage increases. On the contrary, it would ensure that a wage rise really was fully worth while, not eaten away by rising prices. It would mean a genuine increase in the wage-earner's standard of living.

Although the 1960s saw the development of several moves in this direction, e.g., the National Board for Prices and Incomes in 1965, which assessed the justifications made for price and wage increases (in some fifty or so industries reports were issued—car batteries, television rentals, nurses' pay, etc.), the basic assumption that this body (now defunct) made was that national output would increase by around $3\frac{1}{2}$ per cent per year and that wage increases would not exceed this. (There would be exceptions for those regarded as poorly paid.) Even so, such an assumption failed to hold after the disastrous increase in foreign oil import prices of October 1973 which, as we saw already, set in motion a rapid inflationary cycle leading to a complete reassessment of prices and incomes. Although it had already taken powers in 1966 and later under Prices and Incomes Acts to hold up wage settlements which appeared to exceed the norm set, the Government was faced during 1974–76 with a new situation.

Inflation, as we have seen, harms the individual on a fixed income, but we also saw that it could, and did, harm the mass of the working people. Since 1973 despite massive wage increases the real value of the 'take-home' pay of many workers has declined. Although all Western nations suffered the inflation caused initially by these oil price increases, not all the countries suffered equally. Since Britain is a trading nation dependent on selling her goods abroad it is essential that the prices of British goods are not rising any higher or faster than those of her immediate competitors. Unfortunately this is what has happened. Britain's inflation has led to rises in consumer (and inevitably export) prices far higher than those of Italy, France, or Japan, and over three times the rates of our close competitor—West Germany.

Strenuous efforts have been made by the Government to control both prices and wages, e.g., as from 1 August 1975 the ceiling for wage increases for one year ahead was set at £6 per week, and even then anyone earning over £8500 was debarred from receiving any increase at all. In addition, the White Paper 'Attack on Inflation' applied strict price controls including a veto on any attempt to pass on more than the agreed wage increase to the consumer in higher prices. The whole range of government policies is now being pursued to defeat inflation. In Phase II of the Pay Policy, i.e., for the year 1976–77 the Government agreed an average rise of $4\frac{1}{2}$ per cent in wages (£2·50 minimum to £4·00 maximum) with 5 per cent for those earning between £50 and £80 per week.

With the agreement of the TUC the Government pursued a policy aimed at bringing inflation down to under 10 per cent in 1977. Despite the high unemployment caused by a worldwide cutback in trade and the expectation that this would bring about lower price levels, success in this area has not yet been achieved.

The trade unions in spite of their cooperation are inevitably suspicious of any government move to cut the real living standards of their members. They suspect that employers are not having profits cut or restricted as tightly as are the workers who have to abide by pay restrictions. Trade unions remember the miners' strike of 1972–73 which caused havoc to the economy but which gave miners a substantial rise in pay during a period of overall pay restraint. No one wants to go back to that or to the power workers' strike—the cost to the country of these was serious. Nevertheless by 1976 there was a feeling among working people that unless 'pay restraint' as a policy could be shown to be fair to both sides of industry, and could be seen to be maintaining a high level of employment, there would be extreme reluctance on the part of trade union members to commit themselves to a permanent policy of government control over wage bargaining. And the feeling has been shared by many employers who, while agreeing the need for wage and price restraint, want to encourage a competitive spirit between the profitable industries and the less profitable firms who are able to keep going only because they do not require to pay the wage increases which would immediately reveal their financial weakness.

Increasing prosperity

From all this we can see the main requirements if Britain is to prosper: first, a continuing growth in exports to enable the food for her people and the materials for her industries to be bought from abroad; second, increases in the amount of production to make more goods available for the export and the home markets, and in the efficiency of production to keep down the costs and so keep down the prices of these increasing quantities of goods. Third, a high rate of investment (and the savings from which this must come) is needed to keep the basic equipment of production expanding and up to date—the essential need if output and productivity are to increase—and, fourth, a stable price level to prevent the gains made being cancelled out by inflation.

Given these things, prosperity is possible. Expanding industries ensure jobs for all. Higher productivity means a bigger quantity of goods available for all, without excessive increases in price; and it would enable higher wages to be earned without inflation—more goods available and higher earnings so that people could acquire more of them. In other words, the standard of living could rise.

But it is easier to list the requirements than to fulfil them: one has only to consider the fate of the National Plan and the difficulties of the Prices and Incomes policy. The material wealth and standard of living have increased but more slowly than they might have done. It is, however, reasonable to remind ourselves that Britain is a fairly wealthy country and is among the top ten of the world's wealthy countries if we take wealth per head as an index of such prosperity. Our main aim now should be to promote our industrial and commercial efficiency so that we can earn the export orders and thus develop our country so that all may enjoy a higher living standard—at home and abroad.

Again we must remember our international role. Only through being prosperous could Britain give more help to developing nations. And to become efficient and prosperous requires skills of production and trading which earn the respect and confidence of our trading partners—and competitors.

8. Social welfare and the citizen

The Welfare State

Britain's system of social services might be described as the community's endeavour to see that no individual is a victim of any of the five great scourges which marked our society in earlier days. These scourges were listed by Sir William Beveridge as want, disease, squalor, ignorance and idleness. The Beveridge Plan (1944) suggested ways of overcoming them, and it laid the foundations of the postwar Welfare State. Legislation putting the Beveridge Plan into effect was passed after the Second World War, and this forms the main basis of the present Welfare State: National Insurance, family allowances, supplementary benefits, and the National Health Service.

Attack on poverty

The efforts on all these fronts are important, but the most prominent has been the attack on want or poverty. This is the great misfortune which even in wealthy nineteenth-century Britain afflicted many people. Moreover, earning good wages cast its own shadow; for there was no security against distress should earnings cease. What Britain hopes to do in her Welfare State is to provide social security. Ideally, the citizen is guaranteed a minimum income sufficient to ensure decent comfort whatever the circumstances: at all events, a minimum which ensures basic subsistence. It is a noble ideal, civilized and humane, even if, in practice, the Welfare State often seems to fall short of it.

Experience and enquiries, especially from the late nineteenth century onwards, revealed that there were a number of circumstances which would reduce a family from decent comfort to poverty. The income of the wage earner might stop suddenly through unemployment, or sickness, or old age. His earnings might not be enough to support the burden of a large family. He might die, leaving a widow and children to struggle along. Sudden heavy expenses—for example, a birth or death in the family—might put too big a strain on income. The Welfare State has set up a system of benefits and services to help people when they find themselves in such circumstances. The idea is not so much to relieve people who have fallen into poverty, but to prevent their falling into it at all by giving assistance at the critical period. Moreover, this assistance is not considered as charity but as the right of the citizen. To emphasize this, it is partly given on the strength of weekly payments by the citizen while he is in regular employment.

National Insurance

These payments form the basis of the 'contributory principle' of the National Insurance Act (1946). To receive benefits, it is necessary to pay contributions. Beveridge considered that this contributory principle was of great psychological value: people drawing benefit did not feel they were accepting charity, even if the contributions they paid were much less than the benefits they received. Nevertheless, as we shall see later, there are also non-contributory benefits available in the Welfare State.

Every working person in Britain has to pay a fixed weekly contribution to the National Insurance Fund. The amount of the contribution varies according to whether the contributor is employed, self-employed, or non-employed. Most workers come in the first category, and in their case the employer also has to pay a weekly contribution on their behalf. He sees to the payment of his employees' contributions, which he deducts from the wages or salary paid.

In return for this weekly contribution, the worker is entitled to a variety of benefits. Should he lose his job, he is entitled to unemployment benefit. If his earnings are interrupted by sickness, he is entitled to a similar weekly sum. When he retires from work altogether, he receives a pension of much the same order. There are other benefits. If the wage earner dies his widow receives a special benefit payment followed by a weekly pension for the rest of her life. There are special death grants to assist with the expenses of a funeral. Likewise, there are special maternity grants to help cover a happier but equally expensive episode in a family's life.

Hence, in return for a weekly contribution, a family is assured of some financial aid in those critical periods which investigations have shown are the most likely to push people down into dire want.

It is not strictly an insurance scheme. If it were, all benefits would be paid out of the proceeds of the contributions. The insurance fund is not sufficient to do this. Benefits paid out always exceed contributions. The difference is made up out of general government revenue, i.e., out of the revenue derived from national taxation.

Until 1961, contributions and benefits were on a 'flat rate' basis, that is, they did not vary according to earnings. In that year, graduated contributions for pensions were introduced, with those earning more paying a higher contribution. In return, these people were entitled to a higher benefit. In 1966, this principle was extended to unemployment and sickness benefits, and in 1975 to maternity allowances. Since 1975, the graduated pension scheme has ceased to operate, and now all contributions and benefits are 'earnings related'. A percentage of the wage is paid in contribution to National Insurance, and benefits are paid according to a formula which includes a flat rate and an earnings-related supplement. There are also additional benefits for dependants (for example, wife and children).

Child benefits, family income supplement, and supplementary benefits

Social insurance alone, as Beveridge saw, could not completely abolish want. There are men whose earnings are not cut off by unemployment or illness, but whose incomes are constantly depleted by the burden of bringing up a large family. There are people whose needs cannot be met by their insurance benefits. Persistent ill-health cannot be adequately met by sickness payments; it is a medical problem and demands a medical solution, not cash payments. Finally, social insurance can work only if the unemployment rate is low. Benefits can tide people over a short spell out of work, but mass unemployment with millions drawing benefits and needing aid for years on end would disrupt any insurance scheme. Britain's social security system tries to provide against these things as well as against loss of earnings.

The object of the Family Allowances Act (1945) was to see that children in large families do not go short of essentials. The Act aimed to ease the strain by providing for weekly allowances to every family with two or more children. These allowances were originally 40p a week for the second child, and 50p for each additional child. In April 1977 family allowances were replaced by 'child benefits', which now include the first child. The rate is £1 per week for the first or only child and £1·50 for the second and subsequent children.

This is not an insurance scheme. Payments are made from government funds, i.e., they come out of taxes, not out of contributions. They are paid to all families, no matter what their income. Family Income Supplement is also paid to families with small incomes.

The National Assistance Act (1948) was meant to help cases of special hardship. For most people insurance benefits are sufficient, but not for the handicapped, the crippled, the blind, or the homeless. There are those whose needs are such that their pension or unemployment benefit is insufficient to keep them out of poverty. National assistance was introduced as a kind of safety-net to support those people who are not held up by the National Insurance scheme. Like family allowances, this was not an insurance scheme. To get assistance someone had only to show that he or she needed it.

Under the pressure of inflation and rising prices, pensions and unemployment benefits were often inadequate, so that by the 1960s over two million people were applying for national assistance to make up the difference. Moreover, enquiries established that even more were entitled to do so, especially old age pensioners, but did not claim assistance either because they did not know how to set about it or felt there was something shameful about asking for 'assistance'. Nor were the assistance rates, despite increases, themselves always adequate.

A new Social Security Act in 1966 made an attempt to deal with the problem. National assistance was abandoned and replaced by a system of supplementary benefits or allowances. A new body, the Supplementary Benefits Commission, set up inside the Department of Health and Social

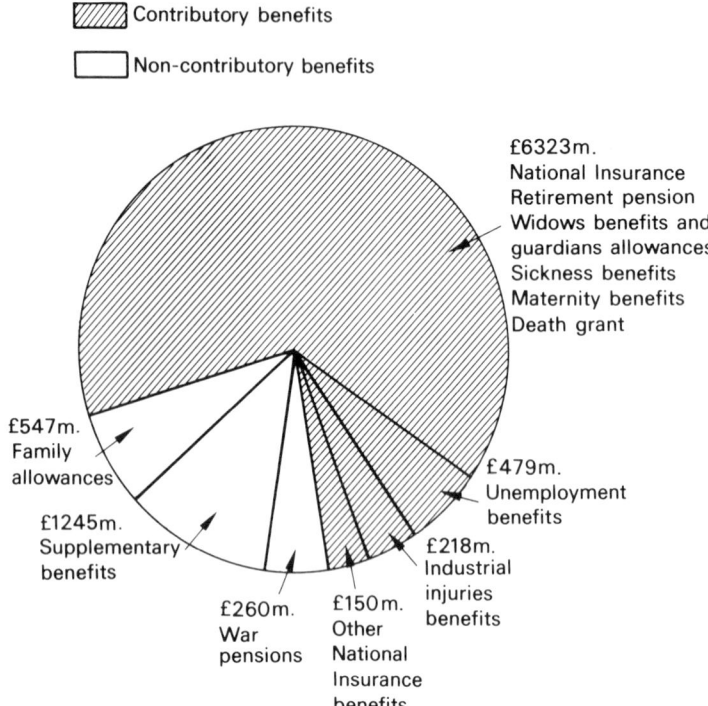

Fig. 8.1. Expenditure on social security benefits, 1975/76 (total value of payments: £9222 million). (Source: *CSO Annual Abstract of Statistics* 1976, HMSO, 1976)

Security, took over responsibility for administering the scheme. The moves were partly to simplify procedure by reducing the variety of authorities involved. These had often proved bewildering to applicants for assistance. The change of name from national assistance, and the provision of allowances through the same department which operates the insurance scheme, signifies more than administrative convenience. It removes some of the stigma which the name national assistance, and its administration through a separate body, aroused in sensitive people.

The scale and cost of social security schemes is very great. It is the largest single item of public expenditure, and amounted to £9222 million in 1975, or one-sixth of the total. Figure 8.1 shows how this sum was distributed among the main benefits and allowances.

National Health Service

The connection between the National Health Service and the problem of poverty may not seem very obvious, but it is important. Good medical services are as vital as good food in keeping up physical strength, but they are more likely to be neglected by people who are hard pressed for money. Illness prolonged for want of early attention can keep a person off work for a long spell, thus interrupting his earnings and depressing his standard of living. And doctors' bills and expensive drugs soon exhaust the savings of an average family. For such reasons Beveridge insisted that a free, comprehensive medical service, providing the best medical attention for all who needed it, was an essential part of a social security system.

The NHS: finance and organization

The National Health Service is not an insurance scheme. A small part of our weekly contributions to National Insurance does go to help pay for the Health Service, but this covers only about 10 per cent of the costs. Another 4 per cent comes from charges made for some parts of the Service and from rates imposed by the local authorities to help pay for the parts of the Service they administer. But about three-quarters of the total cost is paid for by the Government out of money raised through taxation. The service is open to any resident in this country, whether he or she pays National Insurance or not. It is not compulsory, but in fact nearly all doctors have joined it and nearly all the population uses it.

The Health Ministers (the Secretary of State for Social Services in England, and the Secretaries of State for Scotland and Wales) are responsible for the operation of the Service as a whole, and to assist them they have the advice of the Central Health Services Council (England and Wales) and the Scottish Health Service Planning Council. Since 1974 the Health Service has been organized on the basis of health authorities (England and Wales), or health boards (Scotland), general practitioner and dentist services, hospitals, and community medicine. Before 1974, these three branches of the health provision were administered separately.

The public is represented on health councils, which, although not elected, act as a channel of communication between the health authorities and the public, and report on questions concerning the Health Service in their area.

General medical treatment is provided by doctors who are responsible to the family practitioner committees of the area health authorities/boards. From the

Scotland

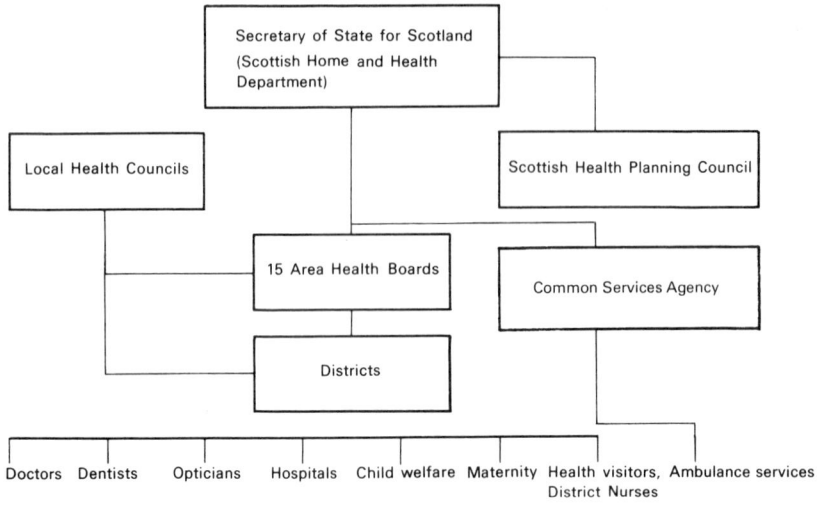

England and Wales

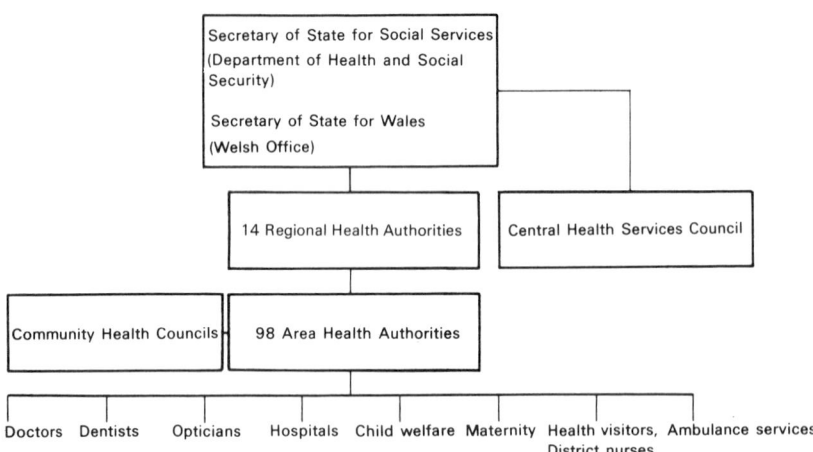

Fig. 8.2. Organization of the National Health Service

list of doctors, the patient is free to pick the one he wants to attend him. The doctor, in turn, has the right to refuse to accept a person on his list of patients. He is paid by the Government according to the number of patients on his list. The patient pays nothing for the doctor's services, no matter how often he makes use of them.

At first there was no charge for prescriptions either, but a small fee was introduced in 1952, and this has been raised several times since. This was partly to keep down expenditure which was proving higher than had been anticipated, and partly to permit more to be spent on other parts of the Health Service. The charge by no means represented the full cost of the drugs and medicines prescribed and was easily borne by most people. Many disapproved nevertheless. They saw it as a retreat from the original idea of a free medical service, and feared that the charges would be a serious burden to poorer people in bad health. Thus the very people who most needed the Service would be discouraged from using it. The Labour Government, who felt this most strongly, abolished the charges in 1964. In 1968, however, they were reluctantly obliged to reintroduce charges as part of their programme to keep public expenditure down during the economic difficulties.

The teeth and eyesight services, which were also free at first, were swamped with demands for false teeth and spectacles. This was largely because many people in Britain had long needed, but never had, optical and dental treatment. But it was felt that some were abusing the services, getting spectacles because they were free, not because they really needed them. To discourage such abuses, charges were brought in in 1951, so that now people have to pay part of the cost of dental treatment and spectacles. Again, the patient still gets a bargain, but it is believed that some who really need attention are deterred by the cost.

Second, the Health Service provides hospital and specialist treatment. Until 1945 Britain's 3000 hospitals were run by hundreds of different bodies. People using them had to pay, though there were Poor Law institutions giving free treatment and many others had special schemes under which cheap treatment was available. A bigger drawback than the costliness of hospitals was their dependence on voluntary contributions from private subscribers. These were often insufficient to meet the growing costs of running the hospitals. They would certainly have been inadequate to pay for the restoration of buildings after the Second World War, or for the costly new equipment and appliances that had been developed in wartime. By the Act, therefore, hospitals were taken over from these private bodies and put under the control of Health Ministers. It is their duty to see that hospital accommodation and treatment, including the services of all kinds of medical specialists, are available free for all who need them. Hospitals, like the other health services, come under the administration of the health authorities and boards. There are fourteen regional health authorities and ninety area health authorities in England, eight area health authorities in Wales, and fifteen health boards in Scotland. These are far fewer in number than the old regional hospital boards and hospital management committees, and doctors often complain of distant authority. At the same time, however, it is now easier to relate one part of the Health Service to another.

For example, the Health Service now includes the former local authority services such as district nurses, midwives, and health visitors. It also runs the

Table 8.1. Public expenditure on the National Health Service: United Kingdom. (Source: *Facts in Focus*, 3rd edn, Penguin, 1975)

	£ million		
	1964/65	1969/70	1974/75
Current expenditure			
Central government			
Family practitioner services:			
General medical	95	148	256
Pharmaceutical	133	204	383
General dental	68	92	185
General ophthalmic	20	28	42
Administration	6	11	16
Hospital and community health services:[1]			
Hospital running expenses	638	964	2758
Administration and other expenses	37	112	119
less payments by patients:			
Hospital services	−8	−11	−25
Pharmaceutical services	−25	−19	−27
Dental services	−12	−17	−34
Ophthalmic services	−8	−11	−17
Total	−53	−58	−103
Departmental administration	11	17	46
Other services	10	18	82
Local health services expenditure[2]	104	117	—
Total current expenditure	1069	1653	3782
Capital expenditure			
Central government	82	135	286
Local authorities	12	9	—
Total capital expenditure	94	144	286
Total expenditure			
Central government	1047	1671	4068
Local authorities[2]	116	126	—
Total public expenditure	1163	1797	4068

1. Including the school health service from 1 April 1974, previously included in education.
2. On 1 April 1974 local authority health services became the responsibility of central government and from that date are included under the heading of community health services.

school health service and clinics where mothers with infants can get advice, attention, and cheap welfare foods.

There are many ways in which people want to see the Health Service improved. There is a great need for more hospitals and for better accommodation in existing ones. Our hospitals can hold about half a million patients. Many hospitals are over one hundred years old, and not enough new ones are being built. There are still shortages of hospital staff of all kinds—doctors, specialists, nurses. In the general service, many doctors have to take more patients than they can really cope with. Not many health centres have been built in the twenty years since they were advocated.

The trouble has been the cost. In the early years of the Health Service there was great alarm at the way this was mounting. But its proportion of the national wealth has stayed much the same, and in terms of spending on the social services its share has dropped. In the earlier days it took the lion's share; now National Insurance benefits and education each take more than National Health. There are areas where spending has mounted exceptionally fast, notably pharmaceuticals.

Whatever its shortcomings, the Health Service has brought great benefits to the British people. There are few families in the land who have not had cause to be thankful for it in the last thirty years. There is no part of the Welfare State for which the British have a higher regard.

Unemployment and its causes

One of the most serious causes of distress is the loss of employment. When a man loses his job he loses his income, so that the livelihood of his family is immediately endangered. National Insurance and supplementary benefits ensure that some money still comes into the household, but this is unlikely to be as much as the breadwinner was earning.

Unemployment has been at a high level in recent years in Britain, and Governments are very sensitive about their responsibilities in the matter. Lord Beveridge stressed that no insurance scheme could withstand the strain imposed by mass unemployment. The economist J. M. Keynes (Lord Keynes) made a lifelong study of unemployment, and as a result much more is known about the different kinds and their causes.

Britain has been particularly badly hit by 'structural unemployment' and 'cyclical unemployment'. In the former, older industries decline and men employed in it lose their jobs. If new industries arise they may be able to absorb the men displaced from the old one. But if they demand quite different skills, or are based in a different part of the country, this solution may not be practicable.

In industries heavily dependent on export markets, a decline in demand abroad may oblige them to cut down production and therefore pay off some of their employees. If the decline continues and the market is permanently lost, then unemployment in that industry increases without even the consolation of a new alternative growing to absorb the displaced men.

A very serious type of unemployment, 'cyclical unemployment', has often come about through a periodical and general fall-off in the demand for capital goods such as ships, heavy machinery, and engines. These are durable items, not needing constant replacement as shirts or groceries do. Consequently, spells of busy production when businesses are renewing capital equipment are often followed by spells of idleness when many workers in the heavy industries are paid off. This slump reacts on associated ones such as iron and steel and coal, much of whose production has been for these industries. The demand for their product drops, they cut production and discharge men. The people thrown out of work have less money to spend on consumer goods, so that industries producing these also find demand is falling, reduce output and pay off men. Finally, this general fall-off in business tends to increase depression by making manufacturers who were considering renewing their capital equipment more reluctant to spend the money when demand is declining.

Table 8.2. Rates of unemployment: analysis by regions. (Source: *CSO Annual Abstract of Statistics*, HMSO, 1976)

	1965	1970	1975
		Percentage	
United Kingdom	1·5	2·6	4·2
Great Britain	1·4	2·5	4·1
England	1·1	2·3	3·8
North	2·5	4·7	5·9
Yorkshire and Humberside	1·1	2·9	4·0
East Midlands	0·9	2·2	3·6
East Anglia	1·3	2·1	3·5
South East	0·8	1·6	2·8
South West	1·5	2·8	4·7
West Midlands	0·7	2·0	4·1
North West	1·6	2·7	5·3
Wales	2·5	3·9	5·6
Scotland	2·9	4·2	5·2
Northern Ireland	6·0	6·8	7·9

On top of 'structural' and 'cyclical' unemployment, the Balance of Payments deficit and high inflation rates have caused governments to cut public expenditure, and this has made more people unemployed. Unemployment rates are not the same throughout the country, and some parts are relatively well off (see Table 8.2). The south of England, for example, and the areas in Scotland near the North Sea oil developments have had low rates. But Clydeside, the north of England, and even the Midlands, have been badly affected.

Creating full employment

The tragic experience in the years between the wars lies behind the determination of Governments after 1945 to maintain full employment. The main direction of policy is to regulate demand, both to prevent it shooting too high in busy periods and dropping too low in the slacker ones. When the demand for capital goods increases rapidly and the industries expand, the danger of overexpansion becomes serious. The higher production has risen, the steeper the subsequent fall when demand drops. At busy periods, then, Government tries to damp down the expansion by making it harder to borrow money, i.e., by increasing the Minimum Lending rate (see page 146). Firms then think more carefully about new building and equipment. On the other hand, when the demand for capital goods seems to be falling too rapidly, the Government tries to check the decline by making it easier to borrow money, thus encouraging firms to renew equipment and extend plant while they can get good terms. Thus the capital goods industries get more orders and the decline is checked.

Moreover, the Government itself is a big spender of money on capital goods, and by regulating its own spending in the same way that it advises businessmen to do, it can affect the situation. It may hold back spending on roads, schools, hospitals and the nationalized industries in order to correct the balance of payments deficit or control inflation. In such a situation the economy is 'overheated'. On the other hand, if unemployment rises too high and demand is too slack, the Government can increase its expenditure, thereby providing new jobs for many people, who therefore receive a full pay packet every week. Thus the purchasing power of the community is kept higher than it would otherwise have been, and the demand for consumer goods in turn does not fall off as steeply as would have been the case without Government intervention.

Again, Government as well as being a huge spender of money, also controls taxation policies. By its use of these it can increase or diminish the amount of money people have available for spending. Hence by, say, a reduction of Income Tax or by an increase in social security benefits, it can increase the amount of purchasing power in the community, i.e., can increase demand. A combination of the two methods—maintaining government expenditure at a high level and remitting taxation—would mean an enormous increase of purchasing power and so keep demand high. It would, of course, mean an unbalanced budget, and while 'deficit budgeting' is a recognized remedy in a depression, Britain's Balance of Payments problem and its high rates of inflation in the 1970s set limits to the use of such a policy.

Postwar Britain has managed to avoid cyclical mass unemployment, although unemployment reached high levels again in the mid-1970s (see Table 8.2). Some part of this unemployment results from apparent temporary difficulties for some firm or industry (e.g., shipbuilding or car manufacture). In these cases, the Government might impose a protective tariff or quota to give the industry a breathing space, or provide subsidies to tide it over and avoid the need to pay off workers. But this is not advisable if the unemployment is structural, as much postwar unemployment has been. Industries like coal and cotton, for instance, have been contracting because other more attractive rival products have appeared, or native producers or rival traders have snatched away for good the wide markets which once meant employment for British workers. Within industries which are not declining in this sense, there has often been technological unemployment. An industry may go in for more automation, for instance, and become in consequence more productive and thriving than ever, but require fewer workers than before. The result, from any of these developments, is to make some workers redundant—a familiar word in Britain today. Coal, cotton, railways have all had to run down their work force. With these problems of redundancy, Governments prefer to accept the inevitable, especially when it is also desirable. There is not much future for anyone in resisting the kind of change which will make for greater prosperity all round. The policy is to ease the position of redundant workers and try to provide them with jobs with a more promising future. In 1964 the Contracts of Employment Act entitled workers to a certain period of notice before dismissal. Under the Redundancy Payments Act of 1965, men and women made redundant receive lump sums of money varying according to their years in the industry. Trade unions, seeing redundancy coming, have usually persuaded employers to soften the blow by, for instance, not replacing older workers as they retire.

When the redundancies fall heavily in a certain area Government may, by using the powers we have already seen, try to steer some other industries into the area to provide alternative work. It is unlikely that the redundant textile worker, say, will have the skills required for the alternative work offered him, and therefore, Government makes provision for retraining him. The Industrial Training Boards, established under the 1964 Act, train adult workers. There are also over fifty 'skill centres' (SCs), offering courses in a variety of trades under the Training Opportunities Scheme (TOPS), especially those trades where skilled labour is in short supply. Redundant workers, ready to move to a new area, are entitled to financial help: lodging allowances, help with removal costs, fares home, and so on.

For the person who is out of work but whose trade is still a going concern, the main object is to help him find employment quickly. Social security benefits ensure him some income, but this family is likely to have a thin time unless he finds another job. The main way in which this is done in Britain today is through the Employment Offices and Job Centres under the control of the Manpower Services Commission, established in 1973. These are offices where the unemployed can register, indicating the type of work they have done, can do, or want to do. At the same time, employers report to the Job Centres the jobs they have available and the type of workmen they require. Thus those who want jobs and those who have jobs to offer can be put in touch with one another. In this way a man can find work more quickly than he could by tramping hopefully around from one factory to another.

Young people in search of a job are helped by local authorities, through a Vocational Guidance Service and Employment Service. The officers circulate information about jobs and careers to the schools, arrange visits to factories and shops, interview children to find out their interests, and help them find suitable work. They keep an eye on the new young workers in the settling-in stages and give guidance over the difficulties that are likely to arise during this period.

Without these government activities, the unemployment rate would doubtless have been a good deal higher than it has been, but Britain still has serious problems relating to the decline of older industries, and the need for retraining of workers in new jobs. The existing schemes do not match up to this situation, nor is it possible any more to consider full employment to be the main priority of the Government. Just as important is controlling the rate of inflation and rectifying the Balance of Payments deficit.

The meaning of poverty today

Remedies have been found for the main causes of poverty in the past. Poverty through unemployment, low wages, and large families has been relieved by redundancy payments, unemployment benefit, higher wages, and child benefits. Poverty through sickness has been checked through the National Health Service and sickness benefit payments. Poverty through old age or loss of the breadwinner is eased by old age pensions and widows' benefits. Special cases are met by supplementary benefits. When he is born, while he is at school, when he is out of work, too ill or too old to work, and when he dies, the British citizen has an assurance of aid to keep him and his dependants from poverty. He enjoys, it is said, 'Social security from the cradle to the grave'.

Even without setting our sights higher, there are still plenty of hard-pressed people in our society. Old age pensioners in particular often have a hard time of it, as their fixed incomes, small enough at best, have become worth still less through the rapid, continuing rise in prices. The high rates of unemployment in the 1970s mean that many families are living on social security. Conditions in the cities have deteriorated as the costs of services have soared and the wealthier citizens have moved out to the suburbs so that they no longer pay rates to the city council. Areas of 'multiple deprivation', with high unemployment, slum housing, and poor health are common in the older towns. Government programmes of 'urban renewal' try to tackle these areas, but the general economic conditions in the country as a whole have limited their success.

Housing

Governments are particularly concerned to improve housing conditions, and local authorities build large numbers of 'council houses' to provide cheap homes for rent. About half of all houses built today are provided by public authorities (mostly local councils), with the remainder privately owned or owned by housing associations and societies. Rents are kept low through subsidies in the case of council houses, and there are rent rebates for those with low incomes. Houses rented privately are subject to rent regulation under the Rent Act (1965). A 'fair rent' may be fixed by independent rent officers, at the request of the landlord or tenant. Those who buy their own houses with the aid of a mortage from a building society get an allowance for the interest in their income tax liability.

Thus, nearly all types of houses are covered by government aid. But the problem of widespread bad housing remains. In part this is due to the age of many houses in the older parts of the cities. Landlords often feel that rents are not high enough to cover the costs of improvements but they are unable to raise them. Eventually, these houses have to be pulled down.

Vast council house estates were built in the 1950s and 1960s, often without much regard for amenity or good architecture. Now many of these estates rank as slums, and tenants are difficult to find for them. Other estates, with 'high-rise flats' have proved unpopular with many people, although they have good standards of accommodation. The problem here is the virtual isolation of tenants in their flats, and the lack of community feeling. Nevertheless, long waiting lists exist for council houses in many areas, and for most people they are the only type of house that can be afforded.

The private sector has been building a growing number of houses since the 1950s, but these houses are for sale to would-be owner occupiers. They are not cheap, and are only within the reach of those people who are able to raise a mortgage. Building societies are only prepared to consider people with a certain level of income and with good prospects of continuing to enjoy that level. Usually, a large deposit on the price is required.

Privately rented houses have declined in numbers, largely for reasons mentioned before. In 1951 they were 52 per cent of all houses, but in 1974 they were only 17 per cent. The private landlord seems to be nearly a thing of the past, but housing associations have become more popular. Tenants form themselves into an association to build and rent flats, and receive assistance from the Government's Housing Corporation. There are now a quarter of a million houses of this kind in Great Britain, but this is only 4 per cent of the total.

Housing conditions have improved greatly since 1945. Houses classed as 'unfit' amounted to only 7 per cent in 1971 in England and Wales, and, although conditions are generally worse in Scotland, in 1971 the Census showed that 86 per cent of houses there possessed the basic amenities of hot and cold water, inside toilet, and bath with 82 per cent in England and Wales. Nevertheless, there is still much overcrowding in Scottish homes, and many properties are over 80 years old (see Table 8.3).

Town and country planning

Since the Second World War, public authorities in Britain have assumed responsibility for the use of the land in their district, and are trying to control

Table 8.3. Housing amenities and overcrowding: Scotland and Great Britain 1971. (Source: *Census of Population: Housing Table 1971*, HMSO)

	Percentage of households having exclusive use of:				Percentage of persons living at density greater than 1½ persons per room in:			
	Hot water %	Fixed bath or shower %	Inside w.c. %	All three amenities %	Owner-occupied housing %	Local authority/ public sector %	Private unfurnished rental, %	Private furnished rental, %
Scotland	92	86.8	92.7	86.3	6.3	15.2	14.4	13.2
England and Wales	91.6	87.9	84.7	82.1	1.3	4.4	3.1	11.8

and plan the development of towns. The Town and Country Planning Acts give central and local government wide powers to regulate development. Local authorities have to survey their district and prepare detailed development plans showing their proposals for about twenty years ahead. They show which parts are to be kept as farmland, which are planned as residential, where new factories, shopping centres, or schools will be sited, where new roads will run, where open spaces are to be preserved. Special attempts are made to retain open countryside all around the town—*green belts*—so that dwellers in the older, central districts are not completely denied the pleasure of the open air by an unbroken outward sprawl of built-up areas.

In a big city, like Birmingham or Glasgow, the policy of keeping open spaces parkland, and a green belt clashes with the need for ground on which to build houses. Many feel the latter is the more urgent need, and open spaces a luxury which must be abandoned. Schemes for building upward instead of outward—flats and skyscrapers instead of low horizontal buildings that 'waste' land—only go part of the way to meet the need. To get over the difficulty, the policy of overspill and new towns is favoured by many, and the New Towns Act (1946) makes provision for this.

The idea is that many city dwellers should move, not to new houses on the present outskirts of the city or in its green belt but away from the city altogether. They would go either to one of the many small towns which are ready to receive them—overspill areas—or to a new town which is built from scratch to accommodate them. Houses are built for the newcomers and jobs provided, either by the migration of firms from the city or by the establishment of new firms and industries in the new areas.

The attractions of the scheme are numerous. The city's own housing problem is eased, its open spaces preserved, its spread checked, and the growing congestion of people reduced.

Moreover, new towns and small towns can be planned as present ones were not. The work area can be convenient to, but quite apart from, the residential part; schools and shops can be set up near the homes but away from main traffic routes; through traffic can be routed around the town, preventing the jams that constantly mar our older towns and reducing road casualties. The overspill towns benefit from the prosperity brought by the bigger population and new industry. The whole economy benefits from the wider dispersion and better distribution of industry.

So far, thirty-two new towns have been set up in Britain. There are five in Scotland—East Kilbride, Cumbernauld, Glenrothes, Livingston, and Irvine. Every year Glasgow families are being rehoused outside the city, and efforts are made to persuade firms and industries to move out of the city more readily. By 1976, however, opposition was growing in Glasgow to the setting up of yet another new town nearby, at Stonehouse. It was felt that the city itself would lose funds from the regional local authority to build the roads, schools and amenities in the new town, which would otherwise have gone to urban renewal in Glasgow. The Government soon agreed with Glasgow, and the new town scheme was cancelled.

Living in new towns has special problems. People miss their relatives or neighbours, and regret the loss of the variety and shops of the city. In time, however, the new places lose their rawness, and develop their own character and community spirit as buildings go up, clubs become organized, and the inhabitants get to know each other better.

Within the old towns there is no chance of beginning with a clean slate, but large improvements have been made. Many old office blocks and shops in the centres of cities have been cleared away, and new ones built. New motorways and ring roads have been constructed, to accommodate the ever-increasing volume of traffic. Supermarkets, and even hypermarkets, have largely replaced the old shops, because of the ease of travel and cheapness and variety of the goods on sale.

A hundred years ago people feared that city life would be impossible because of the many deaths caused by disease. It looks as if the role of disease as the killer of townspeople in the nineteenth century is being taken over by the car and lorry in the twentieth century.

Education

Education is a social service looked after by the community, through its central and local government authorities. There are four systems—one each for England, Wales, Scotland, and Northern Ireland. They developed in different ways, have a different structure of schools, and are regulated by separate Acts of Parliament. Inside each there are various types of school, run and financed in different ways. But all at least have this in common: that over the last hundred years the Government has come to play a much bigger part in organizing and financing their education systems; and their notions of education have grown enormously.

It is seen now not as something crammed once and for all into an eleven-year stretch of childhood, but as a process that continues long after school has been left behind. In scope it has broadened from the simple learning of the so-called 'Three Rs' (reading, writing, arithmetic) to embrace not only more academic subjects but a wide variety of activities: hobbies and school orchestras, drama clubs and camping holidays, art appreciation and subsidized visits to other countries. It extends to the child's physical welfare as well as his mental training. And all this is not the privilege of a few, but is open to all.

While this general education policy holds good for all Britain, different parts of the country, as has been said, have their own systems for carrying it out in practice.

In Scotland most education is of the public kind, paid for from public funds and run by public authorities. These are, first, a department of the central government—the Scottish Education Department—under the Secretary of

State for Scotland, and second, twelve local education authorities—the Education Committees of the Regions and Island Councils.

The job of the Education Committees is to see that provisions are made in their area for children to get the education that Acts of Parliament say they must have. They have to see that enough schools are made available, and that the education inside them is suitable. They appoint the teachers and pay their salaries. They see that all children who should be attending school do so. They provide school meals and organize transport to schools for pupils who need it.

The Scottish Education Department supervises and guides this activity. It provides much of the money the local authorities spend, and naturally needs to feel sure this money is properly spent. Their schemes for providing education, e.g., proposals for new schools, have to be approved by the Secretary of State. They must run their schools according to general regulations which he makes, i.e., the Schools Code. This deals with such things as the size of classes and the kinds of education to be provided.

The Department outlines the main work schemes to be followed. No pupil can sit for the Scottish Certificate of Education unless he has followed a course approved by the Department. Inspectors from the Department (the HMIs) visit the schools and report on premises, equipment, work standards, and so on. The Scottish Education Department also lays down the qualifications teachers must have, and regulates their salaries.

All these schools, supported by public money, provided and managed by public authorities, are called in Scotland public schools (the term in England means something very different indeed.) There are over 3000 Scottish public schools, and about 95 per cent of Scotland's 900 000 schoolchildren are educated in them. Education in these schools, whether primary or secondary, is free.

Education need not end for any pupil when he or she leaves school The secondary pupil who passes sufficient examinations may carry on his full time education at one of the forty-four British universities. Even without school-leaving qualifications, a student may pursue a course at the Open University, which commenced operations in 1971. The other forms of higher and further education have expanded too, and these include polytechnics, central institutions in Scotland, and colleges of further education.

The scale of the education system in Britain is large: there are nearly twelve million pupils and students in full-time attendance at schools and colleges, and in 1974–75 about 13 per cent of all public expenditure was devoted to it—the largest item after social security. It is easily the biggest item of expenditure for the regional (Scotland) and county (England and Wales) local authorities.

Arguments still rage as to the best forms of schooling, and as to the priorities for spending the different levels of education. The main issue is whether comprehensive schools are to be preferred to selective schools, at the secondary level. By 1976, nearly all state schools in Britain were comprehensive, while the independent schools were selective. Deciding whether to spend more on universities than on polytechnics, or to devote a greater share of resources to nursery schools at the expense of other types of school remain tricky problems for the policy-makers. So, too, is regulating the supply of teachers. Until 1976 it was considered that there was a shortage of teachers, but in that year many newly qualified teachers were unable to get jobs, because of the cuts in public expenditure. No clear consensus of educational matters was present in the 1970s, and many of the idealistic reforms of the 1960s had lost some of their attraction.

Table 8.4. Education services in Great Britain (Source: CSO Annual Abstract of Statistics 1976, HMSO)

	1964/65	1974/75
Total school population	7 966 409	9 978 484
Full-time teachers	391 130	546 670
Number of full-time university students	138 711	250 565
Total in further education	546 405	439 423

Table 8.5. Public expenditure on education (Great Britain) (Source: CSO Annual Abstract of Statistics 1976, HMSO)

	1964/65 (£million)	1974/75 (£million)	1975/76 (£million)
Schools maintained by education authorities			
Nursery and primary education	346	1252	
Secondary education	385	1434	3725
Special education	21	113	
Further and adult education	166	604	769
Teacher training	50	185	224
Universities	120	417	548
Total current expenditure	1359	4809	6267
Total capital expenditure	277	594	735
Total public expenditure	1636	5403	7002

Nevertheless, it is plain that educational spending is likely to go on increasing. More children are staying longer at schools. Many schools are still housed in ancient, inadequate buildings. Many classes are too large. If, in addition, primary education is improved, new comprehensives built, and university places increased, then the cost of education must go up still more.

Social welfare today

The Welfare State, or more generally Britain's system of social security and social services, has always been a subject of debate. After thirty years of existence in its present shape, questioning of it has grown, among friends as well as critics. (Table 8.6 shows the costs of various services.)

Among the latter are those who disapprove of the whole idea. The kinds of objection they make are that it inflates the role of the State, and this is dangerous as the State is the enemy of personal liberty; that it encourages layabouts, who get an easy living on the backs of others; that in making such wide provision it has a demoralizing effect, removing the incentive to individual effort and foresight; and that while there might be something to be said for it in time of depression, there is less need for it in a prosperous society, where individuals are in a position to make provision for themselves.

Table 8.6. Expenditure on social services, 1975/76. (Source: CSO Annual Abstract of Statistics, HMSO, 1976)

Social service	£ million
National Insurance and industrial injuries	7 020
Education	7 002
National Health Service	5 471
Housing	4 500
Supplementary benefits	1 245
Family allowances	547
School meals, milk, welfare foods	427
War pensions	260
Family income supplement	14
Attendance allowance	100
Non-contributory pensions	36
Total	26 622

These points are not necessarily absurd or unreasonable, but they are open to rejoinder. It is true that the State can be, and often has been, the enemy of individual liberty; but to identify the State automatically as this is too facile. Very often it has proved the friend of individual liberty. A landlord, exercising his personal liberty, may virtually remove that of his tenants by the charges and conditions he imposes; when the State steps in and legislates to prevent him from doing this, it is limiting his freedom, but it is enlarging that of his tenants.

Again, it is true that the system may be exploited by some individuals. But these, though they may make the headlines, are the exceptions. There is no reason to believe that the British people are lazier or more workshy than at any other period of their history; or that they prefer to scrape along on benefits rather than earn a decent wage. The existence of parasites argues at most for action to check them: it is not an argument for abandoning the system.

We need only look at figures or photographs to see the difference between Britain's children today and seventy years ago. They are bigger, healthier, and better cared for. They enjoy far more opportunities of education, more attractively presented in far more pleasant buildings. The nation's level of health is higher, most people are better housed and have higher standards of living.

At the same time, we have seen how in one area after another there are shortcomings which need remedying. There are people far from affluent in our affluent society. The very prosperity which they do not enjoy makes their lot at once more poignant and more difficult to bear. There are, in particular, the elderly and the children in large families with low incomes. We need more hospitals and schools, and better equipped ones. The housing problem in the cities remains unsolved. There are groups and areas which need not equal treatment but an 'unequal' extra large share of resources if they are to have an equal chance in life. And outside these crucial material fields, Britain as yet spends very little money on the cultural welfare of the people. For most people Britain today is a better society to live in than it was thirty years ago: for many the scope for improvement is still large.

9. Industrial relations

Then and now

The average worker in Britain today works just under 40 hours a week without overtime, and four or five hours extra with overtime. The working week is usually five days, and there are over three weeks holiday in the year for manual workers, with more for non-manual workers. This is in addition to public holidays. The average weekly wage in 1977 was £80 for male manual workers. The conditions in his factory or workshop must conform to standards of

---

Before
1945 From 1802, Acts to regulate child labour in cotton mills, and **Factory Acts** from 1833. Also **Coal Mines Acts, Trade Boards Act**, and **Children and Young Persons Acts**
1948 **Factories Act** giving special attention to welfare of the under 18s
1950 **Shops Act**: regulates closing hours and working conditions, especially of young employees
1954 **Mines and Quarries Act**: pulls existing laws together and lays down principles of safety, health, and welfare
1956 **Agriculture (Safety, Health and Welfare) Act**: the farmworkers' Factory Act
1961 **Factories Act**: to secure health, safety, and welfare
1963 **Offices, Shops, Railway Premises Act**: to secure health, safety and welfare
1963 **Contracts of Employment Act**: gives right to minimum period of notice before dismissal
1965 **Redundancy Payments Acts**: give rights to lump sum payment if job ceases
1969 to exist
1968 **Race Relations Act**: makes it illegal for employer to discriminate on grounds of race, colour or national origin
1970 **Equal Pay Act**: upholds principle of equal remuneration for men and women for work of equal value, and requires that terms and conditions are as favourable to one as to the other
1972 **Contracts of Employment Act**: requires employer to give worker written information on terms of employment and grievance procedure
1974 **Trade Union and Labour Relations Act**: protection against unfair dismissal
1975 **Employment Protection Act**: strengthens rights of employees
1975 **Sex Discrimination Act**: makes it illegal to discriminate against women

---

Fig. 9.1. Government regulation of conditions in industry

health, safety, and welfare laid down by law and enforced by a large body of inspectors.

One hundred and fifty years ago there was no notion of a limited working day or week. Fifteen or sixteen hours a day, six days a week, no holidays—certainly none with pay: these were the prevailing conditions in much manufacturing industry, and not just for adult men but for the women and children who made up a large part of the working force. Conditions of work in mine and factory were often dangerous, usually unhealthy, and unregulated by any authority.

Table 9.1. Growth of trade union membership

Year	Total membership	
1900	2 022 000	
1910	2 565 000	
1920	8 334 000	The decline in membership in
1933	4 392 000	the early 1930s was a result
1939	6 298 000	of the industrial depression
1946	8 803 000	of those years
1958	9 616 000	
1966	10 111 000	
1976	11 500 000	

The great change has been the result of, first, action by Government to enforce better conditions, and second, the organized efforts of workers themselves in the Trade Union movement. Both changes, however, were assisted by the advance of industry itself: the development of better machinery, the growth of output, and the increase in productivity all made it easier to secure higher wages, shorter hours, and better conditions of work.

There is now a complex set of laws which regulate the terms of employment and working conditions in Britain. As well as the more traditional protection afforded under the Acts regulating the hours of work, wages, and safety conditions in factories, mines and shops, workers are protected from the effects of redundancy, unfair dismissal, and sex discrimination. Another area of legislation concerns the powers of trade unions, and the right to strike, picket, or resort to arbitration. (See Figs. 9.1 and 9.3.)

Human relations in industry

Many employers today provide more than the minimum they are forced to by law: good medical attention, canteens and cheap meals. Some firms have works councils or joint committees on which employees and management are represented. These are not bargaining bodies, where the two sides meet as adversaries, but aim to improve communications so that managements' decisions are outlined and discussed with the workers.

The underlying idea is that people will be happier in their work, and work will be more efficient, if management and employees have confidence in and respect for each other, and cooperate in a team effort. In 1977 the Bullock Report advocated that workers be chosen by trade unions to sit as directors on the boards of large firms. This is sometimes called 'industrial democracy' or 'worker participation'. The implications of implementing such a report would be far reaching for British industry.

The rise of the trade unions

While minimum standards of health, safety, and welfare are laid down by Acts of Parliament, the normal way of arranging terms of employment—wages and hours of work—is by negotiation between the employers and the workmen concerned. This is where the Trade Union movement has made its great contribution to the advance from the position 150 years ago.

A trade union is an association of wage earners whose object is to improve the conditions of their working lives. As long as terms of employment were settled between an employer and an individual workman, the latter's position was weak, especially in times of unemployment. The employer could dictate his own terms, which the workman would have to accept or watch the job go to some less demanding man. Whereas, if workmen in some trade were to combine and agree to stick by the same demands, then their bargaining power was greatly increased.

At first, trade unions or associations were treated as illegal conspiracies, and men joining them were liable to severe penalties. Legislation passed in 1871 and 1875 established the legality of trade unions beyond dispute, and Acts in 1906 and 1913 strengthened the right to strike and carry on political activities, including collecting a 'political levy' to support the Labour Party.

The unions have come a long way since the days when they were regarded as criminal conspiracies, driven to disband or work underground. Their legal standing and their rights are well established. Their power and influence have never been greater. They have spread far beyond the ranks of the skilled craftsmen, where their early activity was centred. From 1890, unions of unskilled workmen began to appear. Then they spread to the non-manual workers: teachers, local government workers, civil servants.

At present over eleven million people, i.e., about 45 per cent of the working population, belong to a union. Union funds amount to hundreds of millions of pounds. Governments consult unions carefully, employers treat them with respect. They wield a powerful influence on one of the two main political parties, the Labour Party. Their leaders are better known and more often in the public eye than most politicians, play a prominent part in public life, and are honoured by knighthoods and peerages.

Unions: types and organization

In 1973 there were 495 trade unions in Britain, although four-fifths of all trade unionists were in the twenty-four largest unions, with a membership of over 100 000 each, and under 1 per cent were in the 253 smallest unions which had under 1000 members each. (See Fig. 9.2.)

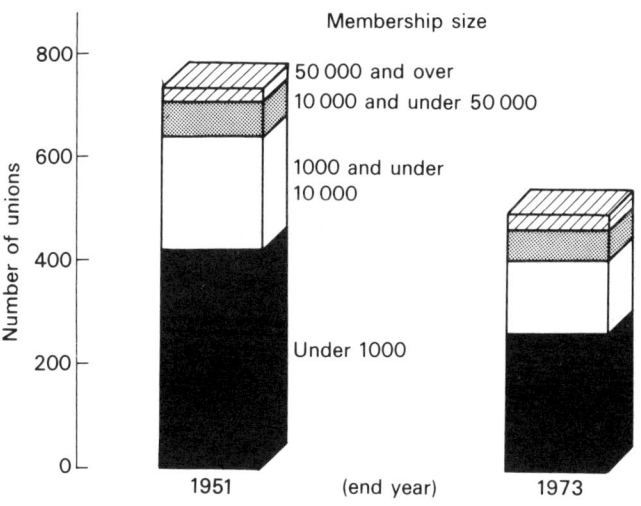

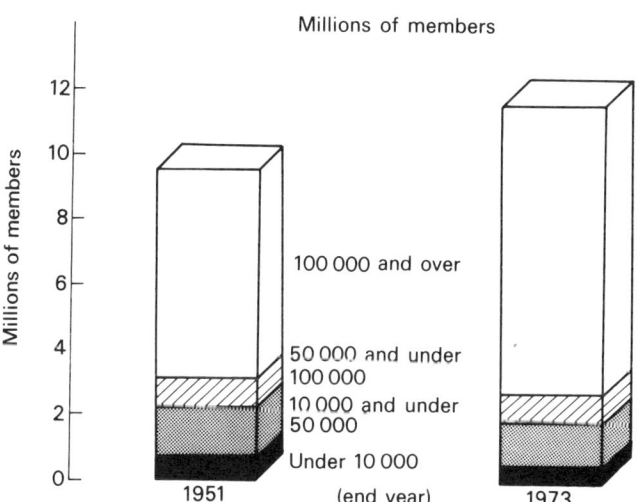

Fig. 9.2. Trade unions membership: United Kingdom. (Source: *Facts in Focus*, 3rd edn, Penguin, 1975)

There are three main types: first, there are craft unions, which are organized on the basis of a single skilled craft or trade, such as the National Union of Sheet Metal Workers, Coppersmiths, and Heating and Domestic Engineers; then there are industrial unions, which cater for all workers within a particular industry, whatever their craft or unskilled job, such as the National Union of Mineworkers; third, there are the general unions, which cater for all workers, especially unskilled, in a wide range of industries such as the Transport and General Workers' Union.

The picture is not really as neat as this. There is, for instance, the National Union of Railwaymen, which must be regarded as an industrial union but does not represent the engine crews who have their own Associated Society of Locomotive Engineers and Firemen. The Amalgamated Union of Engineering Workers is a craft union, but includes many unskilled and semiskilled men. It was once hoped to organize all unions on the lines of industrial unions, but long-established unions are loath to give up their separate identity. Thus in the shipbuilding industry there are still about twenty separate unions.

Trade unions have their differences of organization, too, though the general lines are similar. In most the basic units are the local branches. All members of a union belong to a branch in their neighbourhood.

A man's branch, however, may be quite a distance from his home, and many of its members work in different places or industries. So, to many trade unionists today the unit of their union organized in their factory is more important than the unit organized in their neighbourhood, i.e., their branch. Hence the growing importance of the shop steward, who represents the members of his union in a particular workplace. He is elected by them as a man they know and trust; he takes up their grievances with the management promptly and on the spot. He is often, therefore, a more real figure to union

Table 9.2. Membership of the biggest trade unions (1976). (Source: *Whitaker's Almanack 1977*)

Union	Membership
Transport and General Workers' Union (T&GWU)	1 856 165
Amalgamated Union of Engineering Workers (AUEW)	1 204 720
General and Municipal Workers' Union (GMWU)	881 356
National and Local Government Officer's Association (NALGO)	625 163
National Union of Public Employees (NUPE)	584 485
Electrical, Electronic and Telecommunication Union/Plumbing Trades' Union (EETU/PTU)	420 000
Union of Shop, Distributive and Allied Workers (USDAW)	377 302
Association of Scientific, Technical and Managerial Staffs (ASTMS)	374 000
National Union of Teachers (NUT)	281 855
Union of Construction, Allied Trades and Technicians (UCATT)	274 786
National Union of Mineworkers (NUM)	261 871

members in the 'shop' than their branch or national leaders. Moreover, since few members ever attend branch meetings, the shop steward is the link between them and the branch. It has been said that 'for most members the shop steward is their only real contact with the union; to many he is the union'. The shop stewards of different unions in a factory usually meet frequently in committees, and their influence is very great indeed.

The branch is still the unit in which most union business is carried out. It collects subscriptions and pays out union benefits. It elects its own officials, takes part, by direct voting, in the election of the union's national officials, and picks delegates to represent it at the union's annual conference, where delegates from all the branches meet together. The branch also sends up proposals about union policy for consideration at the conference.

The conference debates and votes on these proposals, thus deciding what the union's policy will be for the coming year: whether to seek a wage increase, whether to aim at longer annual holidays or a shorter week, what to do about some special problem. To see to the carrying out of the decisions during the coming year, a national executive is elected (either by the delegates or by the branches). This usually holds office for a couple of years. The branches also elect, by direct vote, the general secretary or president.

His job, whether he is called general secretary or president, is to see that the policies decided by members through their delegates at the annual conference are carried out; and he is answerable to the executive. Whereas the latter is elected for a year or two only, the general secretary is elected for life. And whereas the executive is comprised of 'part-timers' who carry on with their trade during the year, he is a full-time union official. Consequently, if he is a strong personality he can exercise a very powerful influence in the union's affairs. These are the men whose names and faces the public comes to know, men like Jack Jones and Clive Jenkins.

Each union is independent and makes its own decisions, but for certain purposes numbers of them often join together. The separate unions in the building trade have their National Federation of Building Trades' Operatives; the printing and publishing unions cooperate in the Printing and Kindred Trades' Federation. These bodies often negotiate for all the unions concerned.

Different unions often come together locally. The branches of various unions in a district usually link up in a trades council, to which each sends representatives. They meet about once a month, consider matters of common interest, and take a special interest in local affairs.

The Trades Union Congress

The most important federation of the unions is the Trades Union Congress, the central institution of the movement. Since 1868 delegates from each of the unions have met together annually at a conference, or congress, which lasts for about a week. Here delegates consider the affairs of the Trade Union movement generally. They debate proposals submitted by the union representatives. They also elect the General Council, which represents the TUC until the next annual conference, and the general secretary, who holds the job as long as the TUC is satisfied with him.

The TUC has very little formal power. No individual union need be bound by the decisions of the Congress. Even if the TUC decides to recommend wage restraint in the coming year, members are not barred from putting in a wage claim. Again, many of the TUC recommendations deal with government policy. It may criticize the Budget, or even bargain with the Government on its content, as in 1976, when tax allowances were made dependent on the TUC's agreeing to wage restraint. It may call for changes in the law, as for example the repeal of the Industrial Relations Act 1971. The Conservative Government of Mr Heath (1970–74) found it impossible to impose its industrial relations policies against the wishes of the TUC and the largest unions, and the Labour Government which followed put in its programme items suggested by the TUC under the 'Social Contract' agreement of 1973. The agreement was the work of the TUC–Labour Party Liaison Committee, which was set up in 1972 to discuss policies on industrial relations and the management of the economy. Subsequent versions of the 'Social Contract' were produced in 1975 and 1976.

Thus the TUC is a very important body. It owes this to its ability to speak for the mass of trade unionists in Britain. There are 113 organizations (including federations of unions), comprising about eleven million members, represented in the TUC. This makes it the nearest thing we have in Britain to an official expression of the opinions of millions of working men and women.

The TUC works on a very small budget, derived from a small fee for each member of a union belonging to the TUC, boosted by occasional extra payments. Despite this lack of funds, many people today consider that the unions have too much power, and that their leaders are not representative of the workers as a whole. In some occupations, membership of a union is compulsory, and the number of these 'closed shops' has increased during the 1970s, partly as a result of new legislation (Fig. 9.3). This has given rise to fears that individual freedom has been eroded in the interests of collective bargaining strength.

Trade unions and politics

A trade union is an industrial body, not a political party. It accepts as a member any worker whose job or trade entitles him or her to join it. So far as, say, the NUR is concerned, what political party (if any) a member supports matters no more than what church he goes to or what football team he follows. All that matters is that he should be a railway worker and pay his weekly union subscription. The NUR will then do all it can to better his position in the industry: try to secure him more pay, shorter hours, better overtime rates, and so on. And all this can be done by bargaining with the employers in the industry, without bothering much about politics and Parliament.

By the end of last century many unions began to feel that they should pay more attention to the political field as well as the industrial one. Certain cases in the law courts were decided against the unions and made them afraid that the Acts of Parliament which defined the unions' powers were less satisfactory than they believed. They were alarmed, too, lest the employers instead of simply fighting the unions in the industrial arena, e.g., by tough negotiation and possibly 'lock-outs', might seek legislation in Parliament which would undermine the unions. This danger could only be averted in the political arena by Members of Parliament vigilant on behalf of the unions. And, at that time, trade unionists doubted whether either of the big parties, Conservative or Liberal, could be relied on for this.

They were therefore sympathetic to various groups of people—not trade unionists—who were trying to set up a new political party to support the cause of the poorer classes in Britain. This party could watch for, and denounce, any attempt to pass laws injuring the unions, and could get the existing unsatisfactory ones improved. The unions who thought this way—a slight majority of those in the TUC—got together with other interested groups, like the Fabian Society and the Independent Labour Party, and founded the Labour Party.

Not all unions agreed to play this, or any, part in politics. This is a matter which each union decides for itself. If it likes, it can collect a special political subscription from members quite separate from their normal union subscription. This money forms a political fund which the union may use for political purposes: to pay the costs of a candidate's election campaign, as a donation to help a political party build up its organization, to pay for agents, put out party literature, and so on.

Many unions will have nothing to do with this: over one-quarter of the unions in the TUC, for instance, have no links with the Labour Party at all. Moreover, in those unions that do have a political fund, each member decides for himself whether or not he will pay the political subscription. He loses no privileges by refusing to pay the extra political levy, any more than a union which decides not to set up a political fund loses any of its right and privileges. About one-tenth of the members of those unions which do have a political fund do not contribute to it.

In fact, most of the big unions do have a political fund, most of their members do contribute to it, and nearly all use the fund to support the Labour Party. Ever since the founding of the Labour Party, the relations between it and the unions affiliated to it have been close. This is natural enough, as both have a special concern for the working man, though the unions' concern is for him mainly as a worker in industry, while the Labour Party's is for him mainly as a citizen of Britain.

Moreover, the influence of these unions in the Labour Party is powerful; for one thing, the great bulk of the Party's funds comes from the unions. The unions sponsor a large number of Labour MPs—128 in 1975, two-fifths of the Labour total. 'Sponsorship' by a union means that a candidate gets financial help from the union towards his election expenses, and is supposed to represent the union's interests in Parliament. And at the annual conference of the Labour Party, where its policies are debated and decided, delegates from the unions form a large majority. So the voice of the unions is loud and important when it comes to deciding what the Labour Party's programme should be.

Does this mean that the Labour Party is just the mouthpiece in Parliament of the trade unions? It does not. In the first place, the delegations from the various unions often disagree among themselves at the Labour Party Conference about what policies the Party should adopt. The T&GWU may want the Party to take one line, the AUEW may want it to take quite a different one; the NUM delegation may have a third course to propose. So the delegates from other organizations in the Labour movement are not always flattened by the steam roller of a solid trade union majority.

Then, too, the leaders of the Labour Party in Parliament are a persuasive force in the Conference. They are aware that they must appeal to and, if returned to power, must govern for, the country. There are a good number of trade unionists whose unions do not support the Labour Party and whose voices are therefore not heard at the Conference. There are over thirteen million of the working population who do not belong to any union at all. The leaders of the Labour Party do not want to have a party programme that suits only a section of their supporters but has no attraction for large numbers in the country, so they resist any attempts to make the Party adopt too limited a programme.

Collective bargaining

Whatever their type or size, trade unions have the same general aims—to protect and promote the interests of their members as workers in industry. They try to get them better terms of employment: higher wages, a shorter working day and week, longer holidays. They watch working conditions and try to secure improvements. They take up the cause of members who have grievances about the behaviour of employers. They are especially concerned to prevent unemployment among their members. They keep a wary eye on all developments, whether in the general economy of the country or in the work methods adopted in an industry, which might affect their members' jobs.

The usual means adopted by unions to persuade employers to agree to their terms is collective bargaining, i.e., the unions negotiate with employers on behalf of their members instead of leaving members to strike their own individual bargains.

In earlier days the unions negotiated with an individual employer. But as union strength—and so their bargaining power—grew, the individual employer began to feel in a weak position. The natural reaction was for employers, too, to join together in associations and get the same benefits from collective strength as the workmen were getting.

There are now about 1100 of these employers' associations, designed to strengthen their members' hands in dealing with the unions on labour questions. Most of them are local in character, consisting of employers whose firms are engaged in similar industries in one region or district. About fifty of them are national in scope, catering for the employers in one industry—or related industries—throughout the country. The biggest is the Engineering and Allied Employers National Federation; the National Federation of Building Trade Employers is next. Since 1919 employers' associations have had a central body, the British Employers' Confederation, now the Confederation of British Industry, standing to them rather as the TUC does to the unions.

Table 9.3. The language of industrial relations

Free collective bargaining	Negotiations between workers and employers uncontrolled by the Government
Statutory incomes policy	Limits set on wage settlements by Act of Parliament
Unofficial strike	Strike not supported by the trade union
Restrictive practices	Methods of working designed to put pressure on employers, such as: 'go-slow' (attempt to take longer over a job); 'overmanning' (insistence on using more men on a job than the job demands); 'overtime' (work done outside the basic hours of a job, usually for a higher rate of pay); 'demarcation dispute' (dispute as to who does what kind of work)
Productivity Agreement	Wage rise related to increase in productivity
Shop stewards	Elected leader of workers on the 'shop floor'. The leader of shop stewards committee is called the convenor/convener
'Cooling-off period'	Return to work while negotiations or arbitration takes place
Picketing	The attempt to persuade workers not to go to work during a strike. 'Peaceful picketing' is legal, but picketing sometimes leads to scenes of violence
Work-in	Occupation of factory, etc., by workers who have been sacked or declared redundant
Arbitration	The use of an independent body to try to settle a dispute or strike. ACAS (Advisory, Conciliation and Arbitration Service) is provided by the Government for this purpose

Terms of employment in industry are mainly negotiated by bargaining between the employers' associations and the trade unions concerned, within the confines of government pay policy. This is called 'collective bargaining'. In most industries negotiations take place at the national level. The national representatives of the employers' associations and the national leaders of the unions involved in some dispute meet together to discuss, negotiate, and try to reach a settlement. When they do, the settlement applies to the industry throughout the country. But, in addition, there is collective bargaining at the local workplace, which often modifies the national settlement in that factory or shipyard.

Most industries have permanent negotiating bodies on which employers and unions are represented. This enables negotiations to take place more easily, without loss of time in making arrangements. Many of the Joint Industrial Councils were set up on the suggestion of the Whitley Report in 1916 and are sometimes called Whitley Councils.

Table 9.4. Stoppages of work for selected years.

Year	Number of stoppages	Number of workers involved	Number of working days lost
1957	2 859	1 356 000	8 400 000
1969	3 116	1 665 000	6 846 000
1970	3 906	1 800 000	10 980 000
1971	2 228	1 178 000	13 551 000
1972	2 497	1 726 000	23 923 000
1973	2 873	1 513 000	7 100 000
1974	2 922	1 622 000	14 750 000

Should the two sides, whether in a Joint Industrial Council or in special meetings, be unable to agree, there are further avenues open to them. They may ask the independent Advisory, Conciliation and Arbitration Service (ACAS), which offers conciliation in industrial disputes, and may appoint arbitrators if this fails. The Secretary of State for Employment can also appoint a court of inquiry or committee of investigation into a dispute, e.g., the Wilberforce Court of Inquiry in the miners' strike of 1972. The final award of the arbitrators or court does not have to be accepted, though it usually is.

During the 1960s and early 1970s strikes were frequent in Britain, and some were 'unofficial' (that is, they did not have the support of the union). When a union calls its members out on strike, the strike is official. The strikers receive weekly payments from the union's strike fund and can claim supplementary benefits from the state. Since 1974 strikes have been less frequent, owing to the economic recession and the implementation of the 'Social Contract' by the Labour Government and the unions. In return for legislation which they supported, the unions were prepared to exercise wage restraint and to refrain from strikes.

The Government and industrial relations

During the last ten years successive British Governments have attempted to reform the system of industrial relations by altering the legal position of the trade unions, and by closely controlling the right to the 'free collective bargaining' of wage increases. (See Fig. 9.3.)

In the 1960s both the Conservative and Labour Governments were anxious to reduce the large number of 'unofficial' strikes which were damaging both to the economy and to the trade unions themselves. A Royal Commission on Trade Unions and Employers Associations (the Donovan Commission) reported in 1968, and recommended that nationwide agreements be replaced by individual agreements at factory or company level. This had already become general practice, but had led to difficulties since the procedures in case of dispute had not been worked out, resulting in strikes. New procedures were recommended, but it was said that these should not be enforced by law.

1964–70 Labour Governments
1968 **Donovan Commission on Industrial Relations Reports**: rejects legal penalties for unofficial strikes
1969 **White Paper, 'In Place of Strife'**: announces Government's intention to introduce legal penalties for unofficial strikes, compulsory strike ballots, etc. However, Cabinet decides, after facing strong opposition in TUC and Parliament, to drop Bill

1970–74 Conservative Government
1971 **Industrial Relations Act**: new legal penalties against unofficial strikes, and new Court—the National Industrial Relations Court. Widespread opposition from trade unions, especially after fining and imprisonment of strikers
1972, **Miners Strikes**: in February 1974 Mr Heath, the Prime Minister, called an
1974 election because of the strike

1974–Labour Governments
1974 **Trade Union and Labour Relations Act**: repeals most of Industrial Relations Act
1976 **Trade Union and Labour Relations (Amendment) Act**: permits 'closed shop' arrangements (including journalists)
1976 **Dock Work Regulation Act**: extends closed shop area of the docks. However, Government defeated in Parliament on size of the area

---

Fig. 9.3. Government and the trade unions, 1969–76

The Labour Government in 1969 produced a White Paper, *In Place of Strife*, which promised legislation to lay down new procedures in strikes. Unofficial strikers would be ordered back to work for a 'cooling-off' period of 28 days, during which time negotiations would take place. Strikers disobeying the order to return to work would be liable to fines.

The legislation was never passed. Strong opposition to the proposals was raised by the TUC, and the Cabinet decided not to proceed with the Bill. In return, the TUC gave a 'solemn and binding undertaking' that where they considered unofficial strikers to be at fault they would place an obligation on trade unions to take energetic steps to obtain an immediate resumption of work. But this did not commit the TUC to act in all cases, and the 'penal clauses' relating to fines were dropped.

The Conservatives returned to power in 1970, and passed the Industrial Relations Act in 1971. Once more, 'penal clauses' were invoked to uphold new procedures in the event of strikes, and a new court, the National Industrial Relations Court, was established to deal with industrial disputes. Trade unions were invited to 'register' under the Act, but this was not compulsory. The TUC decided to expel unions which did register, and most unions backed the TUC. At the same time, the Act sought to strengthen the 'official' bargaining powers of the unions, and to further protect employees.

The Act was bitterly opposed by the Trade Union movement from the first, and this feeling grew stronger when the new Court fined unions and imprisoned strikers for contempt of court. Industrial relations deteriorated generally, and two miners' strikes, in 1972 and 1974, brought industry almost to a standstill. While these strikes were directed against the statutory incomes policy of the Government rather than against the Industrial Relations Act, the latter had already destroyed any hope that the unions would give positive support to the general economic policies of the Conservatives.

Mr Heath, the Conservative Prime Minister, decided to call an election rather than face a prolongation of the 1974 miners' strike, which had already led to a 'three-day week'. The election result allowed Labour to form the next Government, and that Government quickly set about repealing the Industrial Relations Act. Nevertheless, the Trade Union and Labour Relations Act 1974, which accomplished this, retained some of the features of the 1971 Act relating to protection against unfair dismissal, and the right to belong to a trade union. Further strengthening of the position of the trade unions followed from the implementation of the 'Social Contract' between the TUC and the Labour Party. These included an extension of 'closed shop' agreements, for example in newspapers and the docks.

The regulation of wages by law (a 'statutory policy') was abandoned, largely owing to the opposition of the unions to any curtailment of 'free collective bargaining'. Nevertheless, by 1975 the Labour Government was threatening to resort again to such legal powers if 'voluntary' wage restraint were not agreed. New versions of the 'Social Contract' were negotiated in 1975 and 1976 between the TUC and the Government, and so the legal powers were not invoked.

It may fairly be asked whether, on the evidence of the last ten years, the trade unions, rather than the Government and Parliament, have effectively ruled the country. In support of this view, it can be said that the Conservative Government was unable to ensure that the unions would register under the Industrial Relations Act and that they would cooperate with the Industrial Relations Court. And before that, Mr Wilson's Labour Government was unable to proceed with its reforms as outlined in the White Paper *In Place of Strife*, because of union opposition. Then again, the miners seemed able to 'hold the country to ransom' during their strikes in 1972 and 1974, thus threatening 'revolution', and eventually bringing the Government down.

On the other side, it should be remembered that the changes in the law relating to the industrial relations were in themselves revolutionary, and were considered by the unions to undermine their very existence. Even so, the TUC leaders never advocated that the unions break the law, only that they refuse to cooperate wherever such a refusal was legal. Of course, not all trade unionists took this cautious line, and many sought to bring the Government down by industrial action. That they were able to do so in 1974 by the miners' strike might appear conclusive evidence of the predominant power of the unions. Yet it was the Prime Minister who decided to call an election, and it was the electorate which refused to endorse his policies.

In the years after 1974, the Labour Government was able to impose its policy of severe wage restraint and massive cuts in public expenditure despite the declared opposition of some trade union leaders. These policies were made possible through the operation of the 'Social Contract' (between the Labour Government and the TUC) and the depressed economic circumstances. Their implementation does not support the view that the unions can now exert their power over the Government without agreeing in return to considerable sacrifices from their members. The position of the Government as 'manager of the economy' is not usurped by the unions, for as in industry itself, management–union cooperation is needed to achieve success. In a democracy based on a general consensus among its citizens, a Government cannot afford to act against the strong opposition of one of the most important interests in the country if it wishes to remain in office. Thus industrial relations demonstrate the more general pattern of relationships between organized groups and the Government in Britain, a pattern based on sharing power rather than on domination of one over the other.

10. Government and politics

The Constitution

When we ask 'How is Britain governed?' we are asking how the affairs of this community of 56 million people are run. There has to be some ruling and regulating when people live in groups, even small groups. Somebody makes the regulations—the laws—that all members of the group must observe. Somebody sees to it that these laws are carried out, that the group's affairs are conducted within the framework of these laws. Somebody decides whether or not a member accused of breaking one of these laws has, in fact, done so.

To find out who these 'somebodies' are, how they are composed and appointed, what powers each possesses, what are the relations between them, we turn to the Constitution of the country. The Constitution is (see Fig. 10.1) simply the set of rules that decree how its government is to be organized.

In the case of some countries, e.g., France and the USA, this is easy to do, because their Constitutions were worked out in special assemblies convened for this purpose, and then written down in a single, official document. Copies of this document can be obtained without difficulty.

Britain, however, has no written Constitution of this kind. There *is* a Constitution, but we cannot turn conveniently to one single official document setting out the rules and principles on which government in Britain is based. We can buy any number of books about the British Constitution, but we cannot buy a copy of our Constitution as Americans and Frenchmen can of theirs. Where then are we to find the rules that underlie the working of Britain's system of government?

Some of them can be found written down in actual laws passed at one time or another in the course of centuries. The Bill of Rights in 1689 laid down a number of things that future monarchs could not do. The Act of Settlement in 1701 outlined certain conditions with which the Monarch must comply. The Parliament Act of 1911 set down in writing certain limits on the power of the House of Lords in the making of laws. Various Reform Acts have decreed, from time to time, just which people should have the right to elect Members of Parliament, and the ways in which this was to be done.

Yet, even if we collected together and studied these scattered laws touching the Constitution, we should still see only part of the picture. A great many rules, just as important, have never been enacted as written laws at all. They are simply *conventions* or customs; that is, rules which are not written down 'in the book' but which everyone agrees must be followed in practice. For instance, there is no law stating in black and white that the Queen *must* give her assent to Bills which have been passed in both Houses of Parliament, but there is a convention that she must do so. Any attempt to flout this convention would be just as serious constitutionally as any attempt to ignore a written law, such as the Bill of Rights.

THE BRITISH CONSTITUTION

1. Acts of Parliament
    Parliament Acts
    Representation of the People Acts
    Act of Union 1707
    Habeas Corpus Act 1679

2. The Prerogative of the Crown
    The Crown appoints and dismisses Ministers and Officials
    The Crown makes treaties
    The Crown summons and dissolves Parliament

3. Conventions of the Constitution
    The powers of the Crown are exercised mainly by Ministers
    The Queen must act on the advice of Ministers
    Ministers are responsible to Parliament for their actions
    The sovereignty of Parliament (the Queen must assent to Bills passed by Parliament)

4. Common Law
    Rights upheld by courts, but not derived from Acts of Parliament

5. Parliamentary Privilege
    Freedom of speech of MPs in debate

Fig. 10.1. The British Constitution

This fact that there is no single written law called 'The British Constitution' has one consequence which is useful in practice but adds to the difficulty of understanding the Constitution. It means that changes in the Constitution can come about more easily and less noticeably. Countries with written Constitutions usually incorporate in them very special regulations for making alterations. A law altering the powers of the American President, i.e., altering the American Constitution, has to be done in a special way, more complicated than that for a law altering, say, import duties. But in Britain, a law altering the powers of the Monarch would proceed in exactly the same was as any other laws, e.g., one altering the school-leaving age. Moreover, the conventions of the Constitution, since they are not written down in law to begin with, can change gradually over a period of time. In this case we are often unable to fix the precise date when a new convention became accepted.

Consequently, in the course of centuries, the Constitution has been changed in a piecemeal fashion—a law enacted here, a change of convention accepted there. There has been no tearing up of everything and starting afresh with a blank sheet of paper—as the French have done several times (1870, 1946, 1958).

The practical advantage of this is that Britain can adapt her system of government to suit a changing society with less difficulty than many other countries. But just because changes have come about piecemeal and gradually over centuries, and often have not needed to be embodied in written law because they have been generally recognized in practice, makes the Constitution more puzzling to the student. Old names and old forms may still persist, though the underlying realities may have altered enormously. It is rather like a housewife who has for years kept sugar in the tin labelled tea. She has not bothered to change the label because she knows quite well, as does everyone in the family, that the tin contains sugar.

This is why explanations of the British constitution always involve a great deal of history. We have not the time and space here to go into this at the length it requires, but will have to make do with a briefer statement of the general development and the main stages in it.

Development of the Constitution

The principle changes in the workings of the British Constitution may be summarized in table form:

1. *Decline in powers of the Monarch, and establishment of the sovereignty of Parliament*: Today the Monarch is 'non-political', and performs ceremonial functions. Parliament is the supreme law-making institution, and Governments must have the support of a majority in the House of Commons.

2. *Advent of democracy*: The right to vote in parliamentary elections has been extended by Acts of Parliament from 1832 to 1969, until now all persons over 18 (with minor exceptions, such as members of the House of Lords) can vote.

3. *The decline in the powers of the House of Lords*: The powers of the House of Lords have been reduced by the Parliament Acts of 1911 and 1949. Today, the House of Lords must pass all financial legislation sent to it from the House of Commons, and can delay other Bills for only one year. Life peers were introduced under the Life Peerages Act 1958, and the Peerage Act 1963 allows peers to disclaim their titles.

4. *Growth of the party system*: From the late nineteenth century the political parties have established strong national organizations, which today hold national conferences to debate policy. Linked to the national organizations are the constituency organizations, which choose the candidates for Parliament. Lastly, there are party organizations in Parliament itself, such as the Whips offices and policy committees of MPs. Party discipline is essential to the working of Parliament today.

Election procedure

The importance of parties and of the people in the British system of government can best be appreciated by seeing what happens at a General Election.

At this, which must take place at least every five years, elections are held in every constituency in Britain to decide which individuals shall represent them in the House of Commons. For electoral purposes the country is divided into 635 constituencies, each of which returns one Member of Parliament. Each constituency contains, on the average, about 63 000 electors. Any citizen over the age of 18 can vote in the constituency where he usually resides; only criminals, lunatics, and members of the House of Lords are disqualified from voting. Similarly, any citizen (with a few exceptions) can become a candidate for election to Parliament, though there are two conditions: he or she must get ten electors in the constituency to nominate him as a candidate, and he must put down a deposit of £150 which he forfeits if he gets less than one-eighth of all the votes cast in the constituency. (The deposit discourages frivolous candidates.)

On the day appointed for the election, voters go to the polling stations in their constituency and indicate, by marking a ballot form, which of the various candidates listed on the form they would like to have as their representative in the House of Commons. At the end of the day the ballot-boxes, into which the voters have put their marked forms, are sealed and taken to one centre in the constituency, unlocked, and the votes counted in the presence of the candidates. The one who has the most votes—even if he has only more than his nearest opponent—is successful, and will go to Westminster as Member of Parliament for that constituency.

Electing MPs and choosing a Government

This procedure going on in every constituency means that the people of the country have chosen the 635 men and women who will make up the House of Commons until the next General Election. In view of the importance of the work the House of Commons does, this is no small matter. But it is not, in fact, the only thing the electors have done. They have also decided which party or parties will form the next Government. Since 1945, only the Labour and Conservative parties have been capable of forming a Government, because the smaller parties have had so few MPs. In February 1974, however, the Labour Party did not have an overall majority in the House of Commons, and came to power with the support of the minor parties.

In order to have an overall majority in the House of Commons, a party must have 318 MPs out of the total of 635. In the General Election of October 1974, the Labour Party won 319 seats, but it received only 39 per cent of the vote in the country as a whole. It is thus possible to win a majority of seats in the House of Commons without having a majority of votes in the election.

Why should so many party members be returned to Parliament? Why should there not be a great many non-party people, as was once the case? The main reason is that with over 60 000 electors to be canvassed in a limited period and with limited money, a candidate needs the aid of an efficient—yet inexpensive—organization of helpers to do this. Only the big national parties have these in the constituencies—the local party associations. Therefore, the candidates who have the backing of these organizations in the constituencies have a huge advantage over the independent candidate, conducting his campaign single-handed or with a hastily improvised organization. Since the big parties have these organizations in every constituency, the non-party candidate has only a slender chance of winning.

Just because this help is so valuable, the party association will not give it to a candidate, i.e., will not adopt him as their man, unless they are absolutely sure he is a good member of their party and a loyal follower of the party leaders. In short, in order to get into Parliament at all, it is almost essential to belong to one of the big national parties.

Nevertheless, during the 1960s and 1970s, the two major parties have been successfully challenged by the Liberals and the Nationalists in several seats, and Independents have been elected on occasion. The Liberals first showed their strength in the 1960s, and in the General Elections of 1974 polled around one-fifth of the votes cast. But just as the two big parties are over-represented in the House of Commons in proportion to their votes, so the Liberals are under-represented. In October 1974, they won only thirteen seats, while under an electoral system based on 'proportional representation' they would have had over 100 MPs. In Scotland, the Scottish National Party won 30 per cent of the vote and returned eleven MPs to Parliament out of seventy-five. In Northern Ireland, not one of the twelve MPs belonged to a major party. In Wales, the Plaid Cymru (Welsh Nationalists) won three seats out of thirty-six.

To sum up, the most recent developments in Britain have shown a decline in the strength of the big parties, and a rise in voting for the smaller parties. This change in voting patterns has not been so strongly reflected in changes of seats held in the House of Commons, however, because the 'first-past-the-post' electoral system has exaggerated the strength of the two big parties.

The party struggle

The General Election is conducted in terms of a struggle between the parties.

Table 10.1. General elections

Year	Conservative Votes cast	Conservative Seats won	Labour Votes cast	Labour Seats won	Liberal Votes cast	Liberal Seats won
1945	$9\frac{1}{2}$ million	212	$11\frac{1}{2}$ million	394	$2\frac{1}{4}$ million	12
1950	$12\frac{1}{2}$ million	298	$13\frac{1}{4}$ million	315	$2\frac{1}{2}$ million	9
1951	$13\frac{3}{4}$ million	321	14 million	295	$\frac{3}{4}$ million	6
1955	$13\frac{1}{4}$ million	344	$12\frac{1}{2}$ million	277	$\frac{3}{4}$ million	6
1959	$13\frac{3}{4}$ million	365	$12\frac{1}{4}$ million	258	$1\frac{1}{2}$ million	6
1964	12 million	303	$12\frac{1}{4}$ million	317	3 million	9
1966	$11\frac{1}{2}$ million	253	13 million	363	$2\frac{1}{4}$ million	12
1970	13 million	330	12 million	287	2 million	6
1974 (Feb.)	12 million	296	$11\frac{1}{2}$ million	301	6 million	14
1974 (Oct.)	$10\frac{1}{2}$ million	276	$11\frac{1}{2}$ million	319	$5\frac{1}{4}$ million	13

Seats and votes
Notice that in 1951 and in February 1974 the party which won most votes did not win most seats, and that the Liberals won few seats but had a sizeable vote in the country. The reason is that the British system, with *single-member constituencies* and *simple majorities* produces this 'distortion'.

Example:

Constituency A		Constituency B		Constituency C	
Jones (C)	20 000	Green (C)	20 000	Grey (L)	30 000
Brown (L)	19 000	White (L)	19 000	Gold (Lib)	15 000
Smith (Lib)	10 000	Black (Lib)	7 000	Scarlet (C)	5 000
Cons. maj.	1 000	Cons. maj.	1 000	Lab. maj.	15 000

Conservatives get 45 000 votes, 2 seats
Labour gets 68 000 votes, 1 seat
Liberals get 32 000 votes, 0 seats

It is not just the *total numbers* of supporters that matter, but how they are *distributed* throughout the constituencies.

At the outset of the campaign each party issues its programme, telling the electors in the country what it will do about the main political issues of the time inflation, unemployment, housing, and so on—if the electorate returns enough of its candidates to give it the essential majority support in the Commons. The party leaders explain the programme, appeal for support, and criticize other parties, on television and radio and at public meetings. Throughout the country posters and placards proclaim the party's proposals. The national press prints the programme, discusses it, and reports on the speeches and activities of the leaders of the parties. In each constituency the official party candidate and his many helpers put the programme across in meetings outside factories, by door-to-door canvassing, by loudspeaker vans in the street. The electorate is urged to 'vote Labour', 'vote Conservative', 'vote Liberal', etc. Electors in the constituency are urged not just to vote for Mr Smith or Mr Jones, but for 'Mr Smith, the Conservative candidate', or 'Mr Jones, the Labour candidate'.

Table 10.2. The general election of October 1974

Party	No. MPs elected	Percentage of votes cast
Labour	319	39.3
Conservative	276	35.8
Liberal	13	18.3
SNP (Scottish National Party)	11	2.9
Plaid Cymru (Welsh Nationalists)	3	0.6
United Ulster Unionist	10	
Social Democratic and Labour (Northern Ireland)	1	
Independent (Northern Ireland)	1	3.1
The Speaker	1	
Others	—	
	635	100.0

When these electors are deciding whether to vote for Mr Smith or Mr Jones, they do so in the light of all this. Those who vote for Jones do so not just because he seems a pleasant fellow who will look after the constituency's interests when at Westminster, but rather because Jones is the candidate of the party they hope will win most seats at the election, and thus provide the Government of the country. There may be a local issue, e.g., unemployment, and candidates will have to persuade electors that they will do their best to get this relieved if they are returned to Parliament. Generally, however, the arguments among voters in any constituency are much more likely to be about the merits of the rival programmes and policies offered to the country by the parties. It is the names of the national party leaders that are bandied about, rather than those of the local candidates. A few weeks after the election, many electors will have completely forgotten the actual name of the candidate they voted for; but they will recall quite clearly whether they voted Conservative, Labour or Liberal.

A General Election, then, is not only a method of choosing a Member of Parliament for each constituency, it is also a national contest to decide which of two or three big parties the people want to provide the personnel and policies of the Government for the next few years. In other words, they are indicating who should be the next Prime Minister. The result of the contest depends on the outcome of 635 skirmishes, each on its separate constituency battlefield. Whichever party wins most of the skirmishes has won the election.

Party system in Parliament

When the results of the elections in all constituencies are in, the leader of the party with the largest number of members returned to the House of Commons is invited by the Queen to form a Government. The leader becomes Prime Minister, and selects from among his party colleagues in Parliament those whom he wants as Ministers to run the various departments of government, e.g., Foreign Secretary, and Secretary of State for Scotland. He also chooses the members of the Cabinet. The party with the next largest number of supporters in the Commons becomes the official Opposition to the Government, its leader taking the title 'Leader of Her Majesty's Opposition'.

The Prime Minister and other Ministers sit on the Government Front Bench in the House, on the Speaker's right. Their party supporters fill up the Government Back Benches behind their leaders. Across the floor of the House, directly facing the Government benches, sit the leaders of the party in opposition, with their supporters occupying the benches behind them.

Thus the very seating arrangements in the House of Commons emphasize the party system. For the next four or five years the party argument goes on across the floor of the House, until the next General Election when the party contest is on again in every constituency in the land.

Yet, strictly speaking, the British Constitution knows little of parties. Until 1969, the ballot paper could list only the candidates' names, and say nothing of their party allegiance. In appearance, then, the voter marking his form is just expressing his preference for one individual over others to be his representative in Parliament. But, as often with the British system, the appearance is not the whole reality. In fact, the voter is also expressing his preference for one of two or three possible governments and national policies that are being offered him. It is, then, the people of Britain themselves who decide who shall rule.

The system of government in Britain today, then, might be summarized in the following fashion. Britain is a monarchy but the Monarch no longer exercises much power. The executive power is vested in the Ministers, especially in the Cabinet—the Prime Minister and his most important colleagues. But the Cabinet can only govern if it has the consent and support of a majority in Parliament: it cannot make or change laws, but must ask Parliament to do this; it cannot raise or spend money without Parliament's sanction; its actions and proposals need Parliament's approval; and if it loses its majority support in Parliament it must resign. The Government is therefore accountable or responsible to Parliament; and since Parliament is elected by the people on a basis of universal adult suffrage, the Government is accountable to the people. The final decision as to which of a certain number of alternative governments and policies the country is to have lies with the (adult) people. People who have similar ideas about what kind of government they want, organize themselves into parties to try and secure the return of a majority of Members of Parliament who share their ideas, and thus secure a Government which will be willing and able to run the country as they would like to see it run.

Party ideologies compared

The two political parties which have formed Governments in Britain since 1945 are the Conservative Party and the Labour Party. Although they oppose one another in elections and in the House of Commons, they do not stand for completely opposed policies in every field. They have similar policies in foreign affairs, both agreeing on the need to support the United Nations and the North Atlantic Treaty Organization, and to work for better East–West relations and disarmament agreements. The argument is mainly over which party is more competent to conduct these policies efficiently.

In domestic matters, too, the parties do not always differ, and their practice is often closer than their manifestos might suggest. But there are important differences mainly in the field of social and economic affairs. On the general issue of Government's role in the economy, Conservatives accept that they must provide guidance and regulation. But as far as possible, they would leave private firms free to make their own plans. Labour followers believe that much more control and regulation is needed in the public interest. They would not nationalize all industries, but they did nationalize steel in 1967, and shipbuilding and aircraft manufacture in 1977, against strong opposition from the Conservatives who prefer private enterprise.

The Conservative and Labour Governments of the 1960s and 1970s have had to tackle a high rate of inflation and a large Balance of Payments deficit. The Labour Government introduced 'statutory' (i.e., by legislation) prices and incomes controls in 1966, although these were unpopular with the trade unions. The Conservatives opposed the use of Government controls, and preferred 'free collective bargaining' and unfettered powers for industry to set its own prices and make profits. But soon after their return to power in 1970, the Conservatives resorted to a statutory policy. Labour came to office again in 1974, and this time the Government did not attempt to reintroduce a statutory policy. Instead, it relied on the 'Social Contract' with the trade unions. Nevertheless, the Government warned that without the unions' cooperation, legal powers to restrain wage increases would be sought. In sum, the difference between the parties on the issue of statutory controls versus free collective bargaining might appear to be ideologically fairly clear, but in practice each has been forced by circumstances to adopt a similar policy.

Another example in this area is the reform of the laws relating to industrial relations. The Labour Government in 1969 proposed penalties for unofficial strikes, but abandoned the policy when the trade unions strongly objected; the

Table 10.3. Party preference by sex, age, and social class (Scotland, May 1974). (Source: Opinion Research Centre Survey, *The Scotsman*, 15 May 1974)

Party	All	Sex		Age					Percentage Class			
		Male	Female	18–24	25–44	45–64	65+	AB	C1	C2	DE
Conservative	29	25	33	24	27	26	41	49	38	23	22
Labour	39	40	39	35	36	43	40	23	27	43	48
Liberal	7	6	8	7	8	6	6	6	10	9	5
SNP	24	29	20	33	29	24	13	22	25	25	24
Other	1	1	1	1	—	1	—	—	1	1	1

1. Less than 1 per cent.
Note: Class AB is middle class, C1 lower middle, C2 skilled working class, and DE unskilled and very poor.

Conservatives passed the Industrial Relations Act in 1971 with stronger powers relating to strikes, but intense opposition from the TUC rendered the Act virtually inoperative. Labour repealed the Act in 1974, and the Conservatives did not put its re-enactment on their programme. Thus both parties, after bitter experience, were forced to accept much the same policy on industrial relations.

Both parties accept the idea of the Welfare State and its existing foundations—National Health Service, social security, full employment. The Conservatives are readier to operate some services selectively and to make small charges. They prefer to leave the individual free to spend his earnings, while providing for those in real need. Labour feels that this would mean hardship or humiliation for the needy and that the public provisions would suffer. Economic circumstances have compelled them to postpone or cut back some of their schemes for expansion, and even to introduce small charges in the Health Service, but they have continued to give what priority they can to the social services.

In housing, both agree that there must be more building by local councils and some protection for tenants against unfair rents by private landlords. But again there is a difference of emphasis: the Conservatives slackened the restrictions on some landlords; Labour reimposed them in the Rent Act of 1965. Conservatives encourage the sale of council houses to tenants who wish to buy, Labour often feels this diminishes the stock of council houses without providing enough money to replace them.

In the field of education, also, there are distinct differences of policy between the two parties. Labour maintains that the present English educational system encourages undesirable divisions in society. First, they object to the numerous private schools outside the State system, to which the wealthy send their children. Second, they regard the separation of secondary schools inside the State system into 'grammar' and 'comprehensive' as deepening the sense of public snobbishness and social inequality in Britain, which is the main target of Labour's attacks. The Conservatives defend the variety of schools on the ground that this preserves some freedom of choice for the individual. They believe that a total changeover to the comprehensive system might mean that the high educational standards of the 'grammar' would be lost, children would be penalized, and educational standards would suffer in the name of equality. Labour thinks otherwise.

In general, then, the Conservatives wish to leave as much opportunity and freedom of choice as they can to private enterprise and the individual. They believe that Labour's plans for more controls, regulations and restrictions would shackle the individual, remove incentive, and discourage effort; and that society would then be neither prosperous nor happy.

Labour prefers to emphasize equality and the community. They believe that there can be no real opportunity for all while so many people are handicapped—the badly housed, the underpaid, the old age pensioner; that private enterprise and individualism too often mean that an 'I'm all right, Jack' attitude and a scramble for profits replace a regard for one's neighbours and the public interest.

Supporters and 'floaters'

The Conservative party is strongly favoured by businessmen, employers, property owners, and people who are fairly prosperous—the middle and upper classes. Labour has its strongest following among the working classes and the poorer people in the country. But this is not a hard-and-fast line. The Conservatives win many working class votes, and Labour has many supporters among the middle classes. The Liberals and Nationalists get their supporters in fairly equal proportions from all the social categories.

Throughout the country, each party has its faithful supporters. Each has a solid core of active members who subscribe to the party funds and work to advance the party's cause. In addition, each has many followers who are not active members but who vote faithfully for the party at every election. But there are many people who feel no deep loyalty to either party. These, the 'floating voters', are the objects of attraction to both parties at election time, as the support of enough of them may easily swing the election in a party's favour. But the years between elections are possibly even more important for a party's fortunes than the hectic three-week election campaign. The really devoted party supporter will stay faithful through thick and thin—though even he likes to see his party vigorous and effective. But the less devoted follower or the 'floater' may well be swayed by the impression a party leaves on his mind by its behaviour during the lifetime of a Parliament. If a Government has made some bad blunders, or if the Opposition has behaved feebly, then election promises and campaign propaganda will prove less effective.

Party organization

In organization the parties are broadly similar. In each constituency throughout the country they have their local associations—the constituency parties. These consist of individuals who are such strong supporters of the party that they are willing to give their time and work—without pay—to advance its cause. In Labour constituency parties, certain organizations such as trade unions or socialist societies may also play a part. A constituency party pays subscriptions to the party's funds, selects the party candidate for the constituency, and local members carry out the hard routine work in the campaign, such as door-to-door canvassing. Between elections the constituency party tries, by propaganda, to strengthen the party's position in the constituency, to increase membership and support. It plans for the next fight and organizes fund raising social events.

Each party holds an annual conference to which the constituency parties (and, in the case of Labour, the trade unions and socialist societies) send representatives. These conferences discuss the party's affairs and policies. In the Labour Party the conference, by its decisions, determines what the party policies should be in general. The Conservative Party Conference is not officially the maker of policy; it just expresses opinions which the leaders may, but need not, take into account.

The party associations throughout the country are rather like the supporters clubs formed by the keenest fans of a football team. The team itself, which the supporters encourage and cheer on, is the Parliamentary Party. This consists of the Members of Parliament of the party at Westminster. The Parliamentary Labour Party is more influenced by its supporters (in the annual conference) than the Conservative one is, but both insist on much freedom of action. Like a football team, they need and appreciate the cheers of their fans, but do not feel obliged to follow their advice on strategy and tactics during a match. Each Parliamentary Party selects its own leader. When the party is in power, the leader, as Prime Minister, chooses his own Cabinet colleagues. When in opposition, each has a 'Shadow Cabinet', but whereas Labour elects its 'Shadow Cabinet' the Conservatives allow the leader to choose the team. In the Conservative Party the leaders formulate party policy; in the Labour Party the leaders have to try and persuade the annual conference to go along with them in the policies they favour.

The Liberal Party, the Nationalists, and the Ulster Unionists

Apart from the 'parties of Government' (the Labour Party and the Conservative Party), there are other parties which have attracted considerable support. The Liberal Party was one of the two great political parties at the beginning of the century (the other being the Conservative Party). But it declined in strength until it had only a handful of MPs. Part of the cause of this decline was the formation of the Labour Party in 1900, which appealed specifically to working-class voters.

In the 1960s and 1970s the Liberal Party made something of a comeback, and in the elections of 1974 nearly one-fifth of all voters voted Liberal. It seemed that many people were tired of the major parties, and were looking for a 'third' party with a different approach. In 1977, the Liberals made a 'pact' with the Labour Government to support it in the House of Commons.

In Scotland and Wales, many voters turned to the Nationalists, and in the election of October 1974 the Scottish National Party won 30 per cent of the Scottish vote and returned eleven MPs. In Wales, the Welsh Nationalists (Plaid Cymru) obtained just over 10 per cent of the vote and returned three MPs. One result of this rise in Nationalist voting was the adoption of devolution policies by the major parties. Under Labour's devolution proposals, Scotland would have an Executive, and an Assembly to pass laws relating to Scottish affairs. Wales would have somewhat more limited powers of 'home rule', since there would be no law-making power. This would be retained by Westminster.

In Northern Ireland (Ulster), Home Rule was practised from 1921 to 1972, through the Stormont Parliament and Government. Because of the civil unrest there after 1969, this system of government was 'suspended' and 'direct rule' introduced from London. The voters in Northern Ireland have not returned MPs of British parties to Westminster, but members of Ulster parties. In October 1974, ten United Ulster Unionists, one Social Democratic and Labour, and one Independent were elected.

Some objections to the party system

People often object to the party system. Since we all want the country to prosper, why not do away with parties and just pick the best people for the job? The answer is that we do not all agree on what should be done to make the country prosper, or on who are the best men and women. People have different opinions, and parties are a reflection of this fact.

Moreover, non-party government is less open to scrutiny and criticism; it can easily become one-party government. If the 'best men' are governing, criticism may be denounced as unpatriotic, and we should be on the road to an undemocratic system.

Quite a different criticism of the British party system is that there are not enough parties. It is said that there could be more than two opinions on any subject, so should there not be numerous parties to give each citizen a better chance of finding one that best suits his own opinion?

The argument against this is that with only two or three big parties there is a better chance of a stable and effective Government. If there were to be a dozen parties, each winning a good share of the seats in Parliament, then a Government could only be formed by several of them agreeing to work together—a coalition. However, it would be difficult for that Government to do anything important without offending one or other of the parties in it; and if the offended party were to withdraw its support, the Government would fall. To stay in power, the Government would have to limit its activity to things that would upset none of the parties represented in it. The advantages of a two-party system are that it often permits a stable, effective Government; that the existence of a solid opposition party ensures that the actions of the Government are constantly scrutinized and criticized; and that there is always an alternative Government available, so that the people do have a choice and can change their Government simply and without violence.

Pressure groups

It may seem that the people have only a small and infrequent voice in public affairs. It is they who decide at a General Election which Government they will have, but General Elections normally occur only once every five years. Moreover, once a Government has been installed, it enjoys very wide powers of action. It is not obliged to keep seeking the electorate's approval before making any particular decisions, even on issues which were not envisaged at election time. Yet its decisions may well disturb many people, including those who had voted for it at the election. Is there no way in which people can make their opinions known except by waiting five years and then voting against the Government concerned?

There are, in fact, many channels and methods whereby the Government is made aware of how people feel about its policies. None of them is so dramatic as a General Election, but they do permit a continuing interaction between the rulers and the ruled. Our society is full of pressure groups, organizations representing people with similar interests or opinions, who are prompt to raise their voice on matters which affect them.

Some organizations are based on occupations, e.g., trade unions or professional associations. Others, like the Automobile Association and the Royal Automobile Club are mainly concerned to provide services for people with some common interest; however, the AA and RAC also make protests when government decisions seem to penalize motorists unfairly. Still other organizations cater for people sharing similar beliefs, e.g., the churches: their purposes are spiritual, not temporal, but again they speak out when government proposals involve questions of morality. Then there are groups out to promote some special cause: to prevent cruelty to children, improve prison conditions, abolish blood sports, ban the bomb, campaign for 'decency' on television and radio. Others are set up to achieve a limited purpose, either local or temporary. Tenants may form an association to fight for better amenities or lower rents; local enthusiasts may start a movement to prevent a regiment from being disbanded, to get a railway service restored, to thwart proposals for a new airport in their neighbourhood.

The means of action open to pressure groups are many and varied. Powerful groups, claiming to speak for great numbers or strong interests, may often go directly to the top, i.e., confront and discuss their grievances with the Minister concerned. We constantly hear of representatives of the TUC or important unions meeting members of the Cabinet to put their objections to government schemes for freezing wages, limiting strike action, or forcing reforms on unions. TUC pressure, for instance, played an important part in persuading the Labour Government in 1969 to abandon the legislation it was proposing for tackling unofficial strikes; and to accept instead the TUC's own proposals. The various versions of the 'Social Contract' from 1974 to 1976 illustrate the close cooperation between the Government and the TUC in incomes policy and legislation generally. Again, the political parties and individual MPs are themselves important channels of communication and pressure. While union leaders are closeted with Ministers, the rank and file may be lobbying sympathetic MPs: a batch of these among government supporters may then add their own pressures on Ministers, raising the threat of dissent with the party unless the Government modifies its policies, and may carry this to the extent of speaking and even voting against their leaders in the House. The individual MP is bombarded with letters and deputations from his constituents, and visits his constituency regularly to listen to complaints. These grievances he then takes up with his party leaders, the government department concerned, or in Parliament itself at question time or in debate.

Again, pressure groups may try to make their weight felt through activities designed to show how strongly they feel or win more support for their cause: they may hold processions, public meetings, marches, and demonstrations; they may organize petitions or try to gain sympathetic publicity in the news media.

Consumer protection and citizen action groups

In recent years, organizations designed to protect the interests of consumers and citizens generally have sprung up, and these now play an important part in political and community life. They are badly needed, since the ordinary citizen often feels defenceless in the face of powerful government departments and commercial bodies. Most towns now possess a Citizen's Advice Bureau, which gives help on a variety of problems such as free legal aid and other rights available to the citizen. It is particularly concerned with consumer protection, and supplements the work of the Government Office of Fair Trading. The official National Consumer Council represents the consumer interest to Government and industry, and the privately run Consumers' Association speaks for its 700 000 members. (See Chapter 6, page 141.)

In the local community, there are many 'voluntary' bodies which tackle social problems. Among the best known are Age Concern, Help the Aged, Shelter, Alcoholics Anonymous, the Samaritans, and the numerous organizations connected with the churches. Even in the age of the 'Welfare State', there is still plenty of room for groups which stand up for the rights and interests of the individual and the weaker sections of the community.

The press and broadcasting

The press and broadcasting play an important part in the matter of public opinion. This is not to say that people's opinions are derived simply from newspaper editorials. Their minds are not a blank sheet on which a journalist or broadcaster can imprint whatever opinion he wishes. Personal experience, interests, and beliefs are more important in shaping a man's outlook and views than what some journalist writes. Research suggests that the media are more effective when they reinforce a person's views than when they contradict them. A party political broadcast by Labour is not likely to convert a man or woman who, for a variety of reasons, has long been a Conservative supporter. Perhaps if there were only one newspaper, hammering home the same message, it might effectively indoctrinate people; but Britain has a variety of national dailies and national Sundays with different views on public affairs, none specifically tied to a party. Then there are many magazines and journals that give their readers further viewpoints.

In fact, a great many people are selective readers. They may buy a certain daily because it gives good coverage of horse racing; they may not read beyond the sports section and the reports on the latest murder or robbery. Nor is a Government likely to change its mind just because of what a newspaper says: direct confrontation with a big pressure group is more likely to be effective. But as a forum in which information is made available the media are very important.'The basis of political freedom and the essence of democracy,' wrote The Times in March 1963, 'is the public's right to know.' This presumes a free, full, and fair presentation of information, for by unfairness in selecting what to print or in the way it is put across, newspapers could mislead the public. Some feel that in this area, the freedom of the press to report fully and fairly, British newspapers are endangered.

The danger is seen to lie in two developments, commercialization and centralization. The bulk of popular newspaper circulation is dominated by seven large groups. To start a successful newpaper when the field is so dominated seems impossible. In the 1950s about twenty newpapers gave up the struggle to survive. To survive requires the support of advertisers, but these are interested in big circulations, not newpapers without many readers. So those already enjoying massive circulations or affluent readership attract the indispensable advertising, and so can afford to make themselves still more attractive. But in their pursuit of bigger circulations to hold their advertisers might they not be led away from their task of presenting free and fair information? This is not a case of unscrupulous advertisers deliberately corrupting journalists and editors. It is that, in the pursuit of ever bigger readership figures, newspapers might resort to means at odds with their responsibilities: might ignore minority views; might cut down on important but not very exciting information; might present it in unfair fashion to make it more eye-catching; might avoid critical reporting in some areas lest it upset certain advertisers.

These are dangers; but so is the dislike of authorities for having their secrets revealed. The constant probing by the press, its daily reporting of government activity, does ensure that misdeeds or blunders, important decisions and disputes are not covered up. The press can also provide information on public reactions and so let the Government see how widespread feelings are, even though it may not act on the information. Most papers now make great use of opinion polls on all kinds of topics of public debate. Newspapers, again, can be extremely effective at publicizing individual cases of injustice, which but for them, might have gone unnoticed: the high-handed treatment of some tenant by a local council or private landlord, of some citizen by the police, of some schoolchildren by a headmaster. Likewise a vivid documentary on television can bring home to millions the urgency of a problem more forcibly than pages of statistics, and so create a public mood in which action may be taken.

Effects of public opinion on Government

A Government does not swing wildly to and fro according to whatever wind blows upon it from these organs of public opinion. It has been entrusted with the power to rule, and can insist that whereas these bodies represent the special interest of boilermakers or bankers, Methodists or motorists, the Government has to consider the national interest. Nevertheless, it often takes these pressures into account. Ministers slow down a little on one measure, speed up another, increase aid to some industry, promise to undertake a new enquiry or to modify some scheme. At the very least, the reasons for not changing its mind are made clearer and more public. In numerous ways, then, a Government responds to the opinions to which it is exposed throughout its period of office. Whether or not it is returned at the next General Election depends in part on how it has responded to these opinions. A Government which assumed that the electorate could be ignored between General Elections would receive some sharp reminders at by-elections and perhaps a severe shock at the next General Election.

Some, however, would argue that all this does not provide enough scope for citizens in government affairs. The feeling stems partly from disillusionment with the conduct of recent Governments, whose actions seem, at least in the short run, to diverge from their previous promises. Partly it reflects a concern that the whole business and machinery of government has become so vast and complex that the individual is helpless to influence it. Indeed even some pressure groups have grown so large that members feel their leaders have lost touch with the opinions of the rank and file. Such feelings of frustration are underlined in the provinces because government is centralized and London-based.

Hence there are demands for more participation, i.e., for changes which would permit the ordinary man to feel more involved, to have a bigger say in decisions which affect him. Some moves have been made. Ombudsmen have been appointed to deal with complaints against central and local government departments. Governments have begun to issue 'Green Papers' which are meant to promote discussions on particular matters before they decide what policy to adopt.

The devolution of power to Scotland and Wales is another way of bringing power 'closer to the people', and soon the English regions may follow with their own institutions. Whether such reforms will be enough to satisfy the people in these areas is another matter. Scotland and Wales have nationalist feeling which derives from their history as separate nations. They also want powers to change the economic conditions of their countries, and in Scotland this might mean using revenue from North Sea oil. The Government in London, however, is opposed to using the oil revenues in this way, and there is support for this attitude from the English regions. These regions are worried about their own economic performance, and also look to devolution if only to 'keep up with the Scots'. One of the trickiest problems facing any British Government in the late 1970s is reconciling the needs and desires of the different parts of the country with the principles of unity and fair play for all citizens.

11. Parliament

Strictly speaking, there are three elements in Parliament—the Crown, the House of Lords, and the House of Commons. Acts of Parliament need the concurrence of all three elements. Before a Bill (a proposed law) can become a law it has to be passed by the House of Commons and the House of Lords, and given assent by the Queen. This can be seen from the opening words of any Act of Parliament: 'Be it enacted by the Queen's most excellent Majesty, by and with the advice and consent of the Lords Spiritual and Temporal, and Commons, in this present Parliament assembled, and by the authority of the same.' So the supreme law-making authority in Britain is 'The Queen-in-Parliament'.

Normally, however, when we talk of Parliament we mean just the two Houses, Lords and Commons. In practice this is reasonable, for while the Queen's assent is essential to the enacting of a law, that assent is always given. There is no written law to prevent the Queen from refusing to give her assent, but no monarch has done this since 1707. This is a well-established convention that is just as effective as any written law.

Often we are guilty of more careless thinking and equate Parliament simply with the House of Commons. This is wrong, but it does reflect a basic truth, that the House of Commons is by far the most powerful and important of the three elements in Parliament. In certain kinds of Acts of Parliament, e.g., Finance Bills, the House of Lords has no power at all, and in others its powers are restricted. Since the Monarch has no choice but to assent and the Lords are limited, the real centre of parliamentary power is in the House of Commons.

House of Lords

The House of Lords consists of about 1160 Members, most of whom (about 840) are hereditary peers of the realm. In addition, there are about 325 non-hereditary peers: the two Archbishops of Canterbury and of York, with the twenty-four senior bishops of the Church of England; ten Lords of Appeal and nine retired Lords of Appeal, appointed for life, to help in the judicial functions of the House of Lords; and about 280 life peers and peeresses, created under the Life Peerages Act 1958.

Until the twentieth century the powers of the Lords in legislation were reckoned to be as great as those of the Commons, except that, by convention, they did not interfere with, i.e., amend or reject, Bills dealing with money. In 1909, however, the House of Lords flouted this convention when it refused to pass the Budget of that year. After a bitter controversy, including two General Elections within twelve months, the powers of the Lords were limited by statute in the Parliament Act of 1911. They have since been further limited by the Parliament Act of 1949.

In consequence of this legislation, the House of Lords has no powers where Money Bills are concerned. One month after passing through the House of Commons such Bills receive the Queen's assent and become law, no matter what the Lords think about them. All other Bills the Lords can delay for a time, but if the House of Commons cares to insist, these, too, can become law despite the Lords' objections. In practice, if the Lords reject a Bill passed by the Commons, the latter have simply to pass it again in the next *session* and not less than twelve months later. It then gets the Royal Assent and becomes law.

In sum, then, the powers of the Lords in legislation are very limited: Money Bills they cannot touch, and others they can only hold up for twelve months. In the last resort, the will of the people, as expressed by the majority of their elected representatives, must prevail.

The House of Lords, although restricted in its powers, can still serve a useful purpose. Nowadays, the Commons have so much business to get through that time is hard to find. Many measures, unless of outstanding importance or very controversial, often get scanty consideration. These can sometimes get a much fuller discussion in the less hard-pressed House of Lords, which may suggest improvements in the details of such legislation that the Commons willingly accept. The great majority of peers never attend the House of Lords, but of those who do many have had great experience in public affairs, so that their discussions are frequently both interesting and valuable.

Apart from this, the House of Lords has a special judicial function. It is the final court of appeal in civil cases and criminal cases, except criminal cases in Scotland, which are dealt with by the High Court of Justiciary. When sitting in its capacity as Supreme Court, the House of Lords consists simply of the Lords of Appeal.

Most people today would agree that a second chamber is a useful institution, especially in view of the pressure of business in the House of Commons. But many object to this chamber being a hereditary House of Lords. Objections have also come from active Members of Parliament obliged by heredity to enter the House of Lords, e.g., Lord Hailsham and Lord Stansgate. The Parliament Act of 1911 did envisage a future reform of the composition of the Upper House, but so far people have been unable to agree on the kind of changes that should be made.

One step has been taken by the Life Peerages Act of 1958. This provides for the creation of non-hereditary peerages, so that the country may have the benefit of the wisdom of distinguished men and women, without posterity being burdened by their descendants, who may not inherit their great abilities. Another was the Peerage Act of 1963 which permitted peers to disclaim their peerage: Mr Wedgwood Benn (Lord Stansgate), Mr Hogg (Lord Hailsham) and Sir Alec Douglas Home (Lord Home), did so, although the last two resumed their titles as life peers in 1970 and 1974 respectively.

House of Commons

We have already seen that the House of Commons consists of 635 elected Members of Parliament. Of these, 516 represent English constituencies, 36 Welsh ones, 71 come from Scotland, and 12 from Northern Ireland. Members of Parliament, as we saw, can also be classified according to the parties to which they belong, as well as the constituencies they represent. Once elected, Members normally retain their seats until that Parliament is dissolved as a prelude to a General Election.

Members of Parliament may carry on doing their own jobs as well as their parliamentary duties, though in most cases this is physically impossible. Since 1911, Members of Parliament have been paid a salary. They also enjoy a number of privileges, the most important being freedom of speech in Parliament. There a Member of Parliament can make remarks which, made outside the House, would lay him or her open to a libel charge. This enables Members of Parliament to speak quite openly and freely. This is a point of special importance, since the business of the House is largely done through debates. Members put motions or proposals to the House, which then debates them and finally decides, by a simple majority vote, whether to accept them as they stand or in an amended form, or to reject them. The vote may be taken by 'acclamation', i.e., by listening to the response of 'Aye' from those who favour the motion, then the 'No' from those who oppose it, and deciding which is the greater. Often, however, a futher vote is insisted on (and only a few members need insist) in the form of a division. Members file out of the chamber into the 'Aye' lobby or the 'No' lobby, which are simply corridors running down the length of the chamber and accessible from it by connecting doors. 'Tellers' count the number in each lobby. The figures are reported. The side with the bigger number wins the division and so carries its verdict on the motion under discussion.

In doing its work, Parliament has its own *procedures*—a great many rules and regulations which prescribe the way in which things have to be done. Without these, an assembly of 635 would never get anything done—everyone wanting his particular motion to be discussed, protesting at somebody else's getting priority, squabbling as to whose turn it was to speak. So there are many rules prescribing the order in which the business of a session, the Parliamentary Year, is done: the order of the programme each day, the ways in which motions have to be made, the rules governing debate, how votes and divisions are to be conducted.

Parliamentary procedure is partly an affair of written orders, partly of old established customs. The first task of a new House of Commons is to elect one of its Members as Speaker, who presides over their meetings and sees that procedure is followed. He controls the debates, deciding which Member of several who want to speak shall have the floor, and seeing that Members do not stray too far from the subject of debate.

Voting, like debating, is carried out under the Speaker's direction, and he pronounces the results of the vote. He interprets the rules of procedure and settles any disputes as to whether things are being 'properly' done. Defiance of the Speaker's ruling on a point can lead to the temporary suspension from the House of the defiant member. The House of Lords has its own procedures, the Lord Chancellor playing there the same role as the Speaker does in the Commons.

To appreciate the role of the House of Commons in the British system, it is most convenient to examine the role of Parliament. Since the Commons is the real centre of power in Parliament, it plays the key part in the activities of Parliament as a whole. Parliament has three main functions: to make laws; to control and criticize the executive government; to control the raising and the spending of money.

Making of laws

The making of laws is a very important function, and Parliament is called the *legislature* because it is the law-making body in Britain. The supremacy, or 'sovereignty', of Parliament means that in theory there is no barrier to the power of Parliament from a written Constitution or from other institutions in the country. Parliament, it is said, can 'make a man into a woman' in law, if it wished.

This theory may not be so correct since Britain joined the European Community in 1973. Now, Britain is subject also to the laws of the Community, and Parliament must not pass laws which are contrary to these laws. Moreover, the European Court can declare an Act of Parliament to be inconsistent with the Treaty obligations and laws which Britain has accepted by joining the European Community.

A useful distinction in understanding the function of Parliament in law making is that between legislature *procedure* and legislative *process*. It is necessary to follow the procedures used in Parliament if we want to know how a Bill becomes an Act of Parliament. But the more general process of law making directs our attention away from Parliament to the government departments and interest groups who actually draw up the Bills. For it is true that nearly all Bills are presented to Parliament by the Government with their main provisions already decided, and the function of Parliament is to take them through the various procedures without greatly changing their content. This leads many people to talk of Parliament as a mere 'rubber-stamp'. That would be an exaggeration, but there are only a few examples of Parliament exerting itself against the wishes of the Government. This is because the majority party and the Government are closely bound together by their programme, and Governments expect their supporters in the House of Commons to vote for the Bills which implement that programme. The programme itself may have been drawn up in a party conference, or through consultation with interest groups.

SOME PARLIAMENTARY TERMS

The Legislature
Parliament (House of Commons and House of Lords)
Legislative Procedure
The stages and rules of debate for Bills
Bill
A proposed law, which when passed becomes an *Act*
Private Member's Bill
A Bill proposed by a backbench MP
Backbencher
An MP who sits on the 'back benches'; that is, he is not a member of the Government or of the Opposition 'front bench'
Session
The duration of Parliament's annual sitting
Delegated Legislation and Statutory Instruments
Powers given by Parliament to the Government to make laws, or the detailed operation of Acts of Parliament
European Law
Law derived from the European Community, and passed by the Council of Ministers of the EEC
The 'Ombudsman'
The Parliamentary Commissioner for Administration, who investigates complaints of maladministration
Select Committees
Committees of MPs to investigate government affairs. The most important are the Public Accounts Committee and the Select Committee on Expenditure
Queen's Speech
The Government's programme for the coming session
Question Time
The period when government Ministers answer questions tabled by MPs

---

Fig. 11.1. Some parliamentary terms

The MPs themselves may not have been involved in this *process*, but they must come into the legislative *procedure* of getting the legislation passed through Parliament.

This procedure is laid down in the *Standing Orders* of the Houses of Parliament, and is interpreted in a work of reference called 'Erskine May'. The *stages* used in passing Bills into Acts are shown in Fig. 11.2, and are as follows:

First Reading: Formal notice that a Bill is to be introduced.

operation of the Act, than by Parliament which deals with it while it is simply a proposal on paper.

Some people are uneasy at Parliament surrendering even part of its law-making power in this way. Yet, if it tried to fix all these details itself before passing any Bill, legislation would almost come to a halt. What really matters is that Parliament should retain a close watch and control over the ways in which the power it delegates is used. One safeguard is that any Act which delegates legislative power also defines carefully the limits of its use. Moreover, all Statutory Instruments must lie before Parliament for forty days before going into effect. There is a special committee of Members of Parliament (the Select Committee on Statutory Instruments) which examines these and draws the attention of the House to any that seem to abuse the power delegated. Parliament can then proceed to annul these.

Nearly all Bills are introduced by the Government, but the backbench MP has the chance to introduce a 'Private Member's Bill' if he or she gets near the top in a ballot at the beginning of the session. Special procedures apply to such Bills, which usually succeed only if they are non-controversial, or if the Government is willing to give them time for debate. Some important laws have been passed in this way, including the abolition of capital punishment, the Abortion Act 1967, and the divorce reforms of 1967 (England and Wales) and 1976 (Scotland). As can be seen from these examples, laws affecting moral questions are often left to backbench MPs to introduce.

Since Britain joined the European Community in 1973, Parliament has lost its monopoly of law-making power. Some law is now directly applied in Britain without going through Parliament. This is called 'European Community Law' and results from our adherence to the Treaty of Rome. The EEC Council of Ministers makes laws of different types, but only *regulations* have direct effect in the member-states. *Directives* must be implemented by the British Government, usually in the form of Statutory Instruments. Both Houses of Parliament have set up committees to scrutinize the drafts of these instruments (otherwise known as 'European secondary legislation'). Parliament can merely insist on debating the proposals, thereby influencing the Government's attitude in the Council of Ministers. Once the Council has decided what to do, Parliament cannot reject the application of such law in Britain.

Control and criticism of the Government

Many people regard this function of Parliament as even more important than law making. The Ministers who form the Government are responsible to Parliament, wherein they must retain the support of the majority of Members. It is Parliament's job to see that they do not forget this, by scrutinizing Ministers' activities and calling them to account. Parliament has several ways and opportunities of exercising this control and criticism.

The Commons can show its control in the most dramatic fashion by bringing a Government down. A vote of 'No Confidence' in the Government, or the rejection of an important government proposal, will compel the

Government to resign, for no Ministers can carry on without the support of a majority in the Commons. This is not very likely nowadays because of the party system. It would be very surprising if many members of the Government party joined their votes to those of the minority Opposition party to defeat their own party leaders and turn them out of office. It would be against their own interests to do so. Yet unless they do this, the critics of the Government cannot secure a majority and thus force the Government to resign.

This does not mean that all the debate and argument is futile. The Opposition may dream wistfully of defeating the Government in a key division, but its daily job is to *criticize*, and this is done by talking, regardless of how the vote goes in the end. In debate, Ministers are forced to defend and explain their proposals and their actions: they cannot sit back smugly just because they are sure of a majority when the vote comes to be taken. These debates are widely reported, and the people—who can get rid of the Government at the next General Election—are kept informed of the Government's conduct.

Debate, then, even if it does not persuade the Government to alter a single proposal, serves very valuable purposes. It ensures that all the Government's proposals and actions are discussed openly, not smuggled through or covered up. It keeps the real masters of the Government—the people—well in the picture as to what is going on. It reminds the temporary rulers—the Government—that they *are* temporary, that they are being observed, and that they had better be 'on their toes'. Blunders are exposed, feeble explanations ridiculed, injustices denounced. The total effect of all this, unless adequately countered in debate by the Government, may be to produce the small swing of opinion in the country which is all that is usually needed to bring about a change of government at the next General Election.

Parliament has plenty of opportunities to exercise its function of criticism. One, as we have already seen, comes in the important debates on Second Reading of Bills introduced by the Government.

There are more general occasions, the most important being the debate on the Queen's Speech at the opening of each session. This speech is, in fact, the Government's statement of its policies and the main measures it proposes to introduce in the coming year. The subsequent debate lasts several days, during which the whole content of the speech is subjected to criticism and comment.

Again, in certain circumstances, a Member of Parliament can bring about a debate at very short notice on 'a matter of urgent public importance'.

The Opposition has traditionally been guaranteed time to debate 'the Estimates', or the Government's expenditure programme for the different departments. Today, committees scrutinize the detailed proposals, and the House as a whole uses twenty-nine 'Supply days' to debate general features of the Government's policies. These subjects are chosen by the Opposition parties.

The most celebrated occasion on which Parliament calls Ministers to account is Question Time in the House of Commons. One hour a day for four days a week is devoted to this. Any Member of Parliament can put a question to any Minister about anything for which that Minister is responsible. It may be a matter of national importance, or it may be a personal matter concerning an individual in the Member's constituency. The Member of Parliament may be seeking information, bringing up some grievance or injustice, uncovering some abuse or instance of bad management.

Ministers get notice of the questions they are to be asked, so they have time to prepare their answers. The original question may, however, be followed up with supplementary questions of which no notice is given. Members of Parliament often make their original question apparently harmless, hoping to work in the real sting in supplementaries, so catching the Minister off his guard. But the Minister is an experienced Member of Parliament himself, and with his departmental assistants is accustomed to looking for the catch in 'simple' questions.

Table 11.1. Typical timetable of a parliamentary session

Address	6 days	
Budget and Finance Bills	$15\frac{1}{2}$ days	
Supply	$26\frac{1}{2}$ days	i.e., Finance 46 days
Consolidated Fund and Appropriation Bills	4 days	
Government legislation	62 days	
Special debates (on Government or Opposition motions)	15 days	
Private Members' time	19 days	
Other business	5 days	
	153 days	

Note the large proportion of Parliament's time devoted to (a) Government legislation and (b) Finance.

Again, a Member of Parliament with some grievance—often he is dissatisfied with a Minister's answers to his question at Question Time—can stage his intention to raise the matter 'on the adjournment'. This refers to the practice of setting aside half an hour at the end of every day, when parliamentary business is over, to allow Members to bring up matters for debate.

Again, Members can pass on constituents' complaints of maladministration to the Parliamentary Commissioner for Administration ('the Ombudsman'), who reports his findings to the MP concerned, and to Parliament as a whole. The Ombudsman is excluded from dealing with the police or the nationalized industries, and he cannot consider questions of policy. He has no powers to enforce his recommendations on the Government. In most cases, however, the Government has agreed to follow up his reports. Most of the complaints dealt with by the Ombudsmen relate to tax and social security matters. There are separate Ombudsmen for the National Health Service and for local government, but these receive complaints from members of the public and through local councillors respectively. The Health Service Commissioners (one each for England, Wales, and Scotland) form part of the Office of the Parliamentary Commissioner, and they also report to Parliament.

Control of the raising and spending of money

This power vested in Parliament is another way in which the Government comes under the control of Parliament. Nothing in all Parliament's history was so important as getting accepted the principle that the 'control of the purse' lay with Parliament. More than that, the power lies in the House of Commons. It is not shared with the Lords. No Government can govern without money. Since the Government must get the Commons' consent to the sums it proposes to spend, to the ways it proposes to raise these amounts, and to the actual spending of them, it is powerless without a majority in the Commons to sanction its annual proposals.

It should be remembered, though, that only the Government can *propose* to raise or spend money. The Commons' business is to consider the proposals, and only the Commons can *sanction* the raising or spending of money. Once again, the Government party majority in the Commons means that it will almost certainly get the Commons' consent; but the need to ask for that consent means that the proposals will be carefully scrutinized and criticized before the consent is given.

On the expenditure side, each year the Government produces the Public Expenditure Survey, which projects for five years ahead the plans for public expenditure. At the end of the year this Survey (also called PESC, after the committee which draws it up, the Public Expenditure Survey Committee) is published and debated in the House of Commons. There is a Select Committee on Expenditure in the House (replacing the Estimates Committee), which has a number of subcommittees to consider different subject areas of public expenditure (e.g., defence, social services, trade and industry). The reports from these committees provide much information for debates in the House as a whole on the Expenditure Survey.

On the basis of this Survey, the departments draw up their estimates for the financial year, beginning on 1 April. These estimates are considered, as we saw, by the House, though debate is not tied strictly to Supply. On twenty-nine days the House takes this opportunity of criticizing the shortcomings of government policies, though in the Supply vote itself the Government's supporters carry consent to this proposed expenditure. Not all expenditure needs annual sanction, e.g., judges' salaries and the interest payments on the National Debt. The latter represents money borrowed by Governments from citizens in the past, on which annual interest has to be paid. This expenditure has been permanently authorized by Act of Parliament. So the Government does not need to get fresh permission for it every year.

The ways in which the money to be spent shall be raised are considered by the House of Commons. The Chancellor of the Exchequer introduces a Budget each year in April (he may also issue Supplementary Budgets at other times of the year). In his speech he reviews the nation's finances. He reminds the Commons of the Estimated Expenditure in the coming year (which they reviewed on those days they devoted to the matter of Supply). He then gives his proposals for the changes in taxation he thinks necessary to raise the money.

Most taxes are, in fact, authorized by permanent legislation and do not need annual reconsideration, though every one that the Chancellor proposes to *alter* in any way has to be approved by the Commons. So, too, has Income Tax, whether he proposes to alter it or leave it alone.

There is an arrangement whereby the proposed taxes become effective at once, but their final authorization is not granted without the usual criticism. The Commons will debate the Budget for some days; and even when

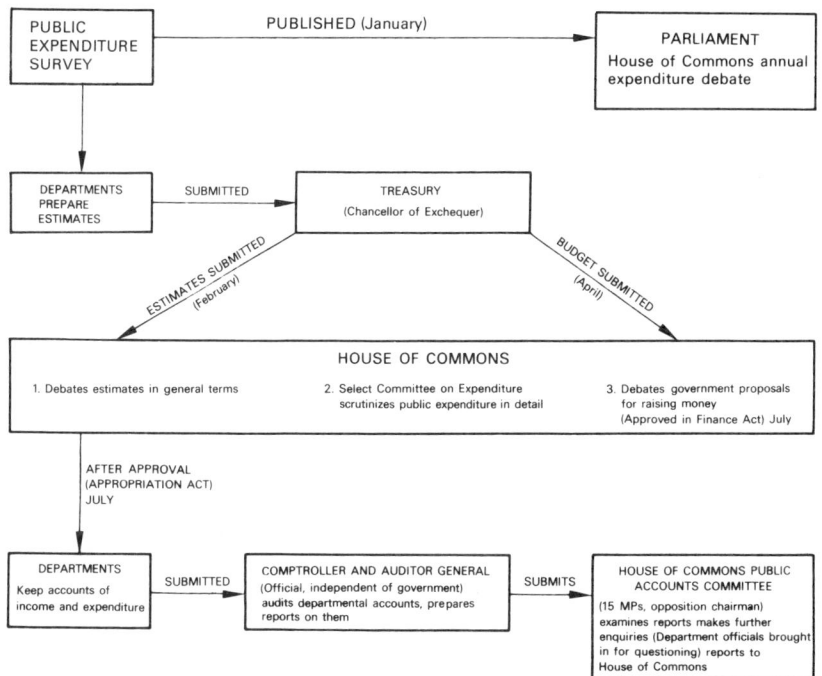

Fig. 11.4. Commons' scrutiny of government spending.

authorized the proposals have to be drafted as a Finance Bill and go through the same stages as any other Bill (except that the Lords cannot touch it). Here again, on Second Reading the whole financial policy of the Government comes under criticism from the House.

Finally, having consented to the Estimated Expenditure and to the ways of raising it, the Commons pass the Appropriation Act. This 'appropriates' the sums granted to the various purposes laid down in the Estimates. The object is to make sure that the Government, once it has been granted permission to spend certain sums, does not then proceed to spend them on things quite different from those outlined in its Estimates.

An annual audit of the accounts of all government departments (showing exactly what has been spent and on what) is carried out by the *Comptroller and Auditor-General*, a special official of Parliament. These Appropriation Accounts, as they are called, and his report on them, go before the Public Accounts Committee, composed of fifteen Members of Parliament with an Opposition Member as chairman. They examine the accounts for instances of wasteful spending by government departments, and their reports may be discussed in the Commons.

Twentieth-century decline?

Several developments, especially in the twentieth century, have lessened the prestige of Parliament and of the ordinary backbench Member. First, there is the growth in importance of the Government and the development of the modern party system. Nowadays the electorate expects the Government to do many things which, a hundred years ago, it did not. The Government, therefore, can justifiably claim the lion's share of Parliament's time for its own business. Moreover, the rigid party system means that Governments need not fear that their measures or their existence will be endangered in Parliament; their support is solid and reliable. The huge amount of business to be done has resulted in restrictions being applied to the time allowed for debate in Parliament. Finally, the Government has come to exercise legislative power and judicial powers.

As for the ordinary Member, not on the front benches of Government or Opposition, there is little time left for him to introduce any private business, once official government and opposition business have claimed their parts of the timetable. He needs luck even to get a chance to speak in a big debate. In what he does say and do he is expected to follow the party line. Party discipline in Parliament is fairly strict. Party officials—the Whips—keep the back-bencher informed of when and how he is expected to support his leaders. He may rebel, but this may lead to the party disowning him; he would then have little chance of being returned to Parliament at any subsequent election.

During the 1970s, further developments in British political history tended towards the weakening of the power of Parliament. Powerful interest groups, especially the trade unions, were able to resist the operation of Acts of Parliament, most notably the Industrial Relations Act 1971. This led Governments to deal directly with the Trades Union Congress in order to get support for their policies. It seemed as if the elected representatives of the people in Parliament were being bypassed in favour of a form of government based on interest groups and the Executive. Some called this the 'corporate state'.

Then, too, some constitutional changes or innovations threatened the supremacy of Parliament. As we have seen, accession to the European Community meant that Parliament no longer had a monopoly over the law-making function. The use of a referendum in June 1975 on British membership of the Community meant that 'direct democracy' had replaced 'representative democracy' on that issue, since the people and not Parliament were being asked to decide what to do. Finally, the introduction of devolution to Scotland and Wales 'transfers' powers from Parliament to new bodies in these countries, although Parliament retains overall 'sovereignty'.

Yet we should not exaggerate these changes. Parliament, as we have seen, still exercises important functions, even if it no longer brings Governments down in defeat as it did a century ago. It is still the great arena in which the battle of political debate is publicly conducted. And on critical occasions the House can still assert itself, as was shown in 1940 when enough Conservative Members turned against the Conservative Prime Minister, Mr Chamberlain, to compel his resignation.

It is the principal forum for political debate in Britain, and it has the function of 'legitimizing' what the Government wishes to do. Party discipline is not as strict as it was, even in the 1960s, and the growth of minor parties has meant that there are often very small government majorities, or no overall majority at all (e.g., after February 1974). This means that the votes of all the MPs are crucial to the passage of Bills, and Governments are more likely to heed the opinions of their backbenchers and MPs of any other parties.

For a time in the 1960s it was thought desirable to reform Parliament by changing the committee system and by altering the powers of the House of Lords. New select committees were established in this period, but the reform of the Lords was defeated in 1969 by a cross-party backbench coalition. In the 1970s there is still talk of reform, and more anxiety about the general decline of Parliament's authority and its place as the focus of respect in public life. The long history of that institution, and its survival through many turbulent periods in the past, ought to give us some optimism about its ability to cope with the apparently fundamental threats to its power and prestige which we have seen in the last ten years.

12. Ministers and civil servants

The Crown and Monarch

In our brief survey of the Constitution we stressed that Parliament does not possess or claim to possess the *executive* power. This is vested in the Crown, which appoints the Prime Minister and members of the Government, the judges (the *judiciary*, or judicial branch), and calls and dissolves Parliament.

The powers of the Crown are today exercised almost entirely on the advice of Ministers of the Crown, and the appointment of these Ministers depends on their having the confidence of a majority in the House of Commons. The choice of a Prime Minister, for example, is clear when one party has an overall majority of seats there. And if a Prime Minister resigns while his party retains a majority in the Commons, the new Prime Minister is chosen by procedures developed within that party, and the name is submitted to the Queen for formal appointment. Before 1965, the Conservative Party did not have clear procedures for appointing a leader, and the Monarch appeared to have some choice. In practice, however, the Queen accepted the advice from the recognized organs of the Party.

The powers of the Monarch are known as the *Royal Prerogative*, and they include the power to grant pardons, to create peers, and give honours (the 'Honours List'). Nearly all these powers are exercised by Ministers of the Government. The Home Secretary or Scottish Secretary, for example, decide on pardons.

Apart from these political and ceremonial functions, the Monarch is important as a symbol of unity for the nation and beyond, for the Queen is also Head of the Commonwealth. Symbols of the Crown are used in Canada, New Zealand and Australia. The Scottish National Party, while pressing for independence for Scotland, wishes to retain Scotland's links with the Crown. Thus, despite the convention that the Queen acts on the advice of the Government, many people distinguish between the Crown and the Government of the day.

Government and Parliament

It is easier to distinguish between the Government and Parliament. Government comes within the 'executive branch', as does the Crown and all 'servants of the Crown', such as the armed services (see Fig. 12.1). Literally, executive means 'carrying out' or 'doing', and once Parliament has passed the laws, the Executive puts them into effect.

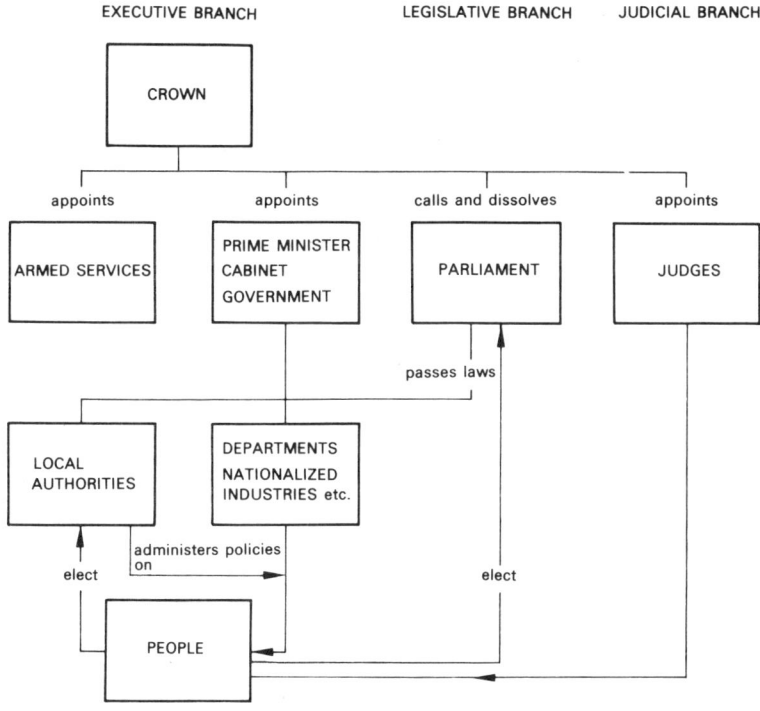

Fig. 12.1. A model of British government

The links between the executive and the legislative branches are very close in Britain. All the Ministers in the Government must be Members of Parliament (a few must be in the House of Lords, the rest in the Commons). The Government must explain and defend its actions and its policies in Parliament. As we saw, most of Parliament's time is taken up with this scrutinizing—debating its proposals for changing the law, for spending money, for raising taxes; questioning Ministers about their actions, criticizing their decisions. And Ministers only retain the executive power so long as they retain the support of a majority in the Commons. If they lose this, they must resign.

Prime Minister and Cabinet: development

The Cabinet and the Prime Minister form the head, or heart, of the Government. Originally the Cabinet consisted of the few select advisers the

Monarch chose to consult rather than summon the large unwieldy *Privy Council*. He presided over their meetings, and was free to take or reject whatever advice they gave him. In the eighteenth cenury, monarchs stopped attending Cabinet meetings, and the Ministers began to discuss and decide matters on their own. Then they developed the practice of sticking together on whatever they decided, and one of them—the leading or 'Prime' Minister—would offer this decision as their advice to the Monarch. As we saw, when this solidarity of the Cabinet rested on the support of a majority in Parliament, the Monarch had no choice but to accept the 'advice' they offered. Thus we arrived at the present position where the Cabinet Ministers are Her Majesty's servants in name only, and where they still 'advise' her, but she must accept whatever they recommend. Henry VIII grew tired of his Minister, Thomas Cromwell, and got rid of him in very final fashion. Queen Victoria detested her Prime Minister, Mr Gladstone, but she had to put up with him and act on the unwelcome 'advice' he used to give.

The Prime Minister

The first step in forming the Government is taken when the Queen sends for the leader of the majority party in the Commons and asks him to become Prime Minister and form a Government.

This is the first task of the Prime Minister. He picks the men and women he wants to act as Ministers in charge of the various departments of government—Environment, Education, Defence, Industry, and so on. He also chooses the few Ministers he wants as members of the Cabinet. All these appointments are entirely in the Prime Minister's hands. He can dismiss any Minister at any time, appoint someone else to the post, and shuffle Ministers around from one department to another. After a spell at Transport, immersed in railways and trunk roads, a Minister may suddenly find himself in the different world of schools, technical colleges, and teachers' salaries at the Department of Education and Science.

In selecting his Cabinet, the Prime Minister naturally wants people who are efficient, but he also likes men and women who get on well together. The Cabinet is a team, and, as in any team, the less brilliant but cooperative person may fit in better than the temperamental star. The Prime Minister usually has his eye on the party, too, for it would not be wise to upset the backbenchers by too many unpopular appointments.

The Prime Minister acts as chairman of the Cabinet and presides over its meetings, which usually occur once or twice a week. He has to deal with differences of opinion in the Cabinet, and try to guide his team to conclusions and decisions that all can accept.

He does not, as a rule, take charge of any special department himself (with the exception of the Civil Service Department), preferring to stay free in order to attend to his general work. In the past, Mr Gladstone, as Prime Minister, did at one time act as his own Chancellor of the Exchequer, and Lord Salisbury combined Prime Minister with being Foreign Secretary. Every Prime Minister is automatically First Lord of the Treasury, but the work of the Treasury is actually done by the Chancellor of the Exchequer. If something very urgent

Table 12.1. Prime ministers and composition of governments

Year	Prime Minister	Composition of Government (support in House of Commons)
1900	Lord Salisbury (Cons.)	Conservative
1902	A. J. Balfour (Cons.)	Conservative
1905	Sir H. Campbell-Bannerman (Lib.)	Liberal
1908	H. H. Asquith (Lib.)	Liberal
1915	H. H. Asquith (Lib.)	Coalition—Lib. and Cons. (War)
1916	D. Lloyd George (Lib.)	Coalition—mainly Conservative (War)
1922	A. Bonar Law (Cons.)	Conservative
1923	S. Baldwin (Cons.)	Conservative
1924	J. R. MacDonald (Lab.)	Labour (needing Lib. support)
1924	S. Baldwin (Cons.)	Conservative
1929	J. R. MacDonald (Lab.)	Labour (needing Lib. support)
1931	J. R. MacDonald (Lab.)	'National'—mainly Cons. and some Lib. and Lab. (Economic crisis)
1935	S. Baldwin (Cons.)	'National'—mainly Conservative
1937	N. Chamberlain (Cons.)	'National'—mainly Conservative
1940	W. S. Churchill (Cons.)	Coalition—All-party (War)
1945	W. S. Churchill (Cons.)	Conservative
1945	C. R. Attlee (Lab.)	Labour
1951	W. S. Churchill (Cons.)	Conservative
1955	Sir. A. Eden (Cons.)	Conservative
1957	H. Macmillan (Cons.)	Conservative
1963	Sir A. Douglas-Home (Cons.)	Conservative
1964	H. Wilson (Lab.)	Labour
1970	E Heath (Cons.)	Conservative
1974	H. Wilson (Lab.)	Labour
1976	J. Callaghan (Lab.)	Labour

came up, the Prime Minister might take charge of it personally; in a crisis, e.g., war, he assumes great powers, as Lloyd George did in the First World War and Winston Churchill in the Second.

The running of the various departments of government is the job of the Ministers in charge, but the Prime Minister is expected to keep an eye on them generally, and to try to settle any differences that might arise between departments. It is the Prime Minister's duty to keep the Queen informed of government business generally: he is the link between Ministers and Monarch.

He has one very special function. The Prime Minister alone advises the

Queen on the time to dissolve Parliament. This is very important, because while a Parliament cannot last more than five years, it does not need to last so long. This means that the Prime Minister can choose the time that suits his party for holding a General Election. Early in the fourth year he may think things are going well—no troubles abroad, a popular Budget at home, the Opposition split by an internal feud—and therefore get a *dissolution* while there is a strong chance of his party being returned and his Government getting another five-year spell in office.

The Prime Minister often acts as spokesman for the Government in the House of Commons on any issue of great importance.

In many appointments, such as bishops and ambassadors, and in the awarding of various honours, the Prime Minister has the real say.

It has been suggested that these powers are so great that Britain today has Prime Ministerial government, not Cabinet government. It is certainly hard to maintain that the Prime Minister is simply 'first among equals' in the Cabinet. He enjoys powers which his colleagues do not.

The power to appoint to (and dismiss from) some hundred desirable government posts, including the Cabinet, makes able, ambitious men and women careful not to offend him. His key voice in deciding on a dissolution helps keep restless backbenchers in line. He is the leader of the national party and this gives him an authority none of his colleagues possesses. Modern systems of communication and the mass media highlight his personal role. The former make it easier for him to undertake dramatic missions: trips to Washington or Moscow for high-level conferences; secret talks on a warship in the Mediterranean; swift plane flights to a crisis zone. The mass media ensure him wide publicity, for he is always news. It is easier for him than for any other politician to make the headlines: news of a move from him draws the press and cameras to Downing Street. Hence a present-day Prime Minister might be tempted to feel that the Government is his personal show, and treat even the Cabinet—apart from a couple of senior colleagues— in a high-handed fashion.

He would, however, be ill advised to do this too confidently, for there are important practical limitations on his powers. His position rests on the majority provided by his party supporters in Parliament. If he upsets too many of them too often, or begins by his activities to appear a liability to the party, they may start looking for another leader. Again, his Cabinet colleagues are themselves important people in the party, often enjoying popularity with some particular section of it. He could, in a showdown, dismiss a batch of them; but would thereby create powerful centres of discontent, weaken the morale of the party, and perhaps increase the electorate's doubts about a divided Government. Of course rebellions do not happen lightly—for the sake of the party, for the sake of office, colleagues will stand a great deal before they rock the boat—but it can happen. The Prime Minister's powers are great, but his continuing to enjoy them depends partly on the skill and care with which he uses them.

The Cabinet

Which Ministers are in the Cabinet, and how many is a matter for the Prime Minister. The usual number is about twenty. Certain Ministers invariably have a place in the Cabinet—the Secretaries of State for Foreign and Commonwealth Affairs, Home Affairs, Scotland, Defence, the Chancellor of the Exchequer, among others. But if a Prime Minister wishes, he can promote to the Cabinet a Minister whose department is not usually included.

The Cabinet is the central organ of the Government. In its meetings it discusses and decides what the Government's policies will be: the schemes the Government is to put before Parliament and which, once endorsed by Parliament, the Government will proceed to carry out. For instance, the Queen's Speech, which outlines to Parliament the things the Government proposes to do in the coming session, is worked out in the Cabinet. All important problems that crop up, and need a policy decision before adoption, go before the Cabinet. All the important legislative proposals of the Government are first discussed by the Cabinet and require its approval before being submitted to Parliament. They only discuss the most important Bills since there is so much government business that the Cabinet would be swamped if it had to make decisions about everything. The individual Minister decides for himself what to do about most of the business of his department. He only brings it up for Cabinet decision if it seems really important.

Differences between departments, unless the Ministers concerned can settle them privately, or the Prime Minister manages to smooth things over, come to the Cabinet for decision. For instance, the Home Secretary might want to give the police force a big increase in pay, but the Chancellor of the Exchequer objects because it will cost too much, and the Secretary of State for Industry fears that the bigger pay for policemen will lure away many young men who were thinking of becoming industrial workers.

Although the Cabinet may include twenty Members, it always acts as one body, on the principle of collective responsibility. However fierce an argument may have gone on in a Cabinet meeting, the decision finally arrived at is considered the decision of the Cabinet as a whole. A Minister who feels badly about a decision can resign his office and go back to being an ordinary backbench Member of Parliament. Mr Cousins, as Minister of Technology, did this in 1966 because he could not accept the Cabinet decision to support a Prices and Incomes Policy, and there have been other resignations since then. Unless the Minister resigns, he or she accepts responsibility for the decision as fully as those Ministers who argued for it, and he must defend it as heartily as any of them. Defeat in the Commons on anything that was decided on in the Cabinet means that the Cabinet must resign as a body. None of its members can claim exemption on the grounds that he had opposed the decision in Cabinet

In fact, no Cabinet Minister is allowed to make it known that he disagreed.

All proceedings in Cabinet are secret, and only the final decision announced as 'Cabinet policy'.

The rule of collective responsibility only applies to matters that have been decided in Cabinet, not to every decision or act of a Minister. If a major policy was rejected, the Cabinet would have to resign; but if the Chancellor of the Exchequer caused a scandal by letting information out before Budget Day—as has happened—only he would have to resign. Many decisions are taken by Ministers without bothering the Cabinet; if these lead to trouble and censure, only the Minister concerned is responsible.

In one respect the idea of collective responsibility has undergone a change in practice. It is still true that the Cabinet must stand together on its decisions, that any Minister not prepared to do so should resign, and that defeat in Parliament on an important Cabinet policy requires the Government to resign or dissolve. But in practice this last position, parliamentary defeat on a matter of confidence, has become extremely unlikely. A century ago it could be said that the Cabinet was collectively responsible to Parliament in the sense that quite often Governments were defeated in the Commons and resigned office in recognition of this parliamentary disapproval. In the twentieth century this is a rare occurrence: 1924 is perhaps the most recent clear case. Developments in the party system have meant that the modern Cabinet can nearly always rely on the support of its loyal majority in the Commons, however big a blunder it may have made. Most Cabinets in this century have given up office in response to an adverse vote in a General Election, not to any defeat in a parliamentary debate. In other words, it is now the electorate, not Parliament, which normally passes the verdict on a Cabinet.

Government departments

The Cabinet, then is a small body that decides policies and deals with major problems. The day-to-day work of running the nation's affairs is carried on through the departments of State, or Ministries. There are about twenty important departments, each of which has a Minister in charge of it. Many members of the Cabinet, as we saw, are themselves Ministers running a department, but there are other posts, e.g., Transport, which do not, as a rule, carry Cabinet rank.

Not all Ministers are in charge of departments. There are four whose departmental duties are very slight, however active they may have been in earlier periods of British history: the Lord President of the Council, the Paymaster-General, the Chancellor of the Duchy of Lancaster, and the Lord Privy Seal. They are still retained, however, because it is useful to have a few Ministers who are free to take on some special job when the Prime Minister wishes them to.

The title of the Minister is usually a clear enough indication of the business of his department, e.g., the Foreign Secretary. One or two may be more puzzling. The Lord Chancellor holds the leading judicial post in England and Wales. He looks after about twenty different offices concerned with legal practice, and advises on many judicial appointments. (In Scotland the leading judicial post is held by the President of the Court of Session.) The law officers in England and Wales are the Attorney-General and the Solicitor-General. They act as legal advisers to the Government and the departments. In important cases they appear in court on behalf of the Government. (In Scotland the law officers of the Crown are the Lord Advocate and the Solicitor-General for Scotland.)

A few departments have, in addition to the Minister, a Minister of State. He is a deputy Minister, helping to carry the workload in departments that are extremely busy, e.g., the Foreign and Commonwealth Office, Scottish Office. All departments have junior Ministers—Parliamentary Secretaries or Under-Secretaries—who relieve the Minister of some work, mainly by standing in for him at Question Time or during debates.

Some departments are responsible for the whole United Kingdom. Others cover only England, Wales, Scotland, or Northern Ireland. A few cover England and Wales only (e.g., the Lord Chancellor's department).

Ministerial responsibility

Whatever the size of scope of his department, the Minister is responsible for it. He is expected to deal with problems and make decisions on any matter that falls within his field, unless it is of such importance that he feels he must bring it up before the Cabinet.

For all the decisions he does take, for all the actions and omissions of his department, the Minister is responsible to Parliament. Even if the decision or deed that raises criticism was the work of some minor official, without the Minister being aware of it, he must still take the responsibility and whatever consequences it has for him.

A century ago the consequences were often a storm of criticism in Parliament and the resignation of the Minister concerned. Nowadays they are rarely so severe. In 1954 the then Minister of Agriculture resigned after criticism of the way his department officials had acted. But more common are cases like the Suez affair in 1956 or the inefficiency in placing government contracts with Ferranti in 1964 and Bristol Siddeley in 1965. All these raised a fierce outcry; they either damaged the country's reputation or involved large losses of public money, but in no case did any 'guilty' Minister resign. Perhaps this partly reflects a more sympathetic view of the difficulty any Minister has of keeping closely in touch with all that goes on in his department these days, when business is so vast, complicated, and often highly technical. But there is no doubt that it reflects the way in which everything today is seen and acted on in party terms. Privately the Prime Minister may be furious with his colleague; later, when the heat has died down, he may quietly drop him from office; but at the time he is unlikely to give the Opposition the chance to enjoy the triumph of forcing a member of the Government to resign. Thus the Government tend to throw the weight of their party majority behind the Minister responsible and save him from censure.

This does not mean that the notion of individual ministerial responsibility has lost all value. The Minister must answer questions about the conduct of his department. He cannot dodge awkward questions by putting the blame on some underling in his Ministry. Moreover, the knowledge that he may at any time have to explain or defend the activities of his department to angry MPs is salutary. He may no longer be in danger of having to resign, but he can still be made to appear foolish or incompetent; and this no Minister likes, especially as the newspapers play up such episodes. So ministerial responsibility still ensures that Ministers are careful about the behaviour of their departments. It may even induce excessive caution by avoiding schemes that are likely to cause embarrassment to the Minister in Parliament.

The Civil Service

A Minister, though a very important person, may not stay long in charge of a department. The Prime Minister may move him from the Ministry of Transport to the Ministry of Education, or perhaps the electorate may turn him and all the other Ministers out of office at a General Election. Does this mean that the business of a department is constantly unsettled, as different Ministers come and go?

It does not, because continuity is provided by the Civil Service. Under the Minister, who is a politician and therefore likely to be removed if his political party does badly in elections, all the staff in government departments are civil servants. They do not hold political appointments, theirs are permanent occupations. The civil servants remain in their posts whichever political party is in power, and whoever happens to be the Minister in charge of their department. It is their duty to serve the Government of the day, whatever their own personal political opinions. Higher civil servants are not, in fact, allowed to take part in national political activities.

In each government department there is a senior civil servant in charge, called the Permanent Secretary, or Permanent Under-Secretary (in contrast to the transient Parliamentary Secretaries). He and his various assistants put their expert knowledge of the department, and their long experience of its affairs, at the service of the Minister. Of course, the Minister officially makes the decisions, because he has to answer to Parliament, but many decisions are in fact taken by civil servants. Just as the Minister will save the Cabinet's time by settling as many things as he can without bothering it, so his higher civil servants save his time. Their long experience enables them to pick out the things that are important or tricky, which the Minister will want to settle, while the more routine affairs they decide themselves.

The Home Civil Service consists of various groups and categories, and those closest to Ministers in the formulation of policy are top-flight members of the Administration Group. This group as a whole contains about 270 000 members, and covers a large variety of duties, from clerical and routine administrative tasks to the coordination and improvement of government machinery. Only a couple of thousand civil servants can be said to share in the formulation of policy with government Ministers.

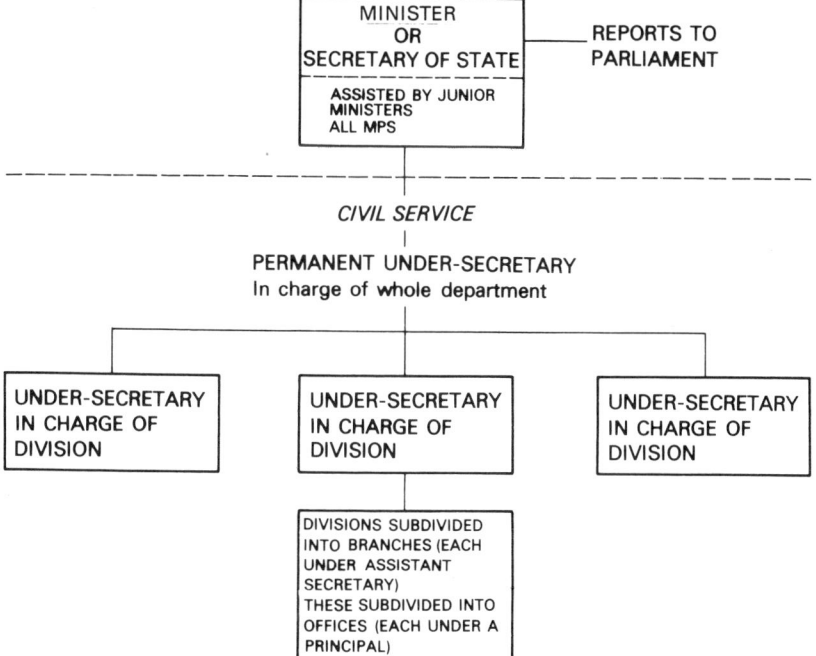

Fig. 12.2. Organization of a government department

All civil servants are recruited by open examination and interview. This is to ensure that the best candidates get the posts, and to avoid the corruption that could creep in if appointments were made by an individual. In the government service, above all other occupations, it is in the community's interest that there should be honesty and impartiality as well as ability.

In 1975, there were about 700 000 civil servants, but this figure included about 177 000 industrial civil servants working in government industrial establishments. About $6\frac{1}{2}$ million people (or about one-quarter of the total workforce) in Britain work in the 'public sector', which also includes the armed services, the nationalized industries, the Health Service, and local government. The State is thus not only 'the Government', but also the major employer in the country.

13. Local government

Scotland

The present system was established in 1975 by the Local Government (Scotland) Act 1973. There are now only 65 local authorities where before there were over 400. These are the nine regions; three island authorities; and 53 districts.

The differences between the types of council lie in the number and importance of the jobs each does, and the area it does them in. The regions and island authorities look after the major services such as education, social work, police, fire, transport, water and 'strategic' planning. The districts' functions include housing, refuse collection, and local planning. The island authorities have most functions, but share some (e.g., police and education) with the regions (see Fig. 13.1).

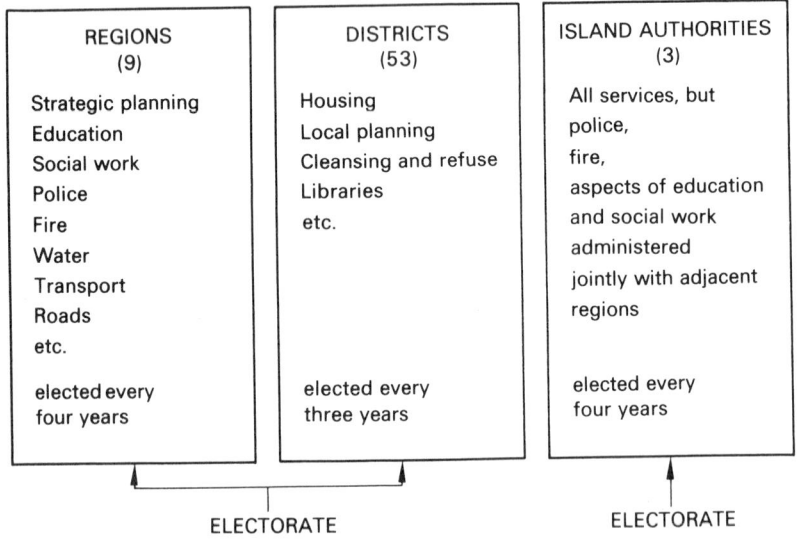

Fig. 13.1. Local government in Scotland

Apart from the local authorities, there are various bodies which represent local opinion and have minor functions. Community councils are elected by the people of areas considerably smaller than the smallest local authorities, the districts. They are watchdog bodies, looking after the interests of places such as small towns or areas within cities. They do not have the power to levy rates, but the District Council gives them finance. Schools councils are another example of this type of body. The parents of pupils in a group of schools elect representatives to a schools council, which takes an interest in the welfare of these schools, and follows up cases of pupils' non-attendance. It should be stressed that only the local authorities are *responsible* for providing local services.

England and Wales

The structure in England and Wales is different in detail, though similar in principle (see Fig. 13.2). It came into being in 1974 as a result of the Local Government Act 1972. There are 53 county authorities and 369 district councils. These are made up as follows: six metropolitan counties (Tyne and Wear; West Midlands; Merseyside; Greater Manchester; West Yorkshire;

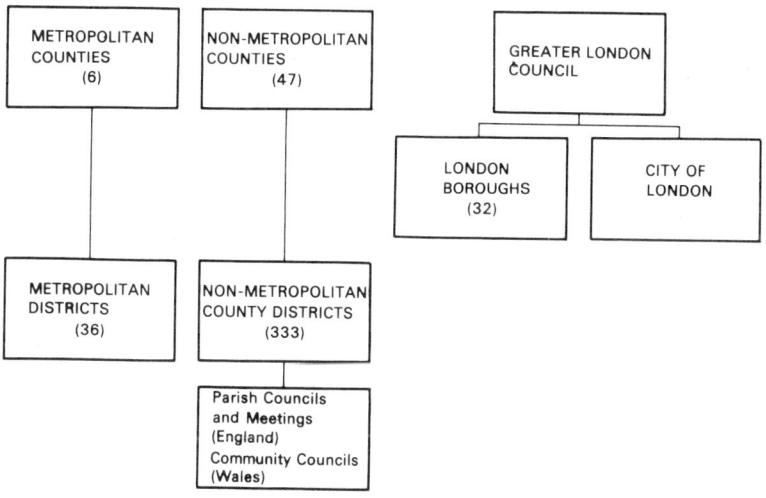

Fig. 13.2. Local government in England and Wales

South Yorkshire), and 36 metropolitan districts; 47 (non-metropolitan) counties and 333 (non-metropolitan) districts. London has its own system, made up of the Greater London Council and the 32 London boroughs and the Corporation of the City of London (this is the historic 'City', which has only 6000 inhabitants).

The distribution of functions between counties and districts varies according to whether it applies to metropolitan or non-metropolitan areas. In the metropolitan areas the district level has more functions than in non-metropolitan areas. In particular, metropolitan districts have education and social services, while in non-metropolitan areas these functions are exercised by the counties. Apart from these, however, major functions such as 'strategic' or 'structure' planning, transport, roads, police, and fire services belong to the counties. Non-metropolitan district councils have local planning, housing, and refuse collection. In London, the Greater London Council is responsible for traffic, major roads, fire, and overall planning. It also administers education in the twelve inner London boroughs and the City of London, through the Inner London Education Authority. The other London boroughs cover education, as well as major services such as housing, social services, and refuse collection. London has special arrangements for the police (Metropolitan Police) and transport (London Transport Executive). The former is responsible to the Home Secretary and not to the Greater London Council, while the latter is appointed by the GLC.

Local government services

The main work of local authorities is to provide and run, in accordance with the relevant Acts of Parliament, those services which they are obliged to supply. They may do more, for some Acts *permit* them to do certain things without *compelling* them, e.g., provide swimming pools. They can also get permission, by special Act of Parliament, to carry out some special task, such as organizing their own public transport system.

Local government services can be classified in the following way. First, there are what are called the environmental services, that is, those concerned with making safe and improving the people's surroundings. These include the public health and sanitary services, under which the council sees that drains and sewers carry the waste water of the town out to sea or to a sewage farm; that the community is supplied with fresh pure water; that houses have supplies piped in; that the streets are cleansed, and that the dustmen call regularly to collect and dispose of refuse; that the atmosphere is kept pure, and that food shops are clean.

Environmental services also include the building, repair, and lighting of streets and bridges, and the planning of the ways in which the land is to be used in the future. Then there is the provision of recreational, cultural, and social amenities, e.g., public parks, tennis courts, and bowling greens; art galleries, museums, and libraries; playing fields, swimming baths, and social centres.

The second group is the protective services, which are largely self-explanatory. The most important are the provision of police forces, fire services, and civil defence. The local authority also sees that dangerous explosives and petrol are safely stored, in accordance with standards laid down in Acts of Parliament.

Third, there are the personal services, designed to help the wellbeing of individuals in the neighbourhood. The most important of these is education. The local authority builds the schools, sees that furniture and equipment are made available, recruits the teachers, and pays their salaries. It supplies the milk that is drunk and the meals that are eaten in schools. It arranges transport for children who need it. In England and Wales it arranges grants for those who wish to continue their education (in Scotland grants come from the Scottish Education Department), provides evening classes and adult education courses for those who cannot study full time.

Housing—the building and letting of houses at cheap rents by the local authority—is another personal service (though, because of the connection between bad housing and the community's health, it might equally well be considered as an environmental service).

Fourth, there are the trading services, in which some local authorities take on tasks that most leave to local commercial firms. They may, for instance, provide their own water supplies, as is the case in Scotland. They may, as in most larger areas, organize their own passenger transport system.

Fifth, the new, larger authorities must produce 'structure plans' and 'regional reports' (in Scotland), for their areas. These cover the creation of employment through attracting industry, the coordination of education, social services, housing, and all the other services in the interests of the area as a whole. It is assumed that some of the initiative will pass from central government to local government under the reformed system, but so far there is no clear evidence of this happening. This is because central government still retains close control over local spending and the standards which local authorities must maintain.

Elections

All these councils are elected bodies. Anyone who is a British subject, over 18, and residing in the area for which the election is being held, is entitled to vote, and to stand for the council. The political parties usually put forward candidates for local elections, just as for parliamentary elections, but there are also many independent candidates. In some councils, nearly all councillors are independents.

The terms of office for the different types of authority vary:

Scotland: Regions, four years; Districts, three years.
England and Wales: Counties, four years; Districts, four years, *either* with one-third of seats elected each year, except when there is a county council election, *or* all elected every fourth year.

After election, the councillors elect from their own ranks the chairman of the council. The titles of this position vary, but the most common are:

	Authority	Title of Chairman
England and Wales	City Districts	Mayor or Lord Mayor
	Other Districts, and Counties	Chairman
Scotland	City Districts	Provost or Lord Provost
	Other Districts, and Regions	Convener

In Scotland, the district and island authorities can nominate up to one-quarter of their membership as *ex officio* Justices of the Peace to serve on the district courts. Formerly, these magistrates were known as 'bailies'.

The committee system

The number of things that the law obliges the council to do is so great that the council as a body could never deal with them all in detail. So the committee system is used. For each main type or department of the council's activity, a committee of a few councillors is set up. In Strathclyde Region, for example, there are thirteen main committees, including an Education Committee, a Social Work Committee, a Water and Sewerage Committee, a Police and Fire Committee, and so on. Each committee studies the running of the services in its department or departments, and makes reports and recommendations about them to the council as a whole. Certain 'lay members' are coopted to serve on the Education Committee. These are representatives of the teachers and the churches. At the head of the committee structure is the 'Policy and Resources Committee', which sets the objectives for the whole council and controls their implementation. It resembles the Cabinet in central government.

The council usually meets about once a month, and most of its time is spent considering the reports that various committees have presented. Every councillor receives copies of the reports well before the meeting, giving him a chance to study them and decide any points he wants to question or dispute.

This means that there is no need to read the reports out loud at the meeting. The Provost can, for example, just mention 'Report of Education Committee, paragraph 1', and, if no councillor wants to raise anything, that part of the report is passed. At 'paragraph 8', one councillor may object to what the Education Committee is proposing; there will be a discussion, and a vote taken. If most support the objector, then the proposal in that section of the report is 'referred back to the Education Committee', which means it has to consider the matter again.

Permanent officials

All the councillors, however, are just ordinary citizens—bus drivers, shopkeepers, schoolteachers, insurance agents. Naturally, they do not have the special knowledge and experience to deal with the details of drainage, water supply, infectious diseases, fire control, and so on.

To advise councillors in their discussion and decisions, and to see that the various services are run in accordance with these decisions, the council employs a number of professional officers who are experts in their own field. Each is appointed as chief officer of the department in which he is especially qualified. He assists and advises the council committee dealing with the affairs of this department. He is responsible to the council for the efficiency with which the department's work is done. Unlike the council which employs them, all these specialist officials are paid a salary.

The most important is the Chief Executive, who acts as the head of a 'management team', and is the main channel of communication between the departments and the council. Other chief officers include the Director of Education (Scotland) or Chief Education Officer (England and Wales), the Director of Finance, the Director of Social Work (or Social Services), the Firemaster, the Chief Constable, and so on. They head teams of officials in their respective departments, but come together in a system of 'corporate management' under the Chief Executive. This means that instead of reporting only to the relevant committee of the council, as in the old system, they now coordinate their activities in an overall strategy for the authority. As we have seen, this is matched on the councillors' part by the Policy and Resources Committee.

Where the money comes from

Where do local authorities get the money to pay the cost of the schools, police forces, fire brigades, roads, drains, and the other services they organize for the neighbourhood?

Most of them have a certain income from the property they own, or from charges made for some services: we pay to use the council swimming pools or tennis courts; we pay rent to the council if we live in a council house; we pay fares if we use the council's transport services. But these receipts come nowhere near meeting the bills that have to be paid. Many of them do not cover the cost of the particular service, let alone help pay for others. Council rents, for instance, do not cover the cost of council housing, because the council keeps them as low as possible.

Most of the money comes from rates, government grants, and loans. In other words it comes, ultimately, from the pockets of the citizens themselves, just as the money spent by the central government does.

Rates are a local tax imposed on the occupiers of property, according to the value of the property. The value of each piece of property—houses, shops, factories, shipyards, and so on—in the area is estimated by the Board of Inland Revenue in England and Wales, and assessors appointed by the regions and island authorities in Scotland. This is called the rateable value of each house or shop. By adding these rateable values together, the council know the rateable value of the whole area under its authority. Once it has decided how much money it is going to have to spend in the year, the council can work out what rate per pound of rateable value is necessary to meet this expenditure.

Suppose, for instance, that the total rateable value of the area is £100 million. The council calculates that the cost of providing schools, paying teachers and policemen, repairing roads, and so on is going to be £50 million. Then, to raise this sum from the rates it will have to impose a rate of 50p for every £1 of rateable value. Therefore, if the Valuation Officer or Assessor has valued the house you occupy at £60, you will have to pay 60 × 50p, that is, £30 in rates that year.

For heavy capital expenditure, e.g., building a new town hall or installing a new water supply system, a council usually gets a loan. It needs the permission of the central government for this, which very often advances the loan. The council must pay interest on this.

Receipts, rates, and loans, however, still do not cover the cost of a council's work. The rest comes out of grants made to the council by the central government (which gets its money from taxes on the citizens of the country as a whole). More than one-third of local government spending in Scotland is covered by government grants.

The grants are of different types. There are specific grants, where the Government agrees to help meet the cost of certain services run by the local authority, e.g., police. Then there are Rate Support Grants. These are in three parts. One ('domestic') is given to enable the household rate to be reduced. Another ('needs') is given largely on a basis of population. The third ('resources') helps authorities with lower than average rateable value. Local authorities differ widely among themselves in their rating resources. Some contain many valuable houses, shops, and factories, and can therefore obtain a good deal of money in rates. Others have much older and shabbier property, the value of which is small and therefore produces very little in the way of rates. To the less affluent authorities, the Government pays this 'resources' grant to bring them a bit nearer to the level of the more prosperous ones. Without this, the people living in the poorer areas would have to make do with services—schools, roads, sanitation—a lot less adequate than their more fortunate neighbours.

All this amounts to an enormous sum of money. In all, local authorities in the United Kingdom spent £14 000 million in 1974, or 30 per cent of all public expenditure. Strathclyde Region planned to spend £547 million in 1976–77, and Glasgow District £58 million (see Table 13.1).

Where the money goes

The biggest single item of expenditure is education, which accounts for about a half of local government spending. Other big items are social services, housing, highways and transportation, and cleansing and environmental health.

Table 13.1. Strathclyde Region and Glasgow District budgets, 1976/77

Service	Net expenditure (£)	Gross equivalent Rate per £ (pence)
Strathclyde Region		
Education	313 208 650	201
Police and Fire	35 619 340	23
Highways and Transportation	47 998 200	31
Water and Sewerage	27 588 670	18
Social Work	61 923 500	40
Administration	23 813 430	15
Provision for price increases, etc.	32 000 000	21
Other services	4 815 450	3
Total	546 967 240	352
Less Income		
Rate Support Grant	369 645 000	238
Grant in lieu of Rates	3 300 000	2
Opening surplus	1 597 240	1
Total	374 542 240	241
Balance met by Rates	172 425 240	111
Domestic Water	11 280 660	13
Glasgow District		
Leisure and Recreation	10 551 010	17
Housing	12 138 465	20
Cleansing and Environmental Health	15 576 076	25
Libraries and Museums	4 951 260	8
Planning and Building Control	6 124 400	10
Administration	5 857 800	9
Other services	2 716 883	4
Total	57 915 894	93
Less Income		
Rate Support Grant	14 500 000	23
Grant in lieu of Rates	580 000	1
Transfer from Reserve	1 000 000	2
Total	16 080 000	26
Balance met from Rates	41 835 894	67

As this is all public money, great care is taken to control its use. The council prepares its budget annually, and has to keep to that estimated expenditure. The accounts must be kept carefully and in detail. Every year auditors go over the accounts. These accounts have to be published, and any ratepayer may examine them and complain to the auditors if he is not satisfied.

Relationship of local authorities to the central government

What is the relationship of local authorities to the central government? In several respects this is determined by Acts of Parliament. All existing local authorities were set up by Acts of Parliament to carry out certain tasks, and the extent of their powers to deal with these tasks is defined in Acts of Parliament. Acts also define the powers of the Minister in the various fields.

First, as we have seen, much money is granted to local councils by the Government. The Government has to get the approval of Parliament for these grants, just as it does for the sums it proposes to spend on the Army or Navy. The Minister, therefore, must be sure he can justify this expenditure to Parliament. So he has powers to see that the local councils use the money properly and that certain conditions are fulfilled. For instance, much of local council housing is paid for from government grants. The council builds houses and lets them at rents it fixes itself. But if the Minister feels the rents are too low, he can compel the council to raise them. (As he did in the case of Dumbarton in 1960 and Clay Cross in 1973.)

Second, in many services an Act instructs the local authority to carry out the work but places on the Minister the duty of inspecting the work to see that certain standards are maintained, in police and fire services, schools, children's homes, etc.

Third, in many cases the things a council proposes to do in carrying out its work need the Minister's approval before they can be done. For instance, an authority is entitled to draw up its own plans for local development under the Town and Country Planning Act. but the same Act says that these plans must first be submitted to the Minister for approval.

We can see from education an instance of a division of powers in running a service. The school-leaving age is fixed by law. Neither the council nor the Minister can make children stay on after reaching this age; only Parliament, by changing the law, can do this. Both the council and the Minister are only concerned with seeing that the present law is carried out. It is up to the council to see that facilities are provided to enable the children in its area to have the education the law says the must, i.e., it has to provide enough schools and recruit teachers to staff them. But the qualifications the teachers must have, and the salaries they should get, are matters for the Minister. Strathclyde may be willing to pay its teachers more money, but, without the Minister's permission, it cannot do so. If councils could fix qualifications, salaries, and standards on their own, the quality of education might vary enormously. The

Secretary of State has to look after the educational services as a whole, and therefore these things are under his control.

The tendency in recent years has been for the central government' power to increase. This has come about in two main ways. One is the transfer to the central government of many functions which used to be carried out by the local authorities. Relief of poverty was once the major task of local authorities; now the Department of Social Security sees to this. Gas and electricity, often provided by local authorities in the past, are now supplied by boards appointed by the Government. Many local authorities used to run hospitals; these were transferred to the care of health authorities or boards under the central government.

Second, the cost of local services has grown enormously of late, with the result that local authorities have had to turn more and more to the central government for grants. As the proportion of local government finance provided by the central government has grown, so, naturally, has the power of Whitehall over the town halls of Britain.

Generally, the local and central authorities cooperate to advance the important services in which both has a part to play. There are occasional disputes; there have been some sharp clashes between certain councils and the Government. But, on the whole, mutual understanding has marked the relationship since the two authorities are, in fact, partners, not rivals.

Changes in the future

The local government system has come in for a good deal of criticism and scrutiny in recent years. This is despite, or even because of, the reorganizations which took place in the mid-1970s.

These reorganizations were concerned to make local government more efficient, but they meant the establishment of larger authorities which were inevitably more distant from the people. The number of councillors was drastically reduced, but the number of officials actually grew. It is not to be wondered at that many people were heard complaining of 'distant bureaucracy'.

Then again, the new system seemed to be unduly complex, with a 'two-tier' structure of counties and districts in England and Wales, and of regions and districts in Scotland. The confusion between the functions allocated to each level led to inefficiency and rivalry between the authorities, which it had been the intention of the reforms to eliminate. Some now yearned for a return to the 'all-purpose' authorities, and in Scotland the vast regional councils became especially unpopular.

Behind much of the complaint was the soaring cost of local government services, with the corresponding steep rise in the rates. A committee was set up to seek new sources of finance for local government (the Layfield Committee), and it reported in 1976 that a local income tax was a possibility, although it would be expensive to collect. The Government, however, was in no mood to introduce such a tax, and the dependence of local government on central grants goes on.

Apart from finance, there is a general feeling that central government is unwilling to allow any new freedom to local authorities. So much of government policy has to be carried out at local level that there is little room for independent policy-making in local government. When councils resist the Government, as they have done on rents and comprehensive schools, they are soon brought to heel, for Parliament can determine what they may or may not do. This is a centralized system of government, which aims to produce equality of services throughout the country. We in Britain cannot really decide whether we value such equality more than we value local democracy and local differences. Until we make up our minds, the present system is likely to continue.

14. Maintenance of law and order

The law is the whole body of rules and regulations by which the people in a community must abide. Laws govern the conduct of individuals towards their fellow citizens, defining the obligations each owes the other and the rights they are entitled to claim.

Without laws, the prospect of leading our normal everyday lives in society would vanish. Our confidence that we have a right to do one thing, or are free to do another, is only justified because there are laws which uphold these rights and freedoms. For example, without laws on road conduct our right to drive on when the lights are green would be no more valid than that of our neighbour to do so when they are red. In effect, traffic lights themselves mean nothing without regulations that lay down the way they must be used. In a society without law, the individual has no rights beyond those he is personally strong enough to enforce, no safety for his person or his property beyond what he himself can provide. Such a society lacks the order and security we need if we are to lead an ordinary peaceful life: the purpose of law is to provide these.

Criminal Law and Civil Law

The obligations which the law imposes on us are of two kinds. First, there are those whose breach is considered harmful to the community as a whole, not just to one particular individual. These constitute the Criminal Law. Assault, burglary, murder, drunken driving, for instance, are all classed as offences against the community, i.e., crimes. Officials acting on behalf of society will track down the offender and bring him to justice, and other public officials will conduct the case against him on behalf of the State—'the case for the Crown'.

Second, there are obligations the breach of which is considered an infringement of the rights of some particular individual, but not damaging to the community in general. These make up the Civil Law. Even if there were no crimes, there would still be plenty of private disputes between individuals over who had the right in some matter. Smith's dog may have ruined Brown's rose bushes; Mrs Jones may feel she has been unfairly provided for in her late husband's will; a workman claims he has been injured through his employer's negligence. In such cases the aggrieved person can arrange to have the case tried, and any wrong done to him put right. But if he does not take action nobody else will, for these are private disputes—'Brown *v*. Smith'.

Scottish Law and English Law

The law in Britain is not, however, the same throughout the whole island. Scotland, as an independent country, developed her own legal system, and it was agreed under the Treaty of Union in 1707 that she should retain this. In England, the Common Law (i.e., the law which was common to the whole Kingdom, as distinct from the varied local systems of law which prevailed in different parts before the establishment of any Common Law) was built up on the decisions made by the judges in the courts; later judges always looked for guidance in their decisions to the judgments of their predecessors in similar cases. In Scotland, the Common Law was based on general principles of law, borrowed from European, especially Roman Law, experience; judges made their decisions in the light of these guiding principles, not in the light of what an earlier judge had decided.

Two hundred and seventy years of Union have helped to bring the two systems closer. For one thing, most new laws in modern times have been made by Acts of Parliament which usually affect England and Scotland alike. Once an Act lays down the legal position, this overrules whatever the Common Law may have said before there was a statute covering the matter.

Second, both Common Law and Statute Law have to be interpreted by a judge. This can be a tricky business: even a carefully worded law may leave room for argument over how it should apply to a particular case. So there are often appeals against one judge's decision to a higher court. These appeal decisions are of great interest to all judges, Scottish as well as English, and influence them in their own decisions thereafter.

Nevertheless, differences still remain, for instance, in the laws of landholding, and inheritance. And, as we shall see, there are differences in court systems and procedures.

The police

It is not enough for laws to exist. They have to be enforced in practice. In Britain there are two main enforcers of the law—the police and the law courts.

The job of the police is to prevent crimes being committed, to investigate them when they are, and to arrest and bring for trial the person they believe committed the offence.

There is no national police force under a 'Ministry of Police' in Britain; people were loath to let such a force come under the direct and complete control of the central government. Instead, there are about fifty-one separate, independent police forces organized on a local government basis. The counties in England and Wales and the Regions and Island authorities in Scotland are the basic units. Each appoints its own chief constable, though it must get the approval of the Home Secretary, or Scottish Secretary of State. Each sees to the recruiting, running, and paying of its own police force, though the central government lays down certain standards of efficiency, regulates salaries, and maintains inspectors who report to the Minister on the condition of the local forces. London has the Metropolitan Police, which is responsible to the Home Secretary, and Northern Ireland has the Royal Ulster Constabulary (RUC) under the Police Authority for Northern Ireland.

Britain has been careful to prevent the police becoming a power on their own. They are given special powers—notably those of arresting people—to enable them to do their work efficiently. These powers are severely limited. For instance, the police cannot arrest a person (unless caught 'in the act') without first getting a warrant from a magistrate permitting them to do so. They cannot enter premises without permission unless they obtain a similar authority. If they do arrest someone, they must bring him before a magistrate within twenty-four hours and (except in Scotland) charge him with some specific offence. In their conduct towards an accused man and in their attempts to obtain statements from him, they have to operate according to strict rules. Their job is solely to arrest and bring charges against a person; the decision as to whether that person is guilty of the offence is not for the police to take. In Scotland the police do not bring charges; instead the Procurator Fiscal decides whether or not to prosecute. The Procurator Fiscal is independent of the police and acts under the authority of the Lord Advocate, the Government's chief law officer in Scotland.

The courts and the judges

It is the task of the law courts to hear the accusation and the defence against it, to decide whether the accused's guilt has been established, and, if so, to pronounce such punishment as the law prescribes for the offence in question. In civil cases the law courts again try to establish the facts, decide which of the parties is in the right, according to the laws on the subject, and award judgment in his favour.

Which court a case is tried in depends on whether it is a civil or a criminal case and on how serious the matter is.

For minor criminal cases, Scotland has the District Court. This deals only with offences such as 'drunk and disorderly' cases or petty thefts. The magistrates in these courts are known now as Justices of the Peace, and some are councillors in the District Councils (formerly called 'bailies'). Others are appointed by the Secretary of State for Scotland. The Justice of the Peace is not usually a qualified lawyer, though he may undergo some legal training after appointment. In Glasgow, there are three legally qualified, full-time 'stipendiary magistrates', instead of JPs. The offences dealt with in District Courts are small, often demanding common sense rather than legal learning (there is always a

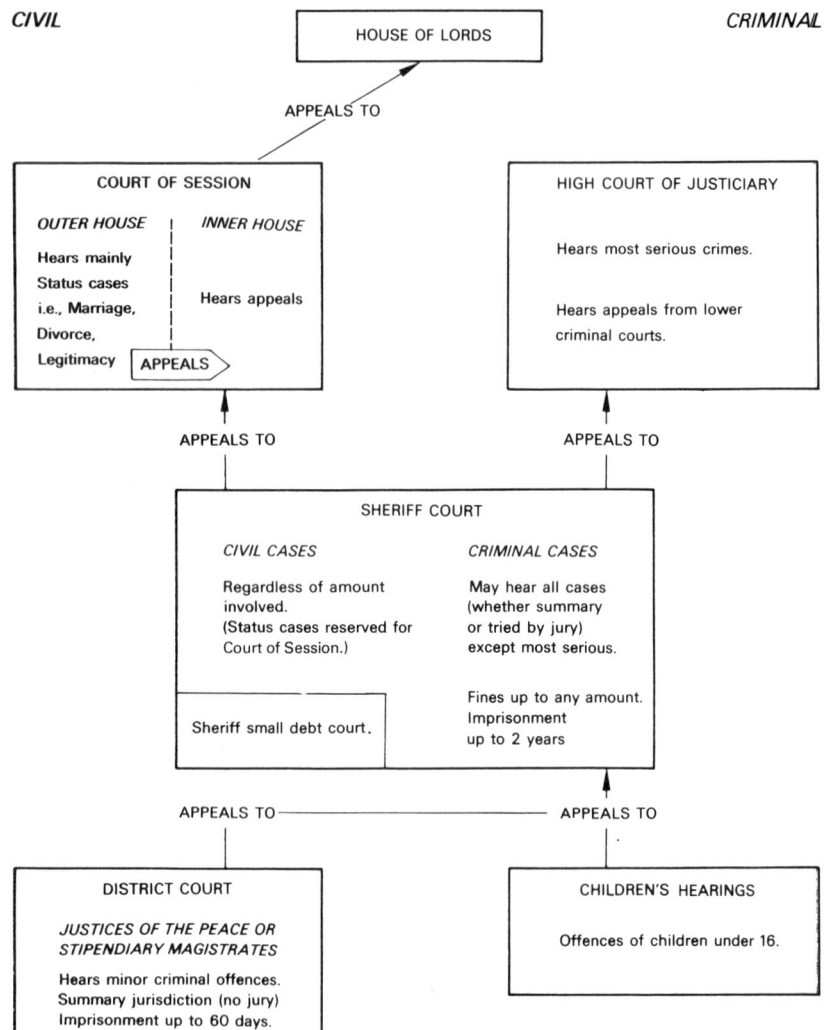

Fig. 14.1. Main courts of law in Scotland

court official with legal qualifications to advise on any awkward points of law that may arise); the penalties they can impose are very limited, and appeals against their decisions are heard in a higher court.

Children under 16, and in some cases between 16 and 18, who have committed minor offences, are dealt with in Children's Hearings, which consist of three members of the community. The 'Reporter' of the Hearing decides if a child should be brought before it, and the Hearing then decides what measures of compulsory care (if any) should be adopted. If the grounds for referring a

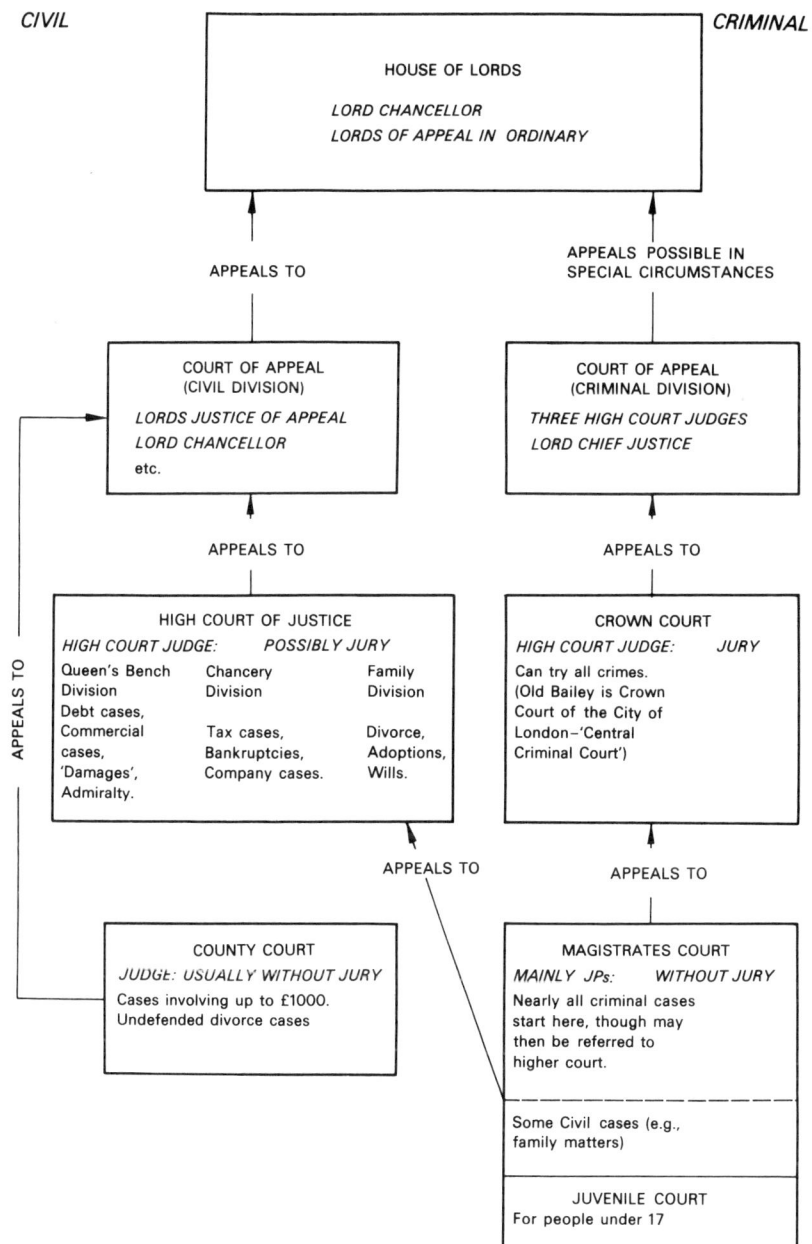

Fig. 14.2. Main courts of law in England and Wales

case to the Hearing are not accepted, the case must first go to the Sheriff Court for proof, and the Sheriff Court can also hear an appeal from the decision of a Hearing.

The principal courts in Scotland are the Sheriff Courts. The Sheriff is the judge in these courts, and he is a fully qualified lawyer with long experience as an advocate or solicitor. These courts can try a wide range of cases, both criminal and civil. In criminal cases only the gravest offences, such as murder and treason, are beyond the range of the Sheriff Court. In civil disputes it can try any case, no matter how much money may be at stake. In both, appeals against the court's judgments may be made to higher courts

The High Court of Justiciary is the supreme criminal court in Scotland. It alone has power to try the most serious criminal cases. Often called the Scottish Court of Criminal Appeal, it also hears appeals against judgments given in the lower courts. From its decisions there is no appeal.

The Court of Session is the supreme civil court. Part of it (the Inner House) is simply an appeal court, considering appeals against judgments given in the other civil courts. Another part (the Outer House) does not hear appeals, but deals with certain civil cases, notably divorce actions. From any decision in the Court of Session, however, a further appeal may be made to the House of Lords.

The judges—twenty of them—in these supreme courts are appointed, by the Scottish Secretary, from the most experienced advocates; and once appointed they are practically irremovable.

The English court structure, as you can see from Fig. 14.2, is more complicated. But here, too, it is a question of the type of case (civil or criminal) and its gravity. The lower courts, dealing with a mass of small cases, are presided over by people who are not qualified lawyers, whereas in the higher courts the judges are all drawn from the most experienced members of the legal profession.

In any system of justice a great deal depends on the judges who hear the cases. In some countries (and in Britain in the past) the judges are under the control of the executive, and so are often under pressure from it to give judgments to suit it instead of according to the laws. In Britain we are anxious to keep the judges free from such political pressures, and by now this principle of judicial independence is well established. The judges are appointed by the Executive, but they cannot be dismissed by it. In England and Wales they can only be removed if both Houses of Parliament present an address to the Crown requesting this, and the Crown agrees. (In Scotland special legislation would be needed.) The procedure has not been used since it was laid down in 1701. Thus no judge need be influenced in his decisions by any fears of losing his position through displeasing the Government.

In addition, a judge's salary is permanent; it does not need to be agreed to every year by parliament, as most public expenditure does. He is a member of the legal profession, which is long established, well organized, sets its own high standards for members, and is a proud defender of its independent traditions. Judges can therefore deliver their judgments on the merits of the case, with the law itself as the only authority they recognize.

Criminal procedure

The procedure by which the courts reach their verdicts often seems laborious and long drawn out. But time taken in establishing the fact as carefully as possible is not time wasted, especially in more serious criminal cases. Every effort has to be made to guard against an innocent man being condemned, or against any man being condemned without having a fair trial.

The principle from which all criminal cases start is that the accused is innocent until proved guilty. The proof must be shown in an open court, to which the public and the press are admitted. And it must be demonstrated by the evidence of witnesses under oath to tell the truth. The court has strict rules about evidence, designed to ensure a fair trial. It will not accept statements made by the accused, which incriminate him, unless it is sure these were fairly obtained. Nor will it permit evidence showing he has previously committed similar offences, for he is not on trial for these, and such evidence would only prejudice his chances; some years ago, a newspaper which printed such information about a man on trial for murder was fined £10 000. Witnesses may testify only to facts of which they have direct knowledge: what they have heard others say (hearsay evidence) is not accepted as evidence. And in Scotland the evidence of one witness alone is not sufficient to convict the accused.

The accused is entitled to hear and cross-examine all of the prosecution's witnesses, and to produce witnesses in his own defence. He is entitled to a legal adviser to conduct his defence, and will be provided with one at the public expense if necessary.

If it is a minor offence heard in a Magistrates Court (and often in Sheriff Courts, too), the case is dealt with by summary jurisdiction. This means that the magistrates or sheriffs themselves decide, after hearing the evidence, whether the accused has been proved guilty of the offence, and pass sentence accordingly. In cases of these 'summary' offences there is no jury.

Jury system

In all serious crimes (indictable offences), however, the accused is entitled to demand trial by jury. This is another of the safeguards against injustice, although originally this was not the purpose. It means that the man's guilt has to be proved to the satisfaction of a number of ordinary people, not just to that of a single judge. They have no special interest or knowledge that might prejudice them against the accused; he is entitled to object to any proposed juror whom he thinks might be prejudiced. Since the jurors are ordinary people unused to the criminal courts, they are likely to be impressed with the seriousness of what they are doing, not hardened to it by daily experience—a good precaution in view of what is at stake.

Any householder may be summoned to serve on a jury, which consists of twelve people in England, fifteen in Scotland. The jury's task is to decide, after considering the evidence presented by both sides in court, whether or not the accused did commit the offence with which he is charged. The judge will deal with any questions of law that arise, such as explaining to the jury what the law means by 'manslaughter' or 'reasonable doubt'; he will also summarize for the jury's benefit the evidence put forward by both sides. And when the jury returns its verdict, the judge passes sentence on (or acquits) the accused. But the decision whether the man is guilty or not guilty is purely a matter for the jury. The jury retires to a private room to discuss the evidence and reach a verdict. In England this must be either 'Guilty' or 'Not Guilty'; but in Scotland there is a third choice, 'Not Proven', which brings acquittal just as 'Not Guilty' does. In England, at one time, the jury had to be unanimous in its verdict; now, however, in both England and Scotland, it is enough if a majority of jurors are in agreement.

Finally, even if found guilty after this careful procedure a man may still appeal against his conviction or sentence, and the judges of the Appeal Court will consider it.

Civil procedure

In certain civil cases there may be a jury if either side wants one, but normally civil disputes are heard by the judge alone. Bringing up a civil action is a matter for the individual, not for the police; he does this through a solicitor, who arranges for the case to be heard. Procedure in court, however, is similar to that in a criminal case, though there is no 'prisoner in the dock'. Each side, plaintiff and defendant, sets out its case, bringing forward its witnesses who give their evidence under oath and are cross-examined by the other side. The judge considers the facts of the case as established by the evidence, and determines how the law applies to this set of facts: if, for instance, Smith was seen lifting his dog over the fence of Brown's garden, the law will take a sterner view than if the dog was seen making its own way in; and if it was seen entering through a gate which Brown himself had left open, the law might take a quite different view of the rights and wrongs of the case. The judge then delivers his judgment and sets out his reasons for it. Once again, appeal against his judgment may be made to a higher court.

No one can claim that mistakes have never happened; judges and juries are fallible. But careful procedure does try to reduce the risk of injustice by ensuring a fair trial.

The Rule of Law

The most important thing about the British system of justice is that it embodies what is called the Rule of Law. This means a number of things. It means that no citizen is above the law, everyone is equally and impartially subject to it. Certain people have special powers to allow them to do their duties, e.g., the police. But these powers are limited, and have to be used according to the law. A policemen who exceeds them, for instance, by forcing his way into premises without a warrant, cannot escape by claiming he had to do this in the course of his duty.

No one is exempt from observing the law of the land. Ministers and millionaires, peers and politicians, judges and generals, all have to obey the laws about, say, driving, just as fully as any other citizen. No person or group enjoys any special legal privileges; the law has no favourites.

The Rule of Law also means that no one may be punished unless he has broken the law. The authorities may distrust a man, they may dislike what he is doing, but they cannot act against him unless he breaks a law. Any charge that he has broken it must be proved, in and to the satisfaction of a court of law, with its independent judge and jury. Thus the citizen is shielded against arbitrary treatment at the hands of people in positions of power.

Why it is important

The Rule of Law is the great safeguard of the personal liberties of the individual in Britain. There is no special Act of Parliament which guarantees freedom of speech, freedom of writing, freedom of holding assemblies and meetings. And there are laws which set limits to these freedoms—though they are quite wide limits. If in holding a meeting we create a disturbance, if what we write or say maligns our neighbour or incites people to violence, then we may find ourselves in court, because we have overstepped the limits and broken the law. But, unless we do overstep these wide limits, we are quite free. So long as we do not break a law, the law itself, in the shape of the independent judges and courts, will uphold our personal liberties against any authority, however high and mighty, that tries to deprive us of our freedom.

Freedom from being arrested and imprisoned just because it suits some authority to lock us up, although we have done nothing unlawful, is the most prized of these freedoms. There is a famous procedure providing a remedy against unlawful detention. In England, by a writ of *Habeas Corpus*, anyone detaining a man unlawfully can be compelled to produce him in court so that a judge may decide the case. In Scotland this is carried out by means of a High Court Order. Once again we are back to the Rule of Law: only the courts can order a man to be imprisoned; and they will only do so if it can be proved that he has broken the law. The following example shows how thoroughly this Rule is enforced. It was applied againt the captain of a foreign ship lying in the Thames. He was required to produce in the law courts a Pole whom he had imprisoned on board, and although no British subject was involved, two destroyers and 120 policemen were used to enforce the court's writ.

These guarantees of the individual's liberties are clearly important in our everyday life. The law-abiding citizen can go about his business free from the fear of being suddenly seized by the police, of being locked up for months without trial, of being condemned on a trumped-up charge with no chance to defend himself, of being bundled off secretly to some prison. Many law-abiding citizens in many countries in this twentieth century do not enjoy such feeling of security.

These liberties are essential also to the working of the British system of government. The essence of political democracy in this country is the freedom to choose one set of rulers and policies from a number of alternatives. If this freedom of choice is to mean anything, we need to know what the alternatives are. We need to be free to read and write about ideas and policies, to talk about and listen to alternative programmes, to organize and attend meetings and societies, to argue, to criticize, and to protest. Only under these conditions are we really free to choose the Government we want to make our wishes known. It is significant that these freedoms are always among the first to disappear under a dictatorship.

Some complaints

In recent years, people have been disturbed over certain practices which seem to flout the Rule of Law. The most important is the growing use of administrative tribunals. These are bodies appointed by Ministers—by the Executive—to deal with certain kinds of dispute. There are, for instance, tribunals to deal with claims about the rents charged for furnished houses, claims from applicants for supplementary benefits, appeals against income tax assessments, applications for a licence to operate a vehicle service.

The defence of these special tribunals is that many of the cases do not concern the law, but rather public policy: whether a man should be granted a licence to run a lorry service depends on whether he will be meeting a real need; and this is not something a judge can decide, because it is not a question of law at all. Again, a rent tribunal needs special knowledge, not of law but of economic conditions and the renting practices in the district. Finally, there are so many of these disputes that the law courts could never cope with them—certainly not with their normal careful procedures. Despite these arguments many people are unconvinced. A man might suffer injustice from a tribunal and be unable to appeal to the law courts for redress. The Executive is exercising judicial power, often in cases where it is itself involved. Often tribunal procedure was casual, with no strict rules of evidence and no reasons given for the tribunal's decisions. As a result of an enquiry in 1957, Parliament passed an Act to remedy this. It set up a special council to supervise and report on tribunals. It increased opportunities of appealing from a tribunal to the ordinary courts of law. Tribunal procedure was reformed to make it less objectionable.

As to the ordinary courts, there are two complaints that are almost as ancient as the law itself: justice is too slow and too expensive. More courts and more judges might ease the first complaint—buildings in particular are lacking. Expense is more serious. If a man cannot afford the cost of going to law, then his right to have justice done is limited in practice, however unlimited it might be in theory. But much has been done to remedy this complaint. In criminal cases of any size, legal aid is always available to the accused. In civil cases, legal aid schemes are gradually being extended. At present aid is obtainable in all but the most trivial civil disputes, though the individual has to pay something himself; the amount he pays depends on his financial position. There are special procedures for small claims.

A social problem that has captured the headlines is the increase in crime in Britain during the postwar years. The 'crime wave' has led some people to demand the restoration of corporal punishment (the birch and the 'cat'), which Britain abolished as being degrading and futile. Governments, however, have preferred to pin their faith to more enlightened policies. Capital punishment was abolished in 1969. Support is given to increasing the police force, imposing sterner prison sentences, building more detention centres, and working out treatment which may reform the criminal, not just punish him.

In recent years, many have called for a 'Bill of Rights' to protect civil liberties. In some countries, for example, the United States, these liberties are enshrined in the Constitution, but in Britain they are to be found in ordinary legislation and the Common Law. The sorts of liberties which might be covered in a Bill of Rights are the equal protection of the laws for all citizens, without discrimination on account of race, colour, religion, or ethnic origin; freedom from arbitrary arrest, and the right to a fair trial; property rights; and so on. As we have seen, these are already dealt with in the laws of the country, but some fear that such laws can be changed too easily by a simple vote in Parliament. Moreover, Britain has subscribed to the European Convention of Human Rights, and these rights can be tested in the European Court of Human Rights. It seems illogical that within Britain itself the courts cannot deal with cases of this sort. The advent of devolution may also bring a Bill of Rights nearer, for the rights of citizens throughout the United Kingdom may have to be spelled out. In other words, we might have to adopt something like a written Constitution after all.

Bibliography
For reference or further study

Note: No textbook dealing with contemporary material can possibly encompass all aspects of the topics listed in the contents. For students of current affairs it is essential to refer regularly to a number of reference books and to new editions of periodicals as they are published. A few of these books and periodicals are listed below. There are many more—on all topics—and there is no suggestion that these are the sole or best references for each topic. Critical appraisal of a range of books by students is an essential part of the broad study of contemporary Britain.

General (Reference)
Cassells Parliamentary Directory (Hulke, M., ed.), Cassell, 1975.
Central Office of Information, *Britain—An Official Handbook*, HMSO, Annual
Dictionary of Modern Economics: A Handbook of Terms and Organizations (Second edition), McGraw-Hill, 1973.
Krikler, B. and Laqueur, W., *A Reader's Guide to Contemporary History*, Weidenfeld & Nicolson, 1972.
Pemberton, J. E., *British Official Publications* (Second edition), Pergamon Press, 1973.
Times Guide to the House of Commons, The Times Newspapers Limited. (Published after election of October 1974.)
Yearbook of Social Policy in Britain, Routledge & Kegan Paul, Annual.

1 Britain: change and challenge
Central Office of Information, *Social Trends*, HMSO, Biannual.
Community Relations Commission—*Report*, HMSO, Annual.
Halsey, A. H. (ed.), *Trends in British Society Since 1900*, Macmillan, 1972.
Hardy, G. B., *Future Leisure*, Cassell, 1976.

2A Major industries: old and new
Stuart, Roderick, *Industrial Change—Cause and Consequence*, Blackie, 1977.
British Steel Corporation, *Ten Year Development*, Strategy Cmnd 5226, HMSO, 1973.

2B Energy
Devereux, Michael, *Future Energy*, Cassell, 1976.
Organization for Economic Cooperation and Development, *Statistics of Energy 1964–74*, OECD/OCDE, 1975.

3 Industry: organization and location
Guenault, P. H. and Jackson, J. M., *The Control of Monopoly in the UK*, Longman, 1974.
Reed, R. W., *The Economics of Public Enterprise*, Butterworth, 1973.

4 Scotland: study of a changing society
Countryside Commission for Scotland, *Annual Report*, HMSO
Highlands and Islands Development Board, *Annual Report*, HMSO.
Kennedy, Gavin (ed.), *The Radical Approach*, Palingenesis Press, 1976.
Our Changing Democracy: Devolution to Scotland and Wales, HMSO, 1975.
Webb, Keith, The Growth of Scottish Nationalism, Molendinar Press, 1977.

5 Agriculture and fishing
Food and Agriculture Organization, *The State of Agriculture—World Review*, HMSO, Annual.
Sea Fisheries, *Annual Tables*, HMSO.

6 Commerce, transport and trade
Future Civil Aviation Policy, Cmnd G400, HMSO, 1976.
Williams, Alma, *Educating the Consumer*, Longman, 1975.

7 Economic problems and policies
Brittan, Samuel, *Steering the Economy: The Role of the Treasury*, Penguin, 1971.
Economic Trends, HMSO, Monthly.
Prest, A. R. and Coppock, D. J., *The UK Economy—A Manual of Applied Economics*, Weidenfeld & Nicolson, 1975.

8 Social welfare and the citizen
Abel-Smith, Brian, *Value for Money in Health Services*, Heinemann, 1976
Central Office of Information, *Social Security in Britain* (COI Reference Pamphlet R5455/75), No. 90, HMSO, 1975.
Levitt, Ruth, *The Reorganized National Health Service*, Croom Helm, 1976.

9 Industrial relations
In Place of Strife, HMSO, 1969.
Modern Studies Association, 'Industrial relations', *MOST** No. 10, January 1976.
Williamson, Hugh, *Trade Unions*, Heinemann, 1975.

10 Government and politics
Stacey, Frank, *British Government 1966–75: Years of Reform*, OUP, 1975.
Proudfoot, Mary, *British Politics and Government 1951–70*, Faber, 1974.

11 Parliament
Central Office of Information, *The British Parliament* (COI Reference Pamphlet R5448/75), No. 33, HMSO, 1975.
Central Office of Information, *Parliamentary Elections in Britain* (COI Reference Pamphlet R5513/75), HMSO, 1975.
King, Anthony, *British Members of Parliament—A Self Portrait*, Macmillan, 1974.
Roth, Andrew, *The MP's Chart*, Parliamentary Profiles, 1975.

12 Ministers and civil servants
Blakie, Robert, *The Office of Prime Minister*, OUP, 1973.
Central Office of Information, *Central Government of Britain* (COI Reference Pamphlet R5564/74), No. 40, HMSO, 1974.
Headley, Bruce, *British Cabinet Minister*, Allen & Unwin, 1975.

13 Local government
Buxton, Richard, *Local Government* (Second edition), Penguin, 1973.
Local Government in England and Wales—A Guide to the System, HMSO, 1974.

14 Maintenance of law and order
Jackson, R. M., The Machinery of Justice in England (Sixth edition), CUP, 1972.
Walker, D. M., *The Scottish Legal System* (Third edition), W. Green, 1969.

---

*Write to: The Editor, *MOST*, 13 Ruthven Street, Glasgow.

Questions to consider

Note: These questions have been selected or adapted from various examination papers set over the last few years. It may happen that the text gives no ready answer to some of the questions, in which case the task of investigating appropriate references will provide students with useful practice in the skills of selecting relevant and contemporary information. It might be helpful to readers to consult the bibliography, where such references may be found.

Chapter 1
1. Explain why most of Britain's population live in towns and why a large proportion of the population is concentrated in and around the seven great cities of Glasgow, Newcastle, Liverpool, Manchester, Leeds, Birmingham and London.
 SCE 'O' Grade, 1973
2. It has been suggested that there are three main ways in which racial prejudice and discrimination occur. How could each of the following help to improve race relations? (i) Legislation; (ii) education; (iii) association.
 East Midland Region Examination Board—CSE, 1976

Chapter 2
1. Account for the postwar decline in certain branches of the British textile industry.
 SCE 'H' Grade, 1976
2. Explain how and why production and employment in the motor vehicle industry in the postwar period have been affected by:
 (i) changes in government economic policies; (ii) industrial disputes within the industry and its component suppliers.
 SCE 'H' Grade, 1975
3. Explain the substantial fall in the consumption of coal from 1950–71.
 SCE 'O' Grade, 1974
4. How have the following influenced the supply and transport of oil?
 (i) The closure of the Suez Canal after the 1967 Arab–Israeli War.
 (ii) The decision of the Organization of Petroleum Exporting Countries (OPEC) to increase the price of oil after the 1973 Arab–Israeli War.
 SCE 'O' Grade, 1977

Chapter 3
1. Most of the firms in the United Kingdom are privately owned, but there are a variety of sizes.
 (i) What is a sole proprietor? (ii) What is a limited partnership? (iii) What is a private limited company? (iv) What is a public limited company?
 East Midland Region Examination Board–CSE, 1976
2. Who controls the nationalized industries?
 Oxford Local Examination—GCE 'A' Level

Chapter 4
(a) For what reasons has there grown in Scotland a demand for a greater degree of self-government?
(b) Describe how Scotland is governed at present and explain the major changes proposed by the Labour Government in 1976.

SCE 'O' Grade, 1977

Chapter 5
'There is only half an acre of food-producing land per head of population in Britain yet our farmers produce not only over half our food requirement but have achieved an increase in output of 50 per cent in the last 20 years, despite a reduction in the workforce from 800 000 to 395 000 workers in the same period.'
Describe and explain how each of the following has contributed to the change in production and productivity stated above:
(i) modern farming technology; (ii) improved crops and livestock; (iii) government policies.

SCE 'H' Grade, 1976

Chapter 6
1. (a) What are the responsibilities of the British Airports Authority?
   (b) How does civil aviation affect:
   (i) Britain's Balance of Payments; (ii) the prosperity of the areas in which the airports are located?

   SCE 'O' Grade, 1973

2. (a) Account for the growth in size and skill of the advertising industry and explain how it serves a useful and necessary service to the public.
   (b) Why and how is the public protected from the advertising industry's 'excesses and exaggerations'?

   SCE 'H' Grade, 1976

Chapter 7
(a) Name one *region* (in the United Kingdom) with a rate of unemployment above the national average and give reasons for its unemployment problems.
(b) How does the Government try to attract industry to areas with severe unemployment problems?

SCE 'O' Grade, 1973

Chapter 8
1. What benefits can a UK citizen obtain from National Health and National Insurance?

   East Midland Region Examination Board—CSE, 1976

2. Of the population who live in a British city 25 per cent may be inadequately housed, 15 per cent may be old age pensioners, 7 per cent may be without jobs and 0.5 per cent may be mentally or physically handicapped, all of whom are entitled to some form of government aid or protection.
   (a) Select two of the above groups. For each, explain why they might be in need of aid or protection and describe the help offered by central and local government.
   (b) Why is the Government having difficulties in providing sufficient help

   SCE 'O' Grade, 1977

Chapter 9
(a) For what reasons and by what means have British Governments tried to regulate and gain a greater measure of cooperation from trade unions in recent years?
(b) Why have Governments encountered difficulties in this respect?

SCE 'H' Grade, 1975

Chapter 10
1. What is 'public opinion'? How is it expressed?

Oxford Local Examination—GCE 'A' Level, 1976

2. Compare the central and local organizations of political parties in Britain. What differences exist in the role played by their respective annual party conferences in the making of party policy?

Oxford Local Examination—GCE 'O' Level, 1976

Chapter 11
1. (a) In what ways is Parliament able to examine government actions and legislation?
   (b) What truth is there in the assertion that discussion and debate in the Commons have little effect on the Government?

SCE 'O' Grade, 1974

2. The name 'Whip' comes from the world of hunting. The 'whipper' was the person who kept the hounds in a pack. In Parliament, the 'Whip' does a very similar job.
   (a) What is the function of a Chief Whip in Parliament?
   (b) What is meant by 'pairing'?

Southern Region Examination Board—CSE, 1976

Chapter 12
1. 'For all practical purposes the Prime Minister has now taken over the powers of the Monarch.' Discuss.

Oxford Local Examination—GCE 'A' Level, 1976

2. Explain and illustrate the statement that 'the institution of the Monarchy is one of the strongest factors in the continuance of stable government in Britain'.

University of London—GCE 'O' Level, 1976

Chapter 13
Give a summary of local government structure since 1974 in England and Wales (including London).

University of London—GCE 'O' Level, 1976

Chapter 14
There are many people involved in the process of enforcing the law. What part do the following play?
(i) Solicitor; (ii) Barrister; (iii) Clerk to the Court; (iv) Justice of the Peace.

East Midland Region Board—CSE, 1976

Index

Abortion Act 1967, 249
Act of Settlement 1701, 224
Advertising, 141–2, 240
Advisory, Conciliation and Arbitration Service (ACAS), 220
Aerospace industry, 60
Agriculture, 10–1, 39, 82, 85, 109 et seq.
Agriculture Act 1947, 114
Aircraft, 29–30, 62, 65, 133
Alexander, Professor K., 89
Annual Review, 117
Appropriation Accounts, 254
Area, 1, 82
Automobile Association (AA), 238

Balance of Payments, 81, 113, 118, 157–60, 162–3, 180, 184, 198–9, 232
Balance of Trade, 156
Banking, 142–6
Bank of England, 63, 145–6
Beeching, Dr. R., 59, 62, 128
Beeching Plan 1963, 128, 130
Benefits, 190–3, 201
Benn, A. Wedgwood (former Lord Stansgate) 243, 244
Beveridge, Sir William (later Lord), 189, 190, 191, 193, 197
Beveridge Plan 1944, 189
Bill of Rights, 224, 225, 287
Bills, 246–7
Birth rate, 4, 5
British Aerospace, 62
British Airways, 60, 132, 134
British Gas Corporation, 47
British Leyland, 28, 29, 64, 68, 180
British Rail, 60, 62, 85
British Shipbuilders, 33, 62
British Steel Corporation, 23, 24, 60
British Transport Commission, 60

British Waterways Board, 60, 127
Broadcasting, 239–40
Buchanan Report 1963, 131
Budget, 173, 174, 175, 177–8, 216
Bullock Report 1977, 212

Cabinet, 231, 236, 257–8, 261–2
Canals, 127–8
Central Electricity Generating Board, 52, 60
Chamberlain, N., 255
Chemicals, 36–9, 101
Churchill, Sir Winston, 259
Cities, 3
Citizens' Advice Bureau, 239
Civil aviation, 60, 104, 132–4
Civil Aviation Authority (CAA), 60, 132
Civil Aviation Act, 60, 132
Civil law, 277–8, 280–1, 283
Civil Service, 258, 264–5
Climate, 120–1
Coal, 6, 12, 14, 20, 24, 42–7, 59, 98–9, 200
Coal Industry Act 1973, 47
Coal Industry Nationalization Act 1946, 47, 59
Common law, 278–9
Common Agricultural Policy (CAP), 116, 119–20
Common Fisheries Policy, 100
Common Market (see EEC)
Commonwealth trade, 151–6
Commonwealth Immigrants Act, 5
Concorde, 30, 65, 133, 134
Confederation of British Industry, 219
Conservative Party, 232–6
Consolidated Fund, 172
Constituencies, 227
Constitution, British, 224, 225, 226–7, 287

Contracts of Employment Act, 200
Conurbations, 3, 4
Conservation, 53
Cotton, 34, 70, 99, 200
Courts, 243, 278, 279–84
Cousins, F., 261
Criminal law, 277
Crown, The, 256, 257, 277, 282
Customs and Excise duties, 174, 176 (see also Taxation)

Death rate, 4, 5, 12
Defence, 163, 171, 172
Departments of Government, 262–3, 264, 265
Department of Health and Social Security, 192, 275
Devaluation, 164
Development areas, 74, 79, 81, 88
Devolution, 107, 108, 236, 241, 255
Diet, 8
Distribution, 126
Distributive trades, 134–6

Earnings, 7, 210
East Anglia region, 79, 123
East Midlands region, 79
Economic Planning Regions, 1, 79, 82
Economy, 81, 112–3
Edwards, Sir Ronald, 59
Education, 172, 205–7, 234, 266, 268
Education (Scotland) Acts, 107
Electricity, 31, 43, 52–3, 61
Electricity Act 1947, 60
Electronics, 31, 93, 103
Electricity Board, 98
Emigration, 83–4, 87
Employers' associations, 219
Energy (see Power)
Engineering, 27 et seq., 72, 85, 93

294

England, 1, 26–7, 44–7, 73, 79, 182, 193, 194, 241, 267–75, 278–9, 280, 281, 282
Entertainment, 9
Estimates, 173, 250, 252
European Convention of Human Rights, 287
European Court, 245, 287
European Economic Community (EEC), 100, 116–20, 123, 153, 155–6, 163, 245, 249, 254, 255
European Free Trade Association (EFTA), 154, 155, 156
European Investment Bank, 93
Exports, 14–6, 19, 24, 28, 34, 147 et seq., 164, 188

Fair Trading Act, 141
Family Allowances Act 1945, 191
Farming (see Agriculture)
Firms, 54–7, 65–70, 80
Fishing industry, 100, 123–5
Food, 5, 109, 115 (see also Agriculture)
Free trade, 154

Gas, 6, 42, 47–9, 60
Gas Act 1948, 60
Gas Board, 60, 63
Geddes Report, 32
General Elections, 227–30
Giscard d'Estaing, President of France, 118
Government, 231, 235, 237, 247, 249–55, 262–3, 265
and Parliament, 256–7
Grants, 75–9, 89, 115, 269, 271, 274
Gray, Sir William, 91
Green belts, 204
'Green' pound, 117, 118–9
Gross Domestic Product (GDP), 18, 168
Gross National Product (GNP), 15, 17, 18, 19, 166, 169

Habeas corpus, 285
Hailsham, Lord Quentin Hogg), 243, 244
Health authorities, 193, 194, 195, 275
Health boards, 193, 194, 195, 275, 283
Health Service (see National Health Service)
Heath, Edward, 216
Highlands and Islands Development Board, 89
Hire Purchase Acts 1965, 140
Home, Lord (Sir Alec Douglas Home), 244
Honours, 256
Hospitals, 195, 196, 197

House of Commons, 228 et seq., 242, 244–5
House of Lords, 224, 226, 242–4, 245, 255
Housing, 172, 201–2, 203, 234, 269, 274
Horticulture, 117
Hydro-Electric Board, 52, 61, 88

Immigration, 4–5
Imperial Chemical Industries (ICI), 37, 65, 66, 68, 69
Imports, 14–6, 147 et seq., 157, 163–4
Industrial estates, 77, 91
Industrial Reorganization Corporation, 182
Industrial relations, 210 et seq.
Industrial Relations Act 1971, 216, 222, 234, 254
Industrial revolution, 12–4, 46
Industrial Training Act 1964, 181, 200
Industry, 11, 19 et seq., 54 et seq., 70–3, 80
Industry Acts, 74, 88
Inflation, 16, 162, 180, 182–7, 232
International Monetary Fund (IMF), 159, 160
Investment, 167–70, 188
Iron and steel, 12, 20 et seq., 60, 70, 71
Iron and Steel Act 1967, 60
Iron ore, 6, 20

Judiciary, 256, 263, 278, 279–83

Keynes, J. M. (Lord), 197

Labour Party, 212, 217, 218, 232 et seq.
Land distribution, 122
Law enforcement, 277 et seq.
Law making, 245–9
Law officers, 263, 279
Leisure activities, 9
Liberal Party, 235, 236
Life Peerages Act 1958, 226, 242, 243
Livestock, 111 (see also Agriculture)
Living standards, 5–10, 202
Lloyd George, D., 259
Local Employment Act 1960, 88
Local government, 266 et seq.
Local Government Act 1972, 267
Local Government (Scotland) Act 1973, 266
Lomé, Convention of, 120
London, 267, 279
Lord Chancellor, 245, 263

Marketing, 70, 151
Marketing Boards, 114, 119, 120
Market gardening, 122
Marsh, Sir Richard, 59
Mechanization, 22, 27, 44, 113
Media, 141, 239, 260
Minerals, 6
Minimum Lending Rate (MLR), 146, 162, 186, 199
Mining, 19, 44, 72
Minister, 256 et seq., 263–4, 274, 286
Money Bills, 243, 253
Monarch, 231, 242, 256, 259
Monopolies Commission, 67
Motor industry, 28, 64, 103, 164
Multinationals, 51, 80

National Assistance Act, 191
National Coal Board, 42, 47, 59
National Consumer Council, 141
National Debt, 178
National Economic Development Council (NEDC), 181
National Enterprise Board, 65, 182
National Freight Corporation, 130
National Health Service, 107, 172, 189, 193 et seq., 201, 265
National Income, 6–7, 16–8, 141, 163, 165
National Insurance, 189, 190–3, 201
National Insurance Act, 190
Nationalized industries, 57–65, 81, 146, 171, 181, 232, 265
New towns, 105–6, 204
New Towns Act 1946, 204
North Atlantic Treaty Organization (NATO), 163, 232
North East, 26, 46, 74, 77
North West region, 79
Northern Ireland, 73, 74, 79, 108, 120, 205, 228, 237, 271
Northern region, 79
North Sea gas and oil, 6, 37, 47–51, 101, 160, 241
Nuclear power, 52, 61

Oil, 6, 37, 40 et seq., 48–51, 98, 101–2, 159, 180, 186, 241
Ombudsmen, 241, 251
Opposition, 231, 235, 247
Organizations, 238

Parliament Acts, 224, 226, 243, 247
Parliament, 242 et seq. and Government, 256–7
Party system, 227, 231–9

295

Pay policy, 180, 184–8, 232
Peerage Act 1963, 226, 244
Pensions, 190 et seq.
Plaid Cymru (Welsh Nationalist Party), 108, 228, 236
Police, 266, 268, 272, 278–9
Politics, 224 et seq.
Population, 1, 4, 13, 77, 82
Post Office, 39, 173
Poverty, 201
Power, 12, 14, 34, 40 et seq., 70, 80, 104
Press, 239–40
Pressure groups, 238–9
Prime Minister(s), 257, 258–60
Privy Council, 258
Productivity, 165–7, 183
Public expenditure, 92, 170–3, 192, 196, 207, 252, 253
Public opinion, 240–1

Queen's Speech, 261

Race Relations Act 1965, 5
Race Relations Board, 5
Railway Act 1974, 63
Railways, 128, 130
Rates, 271–2
Redundancy, 161, 200, 201
Redundancy Payments Act 1965, 200
Refineries, 37, 50–1, 98, 101
Regional planning, 73, 74–9, 81
Regions, 1, 2, 79, 241
Rent Act 1965, 234
Resources, 6, 47, 48, 70
Retail trade, 136–40
Roads, 104, 130–2, 172, 205
Robens, Lord, 47, 59, 64
Royal assent, 225, 242, 243, 247
Royal Automobile Club (RAC), 238

Rule of Law, 284–6
Ryder, Lord, 65, 182

Scotland, 1, 28, 73, 74, 77, 78, 79, 82–108, 145, 193, 194, 228, 236, 255, 263, 266, 267 et seq., 278–82
Scottish Development Agency (SDA), 75, 78, 91
Scottish National Party, (SNP), 107, 228, 256
Sex Discrimination Act 1975, 8
Shetlands, 101–2
Shipbuilding, 31–3, 60, 84–5, 96–8
Shops and stores, 136–8, 205
Social Contract, 180, 216, 220, 222, 223, 232, 238
Social Security Act 1966, 192
Social services, 171, 172, 189 et seq., 271
South East, 1, 73, 74, 77, 78, 79, 87
South Wales, 25–6, 46–7, 77
South West region, 1, 79
Speaker, 245, 248
Statutory Instruments, 248, 249
Steel and iron, 20, 60, 70, 96, 232
Stock market, 56, 57, 144
Strikes, 43, 187, 220–2
Supplementary Benefits Commission, 192

Tariffs, 155, 156, 163, 199
Taxation, 7, 53, 162, 170, 174, 175–80, 182, 186, 199
Telecommunications, 31, 39, 64
Textiles, 12, 14, 19, 33–6, 72, 84, 98, 99
Town and Country Planning Acts, 204, 274

Trade, 11, 15, 66, 126 et seq.
Trade Description Acts, 141
Trade Union and Labour Relations Act 1974, 222
Trades Union Congress (TUC), 187, 215–6, 217, 221, 222, 223, 234, 238, 254
Trade unions, 184, 187, 200, 211, 212–5, 218–20, 232, 238
and Governments, 220–3
Traffic, 131, 132, 204, 205
Training Services Agency, 182
Transport, 39, 42, 60, 126 et seq., 172
Transport Acts, 60, 63, 128
Treasury, 146, 173, 177
Treaty of Accession, 119, 123, 249
Treaty of Rome, 249
Treaty of Union 1707, 278

Unemployment, 16, 46, 74, 78, 84, 197–201

Voting, 169, 226 et seq.

Wales, 1, 25–6, 28, 46–7, 73, 74, 77, 78, 79, 108, 193, 194, 205, 236, 241, 255, 263, 267–75, 278, 282
Welfare state, 189 et seq., 234
West Midlands region, 79
Whips, 247, 248, 254
Whitley Councils, 220
Williams, Mrs. Shirley, 141
Wilson, Sir Harold, 222
Wool, 5, 35–6, 99
Work, conditions of, 211

Yorkshire and Humberside region, 78, 79

Modern Studies Topics

The three books in this series were developed to meet the specific needs of the O- and H-grade of the SCE. Of equal relevance, however, are courses leading to GCE O- and A-level and, in particular, the Social Studies modules of BEC courses.

All three books are under the Consulting Editorship of Alasdair G Nicolson, Deputy Principal of Jordanhill College of Education, previously Head of the Modern Studies Department, the originator and initiator of Modern Studies in Scottish schools. Interrelationship is, therefore, ensured and the current three-volume series was developed from earlier editions of *The World Today* and *Britain Today*.

The two-volume series is now extended to a three-volume programme, providing greater emphasis on continental Europe. After Britain's entry into the European Economic Community, the social, economic, and political aspects of life in European countries are receiving more emphasis in the very many courses for which the series was developed.

The individual titles are:

The World Today 4/E Esmond Wright, Director, Institute of United States Studies, University of London
Britain Today 3/E Alasdair G Nicolson, James G Kellas, Reader in Politics, University of Glasgow, and James Tumelty, University of Glasgow
Europe Today Alasdair G Nicolson and Esmond Wright

McGRAW-HILL Book Company (UK) Limited
MAIDENHEAD · BERKSHIRE · ENGLAND

07 084224 8